*Studies in Consciousness / Russell Targ Editions*

Some of the twentieth century's best texts on the scientific study of consciousness are out of print, hard to find, and unknown to most readers; yet they are still of great importance, their insights into human consciousness and its dynamics still valuable and vital. Hampton Roads Publishing Company—in partnership with physicist and consciousness research pioneer Russell Targ—is proud to bring some of these texts back into print, introducing classics in the fields of science and consciousness studies to a new generation of readers. Upcoming titles in the *Studies in Consciousness* series will cover such perennially exciting topics as telepathy, astral projection, the after-death survival of consciousness, psychic abilities, long-distance hypnosis, and more.

BOOKS IN THIS SERIES

*An Experiment with Time* by J. W. Dunne
*Mental Radio* by Upton Sinclair
*Human Personality and Its Survival of Bodily Death* by F. W. H. Myers
*Mind to Mind* by René Warcollier
*Experiments in Mental Suggestion* by L. L. Vasiliev
*Mind at Large* edited by Charles T. Tart, Harold E. Puthoff, and Russell Targ
*Dream Telepathy* by Montague Ullman, M.D., and Stanley Krippner, Ph.D.,
    with Alan Vaughan

RUSSELL TARG EDITIONS

*UFOs and the National Security State* by Richard M. Dolan

STUDIES IN CONSCIOUSNESS

*Russell   Targ   Editions*

# Mind at Large

Institute of Electrical and Electronics Engineers
Symposia on the Nature of Extrasensory Perception

### Edited by

## Charles T. Tart

## Harold E. Puthoff

## Russell Targ

HAMPTON ROADS
PUBLISHING COMPANY, INC.

Hampton Roads Publishing Company, Inc.
1125 Stoney Ridge Road
Charlottesville, VA 22902

434-296-2772
fax: 434-296-5096
e-mail: hrpc@hrpub.com
www.hrpub.com

If you are unable to order this book from your local
bookseller, you may order directly from the publisher.
Call 1-800-766-8009, toll-free.

ISBN 1-57174-320-0
10 9 8 7 6 5 4 3 2 1
Printed on acid-free paper in Canada

Library of Congress Cataloging-in-Publication Data

Mind at large / edited by Charles T. Tart, Harold E. Puthoff, and
Russell Targ.
    p. cm. -- (Studies in consciousness)
Originally published: 1979. With new pref.
 Includes bibliographical references and index.
 ISBN 1-57174-320-0 (alk. paper)
1. Extrasensory perception--Congresses. 2.
Parapsychology--Congresses. I. Tart, Charles T., 1937- II. Puthoff,
Harold E. III. Targ, Russell. IV. Series.
 BF1021 .M56 2002
 133.8--dc21
                                                        2002009616

This book is dedicated to those
courageous and visionary men and
women who have supported psi research
through the past decade.

# Contents

# List of Tables

# List of Figures

# Preface
# The Unknowable End of Physics
Russell Targ

This book, originally published in 1979, contains some of the strongest and most convincing scientific data for the existence of psychic abilities. It is now thirty years since the U.S. government initiated a research program at Stanford Research Institute (SRI) in California to investigate psychic abilities. That twenty-million-dollar program received continuous financial and institutional support for twenty-three years ending in 1995. The findings were published in the world's most prestigious scientific journals (*Nature;*[1] *The Proceedings of the Institute of Electrical and Electronics Engineers [IEEE];*[2] and *The Proceedings of the American Association for the Advancement of Science [AAAS]*[3]). This program to study the applications of psychic abilities survived a formal Congressional investigation in 1978, after which it went on to provide valuable, otherwise unavailable information to almost every branch of the U.S. intelligence community (Defense Intelligence Agency, Central Intelligence Agency, Army Intelligence, etc.) during the Cold War.

The five chapters of this volume devoted to remote perception experiments show that many people have the ability to describe and experience events and locations that are blocked from ordinary perception. This perceptual ability called remote viewing has now been demonstrated and documented in numerous other U.S. and international laboratories. Yet, such psychic abilities have not by any means been accepted as real by mainstream science. Why is this natural human ability for psychic perception still forbidden by the Western scientific gatekeepers?

As one of the scientists who conducted the research, I do not have to *believe* in extrasensory perception (ESP). I have seen it occur in the laboratory on a day-to-day basis for decades. As a physicist, I don't have to *believe in* this phenomenon any more than I have to believe in lasers—with which I have also worked extensively. It is *there*, as demonstrated by dozens of experimental series. What I believe in is good data and replicable experiments. The history of this program, together with some of the recently declassified remote viewing data, is presented in *Miracles of Mind*, which I co-authored with Dr. Jane Katra. The data of this program include countless accurate drawings and descriptions of buildings and structures, made by remote viewers in our laboratory in California, thousands of miles distant from the perceptual targets. The activities and structures we investigated with experienced psychics were in China, Iran, Italy, and the USSR, and there were also hundreds of test targets in the U.S. We showed many U.S. government scientists, military personnel, and officials how to do this perceptual task called remote viewing—right up to, and including, the under secretary of defense.

There is a skeptical community who work tirelessly to save science from the depredations of frauds and charlatans. I applaud them, and think they fulfill a valuable function. However, in science it is as equally serious an error to throw out true, though intermittent, data as it is to accept as true data that are, in fact, false. (For example, neglecting a small and fluctuating signal from a wind-shear detector can cause a plane to crash—as has happened). None of us want to appear silly, gullible, or insane. We would often prefer to risk being wrong with the support of a group than be correct all by ourselves. Even after four hundred years, those who offer scientific opinions contrary to the prevailing paradigm can expect to meet reactions similar to those experienced by those cultural icons, Giordano Bruno and Galileo Galilei, who suffered in the extreme for offering correct scientific opinions about the Earth's motion.

Similarly, there is great cognitive dissonance over psychic abilities. From a recent (June 2001) Gallup poll, we know that more than half the nation's population feel that they have had psychic experiences. However, reporting such experiences is strongly repressed in this society. Parapsychological experiences reside in the usually excluded non-Aristotelian middle of our thought system; they are neither accepted nor non-accepted. They are borderland phenomena challenging the peace, the two-valued causal order, and the very structure of society, and are therefore available only to the courageous and adventurous— definitely not for the timid. They appear to be phenomena of lability and movement, not of inertia or the concrete. For example, a candle flame is much more likely to show the effects of distant mental intention than is a light bulb.

The skeptical community and press tries mightily to suppress parapsychological data and psychic abilities (except in the movies, where they are condemned and ridiculed). But, psi cannot be suppressed, because it occurs as part of nature. All that can be suppressed is our understanding and awareness.

## The Premature End of Physics

In light of recent discoveries in quantum physics, there have been many various recent expressions from notable scientists suggesting that we are approaching the end of the field of physics. For more than a hundred years, these same sorts of claims have been made by leading scientists of the day, and shown to be false. Such assertions are no more true today than in the past. We hear that the so-called end of physics is just a few years away—to be described, as Michio Kaku recently said, "with an equation less than one inch long."[4] Nobel laureate Steven Weinberg recently wrote a long essay in *The New York Review of Books,* describing his "search for the fundamental principles that underlie everything."[5] He said that "science in the future may take a turn that we cannot now imagine. But I see not the slightest advance sign of such a change." He seems to be saying that everything of importance that will ever be known is already known and understood.

In the late 1800s, Lord Kelvin, the distinguished English physicist who was the first to understand heat energy, made a similar, and now famous, statement that physics was complete, except "only two small clouds remain on the horizon of the knowledge of physics." The two clouds were, first, the interpretation of the results of the Michelson-Morley experiment, which did not detect any effects of the hypothesized ether, and second, the failure of then prevailing electromagnetic theory to predict spectral distribution of black body radiation—which led, respectively, to the development of Albert Einstein's relativity theory and Max Plank's quantum mechanics.

In 1975, Weinberg declared at Lawrence Berkeley Laboratory, "What we want to know is the set of simple principles from which the properties of particles, and *hence everything else,* can be deduced." At Cambridge University, in 1980, astrophysicist Stephen Hawking told his audience, "I want to discuss the possibility that the goal of theoretical physics might be achieved in the not-too-distant future: say by the end of the [twentieth] century. By this I mean that we might have a complete, consistent, and unified theory of physical interactions that would describe *all possible observations.*"

It appears that this hubris is still with us today. I believe that these statements are not only untrue, but logically impossible and misleading. Will there be an end to mathematics? To biology? To history? Will the human mind withdraw from science? Does curiosity ever achieve completion? I think not! A thousand years from now, our current views of physics will seem as primitive as the phlogiston theory of combustion seems to us today.

With these examples of blind spots and short-sightedness from brilliant and famous scientists, I think it is time to tell the truth about psychic abilities. They are a part of our scientific landscape, even though we do not yet well understand their mode of operation. Still we can say that physically they appear to be non-locally interconnected and non-energetic in nature, and psychologically, they can definitely be seen to be holistic and non-analytic (accurate shapes and forms, but few names).

After centuries of academic bombast, we are finally coming to recognize how tentative so-called scientific truth really is. In a scientific world increasingly governed by laws of "indeterminacy" (the uncertainty principle of Werner Heisenberg), "nonlocality" in physics (discovered by Einstein and proved by John Bell), and in "incompleteness" (possibly the greatest theorem in all of mathematics, proved by Kurt Gödel in 1931), it is *logically* impossible to know that we have ever reached the end of physics. The end of physics is as unknowable, as Gödel showed, as the completeness of *any* axiomatic system. Thus we are beginning to find ample metaphysical and philosophical room for the experience of psychic abilities.

Researcher Louisa Rhine found that by far the most common psychic event to appear in the lives of average people is a precognitive dream.[6] These dreams give glimpses to the dreamer of events that he or she will experience in the future. From laboratory data we learn that precognition occurs, and it is important to note that these studies demonstrate that precognition of future events is *just as successful as ordinary, real-time ESP.* In laboratory studies, these abilities are far from perfectly reliable—more like sixty percent, for remote viewing. However, in two decades of experimental research reported in *The Proceedings of the IEEE,* Prof. Robert Jahn and his colleagues at Princeton University have repeatedly demonstrated that *psi* performance, near and far, present and future, does not measurably vary as a function of either spatial or temporal distance.[7] Their published experiments in remote viewing (included in this book) depart from chance expectation by odds of more than a billion to one (actually $10^{-11}$).

## Distant Healing

Experiments in the area of Distant Mental Influence on Living Systems (DMLS) have been carried out by psychologist William Braud, at the Institute of Transpersonal Psychology in Palo Alto, California, together with anthropologist Marilyn Schlitz, Research Director for the Institute of Noetic Sciences.[8] They have shown, in numerous experiments, that if a person in the laboratory simply attends fully to a distant person whose physiological activity is being monitored, he or she—acting as a sender—can influence the distant receiver person's autonomic nervous system, as indicated by changes in their galvanic skin responses (GSR). In four separate experiments involving seventy-eight sessions overall, a person staring intently at a closed-circuit TV monitor image of a distant participant was able to significantly and systematically influence the remote person's GSR. In these cases, no specific techniques of intentional focusing or mental imaging were used by the person ostensibly causing the influence. He or she simply stared at the "stare-ee's" image on the video screen during the thirty-second trials, which were randomly interspersed with control periods. If one's thoughts are reliably able to affect another person's heart rate and skin resistance at a distance, then this data must be part of any comprehensive theory of reality.

Further, the data showing efficacious distant healing are an even greater threat to the consciousness-neglecting materialist position than are the relatively passive mind-to-mind connections demonstrated by remote viewing or mental telepathy data. For example, if one's thought processes can affect the meter reading indicating one's heart rate, then physics must start thinking seriously about consciousness—nothing is more important or physical to a physicist than his meter readings.

In his 1993 book *Healing Research*, psychiatrist Dr. Daniel Benor examined more than 150 controlled research studies from around the world.[9] He reviewed psychic, mental, and spiritual healing experiments done on a variety of living organisms—enzymes, cell cultures, bacteria, yeasts, plants, animals, and humans. More than half the studies demonstrated significant healing. A landmark study by Fred Sicher, psychiatrist Elisabeth Targ and others was published in the December, 1998 issue of *The Western Medical Journal* describing healing research carried out at California Pacific Medical Center.[10] This research details and describes the positive therapeutic effects of distant healing, or healing intentionality, on men with advanced AIDS. The participants' conditions were assessed by psychometric testing and blood testing at their enrollment, after the distant healing intervention, and six months later, when physicians reviewed their medical charts.

Men with AIDS were recruited from the San Francisco Bay Area. They were told that they had a fifty-fifty chance of being in the treatment group, or the control group. Forty distant healers from all parts of the country took part in the study. None of the forty subjects in the study ever met the healers, nor did they or the experimenters know into which group anyone had been randomized. The treatment group experienced significantly better medical and quality-of-life outcomes (with odds of 100 to 1) on many quantitative measures, including fewer outpatient doctor visits (185 vs. 260); fewer days of hospitalization (10 vs. 68); less-severe illnesses acquired during the study, as measured by illness severity scores (16 vs. 43); and significantly less emotional distress. The study concluded that "Decreased hospital visits, fewer severe new diseases, and greatly improved subjective health support the hypothesis of distant healing."

Two other studies of distant healing have been published in prestigious medical journals. In 1988, physician Randolph Byrd published in *The Southern Medical Journal* a successful double-blind demonstration of distant healing.[11] The study involved 393 cardiac patients at San Francisco General Hospital. And in 1999, cardiologist William Harris of the University of Missouri in Kansas City published a similar successful study with 990 heart patients. His paper appeared in *The Archives of Internal Medicine*.[12]

## Physics and Psi

The implications of psychic abilities, whether it be the in-flow of psychic information or the out-flow of healing intentions, illuminate our observation that we live in a profoundly interconnected world. The most exciting research in quantum physics today is the investigation of what physicist David Bohm calls quantum-interconnectedness, or non-local correlations.[13] In laboratories around the world, it has now been demonstrated repeatedly that quanta of light emitted in opposite directions from a source, and traveling at the speed of light, maintain their connection to one another, and that each photon is significantly affected by what happens to its twin *many kilometers away*.[14] This nonlocal connection between the separated partners occurs instantaneously! This connection at a distance looks remarkably like the surprising connection often reported between identical twins who are separated at birth and raised apart.

This unexpected coherence between distant entities is called non-locality. In writing on the philosophical implications of non-locality, physicist Henry Stapp of the University of California at Berkeley states that this quantum connection could be the "most profound discovery in all of science."[15] From the writings of Bohm and Stapp, it is beginning to appear that one cannot understand quantum mechanics without including consciousness. It appears that the data from modern physics, taken together with the data from psi research, point to the fact that we are connected in consciousness, and this limitless awareness is not subject to ordinary limitations of distance in time or space.

## Implications of Psychic Abilities

Passionate opposition to new ideas often arises from a feeling that one is being attacked. For millennia, philosophers have invited us to try to discover who we really are. In the sixteenth and seventeenth centuries Nicholas Copernicus, Giordano Bruno, and Galileo Galilei were persecuted or murdered because they showed overwhelming evidence that we were not, in fact, special beings at the center of the universe—as everyone had been taught—but rather, inhabitants of what can be seen as a large rock, orbiting a hundred million miles from the sun. People hated that idea. It was an attack on their ego—on who they thought they were. In the nineteenth century, Charles Darwin demonstrated that not only did we not have a special place in the universe, but we were also first cousins to monkeys and chimpanzees—a further assault on our specialness. Another blow to our ego came not much later, when Sigmund Freud showed that much of our being is governed by unconscious processes, of which we are entirely unaware. Psychic abilities further erode these boundaries of the self, by indicating that we are not only very small beings at the edge of the galaxy, but also that the psychic shell separating one of us from another is actually quite porous. As Nobel physicist Erwin Schrödinger wrote in 1942:

> Consciousness is a singular of which the plural is unknown. There
> is only one thing, and that which seems to be a plurality is merely a

series of different aspects of this one thing, produced by a deception, the Indian maya, as in a gallery of mirrors.[16]

Such realizations give rise to a potential telepathic threat of uncontrolled intimacy and a possibly troubling loss of privacy for our smaller self. However, as our personal egos are diminished by scientific advances, our knowledge of our true Self is greatly enhanced. What we discover from the data of psi research is that we are capable of expanded awareness far beyond our physical bodies—that formless, unlimited awareness may be who we really are.

The principle scientific finding, in fact, of the research described here is that there is not yet any known spatial or temporal limit to our awareness. It appears that, in consciousness, there is only one of us here. His Holiness the Dalai Lama has remarked that enlightenment is "no separate existence." The message of awakened spiritual teachers throughout history, as well as the quantum physicists, today reminds us that "separation is an illusion."

## Notes

1. Targ, R., and H. Puthoff. 1974. Information transfer under conditions of sensory shielding. *Nature* 251:602–607.

2. Puthoff, H. E., and R. Targ. 1976. A perceptual channel for information transfer over kilometer distances: Historical perspective and recent research. *Proc. IEEE.* 64, no. 3.

3. Puthoff, H. E., R. Targ, and E. C. May. 1981. Experimental psi research: Implications for physics. In *The Role of Consciousness in the Physical World*, R. G. Jahn, 37–86. AAAS Symposium 57, Boulder: Westview Press.

4. Kaku, M. 2001. The Prophets Conference, Techniques of Discovery. New York City, May 18–20, 2001.

5. Weinberg, S. 2001. The future of science and the universe. *New York Review of Books.* November 15, 2001.

6. Rhine, L. 1954. Frequency and types of experience in spontaneous precognition. *J. Parapsychology* 6:93–123.

7. Jahn, R. 1982. The persistent paradox of psychic phenomena: An engineering perspective. *Proc. IEEE* 70 (2): 136–170. R. Jahn, and B. Dunne. 1987. *Margins of Reality: The Role of Consciousness in the Physical World.* New York: Harcourt.

8. Schlitz, M., and W. Braid. 1997. Distant intentionality and healing: Assessing the evidence. *Alternative Therapies* 3 (6), November.

9. Benor, D. J. 1992. *Healing Research.* Vol. 1. Munich, Germany: Helix Verlag.

10. Sicher, F., E. Targ, D. Moore, and H. Smith. 1998. A randomized double-blind study of the effect of distant healing in a population with advanced AIDS. *Western Journal of Medicine* 169:356–363.

11. Byrd, R. C. 1988. Positive therapeutic effects of intercessory prayer in a coronary care unit population. *Southern Medical Journal* 81 (7 July 1988): 826–829.

12. Harris, W. S., et al. 1999. A randomized, controlled trial of the effects of remote intercessory prayer on outcomes in patients admitted to the coronary care unit. *Archives of Internal Medicine* 159:2273–2278.

13. Bohm, D., and B. Hiley. 1993. *The Undivided Universe.* London: Routledge.

14. Freedman, S., and J. Clauser. 1997. Experimental test of local hidden variable theories. *Physical Review Letters* 28:934–941. W. Tittel, J. Brendel, H. Zbinden, and N. Gisin. 1998. Violation of Bell inequalities by photons more than 10 km apart. *Physical Review Letters* 81 (17): 3563–3566.

15. Stapp, H. 2000. In *The Conscious Universe: Parts and Wholes in Physical Reality,* M. Kafatos, and R. Nadeau, p. 70. New York: Springer Verlag.

16. Schrödinger, E. 1945. *What Is Life.* Cambridge University Press.

# Introduction

## Charles T. Tart, Harold E. Puthoff, and Russell Targ

Although the scientific pursuit of psi may conjure up images of card guessing and dice throwing in laboratory cubicles, this new work involves such activities as computerized extrasensory perception (ESP) tests, psychokinetic interference with radioactive decay, psi transmission to a submerged submarine, and long-distance tracking of a U.S. experimenter in the Soviet Union. The results of these and other experiments, and their associated theoretical interpretations, are presented here. We hope by this means to introduce to the scientist and interested layman alike the current data and theory about these fascinating phenomena.

This volume is a collection of new and provocative papers on psi phenomena presented at two symposia of the Institute of Electrical and Electronics Engineers (IEEE), one of the largest and most prestigious scientific societies in the world. The purpose of these symposia was to bring together prominent scientists from a number of disciplines, particularly the physical sciences, to discuss exciting new data and to present physical models and theories about the nature of psi.

The presentation of such data at symposia held under the auspices of such groups as the IEEE marks a relatively recent change in climate in U.S. science. Throughout the history of science, the appearance of anomalous events has always been a challenge to the conceptual systems of the day, and the observation of psi phenomena in our day is such an anomaly. It has been (and still is) a source of controversy, with some scientists dismissing the existence of psi phenomena on a priori grounds. Now, however, as a result of decades of careful laboratory study of psi events, center stage has shifted from the issue of establishing the existence of psi (which has been adequately answered in the affirmative for those scientists who have studied the data) to the testing of models and theories about the nature and implications of psi. The study of psi has thus come of age and is ready to take its place as a challenging interdisciplinary area within the scientific community at large.

*Psi* is an overall term that refers to a class of interactions between consciousness and the physical world which is as yet unexplained—phenomena that seem paradoxical or paraconceptual to our everyday view of reality. These include the acquisition of information not presented to any known sense and the production of physical effects not mediated by any known mechanism. Psi phenomena are said to occur when a person is in a physical situation wherein all known energies that could provide him or her with information about the outside world through his or her known senses, or could transmit his or her intentions to the environment, are apparently blocked, yet the person's experiences and actions indicate that he or she has knowledge about, or control over, distant places and activities.

Traditionally, four major psi phenomena are usually distinguished: *telepathy* is knowledge of another person's thoughts; *clairvoyance* is direct perception or knowledge of some hidden aspect of the physical world, without the intermediary of another mind; *precognition* is knowledge of either future thoughts or future physical conditions or events that do not yet exist and which we would not ordinarily consider predictable from a knowledge (even a psi knowledge) of current events; and *psychokinesis* (PK) is the creation of effects on the physical world simply by willing them to happen. Many modern experiments cut across these traditional distinctions, however, permitting multichannel input and output. An example is so-called remote viewing, which is discussed in detail in this book. In remote viewing, an isolated subject is asked to describe the location and activity of a target team sent by random number generator to one of many possible remote locations. In this experiment, the subject can obtain part of his or her information from the outbound team by telepathy, part by direct perception of the target scene itself, part by precognition of his or her own later visit to the scene when he or she obtains feedback, and, at least in principle, part by psychokinetic control of the random number generator to yield a target in keeping with his or her a priori biases.

Although the question of the existence of psi phenomena has been statistically settled for some time, the data presented in this book offer further striking evidence for the reality of these phenomena, including their occurrence under strictly controlled laboratory conditions. For example, in Chapters 2 and 3, we present the remote-viewing experiments at Stanford Research Institute (SRI) in which a wide variety of subjects in the SRI laboratory were able to describe accurately the location and activities of distant (traveling) experimenters, often in great detail and even at transcontinental distances.* In Chapter 4, researchers at Mundelein College describe their research on precognitive remote viewing, where subjects in Chicago were able to track reliably the activities of their fellow researcher in his travels through the Soviet Union,

---

*Stanford Research Institute is now officially known as SRI International.

half a world away, and forecast his day-to-day actions a day in advance of the traveler himself. And in Chapter 9, Helmut Schmidt summarizes almost a decade of systematic research in which dozens of subjects have demonstrated their ability to systematically perturb the functioning of microcomputer random number generators by an act of will. These psychokinetic experiments, like the perception experiments, appear to be independent of distance and also independent of the complexity of the device to be perturbed. These data represent robust and repeatable phenomena that will not go away. It is the task of researchers today to work to incorporate them into the mainstream of modern science so that they can take their appropriate places in conventional physics and psychology and lose their "para" designation.

Historically speaking, the study of psi phenomena has had a highly variable career in the scientific community. Research into the existence of psi phenomena began in the last century under the name of *psychic research,* and the founding of the Society for Psychical Research in London in 1882 by a group of prominent scientists and scholars was an historic event. The work of J. B. Rhine and his colleagues at Duke University, starting in the 1930s, was highly influential in shaping parapsychology in this country, with its present form of heavy reliance on standardized, repeated "guessing" tests and statistical evaluation of results. The work of Rhine and his colleagues was extremely provocative to the scientific community when it was first published in 1934.[1]

The initial response of the scientific community to the Duke findings was the appropriate one for science when a radical new claim is made: as Honorton reports, there were some 60 critical articles raising methodological questions about the psi studies and some 50 experimental studies, two-thirds of which were independent replications by researchers other than the Duke group.[2] Valid methodological criticisms were accepted by the researchers, and experiments were refined to meet them: psi results kept coming in.

Honorton reports that 88 percent of further Duke studies and 61 percent of the independent replication studies showed statistically significant evidence for psi. Compared to the replication rate of *less than 1 percent* for conventional psychological experiments, the degree of replicability of psi experiments was quite remarkable.[3] Although psi results could not be produced on demand 100 percent of the time, the large majority of the studies were positive; indeed, the evidence for psi phenomena is far better than many accepted psychological phenomena.

In terms of normal scientific procedures, a curious thing then happened. When an anomalous but important phenomenon has been repeatedly demonstrated with good methodology, scientists ordinarily turn increasing attention to it until it is either thoroughly understood and integrated into the current scientific framework or until it initiates a revision in that framework—what Kuhn calls a "paradigm revision."[4] What happened instead was that the scientific community essentially repressed psi phenomena. From the early 1940s until a few years ago, parapsychological experiments were almost never published in the general scientific literature. It was not that manuscripts were not submitted to the orthodox journals but rather that they were frequently rejected for clearly prejudiced reasons. (One rejection letter from *Science* began with, "Most of our readers do not believe in the existence of ESP," as if belief had anything to do with it.) Therefore, the investigators of psi developed a number of special journals to circulate their reports among themselves, but these journals were little known to the general scientific community. Scientists who wanted to investigate psi phenomena were actively discouraged from doing so: some lost jobs or promotions, and grant money was not forthcoming from the usual channels supporting scientific research. The general scientific community was clearly not ready to consider either the evidence for psi or its implications, and the personal and emotional attachment of scientists to their current world views was not going to be disturbed by the evidence. Psychologically, this sort of response is a common human reaction, and it is understandable, but it is bad science.

Over the decades, however, this attitude has begun to change. One reason is that we have finally come close to having repeatable psi experiments. Although there is no known procedure that will produce significant psi results 100 percent of the time regardless of conditions, we do have some experimenters and some laboratories who now experience the *un*successful experiment as the exception. We mentioned earlier that 61 percent of the early independent replications of the historic Duke psi experiments were successful. More recently, Honorton surveyed 89 experimental studies carried out over a 30-year period (1945–75) where various internalized attention states, such as hypnosis or meditation, were tested for their effects on psi functioning and found that 66 percent of the studies found significant psi effects.[5] Honorton has also reported statistically significant success in 39 out of 54 experiments in which subjects attempted to perturb electronic random number generators with PK.[6] Chapter 9 illustrates this kind of research. The SRI research with remote viewing has been so successful with respect to replication at SRI that a subject who shows no signs of success at all is considered rare (see Chapters 2 and 3). One of the editors (Charles T. Tart) has reviewed the literature on the provision of immediate feedback of results to subjects and argued that it eliminates the usual decline of psi with repeated work in the laboratory and may allow some subjects to improve their psi abilities.[7] As we perfect the techniques for getting reliable, high-level psi performance, we can expect to make much more rapid progress in experiments that ask questions about the nature of psi.

Although the work discussed here has achieved a very high level of replicability, a word of caution is in order. We want to remind potential investigators that psi effects involve real, living people, and the conditions necessary to help these people manifest psi under experimental conditions are far from understood. In the last decade, the field of psychology has become painfully aware of the issues of experimenter bias or experimenter influence (see Silverman's excellent book for a review of this literature).[8] It is now a useful rule of thumb in psychological experiments to assume that the experimenter is always part of the experiment and that his or her personal qualities and style of interaction are likely to affect the subjects and the experimental outcome.

This caution is even more true in psi research, where we postulate the existence of largely unknown information channels between experimenter and subject, information channels we have no idea of how to control with current knowledge. Investigators of psi phenomena have begun to examine the possibility of experimenter effects in some detail.[9] Indeed, Tart has argued that traditional experimental designs that involve keeping a subject ignorant of experimental conditions or, worse, actually misleading or deceiving him or her may be quite invalid.[10] Thus, we believe that psi experiments cannot be done "mechanically." We wish we could specify the characteristics of successful experimenters, for there are a number of them who regularly elicit psi in their experiments, but that is a major research problem for the future, and at this point, we can only remind the potential investigator to be sensitive to these human interactions.

With these complexities beginning to be appreciated, it appears that the general scientific community has evolved to the point where it is willing to examine not only the evidence for the existence of psi but to begin to discuss and study its nature. One of the first signs of this increasing maturity was the acceptance of the Parapsychological Association as a member society of the American Association for the Advancement of Science (AAAS) in 1969. Another of the indications was the publication of a report on psi research by two of the editors in *Nature,* a leading general scientific journal.[11] The following quote from a special editorial preceding the article is instructive.

> We publish this week a paper by Drs. R. Targ and H. Putholf (page 602) which is bound to create something of a stir in the scientific community. The claim is made that information can be transferred by some channel whose characteristics appear to fall "outside the range of known perceptual modalities." Or, more bluntly, some people can read thoughts or see things remotely.
>
> Such a claim is, of course, bound to be greeted with a preconditioned reaction amongst many scientists. To some it simply confirms what they have always known or believed. To others it is beyond the laws of science and therefore necessarily unacceptable. But to a few—though perhaps to more than is realised—the questions are still unswered, and any evidence of high quality is worth a critical examination.[12]

The *Nature* article generated enormous controversy. For many scientists, it was their first exposure to the fact that psi phenomena were being seriously researched by credible scientists at respectable institutions.

This interest on the part of the general scientific community led to a demand for more information about psi research. A number of our colleagues have responded to that demand and provided valuable information to the general scientific community about contemporary research. One specific response that eventually led to this book was a major article describing parapsychological research by two of the editors (Harold E. Puthoff and Russell Targ) in the March 1976 *Proceedings of the IEEE*, a major circulation journal in the scientific community.[13] An updated version of this article constitutes Chapter 2 of this book. Interest in this article led to an invitation to the authors to keynote the 1976 IEEE International Conference on Cybernetics and Society in Washington, D.C., an address for which they received the Franklin V. Taylor award for the best presentation at the conference. This was soon followed by an invitation to Targ to organize a special evening highlight symposium on the "State of the Art in Psychic Research" at the Electro 1977 National Convention of the IEEE. More than 1,500 IEEE members attended that session from 8 in the evening until past midnight, and this after a full day of technical papers and with all the tourist attractions of New York City in competition! Chapters 1, 5, 6, and 11 are revised and updated versions of those papers. The further interest generated by these events resulted in an invitation to Puthoff to organize a technical session for the 1977 IEEE International Conference on Cybernetics and Society in Washington, D.C., a year after the initial keynote address to the same conference. Chapters 3, 4, 7, 8, 9, and 10 are updated versions of these papers.*

It is our hope that this book will serve several purposes. First, it provides an up-to-date assessment of some of the most exciting research trends in the scientific study of psi. Many of the results are not only of intellectual or theoretical significance—they are quite large-scale, powerful psi effects rather than slight, though statistically significant, deviations from chance. Second, the presentations illustrate the wide significance of psi phenomena to many fields and underline the need for interdisciplinary approaches. Thus, the editors address this book primarily to the general scientific community (and the curious reader of any background) rather than simply to the parapsychological community. Third, psi phenomena are often viewed as sometimes irrational or supernatural, apparently beyond the current scientific conceptual system. We believe that this view is unwarranted; we feel psi phenomena are certainly lawful and potentially comprehensible, even if some of the laws and systematic principles that will be developed for understanding psi may be qualitatively different

---

*For Chapters 7 and 8, we have substituted less technical, expanded versions of these papers than those given at the meetings, with the authors' permission, to enhance readability for a more general audience.

from current known laws. We especially believe it is important to sharpen our understanding of exactly how psi phenomena do or do not conflict with various aspects of modern physics, and much effort is devoted to that task in this book. We suspect that some psi phenomena may turn out to be compatible with straightforward extensions of modern physics. Since some phenomena may prove not to be compatible, discovering the points of fit and conflict empirically will be vitally important. Such discoveries will not only involve enhancing our understanding of psi but will provide a better understanding of the fundamental properties of the universe.

Compared with the enormity of the questions, our current knowledge is very small. But the potential for progress is there, and it is exciting. We invite the reader to join us as we look over recent developments in psi research and the relationship of psi to the physical world.

## Notes

1. J. B. Rhine, *Extrasensory Perception* (Boston: Boston Society for Psychical Research, 1934).

2. C. Honorton, "Has Science Developed the Competence to Confront Claims of the Paranormal?," in *Research in Parapsychology 1975,* ed. J. Morris, W. Roll, and R. Morris, pp. 199–223 (Metuchen, N.J.: Scarecrow Press, 1976).

3. J. Bozarth, and R. Roberts, "Studying Significant Significance," *American Psychologist* 27 (1972): 774–75; and T. Sterling, "Publication Decisions and Their Possible Effects on Inferences Drawn from Tests of Significance—or Visa-Versa," *Journal of the American Statistical Association* 54 (1959): 30–34.

4. T. Kuhn, *The Structure of Scientific Revolutions* (Chicago: University of Chicago Press, 1962).

5. Honorton, op. cit.

6. C. Honorton, "Replicability, Experimenter Influence, and Parapsychology: An Empirical Context for the Study of Mind" (Paper delivered at meeting of American Association for the Advancement of Science, Washington, D.C., 1978).

7. C. Tart, *Learning to Use Extrasensory Perception* (Chicago: University of Chicago Press, 1976).

8. I. Silverman, *The Human Subject in the Psychological Laboratory* (New York: Pergammon Press, 1977).

9. C. Honorton, M. Ramsey, and C. Cabibbo, "Experimenter Effects in Extrasensory Perception," *Journal of the American Society for Psychical Research* 69 (1975): 135–50; J. Kennedy, and J. Taddonio, "Experimenter Effects in Parapsychological Research," *Journal of Parapsychology* 40 (1976): 1–33; R. White, "The Limits of Experimenter Influence on Psi Test Results: Can Any Be Set?," *Journal of the American Society for Psychical Research* 70 (1976): 333–70; R. White, "The Influence of Persons Other Than the Experimenter on the Subject's Scores in Psi Experiments," *Journal of the American Society for Psychical Research* 70 (1976): 133–66;

and R. Thouless, "The Effect of the Experimenter's Attitude on Experimental Results in Parapsychology," *Journal of the Society for Psychical Research* 48 (1976): 261–66.

10. C. Tart, "Towards Humanistic Experimentation in Parapsychology: A Reply to Dr. Stanford's Review," *Journal of the American Society for Psychical Research* 71 (1977): 81–102.

11. R. Targ and H. Puthoff, "Information Transmission Under Conditions of Sensory Shielding," *Nature* (October 1974): 602–7.

12. "Investigating the Paranormal" (editorial), *Nature* 251 (1974): 559–60.

13. H. Puthoff and R. Targ, "A Perceptual Channel for Information Transfer Over Kilometer Distances: Historical Perspective and Recent Research," *Proceedings of the IEEE* (March 1976): 329-54.

# Introduction to Chapter 1

Many observers have noted that the experience of being an astronaut appears to change people. There is something about seeing the whole earth at once that destroys one's usual piecemeal views of human problems and demands a more holistic or integrated approach. Much of the data and theory presented in this volume consist of new observations and ideas that are not yet integrated with each other because we do not yet know how to relate them. Astronaut Edgar Mitchell, in this provocative chapter, shares his thinking and speculation about the large-scale implications and social effects of psi phenomena.

He points out that while individuals with psi abilities may be extraordinary and seem to be rare, it is the pursuit of the extraordinary and gifted individuals of every type that is the greatest strength of a society. How will our society maintain its forward movement for the future if we do not seek out, develop, and cherish the extraordinary? Some societies appear to be more aware of this dynamic than others. In the Soviet Union, where the pursuit of excellence and support for the gifted is considered a national goal, a number of sources have indicated that a nationwide search for psychically talented individuals is being carried out. If Mitchell's plea is heeded, we can get on with the business of developing our most precious national resource—gifted individuals.

## About the Author

**Edgar D. Mitchell,** Sc.D., is the founder and past president of the Institute of Noetic Sciences in Menlo Park, California, an organization devoted to studying expanded human potential. His training has been in engineering, aeronautics, and astronautics, and he was the pilot of the Apollo 14 lunar-landing module. While in earth orbit after returning from the moon, Mitchell carried out the first ESP experiment ever conducted from outer space to earth, with successful results. He is widely known for his lectures on human potential and parapsychology, and coedited the book *Psychic Exploration* with John White in 1974. He is currently a consultant with Information Science.

# 1

# A Look at the Exceptional

**Edgar D. Mitchell**

An inherent danger for a maturing democratized society is that the pursuit of egalitarian goals creates neglect of the very characteristics that allow attainment of success, that is, the pursuit of excellence, emphasis on creativity, and nurturing of those exceptional human beings who possess the rare talents needed in the vanguard of human progress. Without such talents being utilized by leadership throughout history, mankind would still be struggling in the dark ages. If a modern society fails to continually cultivate those areas where creative intelligence can mature into exceptional capabilities, the society will find itself slipping back toward the more primitive values and institutions characteristic of mundane leadership.

Noble social goals to improve the lot of the least talented cannot possibly succeed without developing the highest capabilities of the most talented who can lead the way.

> To give a fair chance to potential creativity is a matter of life and death for any society. This is all important because the outstanding creative ability of a fairly small percentage of the population is mankind's ultimate asset and the only one with which Man has been endowed.[1]

To emphasize this need—whereas U.S. federal expenditures for social betterment are hovering near the 50 percent mark of the *total* budget of about $400 billion, the most recent figures show only $2.56 million devoted to training, understanding, and research of "gifted" individuals and their exceptional talents. This is approximately .0013 percent of the federal expenditures for achieving social goals and is a distressingly small investment considering the magnitude of the problem.

The creative, cognitive, and intellectual potential of the human mind is vast and of almost limitless variation. On the other hand, the characteristics that distinguish the unusual talent from mediocrity are not at all understood. In fact, some of the unusual talents possessed by a few are not even believed, much less understood. It is toward such understanding and what it could achieve that this author's effort is devoted.

## Extraordinary Capabilities

A century of competent but always controversial research by dedicated men and women of science demonstrates convincingly, for those who will study the record, that a variety of extraordinary capabilities are indeed facts of our existence. Further, it seems that human beings are usually, and probably always, the causative agents. Not only is the range of verifiable events quite large but the lines of evidence point to little understood properties of our human mental machinery as the perpetrator of, or at least collaborator in, these events. They have been inappropriately described as *miraculous, paraphysical, paranormal, supernatural, spirits,* and other such terms that make a traditionalist's skin crawl. For this reason, it is important to dispel any notion that this chapter will give strength to ideas of "unnaturalness." Let us attempt to cut through superstition and myth and get to the crux of the matter regarding cause, but keeping in mind that *natural* does not necessarily imply a "material" or conventional viewpoint—quite the contrary.

To the extent that each of the reported capabilities is valid and observable, it is part of the natural order of the universe, which people in science attempt to understand. There are no unnatural or supernatural phenomena, only very large gaps in our knowledge of what is natural, particularly regarding relatively rare occurrences. We should strive to fill those gaps of ignorance. The fact that claims about many phenomena have associated with them a high "giggle factor" and have historically attracted an unsavory assortment of cranks, quacks, frauds, and charlatans who prey upon the gullible should not deter the dedicated investigator from seeking the truth. Let it be remembered that in the world of science, the methods and the subjects one must use for observations are not always neat, clean, and tidy. In its infancy, pathology was dependent upon grave robbers, and microbiology is indebted to contents of the chamber pot in order to gain knowledge about human functioning. No less onerous is the environment of the contemporary investigator who chooses to study the functioning of extraordinary human mental processes.

Only recently, after many years of effort by a handful of dedicated investigators, has it been possible to bring certain investigations out of the closet and to publish research results in prestigious professional journals. This fact reflects equally the perseverance of the investigators and the entrenched rigidity of our scientific traditionalism.

With all candor, however, it must be stated that of the varied forms of extraordinary mental activity, the most shunned of which bear that distressing label *psychic,* only a few have yet achieved a sufficient level of scientific control and scrutiny to be repeatably demonstrable under laboratory conditions. Some that meet the test are telepathy, precognition, clairvoyance, and, now, remote viewing, which perhaps includes several of the other categories. These forms of activity rightly deserve to be accepted and explained by the scientific community at large.

There are numerous other events, however, which are quite real but relatively more rare, and which have proven to be more difficult to control. These have yet to be adequately documented in the manner required by our traditional methodology. This is true as much because of the limitation of our methods and concepts as the rarity of events. We must remember that it is not nature's task to adapt to our rigid, and often erroneous, preconceived notions but rather our task to be sufficiently creative and intelligent to understand the myriad clues nature gives us. The experienced field investigator who has traveled to different parts of the world to observe and measure in situ those individuals who possess these extraordinary faculties should be heeded. Many have arrived at the conclusion that in fact, *all* the various reported events can be, and often are, genuine occurrences. I refer in these cases not only to prodigious feats of computation and memory but, more specifically, to major psychokinetic phenomena that have been observed and reported by reliable investigators. None of these has as yet been sufficiently studied under laboratory conditions. It is this author's contention, however, that in the fullness of time, the entire class of psychokinetic events will be learned and brought under the conscious control of a sufficiently large sample of individuals that field studies can move into the laboratory, where more careful scrutiny is possible.

It is because many experienced observers agree strongly with the view that all the mental functions now considered extraordinary will, in due course, be made more ordinary that it is time to speculate about what this will mean to our social functioning and institutions. Is there an obvious impact not only on our thinking and way of daily life but, also, on our values?

Toward that end, let us analyze that class of extraordinary human mental functioning often referred to as *psychic* and, from the sparse knowledge we currently have, speculate what is likely to happen should this class of events move out of the realm of extraordinary and become more accepted and, perhaps, more available.

## Types of Extraordinary Capabilities

Preliminary indications are that the potential for psychic functioning is, like musical talent, widely but not uniformly distributed. Further, in the Western cultures, there are good indications that it has been suppressed as being evil or, alternatively, psychotic. Like other talents, it requires a certain level of skill and technique, which apparently can be developed with proper training and perseverance. The degree to which an individual or group of individuals can become more proficient in psychic functioning and the factors that govern proficiency are still not clear. One should not lightly dismiss the admonitions of mystics of nearly every culture who seem, as a group, to be the most proficient. They urge caution and have for centuries cloaked their rites in secrecy and ritualistic language. In order to gain the forbidden knowledge, they prescribe ascetic disciplines of behavior and training to safely achieve the emotional stability and spiritual purity necessary for proficient functioning. Whether these precautions are valid or whether they serve merely to preserve the status and mystique of the elite few is a proper subject for conjecture.

For the purpose of this speculation on societal implications, assume that satisfactorily safe training can be effected and permit us to classify the events into the following categories:

1. Animate awareness: this includes the traditional categories of telepathy and pre- and postcognition and includes the subsets of self-awareness and awareness of other animate life forms.

2. Matter awareness: this also includes traditional categories but is distinguishable from Category 1 in that the information received pertains to other than the animate universe.

3. Animate control: this category is concerned with the active processes of exerting direct or indirect influence on another individual or group of individuals by extraordinary means and includes, as a subset, control of other forms of animate life. It also includes, as a subset, the ability to control one's own physical mechanisms beyond the boundaries currently understood in classical psychology and physiology.

4. Matter control: this category includes the traditional notion of telekinesis, or PK, as applied to the inanimate universe.

I have chosen to use these categories rather than the traditional parapsychological terminology because they represent an ascending order of rarity and complexity, not only in interpretation but also in the implications they produce for the social order.

It is not the purpose here to deal extensively with the scientific implications of these categories. These issues can be discussed far more capably and succinctly by persons highly skilled in such disciplines as theoretical physics, mathematics, neurophysiology, and psychology. I shall touch upon the scientific question only briefly by suggesting that the crucial issue is whether or not these events can be formalized within the confines of classical theories. All would breathe a sigh of relief if this were found to be true. On the other hand, there is no compelling reason to believe that our knowledge of the universe is so complete that in the short century of modern scientific inquiry, we have completely ferreted out all of nature's secrets.

It is reasonable to hope that Categories 1 and 2 and some phenomena in Category 3 could be explained within the classical structure or by modest extrapolations therefrom. On the other hand, it is exceedingly difficult to understand how Category 4, consisting of "mind over inanimate matter," can be understood without major reworking and expansion of current concepts about the fundamental nature of matter and, additionally, some new insights about the nature of mind.

It is the author's personal bias that as a result of the study of Category 4 events, the idealist model (that is, that consciousness and thought represent the fundamental action principle of the universe) will be essential for explaining these events. (The competing models are the materialist model, in which matter is the fundamental "stuff" of the universe, and the dualist model, in which matter and thought are separate and distinct realms.)[2]

However, rather than preempt here the theoretician's job of explaining such events, it will suffice to suggest that in due course, all four categories will be established as valid and will require explanation. Personal observations to date convince me that all these categories are a part of the natural order of an evolving universe. They will be developed in sufficient measure during coming generations to exert influence for the betterment or destruction of our social system.

## Social Consequences

To digress, a further discussion of the four individual categories previously mentioned will facilitate in understanding them.

Category 1 is concerned with awareness of, and perceptiveness about, other living systems. This awareness appears to extend the boundaries of conventional notions about space, time, and information flow. An individual with fully developed perceptual capabilities could, at will, be aware of the feelings, emotions, and thoughts of other individuals. The limits of information resolution and the range of subject matter that can be perceived in this manner have yet to be explored. However, the remote-viewing experiments of Puthoff and Targ give some indication that the distance, range, and resolution of information transferable between cooperating persons is considerable.[3]

Not only is objective information transferable from mind to mind, but the condition of the transmitting system is also usually discernible. Is it healthy, is it comfortable, is it honest, or is it lying? What would it be like to live in a society where one's inner feelings, state of health, and covert motivations could be perceived directly?

Duplicity, dishonesty, and deception would no longer be useful characteristics. With awareness *fully* developed in a social structure, individuals would either become totally honest, with life as an open book, or become paranoid from one's baser motivations being continually perceived.

The diplomatic, political, military, and promotional games that society currently enjoys, and upon which much institutional interaction is based, would, of necessity, fall apart. The alternative would be an "awareness race," in which adversaries would engage in the self-defeating practice of keeping score and outmaneuvering the other's deceptions. This would differ from current practice only in the speed and directness with which it took place.

An important element of animate awareness is deeper *self*-awareness. Achievement of greater awareness of other living systems is not as likely to occur without first, or at least concurrently, achieving greater self-awareness. Being able to discern accurately and honestly one's own condition, needs, and motivations may, in the final analysis, be the most important social advance to evolve from our exploration of extraordinary mental functioning.

If an individual can accept the events and implications of Category 1, then Category 2 is only a small step forward. This category *directly* implies a notion that modern society is approaching from a different viewpoint—that notion is the interconnected and interdependent relationships of *all* matter.

Ecological studies are convincing even the most ironclad pragmatist that man cannot, with impunity, tinker with the delicate balances in nature. Recognition of the interdependency of seemingly unrelated systems suggests that there is no closed system smaller than the entire universe. Although many systems appear substantially independent, there always can be found a small flow of energy or information across the boundaries that influences the processes of the system and creates change.

Category 2 awareness suggests that information about the "states of matter" can be directly perceived by the human organism by, as yet, unknown processes. To cite a practical example, the studies by Dean on executive ESP show a strong correlation between the decision-making abilities of successful executives and their ability to precognize a random ordering of numbers subsequently selected by a computer.[4] From this study, it would seem that successfully guessing the future needs of a company requires some of the same skills required for successfully guessing the outcome of random inanimate events. For this to happen, some information flow from the matter and from the future event must take place so that it can be perceived by the human organism. If one develops this notion to its logical extreme, one arrives at the concept that *any* information about the universe and its functions is *directly knowable* to a talented and trained individual who chooses to obtain such information.

As has been previously stated, questions about who can be trained, transfer mechanisms, limits of resolution, and bit rates, for example, have yet to be answered. However, broadly speaking, the implication of Category 2 awareness is but an extension of Category 1, namely, that the universe is an "open book" to those who become trained to read it. Many current ideas and priorities at all levels of social and institutional functioning with regard to secrecy, proprietary information, and decision making will, of necessity, require modification.

One is challenged to ask at this point, "Is mankind ready for this?"

Category 1 and Category 2 awarenesses are essentially concerned with the passive process of gaining information by *direct cognition, direct perception, intuition,* or any number of other terms that are more or less applicable to these little understood processes. Both categories imply vastly expanded awareness functions available to some, perhaps many, humans through mechanisms yet to be formally explained. The forgoing speculations about what one might expect if large numbers of humanity could develop these abilities to a high art represent a deduction carried to its limit. The truth is probably less dramatic and probably lies short of the limit, at least in the foreseeable future.

As dramatic as the previous discussion of passive processes may seem, it pales in comparison with the implication of the active process of Categories 3 and 4.

Category 3 is direct control of animate systems. Keep in mind that in today's world, humans attempt to control the animate universe through the usual channels of communication, with appeals to reason, law, and self-interest. Where such appeals fail, resort is made to manipulation and coercion. Category 3 only adds another tool to our bag of tricks, a tool realized by consciously changing the information flow of Category 1 from a passive process of awareness to an active process of projection. All of the benefits and detriments currently enjoyed by humanity are accentuated by addition of this powerful means of direct influence. The opportunity for beneficial assistance seems great, but the opportunity for coercion and manipulation of the unaware seems even greater. Perhaps the most important beneficial aspect of Category 3 is the implication of greater control of the individual's own organism.

The traditional notion is that humans are limited in conscious control of the self by many physical and psychological factors. Certainly, studies in biofeedback, meditation, hypnosis, and guided imagery suggest that control can be greatly extended beyond what has been considered possible—perhaps, down to the level of individual cells in the body. If such techniques can become well developed, the implication for self-improvement, health, well-being, wisdom, and fulfillment are quite profound.

It should go without saying that the proper training technique for gaining control of Category 3 capabilities is to *first* learn to control self and then, cautiously, extend one's boundaries out toward the rest of the animate universe. (Nature's wisdom regarding man will hopefully prevent any other approach.)

Category 4 is the control of inanimate matter. This, of course, is the most provocative, most rare, most controversial, and least understood of capabilities. The Western world still does not generally accept this type of functioning as a part of reality. However, it is analogous to the "white crow" problem in logic. Finding just one of the set proves that the set exists. Similarly, finding just one bona fide case of mind over inanimate matter proves that such control exists. Finding additional individuals capable of such control poses untold problems, challenges, and implications for the belief systems that shape our reality. In the minds of many capable field investigators, the traditional paradigm has already been shattered.

The practical implications of this are probably small, since few are likely to develop such capabilities to a high proficiency. The profundity of the issue lies in the implications to our system of thought about the nature of man, the universe, and reality. In spite of the relative rarity of these events, the question must be asked, Could it be that we, each one of us, every day, by our thoughts are subtly influencing our environment, our reality, our universe without consciously knowing it, or is this type of control strictly the province of a few rare individuals who possess this unique capability?

My purpose in presenting these ideas was to ask the provocative question, to illustrate with the extreme example, and to examine the broad implications of what must be considered "extraordinary events." It is left to the reader to fill in the gaps and to ask questions regarding day-to-day implications for such fields as medicine, business, politics, and education. Such exercises are illuminating, startling, and very much worth doing. These ideas present significant challenges to those interested in the progress of knowledge.

Whatever the thoughts one holds about the events and the research presented in this volume, it is important to keep in mind the following facts: (1) the "white crow" exists, (2) the attention devoted to the study of extraordinary human functions is still appallingly little, and (3) Toynbee's quote at the beginning of the paper can be summed up as, "Where do we go from here?"

## Notes

1. Arnold J. Toynbee, "Is America Neglecting Her Creative Minority?" *Accent on Talent,* vol. 2 (January 1968).

2. Edgar D. Mitchell et al., *Psychic Exploration: A Challenge for Science* (New York: G. P. Putnam's Sons, 1974).

3. H. Puthoff and R. Targ, "A Perceptual Channel for Information Transfer over Kilometer Distances: Historical Perspective and Recent Research," *Proceedings of IEEE* 64 (March 1976): 329–54.

4. Douglas E. Dean and John Mihalsky, *Executive ESP* (Englewood Cliffs, N.J.: Prentice-Hall, 1974).

# Introduction to Chapter 2

The work of J. B. Rhine and his colleagues at Duke University in the 1930s, which included dozens of careful laboratory experiments that strongly indicated the existence of ESP, greatly excited the scientific community. There were several years of heated debate, as well as strenuous attempts to disprove the ESP results, but these efforts met with little success on the level of logical argumentation. Methodological criticisms were answered by Rhine, and confirmation of the basic results occurred in a large number of other laboratories.[1] The scientific world, especially the still insecure psychological community, was not yet ready to accept these results, and until very recently, there has been what one sociologist has called a "kind of high-class prejudice" against ESP results.[2] They were simply not mentioned in mainstrearn scientific journals, and articles containing such results were not accepted for publication. The rejection was usually based on some variant of the argument that since there could not be any such thing as ESP, an experiment that showed it had to be flawed, even if no flaw could be found: The handful of scientists who continued working in parapsychology developed a parallel journal structure for disseminating results, but these specialty journals are largely unknown to the general scientific community.*

The following chapter by Harold Puthoff and Russell Targ was first published as an article in 1976 in the *Proceedings of the IEEE,* a journal of wide circulation in the general scientific community. Aside from the importance of its content, its publication, linked with the slightly earlier publication of a psi research paper in *Nature,*[3] represented a new openness and interest in the

---

*These are the *Journal of the Society for Psychical Research* (London), the *Journal of the American Society for Psychical Research* (New York), the *Journal of Parapsychology* (Durham, N.C.), the *International Journal of Parapsychology* (New York, now defunct), and the *European Journal of Parapsychology* (Utrecht).

general scientific community toward parapsychological phenomena. This openness and interest was a reflection of increased cultural interest in expanded human consciousness, as well as stemming from increasing awareness in the physical sciences of the role that the human observer and consciousness might play in developing a comprehensive picture of the universe.

Following a brief overview of scientific parapsychology, the authors report on their remote-viewing experiments, in which a wide variety of people have been enormously successful in describing events occurring at considerable distances from them. These experiments are quite stimulating in suggesting new directions for parapsychological research, as well as requiring an expanded conception of both the nature of the human mind and the nature of the universe. The authors do not deal simply with generalities and puzzles but, rather, present much specific material on the relation of parapsychological phenomena to modern conceptions in the physical sciences.

## About the Authors

**Harold E. Puthoff,** Ph.D., is a physicist whose early research work was in nonlinear optics and quantum electronics. He is a patent holder in the area of lasers, has published numerous technical papers in that area, and is the author (with Richard Pantell) of a widely used textbook, *Fundamentals of Quantum Electronics.* For the past five years [1974–1979], he has worked on the scientific study of parapsychological phenomena at SRI International in Menlo Park, California. Recent articles on parapsychological phenomena in *Nature* (October 1974) and *Proceedings of the IEEE* (March 1976), coauthored with Russell Targ, have been the first major articles on this subject to appear in leading general science journals in many years. Puthoff also coauthored the book *Mind-Reach: Scientists Look at Psychic Ability* with Russell Targ, making five years of research on parapsychological phenomena at SRI available to the general public.

**Russell Targ** approaches parapsychological research from a background in magic, as well as his formal training in physics. He is widely known for his work in both high-power laser development and microwave physics and is an inventor of the tunable plasma laser. His *Mind-Reach* book, coauthored with Puthoff, has been translated into more than half a dozen languages since its 1977 publication, and his and Puthoff's technical papers have been enthusiastically received by a wide professional audience. Targ is cofounder with Charles T. Tart of the Parapsychology Research Group, of which he has been President since 1963, as well as being a Senior Research Physicist at SRI International in Menlo Park, California.

# 2

# A Perceptual Channel for Information Transfer over Kilometer Distances: Historical Perspective and Recent Research

## Harold E. Puthoff and Russell Targ

"It is the province of natural science to investigate nature, impartially and without prejudice."[4] Nowhere in scientific inquiry has this dictum met as great a challenge as in the area of so-called extrasensory perception, the detection of remote stimuli not mediated by the usual sensory processes. Such phenomena, although under scientific consideration for over a century, have historically been fraught with unreliability and controversy, and validation of the phenomena by accepted scientific methodology has been slow in coming. Even so, a recent survey

---

This work was supported by the Foundation for Parasensory Investigation and the Parapsychology Foundation, New York, New York; the Institute of Noetic Sciences, Palo Alto, California; and the National Aeronautics and Space Administration, under Contract NAS 7-100.

Most of this chapter originally appeared under the same title in the *Proceedings of the IEEE* 64 (1976): 329–54, and is reprinted here by permission of the IEEE.

The authors wish to thank the principal subjects, Hella Hammid, Pat Price, and Ingo Swann, who showed patience and forbearance in addition to their enthusiasm and outstanding perceptual abilities. We note with sadness the death of one of our subjects, Pat Price. We express our sincere thanks also to Earle Jones, Bonnar Cox, and Dr. Arthur Hastings, of SRI, and Judith Skutch and Richard Bach, without whose encouragement and support this work could not have taken place.

conducted by the British publication *New Scientist* revealed that 67 percent of nearly 1,500 responding readers (the majority of whom are working scientists and technologists) considered ESP to be an established fact or a likely possibility, and 88 percent held the investigation of ESP to be a legitimate scientific undertaking.[5]

A review of the literature reveals that although experiments by reputable researchers yielding positive results were begun over a century ago (for example, Sir William Crookes's study of D. D. Home in the 1860s),[6] many consider the study of these phenomena as only recently emerging from the realm of quasi-science. One reason for this is that despite experimental results, no satisfactory theoretical construct had been advanced to correlate data or to predict new experimental outcomes. Consequently, the area in question remained for a long time in the recipe stage, reminiscent of electrodynamics before the unification brought about by the work of Ampere, Faraday, and Maxwell. Since the early work, however, we have seen the development of information theory, quantum theory, and neurophysiological research, and these disciplines provide powerful conceptual tools that appear to bear directly on the issue. In fact, several physicists are now of the opinion that these phenomena are not at all inconsistent with the framework of modern physics: the often-held view that observations of this type are a priori incompatible with known laws is erroneous in that such a concept is based on the naive realism prevalent before the development of quantum theory. In the emerging view, it is accepted that research in this area can be conducted so as to uncover not just a catalog of interesting events but, rather, patterns of cause-effect relationships of the type that lend themselves to analysis and hypothesis in the forms with which we are familiar in the physical sciences. One hypothesis is that information transfer under conditions of sensory shielding is mediated by extremely low-frequency (ELF) electromagnetic waves, a proposal that does not seem to be ruled out by any obvious physical or biological facts. Further, the development of information theory makes it possible to characterize and quantify the performance of a communications channel regardless of the underlying mechanism.

For the past three years, we have had a program in the Electronics and Bioengineering Laboratory of SRI to investigate those facets of human perception that appear to fall outside the range of well-understood perceptual/processing capabilities. Of particular interest is a human information-accessing capability that we call *remote viewing*. This phenomenon pertains to the ability of certain individuals to access and describe, by means of mental processes, information sources blocked from ordinary perception and generally accepted as secure against such access.

In particular, the phenomenon we have investigated most extensively is the ability of a subject to view remote geographical locations up to several thousand kilometers distant from his or her physical location (given only a known person on whom to target).[7] We have carried out more than 50 experiments under controlled laboratory conditions with several individuals whose remote perceptual abilities have been developed sufficiently to allow them at times to describe correctly—often in great detail—geographical or technical material, such as buildings, roads, laboratory apparatus, and the like.

As observed in the laboratory, the basic phenomenon appears to cover a range of subjective experiences, variously referred to in the literature as *autoscopy* (in the medical literature); *exteriorization* or *disassociation* (psychological literature); *simple clairvoyance, traveling clairvoyance,* or *out-of-body experience* (parapsychological literature); or *astral projection* (occult literature). We choose the term *remote viewing* as a neutral descriptive term free from prior associations and bias as to mechanisms.

The development at SRI of a successful experimental procedure to elicit this capability has evolved to the point where persons such as visiting government scientists and contract monitors, with no previous exposure to such concepts, have learned to perform well; subjects who have trained over a one-year period have performed excellently under a variety of experimental conditions. Our accumulated data thus indicate that both specially selected and unselected persons can be assisted in developing remote perceptual abilities up to a level of useful information transfer.

In experiments of this type, we have three principal findings. First, we have established that it is possible to obtain significant amounts of accurate descriptive information about remote locations. Second, an increase in the distance from a few meters up to 4,000 kilometers (km) separating the subject from the scene to be perceived does not in any apparent way degrade the quality or accuracy of perception. Finally, the use of Faraday cage electrical shielding does not prevent high-quality descriptions from being obtained.

To build a coherent theory for the explanation of these phenomena, it is necessary to have a clear understanding of what constitutes the phenomena. In this chapter, we first briefly summarize previous efforts in this field in the Background section. We then present the results of a series of more than 50 experimental trials with nine subjects carried out in our own laboratory, which represent a sufficiently stable data base to permit testing of various hypotheses concerning the functioning of this channel. Finally, we indicate those areas of physics and information theory that appear to be relevant to an understanding of certain aspects of the phenomena.

First, however, we present an illustrative example generated in an early pilot experiment. As will be clear from our later discussion, this is not a "best-ever" example but, rather, a typical sample of the level of proficiency that can be reached and that we have come to expect in our research.

Three subjects participated in a long-distance experiment focusing on a series of targets in Costa Rica. These subjects said they had never been to Costa Rica. In this experiment, one of the experimenters (Puthoff) spent ten days traveling through Costa Rica on a combination business/pleasure trip. This information was all that was known to the subjects about the traveler's itinerary. The experiment called for Puthoff to keep a detailed record of his location and activities, including photographs of each of seven target days at 1330 Pacific Daylight Time. A total of 12 daily descriptions were collected before the traveler's return: six responses from one subject, five from another, and one from a third.

The third subject (R. T.) who submitted the single response supplied a drawing for a day in the middle of the series. (The subject's response, together with the photographs taken at the site, are shown in Figure 2.1.) Although Costa Rica is a mountainous country, the subject unexpectedly perceived the traveler at a beach and ocean setting. With some misgiving, he described an airport on a sandy beach and an airstrip with the ocean at the end (correct). An airport building also was drawn and shown to have a large rectangular over-hang (correct). The traveler had taken an unplanned one-day side trip to an offshore island and, at the time of the experiment, had just disembarked from a plane at a small island airport as described by the subject 4,000 km away. The sole discrepancy was that the subject's drawing showed a Quonset hut type of building in place of the rectangular structure.

The above description was chosen as an example to illustrate a major point observed a number of times throughout the program to be described. Contrary to what may be expected, a subject's description does not necessarily portray what may reasonably be expected to be correct (an educated or "safe" guess) but often runs counter even to the subject's own expectations.

We wish to stress again that a result such as the above is not unusual. The remaining submissions in this experiment provided further examples of excellent correspondences between target and response. (A target period of poolside relaxation was identified; a drive through a tropical forest at the base of a truncated volcano was described as a drive through a jungle below a large bare table mountain; a hotel room target description, including such details as rug color, was correct; and so on.) So as to determine whether such matches were simply fortuitous—that is, could reasonably be expected on the basis of change alone—Puthoff was asked after he had returned to blind match the 12 descriptions to his seven target locations. On the basis of this conservative evaluation procedure, which vastly underestimates the statistical significance of the individual descriptions, five correct matches were obtained. This number of matches is significant at $p = .02$, one-tailed, by exact binomial calculation.*

The observation of such unexpectedly high-quality descriptions early in our program led to a large-scale study of the phenomenon at SRI under secure double-blind conditions (that is, target unknown to experimenters, as well as subjects), with independent random target selection and blind judging. The

---

*The probability of a correct daily match by chance for any given transcript is $p = 1/7$. Therefore, the one-tailed probability of at least five correct matches by chance out of 12 tries can be calculated from

$$p = \sum_{i=5}^{12} \frac{12!}{i!\,(12-i)!} \left(\frac{1}{7}\right)^{i} \left(\frac{6}{7}\right)^{(12-i)} = .02.$$

results, presented below, provide strong evidence for the robustness of this phenomenon whereby a human perceptual modality of extreme sensitivity can detect complex remote stimuli.

## Background

Although we are approaching the study of these phenomena as physicists, it is not yet possible to separate ourselves entirely from the language of the nineteenth century, when the laboratory study of the paranormal was begun.

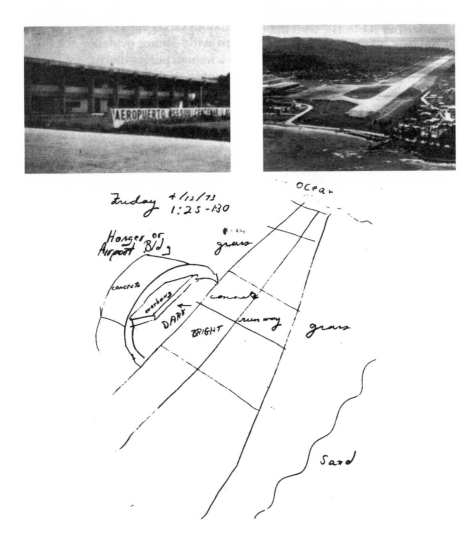

**Figure 2.1** Photographs of airport in San Andres, Colombia, used as remote-viewing target, along with sketch produced by subject in California.

Consequently, we continue to use terms such as *paranormal, telepathy,* and the like. However, we intend only to indicate a process of information transfer under conditions generally accepted as secure against such transfer and with no prejudice or occult assumptions as to the mechanisms involved. As in any other scientific pursuit, the purpose is to collect the observables that result from experiments and to try to determine the functional relationships between these observables and the laws of physics as they are currently understood.

Organized research into so-called psychic functioning began roughly in the time of J. J. Thomson, Sir Oliver Lodge, and Sir William Crookes, all of whom took part in the founding of the Society for Psychical Research (SPR) in 1882 in England. Crookes, for example, carried out his principal investigations with D. D. Home, a Scotsman who grew up in the United States and returned to England in 1855.[8] According to the notebooks and published reports of Crookes, Home had demonstrated the ability to cause objects to move without touching them. We should note in passing that Home, unlike most subjects, worked only in the light and spoke out in the strongest possible terms against the darkened seance rooms popular at the time.[9]

Crookes was a pioneer in the study of electrical discharge in gases and in the development of vacuum tubes, some types of which still bear his name. Although everything Crookes said about electron beams and plasmas was accepted, nothing he said about the achievements of Home ever achieved that status. Many of his colleagues, who had not observed the experiments with Home, stated publicly that they thought Crookes had been deceived, to which Crookes angrily responded:

> Will not my critics give me credit for some amount of common sense? Do they not imagine that the obvious precautions, which occur to them as soon as they sit down to pick holes in my experiments, have occurred to me also in the course of my prolonged and patient investigation? The answer to this, as to all other objections is, prove it to be an error, by showing where the error lies, or if a trick, by showing how the trick is performed. Try the experiment fully and fairly. If then fraud be found, expose it; if it be a truth, proclaim it. This is the only scientific procedure, and it is that I propose steadily to pursue.[10]

In the United States, scientific interest in the paranormal was centered in the universities. In 1912, John Coover was established in an endowed fellowship for psychical research at Stanford University.[11] In the 1920s, Harvard University set up research programs with George Estabrooks; and L. T. Troland.[12] It was in this framework that in 1930, William McDougall invited J. B. Rhine and Louisa Rhine to join the Psychology Department at Duke University.[13] For more than 30 years, significant work was carried out at Rhine's Duke University Laboratory. To examine the existence of paranormal perception, he used the now famous ESP cards, containing a boldly printed picture of a star, cross, square, circle, or wavy lines. Subjects were asked to name the order of these cards in a freshly shuffled deck of 25 such cards. To test for telepathy, an experimenter would look at the cards one at a time, and a subject suitably separated from the sender would attempt to determine which card was being viewed.

J. B. Rhine, together with J. G. Pratt, carried out thousands of experiments of this type under widely varying conditions.[14] The statistical results from these experiments indicated that some individuals did indeed possess a paranormal perceptual ability in that it was possible to obtain an arbitrarily high degree of improbability by continued testing of a gifted subject.

The work of Rhine has been challenged on many grounds, however, including accusations of improper handling of statistics, error, and fraud. With regard to the statistics, the general consensus of statisticians today is that if fault is to be found in Rhine's work, it would have to be on other than statistical grounds.[15] With regard to the accusations of fraud, the most celebrated case of criticism of Rhine's work, that of Price,[16] ended 17 years after it began when the accusation of fraud was retracted by its author in an article entitled "Apology to Rhine and Soal," published in the same journal in which it was first put forward.[17] It should also be noted that parapsychological researchers themselves recently exposed fraud in their own laboratory when they encountered it.[18]

The most severe criticism of all this work, a criticism difficult to defend against in principle, is that leveled by the well-known British parapsychological critic C. E. M. Hansel, who began his examination of the ESP hypothesis with the stated assumption, "In view of the *a priori* arguments against it *we know in advance* that telepathy, etc., cannot occur."[19] Therefore, based on the "*a priori* unlikelihood" of ESP, Hansel's examination of the literature centered primarily on the possibility of fraud by subjects or investigators. He reviewed in depth four experiments that he regarded as providing the best evidence of ESP: the Pearce–Pratt distance series and the Pratt–Woodruff series, both conducted at Duke; Soal's work with Gloria Stewart and Basil Shackleton; as well as a more recent series by Soal and Bowden.[20] Hansel showed, in each case, how fraud *could* have been committed (by the experimenters in the Pratt–Woodruff and Soal–Bateman series or by the subjects in the Pearce–Pratt and Soal–Bowden experiments). He gave no direct evidence that fraud *was* committed in these experiments, but said, "If the result could have arisen through a trick, the experiment must be considered unsatisfactory proof of ESP, *whether or not it is finally decided that such a trick was in fact used.*"[21] As discussed by Honorton in a review of the field, Hansel's conclusion after 241 pages of careful scrutiny therefore was that these experiments were not "fraud-proof" and therefore, in principle, could not serve as conclusive proof of ESP.[22]

In the real world, of course, no experiment in any field of science is completely fraud proof, so Hansel's argument is an absolutist, philosophical one, rather than a scientific argument. In science, data always have priority over theory or a priori convictions. Indeed, Honorton noted that Hansel himself was guilty of the questionable practices he was accusing parapsychological investigators of, for he grossly distorted a drawing of laboratory arrangements in order to make a hypothesis of subject fraud plausible in his criticism of the Pearce–Pratt experiments.[23]

Even among the supporters of ESP research and its results, there remained the consistent problem that many successful subjects eventually lost their ability and their scores gradually drifted toward chance results. This decline effect in no way erased their previous astronomical success, but it was a disappointment, since if paranormal perception is a natural ability, one would like to see subjects improving with practice rather than getting worse.

One of the first successful attempts to overcome the decline effect was in Czechoslovakia in the work of Ryzl, a chemist with the Institute of Biology of the Czechoslovakian Academy of Science and also an amateur hypnotist.[24] Through the use of hypnosis, together with feedback and reinforcement, he developed several outstanding subjects, one of whom, Pavel Stepanek, has worked with experimenters around the world for more than ten years.

Ryzl's pioneering work came as an answer to the questions raised by the 1956 CIBA Foundation Conference on Extrasensory Perception. The CIBA Chemical Company has annual meetings on topics of biological and chemical interest, and that same year, they assembled several prominent parapsychologists to have a state-of-the-art conference on ESP.[25] The conference concluded that little progress would be made in parapsychology research until a repeatable experiment could be found, namely, an experiment that different experimenters could repeat at will and that would reliably yield a statistically significant result.

Ryzl had by 1962 accomplished that goal. His primary contribution was a decision to interact with the subject as a person in order to try to build up his confidence and ability. His protocol depended on "working with" rather than "running" his subjects. Ryzl's star subject, Stepanek, produced highly significant results with many contemporary researchers.[26] In these experiments, he was able to tell with 60 percent reliability whether a hidden card was green side or white side up, yielding statistics of 1 million to one with only 1,000 trials.

As significant as such results are statistically, the information channel is imperfect, containing noise along with the signal. When considering how best to use such a channel, one is led to the communication theory concept of the introduction of redundancy as a means of coding a message to combat the effects of a noisy channel.[27] A prototype experiment by Ryzl using such techniques has proved to be successful. Ryzl had an assistant select randomly five groups of three digits each. These 15 digits were then encoded into binary form and translated into a sequence of green and white cards in sealed envelopes. By means of repeated calling and an elaborate majority vote protocol, Ryzl was able after 19,350 calls by Sepanek (averaging 9 seconds [s] per call) to correctly identify all 15 numbers, a result significant at $p = 10^{-15}$. The hit rate for individual calls was 61.9 percent, 11,978 hits and 7,372 misses.[28] A similar procedure was recently used by Carpenter to transmit the word peace without error in International Morse Code.[29]

The characteristics of such a channel can be specified in accordance with the precepts of communication theory. The bit rate associated with the information channel is calculated from Shannon and Weaver:[30]

$$R = H(x) - H_y(x)$$

where $H(x)$ is the uncertainty of the source message containing symbols with a priori probability $p_i$:

$$H(x) = -\sum_{i=1}^{2} p_i \log_2 p_i$$

and $H_y(x)$ is the conditional entropy based on the a posteriori probabilities that a received signal was actually transmitted:

$$H_y(x) = -\sum_{i,j=1}^{2} p(i,j) \log_2 p_i(j).$$

For Stepanek's run, with $p_i = 1/2$, $p_j(j) = .619$, and an average time of 9 s (seconds) per choice, we have a source uncertainty $H(x) = 1$ bit and a calculated bit rate

$$R \approx .041 \text{ bit/s}$$

or

$$R/T \approx .0046 \text{ bit/s}$$

(Since the 15-digit number [49.8 bits] actually was transmitted at the rate of $2.9 \times 10^{-4}$ bit/s, an increase in bit rate by a factor of about 20 could be expected on the basis of a coding scheme that was more optimum than that used in the experiments.)

Charles Tart, at the University of California, has written extensively on the so-called decline effect. He considers that having subjects attempt to guess cards or perform any other repetitive task for which they receive no feedback follows the classical technique for deconditioning any response. He thus considers card guessing "a technique for extinguishing psychic functioning in the laboratory."[31] He has reported considerable success in eliminating the decline effect with immediate feedback training.[32]

Tart's injunctions of the mid-1960s were being heeded at Maimonides Hospital, Brooklyn, New York, by a team of researchers that included Dr. Montague Ullman, who was director of research for the hospital, Dr. Stanley

Krippner, and, later, Charles Honorton. These three worked together for several years on experiments on the occurrence of telepathy in dreams. In the course of a half-dozen experimental series, they found in their week-long sessions a number of subjects who had dreams that consistently were highly descriptive of pictorial material that a remote sender was looking at throughout the night. This work is described in detail in the experimenters' book *Dream Telepathy.*[33] Honorton is continuing work of this free response type, in which the subject has no preconceived idea as to what the target may be.

In his more recent work with subjects in the waking state, Honorton is providing homogeneous stimulation to the subject who is to describe color slides viewed by another person in a remote room. In this new work, the subject listens to white noise via earphones and views an homogeneous visual field imposed through the use of ping-pong ball halves to cover the subject's eyes in conjunction with diffuse ambient illumination. In this so-called Ganzfeld setting, subjects are again able, now in the waking state, to give correct and often highly accurate descriptions of the material being viewed by the sender.[34] In Honorton's work and elsewhere, it apparently has been the step away from the repetitive forced-choice experiment that has opened the way for a wide variety of ordinary people to demonstrate significant functioning in the laboratory without being bored into a decline effect.

This survey would be incomplete if we did not indicate certain aspects of the current state of research in the USSR. It is clear from translated documents and other sources that many laboratories in the USSR are engaged in paranormal research.[35] Since the 1930s, in the laboratory of L. Vasiliev (Leningrad Institute for Brain Research), there has been an interest in the use of telepathy as a method of influencing the behavior of a person at a distance. In Vasiliev's book *Experiments in Mental Suggestion,* he makes it very clear that the bulk of his laboratory's experiments were aimed at long-distance communication combined with a form of behavior modification, for example, putting people at a distance to sleep through hypnosis.[36]

Similar behavior modification types of experiments have been carried out in recent times by I. M. Kogan, chairman of the bioinformation section of the Moscow board of the Popov Society. He is a Soviet engineer who, until 1969, published extensively on the theory of telepathic communication.[37] He was concerned with three principal kinds of experiments: mental suggestion without hypnosis over short distances, in which the percipient attempts to identify an object; mental awakening over short distances, in which a subject is awakened from a hypnotic sleep at the "beamed" suggestion from the hypnotist; and long-range (intercity) telepathic communication. Kogan's main interest has been to quantify the channel capacity of the paranormal channel. He finds that the bit rate decreases from .1 bit/s for laboratory experiments to .005 bit/s for his 1,000-km intercity experiments.

In the USSR, serious consideration is given to the hypothesis that telepathy is mediated by ELF electromagnetic propagation. (The pros and cons of this hypothesis are discussed below, as well as in Chapter 8.) In general, the entire field of paranormal research in the USSR is part of a larger one concerned with the interaction between electromagnetic fields and living organisms.[38] At the First International Congress on Parapsychology and Psychotronics in Prague, Czechoslovakia, in 1973, for example, Kholodov spoke at length about the susceptibility of living systems to extremely low-level alternating current (ac) and direct current (dc) fields. He described conditioning effects on the behavior of fish resulting from the application of 10 to 100 $\mu$W of RF to their tank.[39] The USSR take these data seriously in that the Soviet safety requirements for steady-state microwave exposure set limits at 10 $\mu$W/centimeter (cm)$^2$ whereas the United States has set a steady-state limit of 10 mW/cm$^2$.[40] Kholodov spoke also about the nonthermal effects of microwaves on animals' central nervous systems. His experiments were very carefully carried out and are characteristic of a new dimension in paranormal research.

The increasing importance of this area in Soviet research was indicated recently when the Soviet Psychological Association issued an unprecedented position paper calling on the Soviet Academy of Sciences to step up efforts in this area.[41] They recommended that the newly formed Psychological Institute within the Soviet Academy of Sciences and the Psychological Institute of the Academy of Pedagogical Sciences review the area and consider the creation of a new laboratory within one of the institutes to study persons with unusual abilities. They also recommended a comprehensive evaluation of experiments and theory by the Academy of Sciences' Institute of Biophysics and Institute for the Problems of Information Transmission.

The Soviet research, along with other behavioristically oriented work, suggests that in addition to obtaining overt responses, such as verbalizations or key presses from a subject, it should be possible to obtain objective evidence of information transfer by direct measurement of physiological parameters of a subject. J. Kamiya, Lindsley, Pribram, Silverman, Walter, and others brought together to discuss physiological methods to detect ESP functioning, have suggested that a whole range of electroencephalogram (EEG) responses, such as evoked potentials (EPs), spontaneous EEG, and the contingent negative variation (CNV), might be sensitive indicators of the detection of remote stimuli not mediated by usual sensory processes.[42]

Early experimentation of this type was carried out by Douglas Dean at the Newark College of Engineering. In his search for physiological correlates of information transfer, he used the plethysmograph to measure changes in the blood volume in a finger, a sensitive indicator of autonomic nervous system functioning.[43] A plethysmographic measurement was made on the finger of a subject during telepathy experiments. A sender looked at randomly selected target cards consisting of names known to the subject, together with names unknown to him (selected at random from a telephone book). The names of the known people were contributed by the subject and were to be of emotional significance to him. Dean found significant changes in the chart recording of finger blood volume when the remote sender was looking at those names known to the subject as compared with those names randomly chosen.

Three other experiments using the physiological approach have now been published. The first work by Tart, a later work by Lloyd, and most recently the work by J. P. Bisaha and B. J. Dunne (see Chapter 4) and E. C. May, Targ, and Puthoff (see Chapter 5) all follow a similar procedure.[44] Basically, a subject is closeted in an electrically shielded room while his or her EEG is recorded. Meanwhile, in another laboratory, a second person is stimulated from time to time, and the time of that stimulus is marked on the magnetic tape recording of the subject's EEG. The subject does not know when the remote stimulus periods are as compared with the nonstimulus periods.

With regard to choice of stimulus for our own experimentation, we noted that in previous work, others had attempted, without success, to detect evoked potential changes in a subject's EEG in response to a single stroboscopic flash stimulus observed by another subject.[45] In a discussion of that experiment, Kamiya suggested that because of the unknown temporal characteristics of the information channel, it might be more appropriate to use repetitive bursts of light to increase the probability of detecting information transfer.[46] Therefore, in our study, we chose to use a stroboscopic flash train of 10-s duration as the remote stimulus.

In the design of the study, we assumed that the application of the remote stimulus would result in responses similar to those obtained under conditions of direct stimulation. For example, when an individual is stimulated with a low-frequency (< 30 Hz) flashing light, the EEG typically shows a decrease in the amplitude of the resting rhythm and a driving of the brain waves at the frequency of the flashes.[47] We hypothesized that if we stimulated one subject in this manner (a putative sender), the EEG of another subject in a remote room with no flash present (a receiver) might show changes in alpha (9–11 Hz) activity and, possibly, an EEG driving similar to that of the sender, or other coupling to the sender's EEG.[48] The receiver was seated in a visually opaque, acoustically and electrically shielded, double-walled steel room about 7 meters (m) from the sender. The details of the experiment, consisting of seven runs of 36 10-s trials each (12 periods each for 0-Hz, 6-Hz, and 16-Hz stimuli, randomly intermixed), have been published.[49] This experiment proved to be successful. The receiver's alpha activity (9–11 Hz) showed a significant reduction in average power (-24 percent, $p < .04$) and peak power (-28 percent, $p < .03$) during 16-Hz flash stimuli as compared with periods of no-flash stimulus. (A similar response was observed for 6-Hz stimuli [-12 percent in average power, -21 percent in peak power], but the latter result did not reach statistical significance.) Figure 2.2 shows an overlay of three averaged EEG spectra from one of the subject's 36 trial runs, displaying differences in alpha activity during the

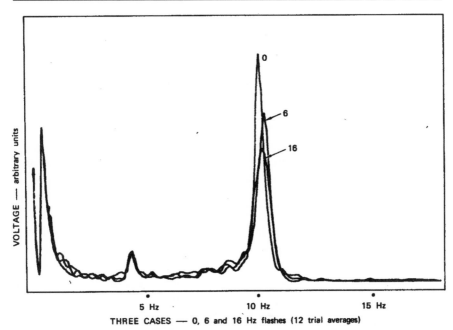

**THREE CASES — 0, 6 and 16 Hz flashes (12 trial averages)**

**Figure 2.2** Occipital EEG frequency spectra, 0–20 Hz, of one subject (Hammid, $S_4$) acting as receiver showing amplitude changes in the 9 to 11-Hz band as a function of strobe frequency. There are three cases: 0-, 6-, and 16-Hz flashes (12 trial averages).

three stimulus conditions. Extensive control procedures were undertaken to determine if these results were produced by system artifacts, electromagnetic pickup (EMI), or subtle cueing; the results were negative.[50]

As part of the experimental protocol, the subject was asked to indicate a conscious assessment for each trial (via telegraph key) as to the nature of the stimulus; analysis showed these guesses to be at chance. Thus, arousal as evidenced by significant alpha blocking occurred only at the noncognitive level of physiological response. Hence, the experiment provided direct physiological (EEG) evidence of perception of remote stimuli even in the absence of overt cognitive response.

Whereas in our experiments we used a remote light flash as a stimulus, Tart in his work used an electrical shock to himself as sender, and Lloyd simply told the sender to think of a red triangle each time a red warning light was illuminated within his view.[51] Lloyd observed a consistent evoked potential in his subjects; whereas in our experiments and in Tart's, a reduction in amplitude and a desynchronization of alpha was observed—an arousal response. (If a subject is resting in an alpha-dominant condition and he or she is then stimulated, for example in any direct manner, one will observe a desynchronization and decrease in alpha power.) We consider that these combined results are evidence for the existence of noncognitive awareness of remote happenings and that they have a profound implication for paranormal research.

## SRI Investigations of Remote Viewing

Experimentation in remote viewing began during studies carried out to investigate the abilities of a New York artist, Ingo Swann, when he expressed the opinion that the insights gained during experiments at SRI had strengthened his ability (verified in other research before he joined the SRI program) to view remote locations.[52] To test Swann's assertion, a pilot study was set up in which a series of targets from around the globe were supplied by SRI personnel to the experimenters on a double-blind basis. Swann's apparent ability to describe correctly details of buildings, roads, bridges, and the like indicated that it may be possible for a subject by means of mental imagery to access and describe randomly chosen geographical sites located several miles from the subject's position and demarcated by some appropriate means. Therefore, we set up a research program to test the remote-viewing hypothesis under rigidly controlled scientific conditions.

In carrying out this program, we concentrated on what we considered to be our principal responsibility—to resolve under unambiguous conditions the basic issue of whether or not this class of paranormal perception phenomenon exists. At all times, we and others responsible for the overall program took measures to prevent sensory leakage and subliminal cueing and to prevent deception, whether intentional or unintentional. To ensure evaluations independent of belief structures of both experimenters and judges, all experiments were carried out under a protocol, described below, in which target selection at the beginning of experiments and blind judging of results at the end of experiments were handled independently of the researchers engaged in carrying out the experiments.

Six subjects, designated $S_1$ through $S_6$ were chosen for the study. Three were considered as gifted or experienced subjects ($S_1$ through $S_3$), and three were considered as learners ($S_4$ through $S_6$). The a priori dichotomy between gifted subjects and learners was based on the experienced group having been successful in other studies conducted before this program and the learners group being inexperienced with regard to paranormal experimentation.

The study consisted of a series of double-blind tests with local targets in the San Francisco Bay Area so that several independent judges could visit the sites to establish documentation. The protocol was to closet the subject with an experimenter at SRI and at an agreed-on time to obtain from the subject a description of an undisclosed remote site being visited by a target team. In each of the experiments, one of the six program subjects served as remote-viewing subject, and SRI experimenters served as a target demarcation team at the remote location chosen in a double-blind protocol as follows.

In each experiment, SRI management randomly chose a target location from a list of targets within a 30-minute driving time from SRI, the target location selected was kept blind to subject and experimenters. The target pool consisted of more than 100 target locations chosen from a target-rich environment. (Before the experimental series began, the director of the Information Science and Engineering Division, not otherwise associated with the experiment, established the set of locations as the target pool, which remained known only to him. The target locations were printed on cards sealed in envelopes and kept in the SRI division office safe. They were available only with the personal assistance of the division director, who issued a single random number selected target card that constituted the traveling orders for that experiment.)

To begin the experiment, the subject was closeted with an experimenter at SRI to wait 30 minutes before beginning a narrative description of the remote location. A second experimenter then obtained from the division director a target location from a set of traveling orders previously prepared and randomized by the director and kept under his control. The target demarcation team, consisting of two to four SRI experimenters, then proceeded by automobile directly to the target without any communication with the subject or experimenter remaining behind. The experimenter remaining with the subject at SRI was kept ignorant of both the particular target and the target pool so as to eliminate the possibility of cueing (overt or subliminal) and to allow him freedom in questioning the subject to clarify his descriptions. The demarcation team remained at the target site for an agreed-on 15-minute period following the 30 minutes allotted for travel.* During the observation period, the remote-viewing subject was asked to describe his or her impressions of the target site into a tape recorder and to make any drawings he or she thought appropriate. An informal comparison was then made when the demarcation team returned, and the subject was taken to the site to provide feedback.

## Subject $S_1$: Experienced

To begin the series, Pat Price, a former California police commissioner and city councilman, participated as a subject in nine experiments. In general, Price's ability to describe correctly buildings, docks, roads, gardens, and the like, including structural materials, color, ambience, and activity—often in great detail—indicated the functioning of a remote perceptual ability. A Hoover Tower target, for example, was recognized and named by name. Nonetheless, in general, the descriptions contained inaccuracies as well as correct statements. A typical example is indicated by the subject's drawing shown

---

*The first subject ($S_1$) was allowed 30 minutes for his descriptions, but it was found that he became fatigued and had little comment after the first 15 minutes. The viewing time was therefore reduced to 15 minutes for subjects $S_2$ through $S_6$.

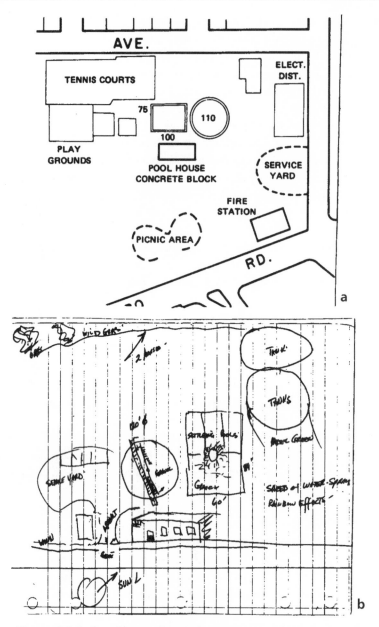

**Figure 2.3** Swimming pool complex as remote-viewing target. (a) City map of target location. (b) Drawing by subject Price ($S_1$).

in Figure 2.3 in which he correctly described a parklike area containing two pools of water: one rectangular, 60 by 89 feet (actual dimensions 75 by 100 feet), and the other circular, diameter 120 feet (actual diameter 110 feet). He incorrectly indicated the function, however, as water filtration rather than recreational swimming. (We often observe essentially correct descriptions of basic elements and patterns coupled with incomplete or erroneous analysis of function.) As can be seen from his drawing, he also included some elements, such as the tanks shown in the upper right, which are not present at the target site. We also note an apparent left-right reversal, often observed in paranormal perception experiments.

To obtain a numerical evaluation of the accuracy of the remote-viewing experiment, the experimental results were subjected to independent judging on a blind basis by an SRI research analyst not otherwise associated with the research. The subject's response packets, which contained the nine typed unedited transcripts of the tape-recorded narratives along with any associated drawings, were unlabeled and presented in random order. While standing at each target location, visited in turn, the judge was required to blind rank order the nine packets on a scale one to nine (best to worst match). The statistic of interest is the sum of ranks assigned to the target-associated transcripts, lower values indicating better matches. For nine targets, the sum of ranks could range from nine to 81. The probability that a given sum of ranks s or less will occur by chance is given by

$$\Pr (s \text{ or less}) = \frac{1}{N^n} \sum_{i=n}^{s} \sum_{l=0}^{k} (-1)^l \binom{n}{l} \binom{i - Nl - 1}{n - 1}$$

where $s$ is obtained sum of ranks, $N$ is number of assignable ranks, $n$ is number of occasions on which rankings were made, and $l$ takes on values from zero to the greatest positive integer $k$ in $(i - n)/N$.[53] (Table 2.1 is a table to enable easy application of the above formula to those cases in which $N = n$.) The sum in this case, which included seven direct hits out of the nine, was 16 (see Table 2.2), a result significant at $p = 2.9 \times 10^{-5}$, one-tailed, by exact calculation.

In experimental trials three, four, and six through nine, the subject was secured in a double-walled copper-screen Faraday cage. The Faraday cage provides 120-decibel (dB) attenuation for plane-wave radio frequency radiation over a range of 15 kHz to 1 GHz. For magnetic fields, the attenuation is 68 dB at 15 kHz and decreases to 3 dB at 60 Hz. The results of rank order judging (Table 2.2) indicate that the use of Faraday cage electrical shielding does not prevent high-quality descriptions from being obtained.

As a backup judging procedure, a panel of five additional SRI scientists not otherwise associated with the research were asked simply to blind match the unedited typed transcripts (with associated drawings) generated by the remote viewer against the nine target locations that they independently visited in turn. The transcripts were unlabeled and presented in random order. A correct match consisted of a transcript of a given date being matched to the target of that date. Instead of the expected number of one match each per judge, the number of correct matches obtained by the five judges was seven, six, five, three, and three, respectively. Thus, rather than the expected total number of five correct matches from the judges, 24 such matches were obtained.

### Table 2.1 Critical Values of Sums of Ranks for Preferential Matching

| Number of Assignable Ranks (N) | .20 | .10 | .05 | .04 | .024 | .01 | .005 | .002 | .001 | .0005 | $10^{-4}$ | $10^{-5}$ | $10^{-6}$ | $10^{-7}$ |
|---|---|---|---|---|---|---|---|---|---|---|---|---|---|---|
| | | | | Probability (one-tailed) That the Indicated Sum of Ranks or Less Would Occur by Chance | | | | | | | | | | |
| 4 | 7 | 6 | 5 | 5 | 5 | 4 | 4 | – | – | – | – | – | – | – |
| 5 | 11 | 10 | 9 | 8 | 8 | 7 | 6 | 6 | 5 | 5 | – | – | – | – |
| 6 | 16 | 15 | 13 | 13 | 12 | 11 | 10 | 9 | 8 | 7 | 6 | – | – | – |
| 7 | 22 | 20 | 18 | 18 | 17 | 15 | 14 | 12 | 12 | 11 | 9 | 8 | – | – |
| 8 | 29 | 27 | 24 | 24 | 22 | 20 | 19 | 17 | 16 | 15 | 13 | 11 | 9 | 8 |
| 9 | 37 | 34 | 31 | 30 | 29 | 26 | 24 | 22 | 21 | 20 | 17 | 14 | 12 | 10 |
| 10 | 46 | 42 | 39 | 38 | 36 | 33 | 31 | 29 | 27 | 25 | 22 | 19 | 16 | 13 |
| 11 | 56 | 51 | 48 | 47 | 45 | 41 | 38 | 36 | 34 | 32 | 28 | 24 | 20 | 17 |
| 12 | 67 | 61 | 58 | 56 | 54 | 49 | 47 | 43 | 41 | 39 | 35 | 30 | 25 | 22 |

*Note:* This table applies only to those special cases in which the number of occasions on which objects are being ranks (*n*) is equal to the number of assignable ranks (*N*). Each entry represents the largest number that is significant at the indicated *p* level.

*Source:* R. L. Morris, "An Exact Method for Evaluating Preferentially Matched Free-Response Material," *Journal of the American Society for Psychical Research* 66 (October 1972): 401. An extended version of the table is available in G. Solfvin, E. Kelly, and D. Burdick, "Some New Methods of Analysis for Preferential Ranking Data," *Journal of the American Society for Psychical Research* 72 (1978): 93–110.

### Table 2.2 Distribution of Rankings Assigned to Transcripts Associated with Each Target Location for Experienced Subject, Price (S₁)

| Target Location | Distance (kilometers) | Rank of Associated Transcript |
|---|---|---|
| Hoover Tower, Stanford | 3.4 | 1 |
| Baylands Nature Preserve, Palo Alto | 6.4 | 1 |
| Radio telescope, Portola Valley | 6.4 | 1 |
| Marina, Redwood City | 6.8 | 1 |
| Bridge toll plaza, Fremont | 14.5 | 6 |
| Drive-in theater, Palo Alto | 5.1 | 1 |
| Arts and Crafts Plaza, Menlo Park | 1.9 | 1 |
| Catholic Church, Portola Valley | 8.5 | 3 |
| Swimming pool complex, Palo Alto | 3.4 | 1 |
| Total sum of ranks | | 16 ($p = 2.9 \times 10^{-5}$) |

*Source:* Compiled by the authors.

## Subject S₄: Learner

This experiment was designed to be a replication of our previous experiment with Price, the first replication attempted. The subject for this experiment was Hella Hammid, a gifted professional photographer. She was selected for this series on the basis of her successful performance as a percipient in the EEG experiment described earlier. Outside of that interaction, she had no previous experience with apparent paranormal functioning.

At the time we began working with Hammid, she had no strong feelings about the likelihood of her ability to succeed in this task. This was in contrast to both Swann, who had come to our laboratory fresh from a lengthy and apparently successful series of experiments with Gertrude Schmeidler at City College of New York, and Price, who felt that he used his remote-viewing ability in his everyday life.[54]

In comparison with the latter two, many people are more influenced by their environment and are reluctant under public scrutiny to attempt activities that are generally thought to be impossible. Society often provides inhibition and negative feedback to the individual who might otherwise have explored his or her own nonregular perceptual ability. We all share an historical tradition of "the stoning of prophets and the burning of witches" and, in more modern times, the hospitalization of those who claim to perceive things that the majority do not admit to seeing. Therefore, in addition to maintaining scientific rigor, one of our primary tasks as researchers is to provide an environment in which the subject feels safe to explore the possibility of paranormal perception. With a new subject, we also try to stress the nonuniqueness of the ability, because from our experience, paranormal functioning appears to be a latent ability that all subjects can articulate to some degree.

Because of Hammid's artistic background, she was capable of drawing and describing visual images that she could not identify in any cognitive or analytic sense. When the target demarcation team went to a target location that was a pedestrian overpass, the subject said that she saw "a kind of trough up in the air," which she indicated in the upper part of her drawing in Figure 2.4. She went on to explain, "If you stand where they are standing, you will see something like this," indicating the nested squares at the bottom of Figure 2.4. As it turned out, a judge standing where she indicated would have a view closely resembling what she had drawn, as can be seen from the accompanying photographs of the target location. It needs to be emphasized, however, that judges did not have access to our photographs of the site, used here for illustrative purposes only, but rather they proceeded to each of the target locations by list.

In another experimental trial, the subject described seeing "an open barn-like structure with a pitched roof." She also saw a "kind of slatted side to the structure making light and dark bars on the wall." Her drawing and a photograph of the associated bicycle shed target are shown in Figure 2.5. (Subjects are encouraged to make drawings of anything they visualize and associate with

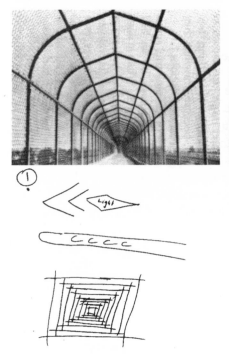

**Figure 2.4** Subject Hammid's ($S_4$) drawing, described as "some kind of diagonal trough up in the air," compared to photographs of target.

the remote location, because drawings they make are in general more accurate than their verbal descriptions.)

As in the original series with Price, the results of the nine-trial series were submitted for independent judging on a blind basis by an SRI research analyst not otherwise associated with the research. While at each target location, visited in turn, the judge was required to blind rank order the nine unedited typed manuscripts of the tape-recorded narratives, along with any associated drawings generated by the remote viewer, on a scale one to nine (best to worst match). The sum of ranks assigned to the target-associated transcripts in this case was 13, a result significant at $p = 1.8 \times 10^{-6}$ one-tailed, by exact calculation (see Table 2.1 and discussion), and included five direct hits and four second ranks (Table 2.3).

Again, as a backup judging procedure, a panel of five additional judges not otherwise associated with the research was asked simply to blind match the unedited typed transcripts and associated drawings generated by the remote viewer against the nine target locations that they independently visited in turn. A correct match consisted of a transcript of a given date being matched to the target of that date. Instead of the expected number of one match each per judge, the number of correct matches obtained by the five judges was five, three, three, two, and two, respectively. Thus, rather than the expected total number of five correct matches from the judges, 15 such matches were obtained.

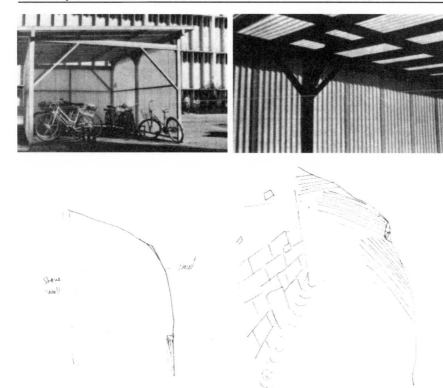

**Figure 2.5** Subject Hammid's ($S_4$) response to bicycle shed target, described as an open "barnlike building" with "slats on the sides" and a "pitched roof," compared to photographs of target.

**Table 2.3 Distribution of Rankings Assigned to Transcripts Associated with Each Target Location for Learner Subject, Hammid ($S_4$)**

| Target Location | Distance (kilometers) | Rank of Associated Transcript |
|---|---|---|
| Methodist Church, Palo Alto | 1.9 | 1 |
| Ness Auditorium, Menlo Park | .2 | 1 |
| Merry-go-round, Palo Alto | 3.4 | 1 |
| Parking garage, Mountain View | 8.1 | 2 |
| SRI International courtyard, Menlo Park | .2 | 1 |
| Bicycle shed, Menlo Park | .1 | 2 |
| Railroad trestle bridge, Palo Alto | 1.3 | 2 |
| Pumpkin patch, Menlo Park | 1.3 | 1 |
| Pedestrian overpass, Palo Alto | 5.0 | 2 |
| Total sum of ranks | | 13 |
| | | ($p = 1.8 \times 10^{-6}$) |

*Source.* Compiled by the authors.

## Subjects S₂ and S₃: Experienced

Having completed a series of 18 remote-viewing trials, nine each with experienced subject $S_1$ (Price) and learner $S_4$ (Hammid), additional replication experiments, four with each subject, were carried out with experienced subjects $S_2$ (Elgin) and $S_3$ (Swann) and learners $S_5$ and $S_6$. To place the judging on a basis comparable to that used with $S_1$ and $S_4$, the four transcripts each of experienced subjects $S_2$ and $S_3$ were combined into a group of eight for rank order judging to be compared with the similarly combined results of the learners $S_5$ and $S_6$.

The series with $S_2$ (Elgin, an SRI research analyst) provided a further example of the dichotomy between verbal and drawing responses. (As with medical literature, case histories often are more illuminating than the summary of results.) The experimental trial described here was the third conducted with this subject. It was a demonstration experiment for a government visitor who had heard of our work and wanted to evaluate our experimental protocol.

In the laboratory, the subject, holding a bearing compass at arm's length, began the experiment by indicating the direction of the target demarcation team correctly to within five degrees. (In all four experiments with this subject, he has always been within ten degrees of the correct direction in this angular assessment.) The subject then generated a 15-minute tape-recorded description and the drawings shown in Figure 2.6.

In discussing the drawings, Elgin indicated that he was uncertain as to the action but had the impression that the demarcation team was located at a museum (known to him) in a particular park. In fact, the target was a tennis court located

**Figure 2.6** Subject Elgin's (S₂) drawings in response to tennis court target compared to photographs of target.

in that park about 90m from the indicated museum. Once again, we note the characteristic (discussed earlier) of a resemblance between the target site and certain gestalt elements of the subject's response, especially in regard to the drawings, coupled with incomplete or erroneous analysis of the significances. Nonetheless, when rank ordering transcripts one through eight at the site, the judge ranked this transcript as two. This example illustrates a continuing observation that most of the correct information related to us by subjects is of a nonanalytic nature pertaining to shape, form, color, and material rather than to function or name.

A second example from this group, generated by $S_3$ (Swann), indicates the level of proficiency that can be attained with prac-

**Figure 2.7** Subject Swann's ($S_3$) response to City Hall target compared to photograph of target.

tice. In the two years since we first started working with Swann, he has been studying the problem of separating the external signal from the internal noise. In our most recent experiments, he dictates two lists for us to record. One list contains objects that he "sees" but does not think are located at the remote scene. A second list contains objects that he thinks are at the scene. In our evaluation, he has made much progress in this most essential ability to separate memory and imagination from paranormal inputs. This is the key to bringing the remote-viewing channel to fruition with regard to its potential usefulness.

The quality of transcript that can be generated by this process is evident from the results of our most recent experimental trial with Swann. The target location chosen by the usual double-blind protocol was the Palo Alto City Hall. Swann described a tall building with vertical columns and "set in" windows. His sketch, together with the photograph of the site, is shown in Figure 2.7. He said there was a fountain, "But I don't hear it." At the time the target team was at the City Hall during the experiment, the fountain was not running. He also made an effort to draw a replica of the designs in the pavement in front of the building and correctly indicated the number of trees (four) in the sketch.

For the entire series of eight, four each from $S_2$ and $S_3$, the numerical evaluation based on blind rank ordering of transcripts at each site was significant at $p = 3.8 \times 10^{-4}$ and included three direct hits and three second ranks for the target-associated transcripts (see Table 2.4).

**Table 2.4 Distribution of Rankings Assigned to Transcripts Associated with Each Target Location for Experienced Subjects, Elgin ($S_2$) and Swann ($S_3$)**

| Subject | Target Location | Distance (kilometers) | Rank of Associated Transcript |
|---|---|---|---|
| $S_2$ | BART Station (Transit System), Fremont | 16.1 | 1 |
| $S_2$ | Shielded room, SRI, Menlo Park | .1 | 2 |
| $S_2$ | Tennis court, Palo Alto | 3.4 | 2 |
| $S_2$ | Golf course bridge, Stanford | 3.4 | 2 |
| $S_3$ | City Hall, Palo Alto | 2.0 | 1 |
| $S_3$ | Miniature golf course, Menlo Park | 3.0 | 1 |
| $S_3$ | Kiosk in park, Menlo Park | .3 | 3 |
| $S_3$ | Baylands Nature Preserve, Palo Alto | 6.4 | 3 |
| | Total sum of ranks | | 15 |
| | | | ($p = 3.8 \times 10^{-4}$) |

*Source:* Compiled by the authors.

## Subjects $S_5$ and $S_6$: Learners

To complete the series, four experiments each were carried out with learner subjects $S_5$ and $S_6$, a man and woman on the SRI professional staff. The results in this case, taken as a group, did not differ significantly from chance. For the series of eight (judged as a group of seven, since one target came up twice, once for each subject), the numerical evaluation based on blind rank ordering of transcripts at each site was nonsignificant at $p = .08$, one-tailed, even though there were two direct hits and two second ranks out of the seven (see Table 2.5).

**Table 2.5  Distribution of Rankings Assigned to Transcripts Associated with Each Target Location for Learner Subjects, $S_5$ and $S_6$**

| Subject | Target Location | Distance (kilometers) | Rank of Associated Transcript |
|---|---|---|---|
| $S_5$ | Pedestrian overpass, Palo Alto | 5.0 | 3 |
| $S_5$ | Railroad trestle bridge, Palo Alto | 1.3 | 6 |
| $S_5$ | Windmill, Portola Valley | 8.5 | 2 |
| $S_5, S_6$ | White Plaza, Stanford (2) | 3.8 | 1 |
| $S_6$ | Airport, Palo Alto | 5.5 | 2 |
| $S_6$ | Kiosk in park, Menlo Park | .3 | 5 |
| $S_6$ | Boathouse, Stanford | 4.0 | 1 |
| | Total sum of ranks | | 20 |
| | | | (p = .08, NS) |

*Source:* Compiled by the authors.

One of the direct hits, which occurred with subject $S_6$ in her first experiment, provides an example of the "first-time effect," which has been rigorously explored and is well-known to experimenters in the field.[55] The outbound experimenter obtained, by random protocol from the pool, a target blind to the experimenter with the subject, as is our standard procedure, and proceeded to the location. The subject, a mathematician in the computer science laboratory, who had no previous experience in remote viewing, began to describe a large square with a fountain. Four minutes into the experiment, she recognized the location and correctly identified it by name (see Figure 2.8). (It should be

**Figure 2.8** Subject's ($S_6$) drawing of White Plaza, Stanford University compared to photograph of target. Subject drew what she called "curvy benches" and then announced correctly that the place was "White Plaza at Stanford."

noted that in the area from which the target locations were drawn, there are other fountains as well, some of which were in the target pool.) As an example of the style of the narratives generated during remote viewing with inexperienced subjects and of the part played by the experimenter remaining with the subject in such a case, we have included the entire unedited text of this experiment as Appendix B.

## Normal and Paranormal: Use of Unselected Subjects in Remote Viewing

After more than a year of following the experimental protocol described above and observing that even inexperienced subjects generated results better than expected, we initiated a series of experiments to explore further whether individuals other than putative "psychics" can demonstrate the remote-viewing ability. To test this idea, we developed a continuing program to carry out additional experiments of the outdoor type with new subjects whom we had no a priori reason to believe had paranormal perceptual ability. To date, we have collected data from five experimental trials with two individuals in this category: a man and a woman who were visiting government scientists interested in observing our experimental protocols. The motivation for these

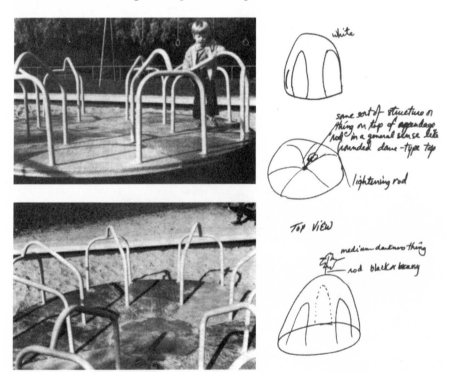

**Figure 2.9** Subject's (V₁) drawing of merry-go-round target compared to photograph of target.

particular experiments was twofold. First, the experiments provide data that indicate the level of proficiency that can be expected from unselected volunteers. Second, when an individual observes a successful demonstration experiment involving another person as subject, it inevitably occurs to him or her that perhaps chicanery is involved. We have found the most effective way to settle this issue for the observer is to have the individual himself or herself act as a subject so as to obtain personal experience against which our reported results can be evaluated.

The first visitor ($V_1$) was invited to participate as a subject in a three-trial series. All three trials contained elements descriptive of the associated target locations; the quality of response increased with practice. The third response is shown in Figure 2.9, where again, the pattern elements in the drawing appeared to be a closer match than the subject's analytic interpretation of the target object as a cupola.

The second visitor ($V_2$) participated as a subject in two experimental trials. In his first trial, he generated one of the higher signal-to-noise results we have observed. He began his narrative, "There is a red A-frame building and next to it is a large yellow thing [a tree—editors]. Now further left there is another A-shape. It looks like a swing set, but it is pushed down in a gully so I can't see the swings" (all correct). He then went on to describe a lock on the front door that he said "looks like it's made of laminated steel, so it must be a Master lock" (also correct).

For the series of five—three from the first subject and two from the second—the numerical evaluation based on blind rank ordering of the transcripts at each site was significant at $p = .017$, one-tailed, and included three direct hits and one second rank for the target-associated transcripts. (See Table 2.6.)

Observations with unselected subjects such as those described above indicate that remote viewing may be a latent and widely distributed perceptual ability.

**Table 2.6 Distribution of Rankings Assigned to Transcripts Associated with Each Target Location for Visitor Subjects, $V_1$ and $V_2$**

| Subject | Target Location | Distance (kilometers) | Rank of Associated Transcript |
|---|---|---|---|
| $V_1$ | Bridge over stream, Menlo Park | .3 | 1 |
| $V_1$ | Baylands Nature Preserve, Palo Alto | 6.4 | 2 |
| $V_1$ | Merry-go-round, Palo Alto | 3.4 | 1 |
| $V_2$ | Windmill, Portola Valley | 8.5 | 1 |
| $V_2$ | Apartment swimming pool, Mountain View | 9.1 | 3 |
| | Total sum of ranks | | 8 |
| | | | (p = .017) |

*Source:* Compiled by the authors.

## Technology Series: Short-Range Remote Viewing

Because remote viewing is a perceptual ability, we considered it important to obtain data on its resolution capabilities. To accomplish this, we turned to the use of indoor technological targets.

Twelve experimental trials were carried out with five different subjects, two of whom were visiting government scientists. They were told that one of the experimenters would be sent by random protocol to a laboratory within the SRI complex and that he would interact with the equipment or apparatus at that location. It was further explained that the experimenter remaining with the subject was, as usual, kept ignorant of the contents of the target pool to prevent cueing during questioning. (Unknown to the subjects, targets in the pool were used with replacement, that is, the same target could possibly be drawn many times rather than used only once. This was because one of the goals of this particular experiment was to obtain multiple responses to a given target to investigate whether correlation of a number of subject responses would provide enhancement of the signal-to-noise ratio.) The subject was asked to describe the target both verbally (tape recorded) and by means of drawings during a time-synchronized 15-minute interval in which the out-bound experimenter interacted in an appropriate manner with the equipment in the target area.

In the 12 trials, seven targets were used: a drill press, a Xerox machine, a video terminal, a chart recorder, a four-state random number generator, a machine shop, and a typewriter. Three of these were used twice (drill press, video terminal, and typewriter), and one (Xerox machine) came up three times in our random selection procedure.

Comparisons of the targets and subject drawings for three of the multiple-response cases (the typewriter, Xerox machine, and video terminal) are shown in Figures 2.10, 2.11, and 2.12. As is apparent from these illustrations alone, the experiments provide circumstantial evidence for an information channel of useful bit rate. This includes experiments in which visiting government scientists participated as subjects (Xerox machine and video terminal) to observe the protocol. In general, it appears that use of multiple-subject responses to a single target provides better signal-to-noise ratio than target identification by a single individual. This conclusion is borne out by the judging described below.

Given that in general the drawings constitute the most accurate portion of a subject's description, in the first judging procedure, a judge was asked simply to blind match only the drawings (that is, without tape transcripts) to the targets. Multiple-subject responses to a given target were stapled together, and thus, seven subject-drawing response packets were to be matched to the seven different targets for which drawings were made. The judge did not have access to our photographs of the target locations, used for illustration purposes only, but rather proceeded to each of the target locations by list. While standing at

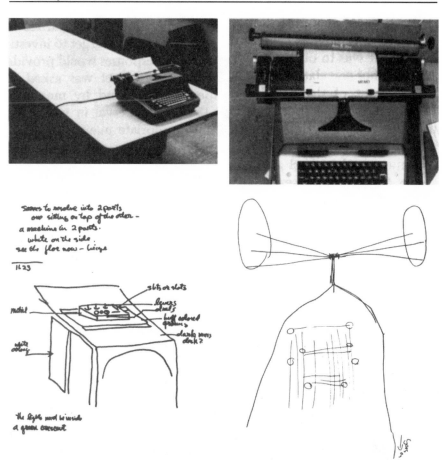

**Figure 2.10** Drawings of a typewriter by two subjects compared to photographs of target.

each target location, the judge was required to rank order the seven subject-drawing response packets (presented in random order) on a scale one to seven (best to worst match). For seven targets, the sum of ranks could range from seven to 49. The sum in this case, which included one direct hit and four second ranks out of the seven (see Table 2.7) was 18, a result significant at $p = .036$ one-tailed.

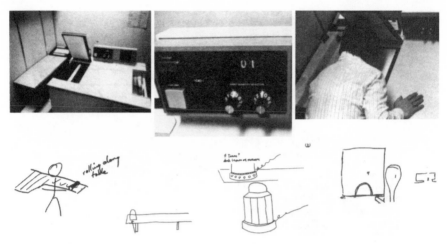

**Figure 2.11** Drawings by three subjects (S$_2$, S$_3$, and V$_3$) for Xerox machine target compared to photographs of target. When asked to describe the square at upper left of response on the right, subject (V$_3$) said, "There was this predominant light source which might have been a window, and a working surface which might have been the sill, or a working surface or desk." Earlier the subject had said, "I have the feeling that there is something silhouetted against the window."

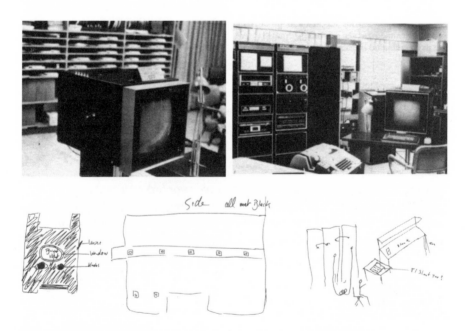

**Figure 2.12** Drawings by two subjects of a video monitor target compared to photographs of target. A) Subject's (S$_4$) drawing of "box with light coming out of it ... painted flat black and in the middle of the room." B) Second subject (V$_2$) saw a computer terminal with relay racks in the background.

**Table 2.7 Distribution of Rankings Assigned to Subject Drawings Associated with Each Target Location**

| Subject | Target | Rank of Drawings |
|---------|--------|:----------------:|
| $S_3, S_4$ | Drill press | 2 |
| $S_2, S_3, V_3$ | Xerox machine | 2 |
| $S_4, V_2$ | Video terminal | 1 |
| $S_3$ | Chart recorder | 2 |
| $S_4$ | Random number generator | 6 |
| $S_4$ | Machine shop | 3 |
| $S_3, S_4$ | Typewriter | 2 |
| | Total sum of ranks | 18 |
| | | (p = .036) |

*Source:* Compiled by the authors.

In the second more detailed effort at evaluation, a visiting scientist selected at random one of the 12 data packages (a drill press experiment), sight unseen and submitted it for independent analysis to an engineer with a request for an estimate as to what was being described. The analyst, blind as to the target and given only the subject's taped narrative and drawing (Figure 2.13) was able, from the subject's description alone, to correctly classify the target as a "man-sized vertical boring machine."

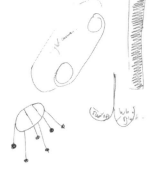

**Figure 2.13** Subject Hammid's ($S_4$) drawing of drill press showing belt drive, stool, and a "vertical graph that goes up and down."

## Summary of Remote-Viewing Results
*Discussion*

The descriptions supplied by the subjects in the experiments involving remote viewing of natural targets or laboratory apparatus, although containing inaccuracies, were sufficiently accurate to permit the judges to differentiate among various targets to the degree indicated. A summary tabulation of the statistical evaluations of these six experiments (involving 51 remote-viewing trials with nine different subjects) is presented in Table 2.8. Five of the six experiments are individually significant at least at the .05 level, with the sixth one being suggestive. Note that the results of individual experiments have been evaluated conservatively on the basis of a judging procedure which ignores transcript quality beyond that necessary to rank order the data packets and which can thus vastly underestimate the significance of the information actually present in the data. Using Edgington's method for combining the probabilities from independent experiments, the probability of observing these six experimental outcomes by chance alone is $7.8 \times 10^{-9}$, one-tailed.[56]

### Table 2.8 Summary: Remote Viewing

| Subject | Number of Trials | p-Value, Rank Order Judging |
|---|:---:|:---:|
| With natural targets: | | |
| $S_1$ (experienced) | 9 | $2.9 \times 10^{-5}$ |
| $S_2$ and $S_3$ (experienced) | 8 | $3.8 \times 10^{-4}$ |
| $S_4$ (learner) | 9 | $1.8 \times 10^{-6}$ |
| $S_5$ and $S_6$ (learners) | 8 | .08 (NS) |
| $V_1$ and $V_2$ (learners/vistors) | 5 | .017 |
| With technology targets: | | |
| $S_2, S_3, S_4, V_2, V_3$ | 12 | .036 |

*Source:* Compiled by the authors.

Thus, the primary achievement of the SRI program was the elicitation of high-quality remote viewing from individuals who agreed to act as subjects. Criticism of this claim could in principle be put forward on the basis of three potential flaws. First, the study could involve naivete in protocol that permitted various forms of cueing, intentional or unintentional. Second, the experiments discussed could be selected out of a larger pool of experiments of which many were of poorer quality. Third, data for the reported experiments could be edited to show only the matching elements, the nonmatching elements being discarded.

All three criticisms, however, are invalid. First, with regard to cueing, the use of double-blind protocols ensures that none of the persons in contact with the subject can be aware of the target. Second, selection of experiments for reporting did not take place; every experiment was entered as performed on a master log and was included in the statistical evaluations. Third, data associated with a given experiment remained unedited; all experiments were tape recorded, and all data were included unedited in the data package to be judged and evaluated.

In the process of judging—attempting to match transcripts against targets on the basis of the information in the transcripts—some patterns and regularities in the transcript descriptions became evident, particularly regarding individual styles in remote viewing and in the perceptual form of the descriptions given by the subjects. These patterns and the judging procedure are discussed below.

*Styles of Response.* The 51 transcripts were taken from nine different subjects. Comparing the transcripts of one subject with those of another revealed that each pattern tended to focus on certain aspects of the remote target complex and to exclude others, so that each had an individual pattern of response, like a signature.

Subject $S_3$, for example, frequently responded with topographical descriptions, maps, and architectural features of the target locations. Subject $S_2$ often focused on the behavior of the remote experimenter or the sequence of actions he carried out at the target. The transcripts of subject $S_4$, more than those of other subjects, had descriptions of the feel of the location, and experiential or sensory gestalts—for example, light/dark elements in the scene and indoor/outdoor and enclosed/open distinctions. Prominent features of $S_1$'s transcripts were detailed descriptions of what the target persons were concretely experiencing, seeing, or doing—for example, standing on asphalty black top overlooking water or looking at a purple iris.

The range of an individual subject's responses was wide. Anyone might draw a map or describe the mood of the remote experimenter, but the consistency of each subject's overall approach suggested that just as individual descriptions of a directly viewed scene would differ, so these differences also occur in remote-viewing processes.

*Nature of the Description.* The concrete descriptions that appear most commonly in transcripts are at the level of subunits of the overall scene. For example, when the target was a Xerox copy machine, the responses included ($S_2$) a rolling object (the moving light) or dials and a cover that is lifted ($S_3$), but the machine as a whole was not identified by name or function.

In a few transcripts, the subjects correctly identified and named the target. In the case of a computer terminal, the subject ($V_2$) apparently perceived the terminal and the relay racks behind it. In the case of targets that were Hoover

Tower and White Plaza, the subjects ($S_1$ and $S_6$) seemed to identify the locations through analysis of their initial images of the elements of the target.

There were also occasional incorrect identifications. Gestalts were incorrectly named; for example, swimming pools in a park were identified as water storage tanks at a water filtration plant ($S_1$).

The most common perceptual level was thus an intermediate one—the individual elements and items that made up the target. This is suggestive of a scanning process that takes sample perceptions from within the overall environment.

When the subjects tried to make sense out of these fragmentary impressions, they often resorted to metaphors or constructed an image with a kind of perceptual inference. From a feeling of the target as an "august" and "solemn" building, a subject ($S_4$) said it might be a library; it was a church. A pedestrian overpass above a freeway was described as a conduit ($S_4$). A rapid transit station, elevated above the countryside, was associated with an observatory ($S_2$). These responses seem to be the result of attempts to process partial information; similarly, this occurs in other parapsychological experiments. These observations are compatible with the hypothesis that information received in a putative remote-viewing mode is processed piecemeal in pattern form (consistent with a low bit rate process, but not necessarily requiring it), and the errors arise in the processes of attempted integration of the data into larger patterns directed toward verbal labeling.

When the subjects augmented the verbal transcripts with drawings or sketches, these often expressed the target elements more accurately than the verbal descriptions. Thus, the drawings tended to correspond to the targets more clearly and precisely than the words of the transcript.

The descriptions given by the subjects sometimes went beyond what the remote experimenter experienced, at least consciously. For example, one subject ($S_4$) described and drew a belt drive at the top of a drill press that was invisible even to the remote experimenter who was operating the machine; another subject ($S_1$) described a number of items behind shrubbery and thus not visible to members of the demarcation team at the site.

Curiously, objects in motion at the remote site were rarely mentioned in the transcript. For example, trains crossing the railroad trestle target were not described, though the remote experimenter stood very close to them.

Also, in a few cases, the subject descriptions were inaccurate regarding size of structures. A 20-foot courtyard separating two buildings was described as 200 feet wide, and a small shed was expanded to a barnlike structure.

*Blind Judging of Transcipts.* The judging procedure entailed examining the transcripts for a given experimental series and attempting to match the transcripts with the correct targets on the basis of their correspondences. The transcripts varied from coherent and accurate descriptions to mixtures of correspondences and noncorrespondences. Since the judge did not know *a priori* which elements of the descriptions were correct or incorrect, the task was complicated, and transcripts often seemed plausibly to match more than one target. A confounding factor in these studies is that some target locations have similarities that seem alike at some level of perception. For example, a radio telescope at the top of a hill, the observation deck of a tower, and a jetty on the edge of a bay all match a transcript description of "looking out over a long distance." A lake, a fountain, and a creek may all result in an image of water for the subject. Therefore, in several cases, even correct images may not help in the conservative differential matching procedure used.

According to our most successful judge, the most successful procedure was a careful element-by-element comparison that tested each transcript against every target and used the transcript descriptions and drawings as arguments for or against assigning the transcript to a particular target. In most cases, this resulted in either a clear conclusion or at least a ranking of probable matches; these matches were subjected to the statistical analyses presented in this chapter.

*Summary*

In summary, we do not yet have an understanding of the nature of the information-bearing signal that a subject perceives during remote viewing. The subjects commonly report that they perceive the signal visually, as though they were looking at the object or place from a position in its immediate neighborhood. Furthermore, the subjects' perceptual viewpoint has mobility in that they can shift their point of view so as to describe elements of a scene that would not be visible to an observer merely standing at ground level and describing what he or she sees. (In particular, a subject often correctly describes elements not visible to the target demarcation team.) Finally, motion is seldom reported; in fact, moving objects often are unseen even when nearby static objects are correctly identified.

A comparison of the results of remote viewing (a so-called free response task) with results of forced choice tasks, such as the selection of one of four choices generated by a random number generator, reveals the following findings.[57] From a statistical viewpoint, a subject is more likely to describe, with sufficient accuracy to permit blind matching, a remote site chosen at random than he or she is to select correctly one of four random numbers. Our experience with these phenomena leads us to consider that this difference in task performance may stem from fundamental signal-to-noise considerations. Two principal sources of noise in the system apparently are memory and imagination, both of which can give rise to mental pictures of greater clarity than the target to be perceived. In the random number task, a subject can create a perfect mental picture of each of the four possible outputs in his or her imagination and then attempt to obtain the correct answer by a mental matching operation. The same is true for card-guessing experiments. On the other hand, the subject in remote viewing is apparently more likely to approach the task with a blank mind as he or she attempts to perceive pictorial information from remote locations about which he or she may have no stored mental data.

Finally, we observe that most of the correct information that subjects relate to us is of a nonanalytic nature pertaining to shape, form, color, and material rather than to function or name. In consultation with Dr. Robert Ornstein of the Langley-Porter Neuropsychiatric Institute, San Francisco, and with Dr. Ralph Kiernan of the Department of Neurology, Stanford University Medical Center, Stanford, California, we have formed the tentative hypothesis that paranormal functioning may involve specialization characteristic of the brain's right hemisphere. This possibility is derived from a variety of evidence from clinical and neurosurgical sources, which indicate that the two hemispheres of the human brain are specialized for different cognitive functions. The left hemisphere is predominantly active in verbal and other analytical functioning, and the right hemisphere predominates in spatial and other holistic processing.[58] Further research is necessary to elucidate the relationship between right hemisphere function and paranormal abilities. Nonetheless, we can say at this point that the remote-viewing results of the group of subjects at SRI have characteristics in common with more familiar performances that require right hemispheric function. The similarities include the highly schematicized drawings of objects in a room or of remote scenes. Verbal identification of these drawings is often highly inaccurate, and the drawings themselves are frequently left-right reversed relative to the target configuration. Further, written material generally is not cognized. These characteristics have been seen in left hemisphere brain-injured patients and in callosal-sectioned patients.

As a result of the above considerations, we have learned to urge our subjects simply to describe what they see as opposed to what they think they are looking at. We have learned that their unanalyzed perceptions are almost always a better guide to the true target than their interpretations of the perceived data.

## Considerations Concerning Time

If the authors may be forgiven a personal note, we wish to express that this section deals with observations that we have been reluctant to publish because of their striking apparent incompatibility with existing concepts. The motivating factor for presenting the data at this time is the ethical consideration that theorists endeavoring to develop models for paranormal functioning should be apprised of all the observable data if their efforts to arrive at a comprehensive and correct description are to be successful.

During the course of the experimentation in remote viewing, subjects occasionally volunteered the information that they had been thinking about their forthcoming participation in a remote-viewing experiment and had an image come to them as to what the target location was to be. On these occasions, the information was given only to the experimenter remaining at SRI with the subject and was unknown to the outbound experimenter until completion of the experiment. Two of these contributions were among the most accurate descriptions turned in during those experiments. Since the target location had not yet been selected when the subject communicated his or her perceptions about the target, we found the data difficult to contend with.

We offer these spontaneous occurrences not as proof of precognitive perception but, rather, as the motivation that led us to do further work in this field. On the basis of this firsthand evidence, together with the copious literature describing years of precognition experiments carried out in various other laboratories, we decided to determine whether a subject could perform a perceptual task that required both spatial and temporal remote viewing.

It is well known and recently has been widely discussed that nothing in the fundamental laws of physics forbids the apparent transmission of information from the future to the present (discussed further below). Furthermore, there is a general dictum that "in physical law, everything that is not forbidden, is required."[59] With this in mind, we set out to conduct very well-controlled experiments to determine whether we could deliberately design and execute experiments for the sole purpose of observing precognition under laboratory conditions.

The experimental protocol was identical to that followed in previous remote-viewing experiments with but one exception. The exception was that the subject was required to describe the remote location during a 15-minute period beginning 20 minutes before the target was selected and 35 minutes before the outbound experimenter was to arrive at the target location.

In detail, as shown in Table 2.9, each day at 10 a.m., one of the experimenters would leave SRI with a stack of ten sealed envelopes from a larger pool (randomized daily), containing traveling instructions that had been prepared but which were unknown to the two experimenters remaining with the subject. The subject for this experiment was Hammid ($S_4$), who had participated in the nine-experiment series replicating the original Price work described earlier. The traveling experimenter was to drive continuously from 10 a.m. until 10:30 a.m. before selecting his destination with a random number generator. (The motivation for continuous motion was our observation that objects and persons in rapid motion were not generally seen in the remote-viewing mode of perception, and we wished the traveler to be a poor target until he reached his target site.) At the end of 30 minutes of driving, the traveling experimenter generated a random digit from zero to nine with a Texas Instruments SR-51 random number generator; while still in motion, he counted down that number of envelopes and proceeded directly to the target location so as to arrive there by 10:45 a.m. He remained at the target site until 11 a.m., at which time he returned to the laboratory, showed his chosen target name to a security guard, and entered the experimental room.

### Table 2.9 Experimental Protocol: Precognitive Remote Viewing

| Time Schedule | Experimenter/Subject Activity |
|---|---|
| 10:00 a.m. | Outbound experimenter leaves with ten envelopes (containing target locations) and random number generator; begins half-hour drive |
| 10:10 a.m. | Experimenters remaining with subject in the laboratory elicit from subject a description of where outbound experimenter will be from 10:45 to 11 |
| 10:25 a.m. | Subject response completed, at which time laboratory part of experiment is over |
| 10:30 a.m. | Outbound experimenter obtains random number from a random number generator, counts down to associated envelope, and proceeds to target location indicated |
| 10:45 a.m. | Outbound experimenter remains at target location for 15 minutes (10:45 to 11) |

*Source:* Compiled by the authors.

During the same period, the protocol in the laboratory was as follows. At 10:10 a.m., the subject was asked to begin a description of the place to which the experimenter would go 35 minutes hence. This subject then generated a tape-recorded description and associated drawings from 10:10 a.m. to 10:25 a.m. at which time, her part in the experiment was ended. Her description was thus entirely concluded five minutes before the beginning of the target selection procedure.

**Figure 2.14** Subject Hammid ($S_4$) described "some kind of congealing tar, or maybe an area of condensed lava ... that has oozed out to fill up some kind of boundaries."

**Figure 2.15** Subject Hammid (S$_4$) described a formal garden "very well manicured" behind a double colonnade.

Four such experimental trials were carried out. Each of them appeared to be successful, an evaluation later verified in blind judging without error by three judges. We will briefly summarize the four trials below.

The first target, the Palo Alto Yacht Harbor, consisted entirely of mud flats because of an extremely low tide (see Figure 2.14). Appropriately, the entire transcript of the subject pertained to "some kind of congealing tar, or maybe an area of condensed lava. It looks like the whole area is covered with some kind of wrinkled elephant skin that has oozed out to fill up some kind of boundaries where [the outbound experimenter] is standing." Because of the lack of water, the dock where the remote experimenter was standing was in fact resting directly on the mud.

Note that the subject has learned not to rush into interpretation as to the nature or purpose of the place. This is a result of our cautioning based on the observation that such efforts tend to be purely analytical and in our experience are almost invariably incorrect. If a subject can limit himself or herself to what he or she sees, the subject is often then able to describe a scene with sufficient accuracy that an observer can perform the analysis for him or her, and identify the place.

The second target visited was the fountain at one end of a large formal garden at Stanford University Hospital (Figure 2.15). The subject gave a lengthy description of a "very well manicured" formal garden behind a wall with a "double colonnade." When we later took the subject to the location, she was herself taken aback to find the double colonnaded wall leading into the garden just as described.

The third target was a children's swing at a small park 4.6 km from the laboratory (Figure 2.16). The subject repeated again and again that the main focus of attention at the site was a "black iron triangle that the outbound experimenter had somehow walked into or was standing on." The triangle was "bigger than a man," and she heard a "squeak, squeak, about once a second," which we observed was a match to the black metal swing that did squeak.

**Figure 2.16** Subject Hammid (S₄) saw a "black iron triangle that Hal had somehow walked into" and heard a "squeak, squeak, about once a second."

**Figure 2.17** Subject Hammid ($S_4$) described a very tall structure located among city streets and covered with "Tiffanylike glass."

The final target was the Palo Alto City Hall (Figure 2.17). The subject described a very, very tall structure covered with "Tiffanylike glass." She had it located among city streets and with little cubes at the base. The building is glass covered, and the little cubes are a good match to the small elevator exit buildings located in the plaza in front of the building.

To obtain a numercial evaluation of the accuracy of the precognitive viewing, the experimental results were subjected to independent judging on a blind basis by three SRI scientists who were not otherwise associated with the experiment. The judges were asked to match the four locations, which they visited, against the unedited typed manuscripts of the tape-recorded narratives, along with the drawings generated by the remote viewer. The transcripts were presented unlabeled and in random order and were to be used without replacement. A correct match required that the transcript of a given experiment be matched with the target of that experiment. All three judges independently matched the target data to the response data without error. Under the null hypothesis (no information channel and a random selection of descriptions without replacement), each judge independently obtained a result significant at $p = (4!)^{-1} = .042$, one-tailed.

For reasons we do not as yet understand, the four transcripts generated in the precognition experiment show exceptional coherence and accuracy, as evidenced by the fact that all of the judges were able to match successfully all of the transcripts to the corresponding target locations. A long-range experimental program devoted to the clarification of these issues and involving a number of subjects is under way. The above four experiments are the first four carried out under this program. Replication of precognitive remote viewing is reported in Chapter 4.

Currently, we have no precise model of this spatial and temporal remote-viewing phenomenon. However, models of the universe involving higher-order synchronicity or correlation have been proposed by the physicist W. Pauli and the psychologist Carl Jung.

> Acausality. If natural law [as usually understood] were an absolute truth, then of course there could not possibly be any processes that deviate from it. But since causality [as usually understood] is a *statistical* truth, it holds good only on average and thus leaves room for *exceptions* which must somehow be experienceable, that is to say, *real*. I try to regard synchronistic events as acausal exceptions of this kind. They prove to be relatively independent of space and time; they relativize space and time insofar as space presents in principle no obstacle to their passage and the sequence of events in time is inverted so that it looks as if an event which has not yet occurred were causing a perception in the present.[60]

We shall see in the next section that such a description, though poetic, has some basis in modern physical theory.

## Discussion

It is important to note at the outset that many contemporary physicists are of the view that the phenomena that we have been discussing are not at all inconsistent with the framework of physics as currently understood. In this emerging view, the often-held belief that observations of this type are incompatible with known laws in *principle* is erroneous, such a concept being based on the naive realism prevalent before the development of modern quantum theory and information theory.

One hypothesis, put forward by Kogan of the USSR, is that information transfer under conditions of sensory shielding is mediated by ELF electromagnetic waves in the 300- to 1,000-km region.[61] Experimental support for the hypothesis is claimed on the basis of slower than inverse square attenuation, compatible with source-percipient distances lying in the induction field range, as opposed to the radiation field range; observed low bit rates (.005–.1 bit/s) compatible with the information-carrying capacity of ELF waves; apparent ineffectiveness of ordinary electromagnetic shielding as an attenuator; and standard antenna calculations entailing biologically generated currents yielding results compatible with observed signal-to-noise ratios.

M. Persinger, of the Psychophysiology Laboratory, Laurentian University, Toronto, Canada, has narrowed the ELF hypothesis to the suggestion that the 7.8-Hz Shumann waves and their harmonics propagating along the earth-ionosphere wave guide duct may be responsible. Such an hypothesis is compatible with driving by brain-wave currents and leads to certain other hypotheses, such as asymmetry between east–west and west–east propagation, preferred experimental times (midnight to 4 a.m.), and expected negative correlation between success and the $U$ index (a measure of geomagnetic disturbance throughout the world). Persinger claims initial support for these factors on the basis of a literature search.[62] Persinger discusses his theories in Chapter 8.

On the negative side with regard to a straightforward ELF interpretation as a blanket hypothesis are the following: (1) appparent real-time descriptions of remote activities in sufficient detail to require a channel capacity in all probability greater than that allowed by a conventional modulation of an ELF signal, (2) lack of a proposed mechanism for coding and decoding the information onto the proposed ELF carrier, and (3) apparent precognition data. The hypothesis must nonetheless remain open at this stage of research, since it is conceivable that counterindication (1) may eventually be circumvented on the basis that the apparent high bit rate results from a mixture of low bit rate input and high bit rate "filling in the blanks" from imagination; counterindication (2) is common to a number of normal perceptual tasks and may therefore simply reflect a lack of sophistication on our part with regard to perceptual functioning;[63] and counterindication (3) may be accommodated by an ELF hypothesis if advanced waves, as well as retarded waves, are admitted.[64] Experimentation to determine whether the ELF hypothesis is viable can be carried out by the use of ELF sources as targets, by the study of parametric dependence on propagational directions and diurnal timing, and by the exploration of interference effects caused by creation of a high-intensity ELF environment during experimentation, all of which are under consideration in our laboratory and elsewhere.

Some physicists believe that the reconciliation of observed paranormal functioning with modern theory may take place at a more fundamental level—namely, at the level of the foundations of quantum theory. There is a continuing dialogue, for example, on the proper interpretation of the effect of an observer (consciousness) on experimental measurement,[65] and there is considerable current interest in the implications for our notions of ordering in time and space brought on by the observation[66] of nonlocal correlation or "quantum interconnectedness" (to use Bohm's term) of distant parts of quantum systems of macroscopic dimensions.[67] The latter, Bell's theorem,[68] emphasizes that "no theory of reality compatible with quantum theory can require spatially separated events to be independent,"[69] but must permit interconnectedness of distant events in a manner that is contrary to ordinary experience.[70] This prediction has been experimentally tested and confirmed in the recent experiments of, for example, Freedman and Clauser.[71]

E. H. Walker and O. Costa de Beauregard (see Chapter 7), independently proposing theories of paranormal functioning based on quantum concepts, argue that observer effects open the door to the possibility of nontrivial coupling between consciousness and the environment and that the nonlocality principle permits such coupling to transcend spatial and temporal barriers.[72]

Apparent time reversibility—that is, effects (for example, observations) apparently preceding causes (for example, events)—though conceptually difficult at first glance may be the easiest of apparent paranormal phenomena to assimilate within the current theoretical structure of our world view. In addition to the familiar retarded potential solutions $f(t - r/c)$, it is well-known that the equations of, for example, the electromagnetic field admit of advanced potential solutions $f(t + r/c)$—solutions that would appear to imply a reversal of cause and effect. Such solutions are conventionally discarded as not corresponding to any observable physical event. One is cautioned, however, by statements such as that of Stratton in his basic text on electromagnetic theory.

> The reader has doubtless noted that the choice of the function $f(t - r/c)$ is highly arbitrary, since the field equation admits also a solution $f(t + r/c)$. This function leads obviously to an advanced time, implying that the field can be observed before it has been generated by the source. The familiar chain of cause and effect is thus reversed and this alternative solution might be discarded as logically inconceivable. However, the application of "logical" causality principles offers very insecure footing in matters such as these and we shall do better to restrict the theory to retarded action solely on the grounds that this solution alone conforms to the present physical data.[73]

Such caution is justified by the example in the early 1920s of Dirac's development of the mathematical description of the relativistic electron that also yielded a pair of solutions, one of which was discarded as inapplicable until the discovery of the positron in 1932.

In an analysis by Costa de Beauregard, an argument is put forward that advanced potentials constitute a convergence toward "finality" in a manner symmetrical to the divergence of retarded potentials as a result of causality.[74] Such phenomena are generally unobservable, however, on the gross macroscopic scale for statistical reasons. This is codified in the thermodynamic concept that for an isolated system, entropy (disorder) on the average increases. It is just this requirement of isolation, however, that has been weakened by the observer problem in quantum theory, and Costa de Beauregard argues that the finality principle is maximally operative in just those situations where the intrusion of consciousness as an ordering phenomenon results in a significant local reversal of entropy increase. At this point, further discussion of the subtleties of such considerations, though apropos, would take us far afield, so we simply note that such advanced waves, if detected, could in certain cases constitute a carrier of information precognitive to the event.

The above arguments are not intended to indicate that the precise nature of the information channel coupling remote events and human perception is understood. Rather, we intend to show only that modern theory is not without resources that can be brought to bear on the problems at hand, and we expect that these problems will, with further work, continue to yield to analysis and specification.

Furthermore, independent of the mechanisms that may be involved in remote sensing, observation of the phenomenon implies the existence of an information channel in the information-theoretic sense. Since such channels are amenable to analysis on the basis of communication theory techniques, as indicated earlier, channel characteristics such as bit rate can be determined independent of a well-defined physical channel model in the sense that thermodynamic concepts can be applied to the analysis of systems independent of underlying mechanisms. Furthermore, as we have seen from the work of Ryzl discussed earlier, it is possible to use such a channel for error-free transmission of information if redundancy coding is used. (See also Appendix A.) Therefore, experimentation involving the collection of data under specified conditions permits headway to be made despite the formidable work that needs to be done to clarify the underlying bases of the phenomena.

## Conclusion

For the past three years, we have had a program in the Electronics and Bioengineering Laboratory of SRI to investigate those facets of human perception that appear to fall outside the range of well-understood perceptual or processing capabilities. The primary achievement of this program has been the elicitation of high-quality remote viewing—the ability of both experienced subjects and inexperienced volunteers to view, by means of innate mental processes, remote geographical or technical targets, such as roads, buildings, and laboratory apparatus. Our accumulated data from over 50 trials with more than a half-dozen subjects indicate the following. First, the phenomenon is not a sensitive function of distance over a range of several kilometers. Second, Faraday cage shielding does not appear to degrade the quality or accuracy of perception. Third, most of the correct information that subjects relate is of a nonanalytic nature pertaining to shape, form, color, and material rather than to function or name. (This aspect suggests a hypothesis that information transmission under conditions of sensory shielding may be mediated primarily by the brain's right hemisphere.) Fourth, the principal difference between experienced subjects and inexperienced volunteers is not that the latter never exhibit the faculty but, rather, that their results are simply less reliable. (This observation suggests the hypothesis that remote viewing may be a latent and widely distributed, though repressed, perceptual ability.)

Although the precise nature of the information channel coupling remote events and human perception is not yet understood, certain concepts in information theory, quantum theory, and neurophysiological research appear to bear directly on the issue. As a result, the working assumption among researchers in the field is that the phenomenon of interest is consistent with modern scientific thought and can therefore be expected to yield to the scientific method. Further, it is recognized that communication theory provides powerful techniques, such as the use of redundancy coding to improve signal-to-noise ratio, which can be employed to pursue special-purpose application of the remote-sensing channel independent of an understanding of the underlying mechanisms. We therefore consider it important to continue data collection and to encourage others to do likewise; investigations such as those reported here need replication and extension under as wide a variety of rigorously controlled conditions as possible.

# Appendix A
# Signal Enhancement in a Paranormal Communication Channel by Application of Redundancy Coding

Independent of the mechanisms that may be involved in remote sensing, observation of the phenomenon implies the existence of an information channel in the information-theoretic sense. As we have seen from the work of Ryzl and Carpenter discussed earlier, it is even possible to use such a (noisy) channel for error-free transmission of information if sufficient redundancy coding is used.[75] Following is a general procedure that we have used successfully for signal enhancement.

We shall assume that the "message" consists of a stream of binary digits (0,1) of equal probability (for example, binary sort of green/white cards as in Ryzl's case, English text encoded as in Table 2.10 and sent long distance by strobe light on/off, and so on). To combat channel noise, each binary digit to be sent through the channel requires the addition of redundancy bits (coding). Efficient coding requires a compromise between the desire to maximize reliability and the desire to minimize redundancy. One efficient coding scheme for such a channel is obtained by application of a sequential sampling procedure of the type used in production-line quality control.[76] The adaptation of such a procedure to paranormal communication channels, which we now discuss, was considered first by Taetzsch.[77] The sequential method gives a rule of procedure for making one of three possible decisions following the receipt of each bit: accept 1 as the bit being transmitted; reject 1 as the bit being transmitted (that is, accept 0); or continue transmission of the bit under consideration. The sequential sampling procedure differs from fixed-length coding in that the number of bits required to reach a final decision on a message bit is not fixed before transmission but depends on the results accumulated with each transmission. The principal advantage of the sequential sampling procedure, as compared with the other methods, is that on the average, fewer bits per final decision are required for an equivalent degree of reliability.

### Table 2.10 Five-Bit Code for Alphanumeric Characters

| Alphabet Letters | Binary Code | Alphabet Letters | Binary Code |
|:---:|:---:|:---:|:---:|
| E | 00000 | Y | 01000 |
| T | 11111 | G, J | 10111 |
| N | 00001 | W | 01001 |
| R | 11110 | V | 10110 |
| I | 00010 | B | 01010 |
| O | 11101 | 0 | 10101 |
| A | 00011 | 1 | 01011 |
| S, X, Z | 11100 | 2 | 10100 |
| D | 00100 | 3 | 01100 |
| H | 11011 | 4 | 10011 |
| L | 00101 | 5 | 01101 |
| C, K, Q | 11010 | 6 | 10010 |
| F | 00110 | 7 | 01110 |
| P | 11001 | 8 | 10001 |
| U | 00111 | 9 | 01111 |
| M | 11000 | . | 10000 |

Note: Alphabet characters listed in order of decreasing frequency in English text. See, for example, A Sinkov, *Elementary Cryptanalysis—A Mathematical Approach* (New York: Random House, 1968). (The low-frequency letters, X, Z, K, Q, and J, have been grouped with similar characters to provide space for numerics in a five-bit code.) In consideration of the uneven distribution of letter frequencies in English text, this code is chosen such that 0 and 1 have equal probability.

Source: Compiled by the authors.

Use of the sequential sampling procedure requires the specification of parameters that are determined on the basis of the following considerations. Assume that a message bit (0 or 1) is being transmitted. In the absence of a priori knowledge, we may assume equal probability ($p$ =.5) for the two possibilities (0,1). Therefore, from the standpoint of the receiver, the probability of correctly identifying the bit being transmitted is $p$ = .5 because of chance alone. An operative remote-sensing channel could then be expected to alter the probability of correct identification to a value p = .5 + $\psi$, where the parameter satisfies $0 < |\psi| < .5$. (The quantity may be positive or negative, depending on whether the paranormal channel results in so-called psi hitting or psi missing.) Good psi functioning on a repetitive task has been observed to result in $\psi$ = .12, as reported by Ryzl.[78] Therefore, to indicate the design procedure, let us assume a baseline psi parameter $\psi_b$ = .1 and design a communication system on this basis.

The question to be addressed is whether after repeated transmission, a given message bit is labeled a "1" at a low rate $p_0$, commensurate with the hypothesis $H_0$ that the bit in question is a "0," or a a higher rate $p_1$, commensurate with the hypothesis $H_1$ that the bit in question is indeed a "1." The decision-making process requires the specification of four parameters.

$p_0$ The probability of labeling incorrectly a "0" message bit as a "1." The probability of labeling correctly a "0" as a "0" is $p = .5 + \psi_b = .6$. Therefore, the probability of labeling incorrectly a "0" as a "1" is $1 - p = .4 = p_0$.

$p_1$ The probability of labeling correctly a "1" message bit as a "1" is given by $p_1 = .5 + \psi_b = .6$.

$\alpha$ The probability of rejecting a correct identification for a "0" (Type 1 error). We shall take $\alpha = .01$.

$\beta$ The probability of accepting an incorrect identification for a "1" (Type 2 error). We shall take $\beta = .01$.

With the parameters thus specified, the sequential sampling procedure provides for construction of a decision graph as shown in Figure 2.18. The equations for the upper and lower limit lines are

$$\Sigma_1 = d_1 + SN$$

$$\Sigma_0 = -d_0 + SN$$

where

$$d_1 = \frac{\log \dfrac{1-\beta}{\alpha}}{\log \dfrac{p_1}{p_0} \dfrac{1-p_0}{1-p_1}} \qquad d_0 = \frac{\log \dfrac{1-\alpha}{\beta}}{\log \dfrac{p_1}{p_0} \dfrac{1-p_0}{1-p_1}}$$

$$S = \frac{\log \dfrac{1-p_0}{1-p_1}}{\log \dfrac{p_1}{p_0} \dfrac{1-p_0}{1-p_1}}$$

in which $S$ is the slope, $N$ is the number of trials, and $d_1$ and $d_0$ are the y-axis intercepts. A cumulative record of receiver-generated responses to the target bit is compiled until either the upper or the lower limit line is reached, at which point a decision is made to accept 0 or 1 as the bit being transmitted.

Channel reliability (probability of correctly determining message being

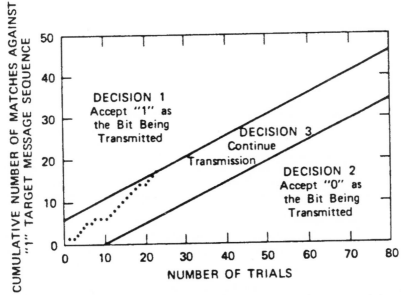

**Figure 2.18** Enhancement of signal-to-noise ratio by sequential sampling procedure ($p_0 = .4, p_1 = .6, \alpha = .01, \beta = .01$).

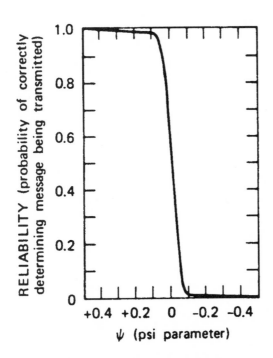

**Figure 2.19** Reliability curve for sequential sampling procedure ($p_0 = .4, p_1 = .6, \alpha = .01, \beta = .01$)

transmitted) as a function of operative psi parameter 0 is plotted in Figure 2.19. As observed, the sequential sampling procedure can result in 90 percent or greater reliability with psi parameters on the order of a few percent.

Implementation of the sequential sampling procedure requires the transmission of a message coded in binary digits. Therefore, the target space must consist of dichotomous elements, such as the white and green cards used in the experiments by Ryzl.

In operation, a sequence corresponding to the target bit (0 or 1) is sent, and the cumulative entries are made (Figure 2.18) until a decision is reached to accept either a 1 or a 0 as the bit being transmitted. At a prearranged time, the next sequence is begun and continues as above until the entire message has been received. A useful alternative, which relieves the percipient of the burden of being aware of his or her self-contradiction from trial to trial, consists of cycling through the entire message repetitively and entering each response on its associated graph until a decision has been reached on all message bits. The authors have used this technique successfully in a pilot study, but a discussion of this would take us beyond the intended scope of this chapter.

From the results obtained in such experiments, the channel bit rate can be ascertained for the system configuration under consideration. Furthermore, bit rates for other degrees of reliability (that is, for other $p_0$, $p_1$, $\alpha$, and $\beta$) can be estimated by construction of other decision curves over the same data base and thus provide a measure of the bit rate per degree of reliability.

In summary, the procedures described here can provide for a specification of the characteristics of a remote-sensing channel under well-defined conditions. These procedures also provide for a determination of the feasibility of such a channel for particular applications.

# Appendix B
# Remote-Viewing Transcript

Following is the unedited transcript of the first experiment with an SRI volunteer ($S_6$), a mathematician in the computer science laboratory, with no previous experience in remote viewing. The target, determined by random procedure, was White Plaza, a plaza with fountain at Stanford University (shown in Figure 2.8). As is our standard protocol, the experimenter with the subject is kept ignorant of the specific target visited, as well as the contents of the target pool. The experimenter's statements and questions are in italics.

*Today is Monday, October 7. It is 11:00, and this is a remote-viewing experiment with Russ Targ, Phyllis Cole, and Hal Puthoff. In this experiment, Hal will drive to a remote site chosen by a random process. Phyllis Cole will be the remote viewer, and Russ Targ is the monitor. We expect this experiment to start at 20 minutes after 11 and run for 15 minutes.*

*It is just about 20 minutes after 11, and Hal should be at his target location by now.*

*Why don't you tell me what kind of pictures you see and what you think he might be doing or experiencing.*

The first thing that came to mind was some sort of a large, square kind of a shape. Like Hal was in front of it. It was a . . . not a building or something, it was a square. I don't know if it was a window, but something like that so that the bottom line of it was not at the ground. About where his waist was, at least. That's what it seemed to me. It seems outdoors somehow. Tree.

*Does Hal seem to be looking at that square?*

I don't know. The first impression was that he wasn't, but I have a sense that whatever it was was something one might look at. I don't know if it would be a sign, but something that one might look at.

*Can you tell if it is on the ground or vertical?*

It seemed vertical.

I don't have a sense that it was part of anything particular. It might be on a building or part of a building, but I don't know. There was a tree outside, but I also got the impression of cement. I don't have the impression of very many people or traffic either. I have the sense that he is sort of walking back and forth. I don't have any more explicit picture than that.

*Can you move into where he is standing and try to see what he is looking at?*

I picked up he was touching something—something rough. Maybe warm and rough. Something possibly like cement.

*It is 24 minutes after 11.*

*Can you change your point of view and move above the scene so you can get a bigger picture of what's there?*

I still see some trees and some sort of pavement or something like that. Might be a courtyard. The thing that came to mind was it might be one of the plazas at Stanford campus or something like that, cement.

Some kinds of landscaping.

I said Stanford campus when I started to see some things in White Plaza, but I think that is misleading.

I have the sense that he's not moving around too much. That it's in a small area.

I guess I'll go ahead and say it, but I'm afraid I'm just putting on my impressions from Stanford campus. I had the impression of a fountain. There are two in the plaza, and it seemed that Hal was possibly near the, what they call, Mem Claw.

*What is that?*

It's a fountain that looks rather like a claw. It's a black sculpture. And it has benches around it made of cement.

*Are there any buildings at the place you are looking at? Are there any buildings? You described a kind of a courtyard. Usually at some places there should be a building, large or small, that the courtyard is about. Look at the end or the sides of the courtyard. Is there anything to be seen?*

I have a sense that there are buildings. It's not solid buildings. I mean there are some around the periphery, and I have a sense that none of them are very tall. Maybe mostly one story, maybe an occasional two-story one.

*Do you have any better idea of what your square was that you saw at the outset?*

No. I could hazard different kinds of guesses.

*Does it seem part of this scene?*

It . . . I think it could be. It could almost be a bulletin board or something with notices on it maybe. Or something that people are expected to look at. Maybe a window with things in it that people were expected to look at.

*What kind of trees do you see in this place?*

I don't know what kind they are. The impression was that they were shade trees and not terribly big. Maybe 12 feet of trunk and then a certain amount of branches above that. So that the branches have maybe a 12-foot diameter or something. Not real big trees.

*New trees rather than old trees?*

Yeah, maybe five or ten years old but not real old ones.

*Is there anything interesting about the pavement?*

No. It seems to be not terribly new or terribly old. Not very interesting. There seems to be some bits of landscaping around. Little patches of grass around the edges and peripheries. Maybe some flowers. But not lush.

*You saw some benches. Do you want to tell me about them?*

Well, that's my unsure feeling about this fountain. There was some kind of benches of cement. Curved benches, it felt like.

They were of rough cement.

*What do you think Hal is doing while he is there?*

I have a sense that he is looking at things trying to project them. Looking at different things and sort of walking back and forth not covering a whole lot of territory.

Sometimes standing still while he looks around.

I just had the impression of him talking, and I almost sense that it was being recorded or something. I don't know if he has a tape recorder, but if it's not that, then he is saying something because it needed to be remembered.

*It's 11:33. He's just probably getting ready to come back.*

## Summary

For more than 100 years, scientists have attempted to determine the truth or falsity of claims for the existence of a perceptual channel whereby certain individuals are able to perceive and describe remote data not presented to any known sense. This chapter presents an outline of the history of scientific inquiry into such so-called paranormal perception and surveys the current state of the art in parapsychological research in the United States and abroad. The nature of this perceptual channel is examined in a series of experiments carried out in the Electronics and Bioengineering Laboratory of SRI. The perceptual modality most extensively investigated is the ability of both experienced subjects and inexperienced volunteers to view, by innate mental processes, remote geographical or technical targets, including buildings, roads, and laboratory apparatus. The accumulated data indicate that the phenomenon is not a sensitive function of distance, and Faraday cage shielding does not in any apparent way degrade the quality and accuracy of perception. On the basis of this research, some areas of physics are suggested from which a description or explanation of the phenomenon could be forthcoming.

## Notes

1. C. Honorton, "Has Science Developed the Competence to Confront Claims of the Paranormal?," in *Research in Parapsychology 1975,* ed. J. Morris, W. Roll, and R. Morris. (Metuchen, N.J.: Scarecrow Press, 1976), pp. 199–224.

2. P. Allison, "Social Aspects of Scientific Innovation: The Case of Parapsychology" (M.A. thesis, University of Wisconsin, 1973).

3. R. Targ and H. Puthoff, "Information Transmission Under Conditions of Sensory Shielding," *Nature* 252 (October 1974): 602–7.

4. J. R. Smythies, ed., *Science and ESP* (London: Routledge, 1967).

5. C. Evans, "Parapsychology—What the Questionnaire Revealed," *New Scientist* 67 (January 1973): 209.

6. A. Gauld, *The Founders of Psychical Research* (New York: Schocken Books, 1968). See also W. Crookes, *Researches in the Phenomena of Spiritualism* (London: J. Burns, 1874).

7. Our initial work in this area was reported in R. Targ and H. Puthoff, "Information Transmission Under Conditions of Sensory Shielding," op. cit., reprinted in *IEEE Communications and Society Newsletter* 13 (January 1975): 12–19.

8. Crookes, op. cit.

9. D. D. Home, *Lights and Shadows of Spiritualism* (New York: G. W. Carleton, 1877).

10. Crookes, op. cit.

11. J. Coover, *Experiments in Psychical Research* (Palo Alto, Calif.: Stanford University Press, 1917).

12. G. Estabrooks, *Bulletin of the Boston Society for Psychical Research* (1927). See also L. T. Troland, *Techniques for the Experimental Study of Telepathy and Other Alleged Clairvoyant Processes* (Albany, N.Y.: 1928).

13. J. B. Rhine, *New Frontiers of the Mind* (New York: Farrar and Rinehart, 1937).

14. J. Pratt and J. B. Rhine et al., *Extra-Sensory Perception after Sixty Years* (New York: Henry Holt, 1940).

15. C. Scott, "G. Spencer Brown and Probability: A Critique," *Journal of the Society for Psychical Research* 39 (1958): 217–34.

16. G. R. Price, "Science and the Supernatural," *Science* 122 (1955): 359–67.

17. G. R. Price, "Apology to Rhine and Soal," *Science* 175 (1972): 359.

18. J. B. Rhine, "A New Case of Experimenter Unreliability," *Journal of Parapsychology* 38 (June 1974): 215–25.

19. C. E. M. Hansel, *ESP—A Scientific Evaluation* (New York: Scribner, 1966).

20. J. B. Rhine and J. G. Pratt, "A Review of the Pearce–Pratt Distance Series of ESP Tests," *Journal of Parapsychology* 18 (1954): 165–77; J. G. Pratt and J. L. Woodruff, "Size of Stimulus Symbols in Extrasensory Perception," *Journal of*

*Parapsychology* 3 (1939): 121–58; S. G. Soal and F. Bateman, *Modern Experiments in Telepathy* (London: Faber and Faber, 1953); and S. G. Soal and H. T. Bowden, *The Mind Readers: Recent Experiments in Telepathy* (New Haven Conn.: Yale University Press, 1954).

21. Hansel, op. cit., p. 18.

22. C. Honorton, "Error Some Place," *Journal of Communications* (Annenberg School of Communications) 25 (Winter 1975).

23. Ibid.

24. M. Ryzl, "Training the Psi Faculty by Hypnosis," *Journal of the American Society for Psychical Research* 41 (1962): 234–51.

25. *CIBA Foundation Symposium on Extra Sensory Perception* (Boston: Little, Brown, 1956).

26. M. Ryzl and J. Pratt, "A Repeated-Calling ESP Test with Sealed Cards," *Journal of Parapsychology* 27 (1963): 161–74; M. Ryzl and J. Pratt, "A Further Confirmation of Stabilized ESP Performance in a Selected Subject," *Journal of Parapsychology* 27 (1963): 73–83; J. Pratt, "Preliminary Experiments with a 'Borrowed' ESP Subject," *Journal of the American Society for Psychical Research* 42 (1964): 333–45; J. Pratt and J. Blom, "A Confirmatory Experiment with 'Borrowed' Outstanding ESP Subject," *Journal of the American Society for Psychical Research* 42 (1964): 381–88; W. G. Roll and J. G. Pratt, "An ESP Test with Aluminum Targets," *Journal of the American Society for Psychical Research* 62 (1968): 381–87; and J. Pratt, "A Decade of Research with a Selected ESP Subject: An Overview and Reappraisal of the Work with Pavel Stepanek," *Proceedings of the American Society for Psychical Research* 30 (1973).

27. C. Shannon and W. Weaver, *The Mathematical Theory of Communication* (Urbana: University of Illinois Press, 1949).

28. M. Ryzl, "A Model for Parapsychological Communication," *Journal of Parapsychology* 30 (March 1966): 18–31.

29. J. C. Carpenter, "Toward the Effective Utilization of Enhanced Weak-Signal ESP Effects" (Paper delivered at American Association for the Advancement of Science, New York, 1975).

30. Shannon and Weaver, op. cit.

31. C. Tart, "Card Guessing Tests: Learning Paradigm or Extinction Paradigm," *Journal of the American Society for Psychical Research* 60 (1966): 46.

32. C. T. Tart, *Learning to Use Extrasensory Perception* (Chicago: University of Chicago Press, 1976).

33. M. Ullman and S. Krippner, with A. Vaughan, *Dream Telepathy* (New York: Macmillan, 1973).

34. C. Honorton, "State of Awareness Factors in Psi Activation," *Journal of the American Society for Psychical Research* 68 (1974): 246–57.

35. *Proceedings of the Second International Congress of Psychotronic Research* (Monte Carlo) (Cotati, Calif.: International Association of Psychotronic Research, 1975).

36. L. L. Vasiliev, *Experiments in Mental Suggestion* (Hampshire, England: ISMI, 1963).

37. I. M. Kogan, "Is Telepathy Possible?," *Radio Engineering* 21 (January 1966): 75; I. M. Kogan, "Telepathy, Hypotheses and Observations," *Radio Engineering* 22 (January

1967): 141; I. M. Kogan, "Information Theory Analysis of Telepathic Communication Experiments," *Radio Engineering* 23 (March 1968): 122–30; and I. M. Kogan, "The Information Theory Aspect of Telepathy," P-4145, mimeographed (Santa Monica, Calif.: RAND, July 1969), p. 4,145.

38. A. S. Presman, *Electromagnetic Fields and Life* (New York: Plenum, 1970); and Y. A. Kholodov, ed., *Influence of Magnetic Fields on Biological Objects* (JPRS 63038 NTIS) (Springfield, Vt.: Joint Publications Research Service, 1974).

39. Y. A. Kholodov, "Investigation of the Direct Effect of Magnetic Fields on the Central Nervous System," in *Proceedings of the First Conference of Psychotronic Research* (JPRS 1/5022-1 and 2) (Springfield, Vt.: Joint Publications Research Service, 1974).

40. D. Mennie, "Consumer Electronics," *IEEE Spectrum* 12 (March 1975): 34–35.

41. W. P. Zinchenko et al., "Parapsychology: Fiction or Reality?," *Questions of Philosophy* 9 (1973): 128–36.

42. R. Cavanna, ed., *Proceedings of the International Conference of Methodology in Psi Research* (New York: Parapsychology Foundation, 1970).

43. E. D. Dean, "Plethysmograph Recordings as ESP Responses," *International Journal of Neuropsychiatry* 2 (September 1966).

44. C. Tart, "Physiological Correlates of Psi Cognition," *International Journal of Parapsychology* 5 (1963) 375–86; and D. H. Lloyd, "Objective Events in the Brain Correlating with Psychic Phenomena," *New Horizons* 1, no. 2 (Summer 1973): 69–75.

45. J. Silverman and M. S. Buchsbaum, "Perceptual Correlates of Consciousness: A Conceptual Model and Its Technical Implications for Psi Research," in *Psi Favorable States of Consciousness,* ed. R. Cavanna (New York: Parapsychology Foundation, 1970), pp. 143–69.

46. J. Kamiya, "Comment to Silverman and Buchsbaum," in Cavanna, ed., op. cit., pp. 158–59.

47. D. Hill and G. Parr, *Electroencephalography: A Symposium on Its Various Aspects* (New York: Macmillan, 1963).

48. T. D. Duane and T. Behrendt, "Extrasensory Electroencephalographic Induction between Identical Twins," *Science* 150 (1965): 367.

49. Targ and Puthoff, "Information Transmission Under Conditions of Sensory Shielding," op. cit.

50. Ibid.

51. Tart, "Physiological Correlates of Psi Cognition," op. cit., and Lloyd, op. cit.

52. K. Osis, "New ASPR Research on Out-of-Body Experiences," *ASPR Newsletter,* no. 14 (1972).

53. R. L. Morris, "An Exact Method for Evaluating Preferentially Matched Free-Response Material," *Journal of the American Society for Psychical Research* 66 (October 1972): 401.

54. G. R. Schmeidler, "PK Effects upon Continuously Recorded Temperatures," *Journal of the American Society for Psychical Research* 67 (October 1973): 325–40.

55. W. Scherer, "Spontaneity as a Factor in ESP," *Journal of the American Society for Psychical Research* 12 (1948): 126–47.

56. E. Edgington, "An Additive Method for Combining Probability Values from Independent Experiments," *Journal of Psychology* 80 (1972): 351–63.

57. R. Targ, P. Cole, and H. Puthoff, "Techniques to Enhance Man-Machine Communication," Final Report, NASA Contract NAS7-100 (Menlo Park, Calif.: SRI, June 1974).

58. R. Ornstein, *The Nature of Human Consciousness* (San Francisco: Freeman, 1973), chaps. 7 and 8; and R. W. Sperry, "Cerebral Organization and Behavior," *Science* 133 (1961): 1749–57.

59. O. Bilaniuk and E. C. G. Sudarshan, "Particles Beyond the Light Barrier," *Physics Today* 22 (May 1969): 43–51.

60. W. Pauli and C. G. Jung, eds., *The Interpretation of Nature and the Psyche* (Bollingen series, no. 51) (Princeton, N.J.: Princeton University Press, 1955).

61. Kogan, "Is Telepathy Possible?," op. cit.; Kogan, "Telepathy, Hypotheses and Observations," op. cit.; Kogan, "Information Theory Analysis of Telepathic Communication Experiments," op. cit.; and Kogan, "The Information Theory Aspect of Telepathy," op. cit.

62. M. A. Persinger, "ELF Waves and ESP," *New Horizons: Transactions of the Toronto Society for Psychical Research* 1 (January 1975): 232–35; and M. A. Persinger, *The Paranormal*, pt. 2, *Mechanisms and Models* (New York: M.S.S. Information Corp., 1974).

63. B. Julesz, *Foundations of Cyclopean Perception* (Chicago: University of Chicago Press, 1971).

64. H. Puthoff and R. Targ, "Psychic Research in Modern Physics" in *Psychic Exploration—A Challenge for Science*, ed. J. White (New York: Putnam, 1974), pp. 522–42; and G. Feinberg, "Precognition—A Memory of Things Future?," in *Proceedings of the Conference on Quantum Physics and Parapsychology* (Geneva) (New York: Parapsychology Foundation, 1975): 54–75.

65. E. P. Wigner, "The Problem of Measurement," *American Journal of Physics* 31 (1963): 6.

66. J. J. Freedman and J. F. Clauser, "Experimental Test of Local Hidden Variable Theories," *Physical Review Letters* 28 (April 1972): 938; and J. F. Clauser and M. A. Horne, "Experimental Consequences of Objective Local Theories," *Physical Review D.* 10 (July 1974): 526.

67. D. Bohm and B. Hiley, "On the Intuitive Understanding of Non-Locality as Implied by Quantum Theory," *Foundations of Physics* 5 (1975): 93–109.

68. J. S. Bell, "On the Problem of Hidden Variables in Quantum Theory," *Review of Modern Physics* 38 (July 1966): 447.

69. H. Stapp, "Theory of Reality," Lawrence-Berkeley Laboratory Report LBL-3837, mimeographed (Berkeley: University of California, April 1975).

70. A. Einstein, B. Podolsky, and N. Rosen, "Can Quantum-Mechanical Description of Physical Reality Be Considered Complete?," *Physical Review* 47 (May 1935): 777; and R. H. Dicke and J. P. Wittke, *Introduction to Quantum Mechanics* (Reading, Mass.: Addison-Wesley, 1960), chap. 7.

71. Freedman and Clauser, op. cit., and Clauser and Horne, op. cit.

72. E. H. Walker, "Foundations of Paraphysical and Parapsychological Phenomena," in *Proceedings of the Conference of Quantum Physics and Parapsychology,* op. cit.; and O. Costa de Beauregard, "Time Symmetry and Interpretation of Quantum Mechanics" (Paper delivered at Boston Colloquium for Philosophy of Science, February 1974) in *Foundations of Physics* (in press).

73. J. A. Stratton, *Electromagnetic Theory* (New York: McGraw-Hill, 1941).

74. Costa de Beauregard, op. cit.

75. Shannon and Weaver, op. cit., and Ryzl, "A Model for Parapsychological Communication," op. cit.

76. P. Hoel, *Introduction to Mathematical Statistics,* 2d ed. (New York: Wiley, 1954), p. 27.

77. R. Taetzsch, "Design of a Psi Communications System," *International Journal of Parapsychology* 4 (Winter 1962): 35.

78. Ryzl, "A Model for Parapsychological Communication," op. cit.

# Introduction to Chapter 3

This chapter describes additional remote-viewing experiments at SRI, including an extension of subject-target separations to transcontinental distances, undertaken to learn more about the range and nature of the phenomenon. The authors further discuss possible physical principles involved in parapsychological effects. An especially valuable feature is a summary table of what is currently known about remote viewing, compiled from the most recent data.

An additional important section of this chapter is one devoted to an examination of various criticisms of the remote-viewing studies that have been put forward by critics. As with J. B. Rhine et al.'s publications in the 1930s, Harold Puthoff and Russell Targ's publication of the preceding chapter, as well as their *Nature* article,[1] caused considerable reaction in the scientific community, ranging from positive reaction to the fact that important questions about parapsychological effects were being studied to criticism as to possible loopholes in the protocols. This give and take is an essential element of scientific procedure. For example, these data were presented at the 1979 Conference of the American Association for the Advancement of Science in Houston, Texas.*

## About the Authors

The biographies of **Russell Targ** and **Harold E. Puthoff** have appeared at the beginning of Chapter 2. **Edwin C. May's** biography appears at the beginning of Chapter 5.

---

*Puthoff, H. E., R. Targ, and E. C. May. 1981. Experimental psi research: Implications for physics. In *The Role of Consciousness in the Physical World*, R. G. Jahn, 37–86. AAAS Symposium 57, Boulder: Westview Press.

# 3

# Direct Perception of Remote Geographical Locations

**Russell Targ, Harold E. Puthoff, and Edwin C. May**

## Long-Distance Remote-Viewing Experiments

### General

After establishing the data base [reported in Chapter 2—eds.] of 51 remote-viewing trials with local targets (sites within a few kilometers), we undertook a series of five trials designed to determine whether an increase in subject-target separation to transcontinental distances would degrade the quality or accuracy of perception.[2] A major motivation for this effort was the desire to begin to accumulate data to examine various hypotheses, for example, whether remote viewing is mediated by ELF electromagnetic waves. Under simple forms of this hypothesis, one would expect a degradation in accuracy as the subject-target distance is increased to several thousand kilometers.[3]

As a secondary goal, we were interested in the real-time data rate, for example, determining the extent to which a remote-viewing subject can track the real-time activities and movements of a known individual in a distant city. Therefore, the subjects were encouraged to describe real-time activity during the viewing period.

The methodology with regard to target selection again was designed to eliminate possible cueing paths. Targets were determined either by random number generator entry into a previously prepared target list unknown to subject and experimenters with the subject or, in one case, on the basis of site selection by an independent, skeptical challenger.

An interesting additional technique that was employed successfully in the first two of the five experimental trials was the use of the DARPA computer teleconferencing network for postexperiment feedback. Access to the computer by the traveling experimenter was by means of a portable terminal. The use of the teleconferencing service allowed the subject in one state (California) to communicate with an experimenter in the other state, New York. The conversational TALK mode available on the DARPA net was used for this purpose in the following manner.

The subject at SRI (supervised) and the experimenters on the East Coast agreed (via computer teleconferencing) to begin an experiment in one-half hour. The purpose of the computer in this experiment was to provide time- and date-stamped permanent records of all communications between the various parties involved in the experiment. These data could be read in real time by any authorized person entering the SRI-AI Tenex (MSG) system.

After logging off the computer, the outbound experimenters used a random number generator to determine which of six locations in the target area would constitute the target to be visited in this experiment. Neither the subject nor the experimenter at SRI knew the contents of the target list, compiled in New York after logging off the computer link. Having selected a target location by the random protocol, the outbound experimenters proceeded directly to the site and remained there for 15 minutes. At the previously agreed-upon start time (one-half hour after breaking computer links), the subject typed impressions into a special computer file established for this purpose.

When the outbound experimenters returned from the target site to the hotel, one of the experimenters made use of a limited-access file to enter his description of the place he actually visited. He then returned to the executive level of the computer and awaited the appearance of the SRI experimenters and subject who could then (and only then) link the New York and Menlo Park terminals. At that time, both files were printed out on both terminals, and both the subject and the outbound team each learned what the other had written.

## Menlo Park to New York City (Grant's Tomb)

Two subjects, $S_7$ and $S_8$, both in California, participated simultaneously in this experiment of Grant's Tomb, which was the first of the two New York City targets. Both subjects independently provided computer-stored records of their impressions, and one made the sketch shown in Figure 3.1.

Subject $S_8$, an SRI systems analyst, said in his opening paragraph: "Outdoors, large open area, standing on and then off asphalt (rough material), dark for a path. A white building, like a ticket booth. Wooden structure, is white in color, and has an arched look about it. There is a large shade tree close to Russ" (outbound experimenter).

Subject $S_7$, closeted in a separate SRI location, began with: "I thought of a high place with a view." The subject continued with: "I saw a tree on your left

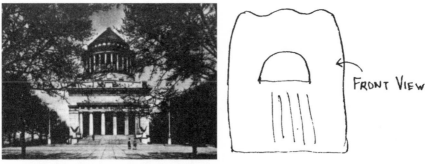

**Figure 3.1** Coast-to-coast remote-viewing experiment. Subject described: "Outdoors, large open area. . . . Shade trees. . . . White building with arches."

in a brick plaza—it seemed to be in front of a building you were entering. . . . I could not clearly identify the activity. A restaurant? A museum? A bookstore? . . . You were looking at coins in the palm of your hand, maybe giving some to Nicky" (son of outbound experimenter). The coins were in fact used to purchase the postcard from which Figure 3.1 was made, and they were given to the experimenter's son, who made the purchase. Both subjects then went on for an additional paragraph to describe details of the activities they imagined to be going on inside the building they saw, details that were partly correct, partly incorrect.

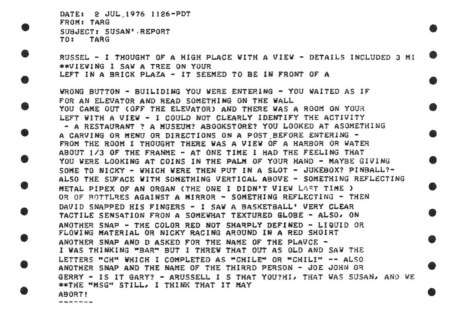

**Figure 3.2** Computer file printout. California–New York long-distance remote-viewing. Target: Grant's Tomb, New York City.

**Figure 3.3** Coast-to-coast remote-viewing experiment with target at Washington Square in New York City.

As an example of the style of narrative generated by a subject during a computer teleconferencing experiment, we include the entire unedited computer-logged text of $S_7$'s response to the Grant's Tomb target in Figure 3.2.

## Menlo Park to New York City (Washington Square Fountain)

In the second experiment, the target, again chosen by random protocol, was the fountain in Washington Square Park. One subject, $S_7$, participated. The subject produced an exceptionally accurate transcript. The photos and the subject's drawing of the fountain are shown in Figure 3.3. The subject began his printout with the following:

> The first image I got at about the first minute was of a cement depression—as if a dry fountain with a cement post in the center or inside. There seemed to be pigeons off to the right, flying around the surface out of the depression. . . . At one point I thought you were opening a cellophane bag. . . . [The experimenters had in fact bought ice cream during the experimental period.] There was also a rectangular wooden frame, a window frame, but I wasn't sure if it was on a building, or a similar structure with a different purpose [a possible correlation from a functional viewpoint to the Washington Square Arch through which the outbound experimenters viewed the fountain toward the end of the experimental period]. All in all, I thought you were in Riverside Park [incorrect analysis].

An SRI scientist, familiar with the New York City area but blind to the target, did, however, identify the target correctly on reading the 20 lines of print-

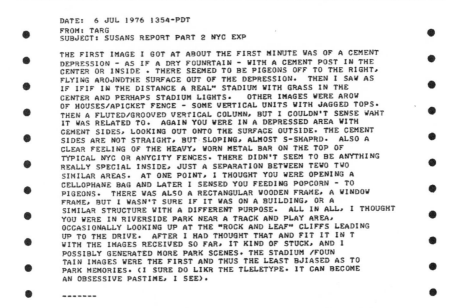

```
DATE:  6 JUL 1976 1354-PDT
FROM: TARG
SUBJECT: SUSANS REPORT PART 2 NYC EXP

THE FIRST IMAGE I GOT AT ABOUT THE FIRST MINUTE WAS OF A CEMENT
DEPRESSION - AS IF A DRY FOUNRTAIN - WITH A CEMENT POST IN THE
CENTER OR INSIDE . THERE SEEMED TO BE PIGEONS OFF TO THE RIGHT,
FLYING AROJNDTHE SURFACE OUT OF THE DEPRESSION.  THEN I SAW AS
IF IFIF IN THE DISTANCE A REAL" STADIUM WITH GRASS IN THE
CENTER AND PERHAPS STADIUM LIGHTS.   OTHER IMAGES WERE AROW
OF HOUSES/APICKET FENCE - SOME VERTICAL UNITS WITH JAGGED TOPS.
THEN A FLUTED/GROOVED VERTICAL COLUMN, BUT I COULDN'T SENSE WAHT
IT WAS RELATED TO.  AGAIN YOU WERE IN A DEPRESSED AREA WITH
CEMENT SIDES, LOOKING OUT ONTO THE SURFACE OUTSIDE. THE CEMENT
SIDES ARE NOT STRAIGHT, BUT SLOPING, ALMOST S-SHAPRD.  ALSO A
CLEAR FEELING OF THE HEAVY, WORN METAL BAR ON THE TOP OF
TYPICAL NYC OR ANYCITY FENCES. THERE DIDN'T SEEM TO BE ANYTHING
REALLY SPECIAL INSIDE, JUST A SEPARATION BETWEEN TEWO TWO
SIMILAR AREAS.  AT ONE POINT, I THOUGHT YOU WERE OPENING A
CELLOPHANE BAG AND LATER I SENSED YOU FEEDING POPCORN - TO
PIGEONS.  THERE WAS ALSO A RECTANGULAR WOODEN FRAME, A WINDOW
FRAME, BUT I WASN'T SURE IF IT WAS ON A BUILDING, OR A
SIMILAR STRUCTURE WITH A DIFFERENT PURPOSE.  ALL IN ALL, I THOUGHT
YOU WERE IN RIVERSIDE PARK NEAR A TRACK AND PLAY AREA,
OCCASIONALLY LOOKING UP AT THE "ROCK AND LEAF" CLIFFS LEADING
UP TO THE DRIVE.  AFTER I HAD THOUGHT THAT AND FIT IT IN T
WITH THE IMAGES RECEIVED SO FAR, IT KIND OF STUCK, AND I
POSSIBLY GENERATED MORE PARK SCENES. THE STADIUM /FOUN
TAIN IMAGES WERE THE FIRST AND THUS THE LEAST BJIASED AS TO
PARK MEMORIES. (I SURE DO LIKR THE TLELETYPE. IT CAN BECOME
AN OBSESSIVE PASTIME, I SEE).

-------
```

**Figure 3.4** Computer file printout. California–New York long-distance remote viewing. Target: Washington Square, New York City

out as it emerged from the computer terminal. (For the complete transcript, see Figure 3.4.)

These experiments provide an elegant demonstration of the utility of the teleconferencing process as a secure data-recording system to provide real-time monitoring of long-distance remote-viewing experiments.

In a more detailed tape recording made after the experiment, but before any feedback, the subject described "cement steps going into the depression, like a stadium, and the rounded edge of the top of the depression as you go up to ground level." These descriptions are not only correct but also show remarkable detail.

## Quantitative Analysis of New York City Target Transcripts

As a beginning in deriving a quantitative estimate of the amount of valid data in a transcript, we have made a detailed analysis of the previous two transcripts generated by a single subject ($S_7$) during the long-distance experiments between Menlo Park, California, and New York City.

To carry out this analysis, each transcript typed by the subject into a computer file was edited to retain only declarative statements spontaneously generated by the subject or responses to direct questions. These statements were collected in groups called *concepts*. For example, if the subject had five references to a condition that could be defined as shady, these would be combined in the concept "shady."

We performed four comparative analyses on the concepts from the two transcripts: Transcript A with Site A; Transcript B with Site B; Transcript A

**Table 3.1 Quantitative Analysis of the Grant's Tomb Transcript**

| Subject's Description (quotes) | Correspondence | (0–10) | Cross Correspondence to Washington Square | (0–10) |
|---|---|---|---|---|
| 1. I thought of a high place with a view | Bluff overlooking river | 10 | Standing in a depression | 0 |
| 2. I saw a tree on your left | Lots of trees | 10 | Nearby trees | 8 |
| 3. In a brick plaza | Plaza looks like brick | 8 | Plaza looks like brick | 8 |
| 4. Building you were entering | Entered tomb building | 10 | No buildings | 0 |
| 5. Read something on the wall | Read informative plaque | 10 | No walls, no reading | 0 |
| 6. Came off the elevator | No elevator | 0 | No elevator | 0 |
| 7. A restaurant? | None | 0 | None | 0 |
| 8. A museum? | It is a museum | 10 | None | 0 |
| 9. A bookstore? | Books and cards are sold | 10 | None | 0 |
| 10. A carving, menu, or directions on a post | Bronze plaque at entry | 8 | None | 0 |
| 11. The room has a view | Room looks down on tombs 30 feet below | 7 | No room | 0 |
| 12. View of harbor or water | View of river | 9 | Large operating fountain | 9 |
| 13. Coins in your hand | Used to buy cards | 10 | Used to buy ice cream | 10 |
| 14. Gave some coins to Nicky (son) | He bought cards | 10 | Does not apply | 0 |
| 15. Nicky put them into a slot | No slot | 0 | Does not apply | 0 |
| 16. Reflecting metal pipes | Could be columns | 6 | Metal pipes in fountain | 6 |
| 17. Bottles against a mirror | None | 0 | None | 0 |
| 18. Something reflecting | Marble and glass doors | 6 | Water in fountain | 6 |
| 19. Basketball or textured globe | None | 0 | Glass globe around fountain | 8 |
| 20. Nicky in red shirt | Correct | 10 | Does not apply | 0 |
| 21. Liquid or flowing material | None | 0 | Water in fountain | 10 |
| | Mean | 6.4 | Mean | 3.1 |

*Source:* Compiled by the authors

## Table 3.2 Quantitative Analysis of the Washington Square Transcript

| Subject Description (quotes) | Correspondence | (0–10) | Cross Correspondence to Grant's Tomb | (0–10) |
|---|---|---|---|---|
| 1. Cement depression | We were in a cement depression | 10 | Tombs are in marble depression | 10 |
| 2. A dry fountain | Operating fountain | 8 | None | 0 |
| 3. Cement post in the center | Cement post plus large pipe | 7 | Tombs in center | 2 |
| 4. Pigeons off to the right | Pigeons were in the park nearby | 8 | No pigeons | 0 |
| 5. Stadium with grass and lights | Scale factor | 3 | Scale factor | 3 |
| 6. Rows of houses, picket fence | Houses with iron fences | 9 | None | 0 |
| 7. Vertical units with jagged tops | Arch supports perhaps | 3 | Columns in front of building | 10 |
| 8. Fluted grooved white columns | Side arch supports | 6 | Columns in front of building | 10 |
| 9. You are in a depressed area with cement sides | Exactly | 10 | Tomb is in a depressed area | 3 |
| 10. Sides are sloping almost S-shaped | Exactly | 10 | Somewhat curved at top | 3 |
| 11. Heavy worn metal | Copper posts in fountain | 7 | Marble railing | 3 |
| 12. A separation between different areas | In and out of fountain | 6 | Above and below in tomb area | 7 |
| 13. You were opening a celophane bag | Yes | 10 | No | 0 |
| 14. You were feeding popcorn to pigeons | Others were | 3 | No pigeons | 0 |
| 15. Rectangular wooden frame …on a building | Could be the arch | 5 | Rectangular building | 3 |
| 16. Riverside Park, tracks and play area | Play area nearby | 3 | Tomb is in Riverside Park | 7 |
| | Mean | 6.8 | Mean | 3.8 |

Source: Compiled by the authors

with Site B; and Transcript B with Site A. Each concept was assigned a rating ranging from zero to ten, depending on the analyst's subjective impression as to whether the concept had no correspondence (a rank of zero) or complete correspondence (a rank of ten) with the target. The cross-matching was to serve as a crude measure of chance or generalized correspondence.

For the Grant's Tomb target site, there were 21 distinct concepts with a mean score $\mu = 6.4$; for the Washington Square site, there were 16 concepts with a mean score $\mu = 6.8$. The individual cross matches were as follows: Grant's Tomb transcript to Washington Square had a mean score $\mu = 3.1$, and the Washington Square transcript matched against Grant's Tomb yielded a mean score $\mu = 3.8$. Table 3.1 shows the detailed analysis for the Grant's Tomb experiment. For each of the 21 concepts (all that were found), we display a summary of the concept, the target correspondence and its related score, and the correspondence with the control target, Washington Square, and its related score. Table 3.2 shows the same data for the Washington Square site and its control target, Grant's Tomb.

The combined score for the direct matches is $\mu = 6.6$, and for the cross matches, it is $\mu = 3.4$, where the means are calculated by direct average. The difference in the means, although not definitive in a statistical sense (because of the large spread), is consistent with earlier qualitative assessments of transcript accuracy of over 50 transcripts. From these means, we would estimate that approximately 66 percent of this one subject's response constitutes an accurate description of the target site, whereas if the data are matched against other target sites, only 37 percent of the response would typically apply. Although crude, this subjective analysis serves as a first step in suggesting a method for further single transcript analysis.

## New York City to Ohio (Ohio Caves)

A third long-distance remote-viewing experiment was carried out under the control of an independent, skeptical scientist. In this case, both SRI experimenters, while attending a conference, agreed to take part in a remote-viewing experiment in which our colleague would select the target.

Under the observation of our challenger, we telephoned subject $S_4$ in New York City and obtained the subject's agreement to participate in a long-distance remote-viewing experiment. The subject was told only that we were located somewhere between New York City and our California laboratory and that shortly we would be taken to a target which we would like to have described. The time for the experiment was set for 2 p.m. Eastern Daylight Time (EDT). We also agreed to call again at 3 p.m. EDT to obtain subject $S_4$'s impressions and to provide feedback as to the actual target.

The scientist took us directly to the Ohio Caverns at Springfield, Ohio, which he had chosen as the target location (see Figure 3.5). We entered the grounds through an entrance arch that opens onto an enormous expanse of lawn, perhaps 20 acres. The caves are located at a depth of approximately 150 feet and are entered through a small building having a long flight of steep stairs. Once underground, we walked through a maze of rock-lined tunnels that lead eventually into a series of rooms lined with calcite stalactites and stalagmites, frosty white and beige crystals formed like icicles. The entire cavern is illuminated by small electric light bulbs attached to the walls. After a 45-minute walk, we exited the caves through a large metal door giving access to a square cross-sectional shaft with stairs leading to the surface.

Following the experimental period, the scientist observer called the subject in New York, 45 minutes after we left the caves. The opening statements of the subject's transcript, as dictated over the phone and posted to the SRI experimenters, is as follows:

> 1:50 PM before starting—Flat semi-industrial countryside with mountain range in background and something to do with underground caves or mines or deep shafts—half manmade, half natural—some electric humming going on—throbbing, inner throbbing. Nuclear or some very far out and possibly secret installation—corridor—mazes of them—whole underground city almost—Don't like it at all—long for outdoors and nature. 2:00 PM—[Experimenters] R and H walking along sunny road—entering into arborlike shaft—again looks like man helped nature—vines (wisteria) growing in arch

**Figure 3.5** Ohio caves: described by subject in New York as "underground caves or mines. . . . Deep shafts. . . . Darker, cool, moist earth-smelling passages."

at entrance like to a wine cellar—leading into underground world. Darker earth-smelling cool moist passage with something grey and of interest on left of them—musty—sudden change to bank of elevators—a very manmade steel wall—and shaft-like inverted silo going deep below earth—brightly lit.

Subject $S_4$ concludes with: "I see a lot of gold and metal and silver—gold glow all over—not much sound—very silent factory—scary—few people—very special."

As if often the case, one observes that the basic gestalt of the target site is cognized and even experienced, for example, the underground caves aspect, while specifics are misinterpreted, for example, the labeling of the location as a nuclear installation.

A second subject ($S_8$), working by himself at SRI, who had agreed in advance to participate in the same experiment by date and time, was less successful with the cavern target. This subject erroneously interpreted early impressions as associated with a museum. As a result, the majority of his transcript, although containing some correct elements, reflects primarily an incorrect analytical interpretation and cannot be said to constitute evidence for paranormal functioning.

## New Orleans to Palo Alto (Northern California Bank Plaza)

Two experimental trials carried out between New Orleans and Menlo Park, California, constitute the final tests of the long-distance series, seven trials of which have been completed to date (all reported here). These last two were carried out with the two subjects who had participated in the first two California-to-New York experiments.

The first trial in this series involved subject $S_7$ in New Orleans viewing activities of a group of three people known to the subject at a location in a Palo Alto/Menlo Park area 2,000 miles away. The subject's principal impression was of an "overhang of a building over their heads . . . also a round gold rim around a sunken depression." The target, a bank building, is shown in Figure 3.6. Principal features of the target include a dramatic building overhang and a rectangular concrete depression with a fountain, in which the water comes out of a circular gold rim. The subject also reported "some kind of fake china flowers mushrooming out of the depression." There were four orange lamps mounted on the gold rim. Finally, $S_7$ reported, "There was a projectile coming toward [one of the outbound experimenters]. Like a ball or frisbee, as if [another experimenter] has tossed him a ball." Actually, the experimenters had found a paper airplane lying on the ground and had thrown it back and forth several times. In fact, the photo of the site taken at the time of the experiment shows the airplane between them. This is one of the few times that a remote-viewing subject has perceived rapid motion at the target site.

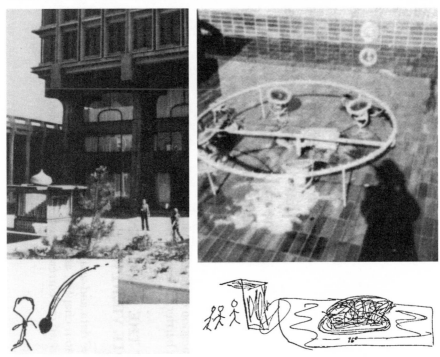

**Figure 3.6** Remote-viewing experiment—New Orleans to Palo Alto, October 30, 1976. Subject described: "the overhang of a building over their heads," and "a round gold rim around a sunken depression.... In the surface of the depression there is some kind of fake china flowers. It's like a bonsai tree mushrooming out of the surface." Later in the transcript the subject said, "There was a projectile coming toward [one of the outbound experimenters]. Some kind of projectile, like a ball or a frisbee. As if [another experimenter] tossed him a ball." (It was a paper airplane.)

## Menlo Park to New Orleans (Louisiana Superdome)

For the final experiment (subject in Menlo Park), it was agreed that at 1200 Central Standard Time on a particular day, the outbound experimenter would choose a target location in his city by random protocol and remain there for the required 15 minutes. During this time, subject $S_8$ in Menlo Park would tape record impressions and make any drawings that seemed appropriate. (The DARPA net was not available because of computer net malfunction.)

The target chosen by randomized entry into a New Orleans guidebook list was the Louisiana Superdome. The outbound experimenter tape recorded the following description as he looked at the building: "It is a bright sunshiny day. In front of me is a huge silvery building with a white dome gleaming in the sun. It is a circular building with metal sides. It looks like nothing so much as

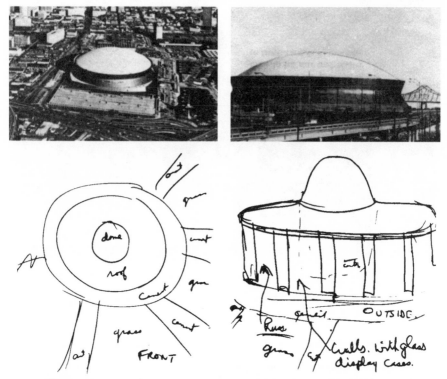

**Figure 3.7** Long-distance remote-viewing experiment—SRI, Menlo Park, to Louisiana Superdome. Subject described lagre circular building with a white dome (October 31, 1976).

a flying saucer. The target is in fact the 80,000-seat Louisiana Superdome stadium."

The subject in Menlo Park described the target as "a large circular building with a white dome." The subject also expressed feelings of wanting to reject what he saw because the dome looked "like a flying saucer in the middle of a city." Some appreciation for this perception can be obtained from Figure 3.7, in which the target is shown together with the sketches that the subject made.

Taken overall, the results obtained in these five long-distance remote-viewing experiments are of roughly the same accuracy with regard to site description as those obtained in local remote-viewing experiments. The descriptions not only contain correct information beyond that expected by chance but also show remarkable detail and resolution. Furthermore, real-time activities are observed and correctly described in a number of instances. Although extensive data must be taken before a final conclusion can be reached, it appears at this point that there is little, if any, degradation in quality of perception as the subject-target distance is increased from a few miles to transcontinental distances. The results obtained on the basis of viewing a New

York site from SRI in Menlo Park, 3,000 miles away, for example, are similar to those obtained in local remote-viewing experiments. Any theory of paranormal functioning put forward at this time should take this insensitivity to distance into account, and any application of paranormal functioning need not, at first, consider distance as a barrier, at least to the range examined.

## State of the Art of Knowledge of Remote Viewing

Given the data and analyses of remote-viewing performance in this and the previous chapter, as well as in other as yet unreported work, we have summarized our current knowledge about the phenomenon in Table 3.3.

## Principles of Physics Potentially Applicable to Psi Phenomena

One of the common objections to the existence of so-called paranormal functioning is that it would seem to be in conflict with the laws of physics. Our investigations, however, have led us to the contrary view, namely, that the data can in all probability be accounted for either within the framework of physics as presently understood or within the framework of extrapolations that have been proposed to account for other (nonpsi) data. In fact, we anticipate that not only can we use physical principles to help us understand psi phenomena but the psi data base will probably shed light on some of the current problems in physics, for example, with regard to the foundations of quantum theory and for geometrical models of space-time events such as exist in relativity theory. In this section, we outline how we are making use of our experimental data base to deduce the relevant physical principles and laws that govern psi functioning.

In addition to attempting to determine whether psi phenomena are generally compatible with the laws and content of physics as presently codified, we are also examining the limits of specific physical theories in modeling psi phenomena. The areas of physics we have under consideration as potentially relevant to modeling psi phenomena include the possibility that remote viewing is mediated by ELF electromagnetic waves;[4] the possible significance for remote viewing of Bell's theorem[5] and the Einstein-Podolsky-Rosen (EPR) paradox of quantum theory,[6] which emphasizes that "no theory of reality compatible with quantum theory can require spatially separated events to be independent,"[7] but must permit interconnectedness of distant events in a manner that is contrary to ordinary experience[8] (experimentally confirmed at the microscopic level);[9] the proper interpretation of the effect of an observer (consciousness) on experimental measurement,[10] of possible significance in PK; the possibility that the causality-reversing tachyon[11] or advanced-potential solutions of physics may play a role in precognition;[12] and the

**Table 3.3 Remote Viewing: State of the Art-Current (1978) Knowledge**

| Characteristic | Known | Unknown |
|---|---|---|
| Target acquisition | Subject can acquire and describe target site on the basis of presence of cooperative experimenter at site | What is necessary for target acquisition (names, maps, pictures, other coordinate systems); whether person unknown to subject can be tracked on the basis of biographical information, pictures, and so forth |
| Target attributes sensed | Descriptive aspects (shape, form, color, material) are described better than analytical concepts (function, name), although at times, the latter come through excellently; written target material correct only occasionally; alphabet target successful only statistically | Whether analytical psi can be trained to levels successful only statistically similar to descriptive psi |
| Time of flight | Information access often appears to be available in essentially "real" time | Time-of-flight of psychoenergetic phenomena; mechanism of propagation |
| Temporal resolution | Real-time activities at the target site are often perceived; experiments have included successful real-time remote viewing to within ten seconds; estimated bit rate ~$10^{-1}$ bits/s; ephemeral, rapid, or repetitive targets more difficult | Extent to which a subject can improve temporal resolution; accuracy of the process; upper limit to bit rate and ability to track targets in motion |
| Spatial resolution | 1 millimeter (mm) | Extent to which subject can improve spatial resolution |
| Distance effects | Accuracy and resolution not a sensitive function of subject-target distance over intercontinental distances | Whether, or at what range, distance effects become important |
| Shielding | Faraday cage or seawater electrical shielding not effective shield | Whether magnetic shielding effective |

| Topic | Description | Areas for future research |
|---|---|---|
| Sensory modalities | In addition to visually observable detail, subjects sometimes report sounds, smells, electromagnetic fields, and so forth, which can be verified as existing, at target locations | The accuracy of nonvisual sensory modalities; other sensory modes available |
| Factors that appear to inhibit success in remote viewing | A prior subject knowledge of target possibilities; absence of feedback; application of ability to trivial tasks (testing for the sake of testing); use of repetitive target sequences | Effects of environmental physical factors; electromagnetic jamming |
| Factors that appear to enhance success in remote viewing | Interest factor for subject; a prori necessity and relevance for obtaining information (seriousness of purpose); presence of a facilitating monitor to ask questions and direct the subject's attention; practice with feedback | Effects of environmental physical factors; electromagnetic generators for targeting |
| Accuracy and reliability | Analysis of remote-viewing transcripts generated by experienced subjects indicates that for a given target site, roughly two-thirds of the subject-generated material constitutes an accurate description of the site, while about one-third is ambiguous, general, or incorrect | Achievement levels to be reasonably expected |
| Use of redundancy to improve signal-to-noise ratio | Redundancy, whereby more than one individual attempts to collect data on a given target, improves reliability by reducing the effect of the biases of individual subjects | Optimum number of subjects for efficient utilization of this approach |
| Robustness of phenomena | Continuing demonstrations at SRI and replications in other laboratories indicate that the capability known as "remote viewing" is a robust human perceptual ability | |

**Table 3.3 Remote Viewing: State of the Art–Current (1978) Knowledge (Continued)**

| Characteristic | Known | Unknown |
|---|---|---|
| Distribution of psychoenergetic capacity in population; identification of good subjects | Abilities appear widespread, though latent; volunteers with no previous history of psychoenergetic functioning exhibit ability in screening experiments, indicating that reliance on the availability of special subjects may not be necessary | Percentage of population with natural talent or trainable; optimum screening procedures; medical or psychological profile of good subjects |
| Improvement potential | Subjects trained over a several-year period have shown improved performance both with regard to accuracy and reliability | Whether near-perfect results as sometimes obtained can become routine |
| Technological considerations | Low-level perturbation of equipments observable during remote viewing (magnetometer, noise, and nuclear decay driven random event generator) | Degree to which phenomena can be stabilized, mechanized, energy stored; to what extent psychoenergetic processes can be amplified by technological means |
| Theoretical considerations | Phenomena characteristics often appear to be at variance with present scientific models | Precise mechanisms responsible for the phenomena; relationship of phenomena to electromagnetic, quantum, and so forth bases of present scientific understanding; whether the data can be accounted for within the framework of physics as presently understood or on the basis of conservative extrapolation that have been proposed to account for other (nonpsi) data |

*Source:* Compiled by the authors.

potential relevance (for a general theory of psi phenomena) of theories based on geometries that provide for a more extended structure of the space-time metric.* To indicate the tenor of our approach, let us consider briefly two examples from this list.

A reasonable first hypothesis is that remote viewing is mediated by ELF electromagnetic waves, a hypothesis that does not seem to be ruled out by any obvious physical or biological facts.

This hypothesis, put forward by I. M. Kogan of the Soviet Union, suggests that information transfer under conditions of sensory shielding is mediated by ELF waves with wavelengths in the 300 to 1,000 kilometer region.[13] Experimental support for the hypothesis is claimed on the basis of less-than-inverse square attenuation with distance, compatible both with earth-ionosphere wave guide mode trapping and with source-percipient distances lying in the induction field range as opposed to the radiation field range; observed low bit rates (.005–.1 bits/s) compatible with the information-carrying capacity of ELF waves; apparent ineffectiveness of ordinary electromagnetic shielding as an attenuator; and standard antenna calculations entailing biologically generated currents yielding results compatible with observed signal-to-noise ratios.

On the negative side with regard to a straightforward ELF interpretation as a blanket hypothesis are the following: (1) apparent high-resolution, real-time descriptions of remote activities in sufficient detail to require a channel capacity in all probability greater than that allowed by a conventional modulation of an ELF signal; (2) lack of a proposed mechanism for coding (and decoding) the information onto the proposed ELF carrier; and (3) apparent precognition data. The hypothesis must nonetheless remain open at this stage of research, since it is conceivable that counterindication (1) may eventually be circumvented on the basis that the apparent high resolution and high bit rate results from a mixture of low bit rate input and high bit rate "filling in the blanks" from imagination; that counterindication (2) is common to a number of normal perceptual tasks and may therefore simply reflect a lack of sophistication on our part with regard to perceptual functioning;[14] and counterindication (3) may be accommodated by an ELF hypothesis if advanced waves as well as retarded waves are admitted.[15]

Experimentation to determine whether the ELF hypothesis is viable can be carried out by the use of ELF sources as targets, by the study of parametric dependence on propagational directions and diurnal timing, by

---

*We wish to acknowledge the technical contributions of Elizabeth A. Rauscher, a consultant to SRI on leave from Lawrence-Berkeley Laboratory, who has done extensive research on physical theories relevant to psi functioning—in particular, work on multidimensional geometries.

experimentation under unusual conditions of shielding (for example, in a submarine),* and by the exploration of interference effects caused by creation of a high-intensity ELF environment during experimentation. All of these are under consideration in our laboratory and elsewhere.

Because of the apparent difficulties with the ELF hypothesis, especially in accounting for the relatively high resolution and data rate of paranormal perception, serious consideration is being given to alternative mechanisms. A more speculative, but promising, hypothesis, which could in principle account for

---

*As of this writing, we have been able to perform two preliminary tests of remote viewing from a submarine. The following is a brief description of results.

The goal of this experiment was to determine whether it was possible to transmit a message to a submerged submarine via the remote-viewing channel. The test was designed to provide not only an opportunity to determine the feasibility of psychoenergetic communication with an isolated individual but also to provide data on the effects of environmental stress on psychoenergetic performance and on the possible shielding effects of several hundred feet of seawater (which is known to be a good shield for all but the lowest frequencies of the electromagnetic spectrum). One hundred and seventy meters of seawater provides more than 20 db attenuation for signals at all frequencies greater than 10 Hz.

The submersible used in the experiment was the Taurus, a five-man underwater vehicle manufactured by International Hydrodynamics Company of Canada. During the experimentation discussed here, the submersible operated submerged in the waters near Santa Catalina Island, off the coast of southern California.

The protocol for the experiment was as follows. A series of six potential messages to be sent was constructed in advance of the experiment. To each message was assigned a San Francisco Bay Area target location. To send a given message, a pair of experimenters comprising a target demarcation team went at a prearranged time to the site linked to the particular message and remained there for 15 minutes. During this period, a subject on board the submersible, monitored by an experimenter blind to the target pool, registered his impressions as to where the demarcation team was, 500 miles away, as per standard remote-viewing protocol. Following the remote-viewing trial, the subject then consulted a packet that contained the list of potential targets (seen for the first time at this point), made a choice as to which target of the set was viewed, and noted the associated message.

Two experiments of this type were carried out, one each with two subjects. For this first experiment, the submersible was at a depth of 170 m in water 340 m deep; for the second, the submersible rested on the bottom in 80 m of water. In both cases, the subjects rendered excellent descriptions of the target sites and had no difficulty in choosing the correct target from the list of six potential targets. Although the subjects indicated that they had experienced some degree of stress due to cramped conditions and seasickness, these environmental factors did not appear to affect the quality of performance deleteriously.

We are grateful for the many significant contributions of Mr. Stephen Schwartz of the Philosophical Research Society of Los Angeles, who as Director of Project Deep Quest (an underwater psychic archaeology experiment), made experimental time on the Taurus available to SRI.

both remote viewing and precognition, was developed in conjunction with Gerald Feinberg of Columbia University. It is proposed that the ordinary Minkowski four-space (three spatial, one temporal coordinates) might simply be the real part of an eight-dimensional complex space-time. For this generalized coordinate model, we let the spatial coordinates $x \rightarrow x + ix'$, and similarly for time, $t \rightarrow t + it'$. Analogous to the expression for the square of the distance between two points in Minkowski four-space,

$$\Delta s^2 = \Delta x^2 - c^2 \, \Delta t^2$$

we take the corresponding expression in the complex eight-space to be

$$\Delta s^2 = \Delta s \, \Delta s^0 = \Delta x'^2 - c^2 \, \Delta t^2 - c^2 \, \Delta t'^2$$

With regard to modeling remote viewing in real time ($\Delta t = 0$), we can construct situations in which the remaining first, second, and fourth terms in the above equation add to zero ($\Delta s = 0$). Therefore, even though there is an ordinary (three-space) separation $\Delta x$ between the two points, the distance in the complex eight-space is reduced to zero. Under the hypothesis that the imaginary (primed) coordinates are accessible to consciousness, reduction of the eight-space separation to zero could in principle provide for a coupling between remote viewer and target site. Given the additional geometrical channels provided by this model, a similar argument can be mounted to account for precognition ($\Delta s = 0$ for $\Delta t < 0$). We thus have the possibility of a geometrical interpretation of the quantum interconnectedness principle, by which events remote in space-time are nonetheless connected by nonlocal correlations[16] or, in this interpretation, by the nature of the fabric of space-time itself.

We are presently pursuing the implications of these and other models. Our goal in these investigations is to develop a theoretical structure to account for the data at hand and to predict new, testable experimental outcomes.

## Conclusions

In this chapter we have further described our investigations into aspects of human perception that appear to fall outside the range of well-understood perceptual/processing capabilities. Specifically, we have examined a phenomenon we call "remote viewing," the ability of certain individuals to access and describe, by mental processes, remote geographical sites blocked from ordinary perception by reason of distance and shielding.

In a series of experiments extending up to 5,000 km we have not observed any degradation in accuracy or resolution as a function of increasing distance. Furthermore, some real-time tracking of the activities of individuals at the target site has been accomplished over these distances. Although the information channel is imperfect, the data generated by the remote-viewing process exceed any reasonable bounds of chance correlation.

In the spirit of the dictum of physicist Richard P. Feynman that experimentation in difficult and controversial areas should be exhaustively self-criticized, we list below the potential criticisms of our experimentation, along with a discussion of each point: criticism and rebuttal.

## Experiment Selection
*Criticism*

The experiments discussed could be selected out of a larger pool of experiments of which many are of poorer quality.

*Rebuttal*

Selection of experiments for reporting does not take place; every experiment is entered as performed on a master log and is included in the statistical evaluations.

## Data Selection
*Criticism*

Data submitted to judges could be edited to show only the matching elements, the nonmatching elements being discarded.

*Rebuttal*

Data associated with a given experiment remain unedited; all experiments are tape recorded, and all data (tape transcripts, drawings, clay models) are included unedited in the data package to be judged and evaluated.

## Cueing
*Criticism*

The study could involve naivete in protocol that permits various forms of cueing (intentional or unintentional).

*Rebuttal*

The use of double-blind protocols ensures that none of the persons in contact with the subject is aware of either the particular target or target pool; similarly, no one in contact with a judge is aware of the target list/subject output correspondence. For example, judges are not taken to target sites by a knowledgeable person but rather proceed to the target sites, unaccompanied, on the basis of written instructions generated without knowledge of subject output.*

---

*Marks and Kammann recently hypothesized that the successful results of the first remote viewing study (with subject Price) might have been due to extraneous cues in the unedited transcript. An independent rejudging of the data taking this possibility into account has refuted their hypothesis.

## Educated Guess

*Criticism*

A subject may be able to guess as to which sites in a given area are likely to be chosen as targets and may have familiarized himself or herself with the locations.

*Rebuttal*

In the statistical judging procedure used, no advantage could be gained *even if a subject were to be given a list of possible target sites beforehand and encouraged to familiarize himself or herself with the locations.* Even in such an extreme hypothetical case (no such procedure was ever used) where a subject could not help but render a set of perfect descriptions of target sites, he or she still had the basic statistical problem of generating blind the correct target/description pair sequence upon which the statistical evaluation is based.

## Target Limitations

*Criticism*

If a subject is given feedback after an experiment that today's target was a fountain, he or she knows that the following target is unlikely to be a fountain, since targets are chosen for unique differentiable qualities.

*Rebuttal*

The target pool in use (> 100 target sites) contains several fountains, several buildings, several parks, and so forth, and therefore, the content of a given target, determined by random entry into the target pool, is essentially independent of the contents of other targets.

## Transcript Generality

*Criticism*

Transcripts generated by subjects are so general as to match anything. ("Sky is blue, grass is green.")

*Rebuttal*

Judging protocol involves *differential* matching. Therefore, true but general statements do not help a judge to *preferentially* assign a transcript to one site as opposed to another.

## "Read-In" Matches

*Criticism*

Given a transcript and a target, a judge can "read in" matches.

*Rebuttal*

*Differential* matching on a *blind* basis allows matches to be "read in" equally for noncorresponding, as well as corresponding, target/transcript pairs and therefore provides no differential advantage.

## Inadequate Handling of Judging Materials

*Criticism*

Preparation of judging materials (transcript typing) may provide opportunity for a "leak," or perhaps degradation of typing ribbon may provide artifactual information as to order of experiments.

*Rebuttal*

Transcript typing is carried out in a random order by individuals kept blind to the key; one-time ribbons are used.

## Post Hoc Photography

*Criticism*

Photographs used to illustrate remote viewing results are taken after completion of the experiments and therefore suffer from the fallacy of post hoc matching.

*Rebuttal*

All blind judging, matching, and statistical evaluation of the results (which is where the scientific issues are decided) are completed *before* photographs are taken; judges do not have access to photographs during their analysis, and therefore, judges cannot be cued into correspondences observed post hoc.

In short, at all times, we and others responsible for the overall program took measures to prevent sensory leakage and subliminal cueing and to prevent deception, whether intentional or unintentional. To ensure evaluations independent of belief structures of both experimenters and judges, all experiments were carried out under a protocol in which target selection at the beginning of experiments and blind judging of results at the end of experiments were handled independently of the researchers engaged in carrying out the experiments. In five years of self- and other criticism, we have not found a way to fault either the experimental protocols or the conclusions derived therefrom.

Furthermore, since the initial publication of our investigations of this remarkable phenomenon,[17] a number of attempts at replication have been carried out in other laboratories,[18] most of which have been successful. One of these is reported in Chapter 4. Therefore, the phenomenon does not appear to depend on unique personality/environment configurations. We are thus led to conclude that remote viewing constitutes a robust phenomenon whereby subjects are able to describe in words and drawings, to a degree exceeding any reasonable bounds of chance correlation, both the location and actions of experimenters placed at undisclosed sites at varying separations from the subjects up to transcontinental distances.

# Summary

In this chapter, we concentrated on recent transcontinental experiments carried out with individuals whose remote perceptual abilities have been developed sufficiently to allow them to describe—often in great detail—geographical or technical material, such as buildings, roads, structures, and natural formations, along with real-time activities of persons at the target site. These experiments, together with our previously established data base of over 50 local (< 20 km) experiments, indicate that (1) although the information channel is imperfect, the data generated by the remote-viewing process exceeds any reasonable bounds of chance correlation, and (2) the extent of physical distance separating the subject from the target site up to transcontinental distances does not appear to significantly affect the accuracy of perception.

# Notes

1. R. Targ and H. Puthoff, "Information Transfer Under Conditions of Sensory Shielding," *Nature* 252 (October 1974): 602–7.

2. Ibid.; H. Puthoff and R. Targ, "A Perceptual Channel for Information Transfer Over Kilometer Distances: Historical Perspective and Recent Research," *Proceedings of the IEEE* 64 (March 1976): 329–54; and R. Targ and H. Puthoff, *Mind-Reach: Scientists Look at Psychic Ability* (New York: Delacorte Press, 1977).

3. I. M. Kogan, "Is Telepathy Possible?," *Radio Engineering* 21 (January 1966): 75; I. M. Kogan, "Telepathy, Hypotheses and Observations," *Radio Engineering* 22 (January 1967): 141; I. M. Kogan, "Information Theory Analysis of Telepathic Communication Experiments," *Radio Engineering* 23 (March 1968): 122; I. M. Kogan, "The Information Theory Aspect of Telepathy" (P-4145), mimeographed (Santa Monica, Calif.: RAND, July 1969); M. A. Persinger, "Geophysical Models for Parapsychological Experiences," *Psychoenergetic Systems 1* (1975): 63–74; and M. A. Persinger, *The Paranormal*, pt. 2, *Mechanisms and Models* (New York: M.S.S. Information Corp., 1974).

4. Ibid.

5. J. S. Bell, "On the Problem of Hidden Variables in Quantum Theory," *Review of Modern Physics* 38 (July 1966): 447.

6. A. Einstein, B. Podolsky, and N. Rosen, "Can Quantum-Mechanical Description of Physical Reality be Considered Complete?," *Phys. Rev.* 47 (May 1935): 777.

7. H. Stapp, "Theory of Reality," Lawrence-Berkeley Laboratory Report LBL-3837, mimeographed (Berkeley: University of California, April 1975).

8. R. H. Dicke and J. P. Wittke, *Introduction to Quantum Mechanics* (Reading, Mass.: Addison-Wesley, 1960), chap. 7, and D. J. Bohm and B. J. Hiley, "On the Intuitive Understanding of Non-Locality as Implied by Quantum Theory," *Foundations of Physics* 5 (1975): 93–109.

9. J. J. Freedman and J. F. Clauser, "Experimental Test of Local Hidden Variable Theories," *Physical Review Letters* 28 (April 1972): 938; and J. F. Clauser and M. A. Horne, "Experimental Consequences of Objective Local Theories," *Phys. Rev. D.* 10 (July 1974): 526.

10. E. P. Wigner, "The Problem of Measurement," *American Journal of Physics* 31 (1963): 6; and E. H. Walker, "Foundations of Paraphysical and Parapsychological Phenomena," in *Proceedings of the Conference on Quantum Physics and Parapsychology* (Geneva) (New York: Parapsychology Foundation, 1975), pp. 1–53.

11. G. Feinberg, "Possibility of Faster-Than-Light Particles," *Physical Review* 159 (1967): 1089.

12. J. A. Stratton, *Electromagnetic Theory* (New York: McGraw-Hill, 1941); G. Feinberg, "Precognition—A Memory of Things Future?," in *Proceedings of the Conference on Quantum Physics and Parapsychology,* op. cit., pp. 54–75; and O. Costa de Beauregard, "Quantum Paradoxes and Aristotle's Twofold Information Concept," in *Proceedings of the Conference on Quantum Physics and Parapsychology,* op. cit.

13. Kogan, "Is Telepathy Possible?," op. cit.; Kogan, "Telepathy, Hypotheses and Observations," op. cit.; Kogan, "Information Theory Analysis of Telepathic Communication Experiments," op. cit.; and "The Information Theory Aspect of Telepathy," op. cit.

14. B. Julesz, *Foundations of Cyclopean Perception* (Chicago: University of Chicago Press, 1971).

15. Feinberg, op. cit., and H. Puthoff and R. Targ, "Psychic Research and Modern Physics," in *Psychic Exploration—A Challenge for Science,* ed. J. White (New York: Putnam, 1974), pp. 522–42.

16. Costa de Beauregard, op. cit.; Julesz, op. cit.; and Puthoff and Targ, in White, ed., op. cit.

17. Targ and Puthoff, "Information Transfer Under Conditions of Sensory Shielding," op. cit.; Puthoff and Targ, "A Perceptual Channel for Information Transfer Over Kilometer Distances: Historical Perspective and Recent Research," op. cit.; and Targ and Puthoff, *Mind-Reach,* op. cit.

18. A. Hastings and D. Hurt, "A Confirmatory Remote Viewing in a Group Setting," *Proceedings of the IEEE* 64 (October 1976): 1,544–45; T. Whitson et al., "Preliminary Experiments in Group Remote Viewing," Proceedings of the IEEE 64 (October 1976): 1,548–51; Jacques Vallee, Arthur Hastings, and Gerald Askevold, "Remote Viewing Experiments through Computer Conferencing," *Proceedings of the IEEE* 64 (October 1976): 1,551–52; J. P. Bisaha and B. J. Dunne, "Precognitive Remote Viewing in the Chicago Area: A Replication of the Stanford Experiment," in *Research in Parapsychology 1976* (Metuchen, N.J.: The Scarecrow Press, 1977), pp. 84–86; B. J. Dunne and J. Bisaha, "Multiple Channels in Precognitive Remote Viewing," in *Research in Parapsychology 1977* (Metuchen, N.J.: The Scarecrow Press, in press), pp. 146–51; J. P. Bisaha and B. J. Dunne, "Multiple Subject and Long Distant Precognitive Remote Viewing of Geographical Locations," *Proceedings of the IEEE 1977 International Conference on Cybernetics and Society* (Washington, D.C., September 19–21, 1977): 514–18; H. Chotas, "Remote Viewing in the Durham Area," *Journal of Parapsychology* 42 (1978): 61–62, E. Rauscher et al., "Remote Perception of Natural Scenes Shielded against Ordinary Perception," in *Research in Parapsychology 1975,* ed. J. Morris, W. Roll, and R. Morris, pp. 41–45 (Metuchen,

N.J.: Scarecrow Press, 1976); S. Allen et al., "A Remote Viewing Study Using a Modified Version of the SRI Procedure," in *Research in Parapsychology 1975,* op. cit., pp. 46–48; D. Marks, and R. Kammann, "Information Transmission in Remote Viewing Experiments," *Nature* 274, no. 5,672 (1978): 680–81; H. Puthoff and R. Targ, "Information Transmission in Remote Viewing Expenments: II" (submitted to *Nature* for publication); and C. Tart, "Reanalysis of SRI Remote Viewing Experiments" (submitted to *Nature* for publication).

# Introduction to Chapter 4

When the SRI work on remote viewing was announced to the scientific community, an enormous amount of interest was generated. One of the reasons for this was that the quantity of psi being manifested appeared much higher than that found in the usual laboratory psi experiment. Since learning how to produce a reliable psi effect on demand in the laboratory is a necessary prerequisite to being able to study its nature, a number of other experimenters and laboratories attempted to replicate the remote-viewing procedure. The following chapter describes one such replication series—the remote-viewing studies at Mundelein College in Chicago carried out by John Bisaha and Brenda Dunne. These include precognitive remote viewing from Chicago of an outbound experimenter traveling in the Soviet Union. These are thoughtful and well-conceived replications of the SRI experiments, which produced quite significant results in their own right, as well as demonstrating further the power of the remote-viewing procedure.

## About the Authors

**John P. Bisaha,** M.A., is an Assistant Professor of Psychology, as well as Director of Planning and Institutional Research at Mundelein College in Chicago. His training is in statistics, computers, experimental design, and sensation/perception. He has taught one of the few accredited college courses in parapsychology in the United States and is especially active in trying to present scientifically accurate information about parapsychology to the public. His and Brenda Dunne's highly successful work with the remote-viewing technique has attracted national attention.

**Brenda J. Dunne,** M.A., is currently a doctoral student studying with the Committee on Human Development at the University of Chicago. She is a graduate, magna cum laude, of Mundelein College, Chicago, with a degree in psychology and humanities. Cofounder and Vice-President of the Midwest

Parapsychology Research Institute, she has been actively engaged in parapsychological research for the past four years, with special emphasis in the area of precognitive remote viewing, and has published several papers in this field. Currently, she teaches courses in parapsychology, altered states of consciousness, biofeedback, creativity, and meditation and conducts workshops on these topics in the Chicago area.

# 4

# Multiple Subject and Long-Distance Precognitive Remote Viewing of Geographical Locations

## J. P. Bisaha and B. J. Dunne

While the phenomenon of precognition has antecedents that reach back to earliest recorded history, empirical experimentation in this aspect of human experience has been relatively sparse, primarily due to the difficulties of designing a replicable experiment. Experimentation in precognitive remote viewing evolved over the past few years as a variation of real-time remote-viewing experiments conducted at SRI, which demonstrated the ability of isolated percipients to describe an unknown target site at the same time that an agent was visiting the randomly selected location.[1] Successful replication attempts have been carried out, not only in real-time remote viewing,[2] but also in a variation of the design, which incorporated precognition by having the percipient describe a target before the target was selected and before the agent arrived at the designated site.[3]

Over 35 trials of this kind have been conducted at our laboratory to date, with more than 15 ungifted and untrained participants following the precognitive protocol. Each has indicated the capability of accurately describing scenes in spite of both spatial and temporal barriers.

Since we believe this ability to be a latent and widespread one rather than an unusual talent of a gifted few, and since real-time remote-viewing experiments have been so successful over long spatial distances,[4] two separate experimental designs were devised in the hope of expanding the original SRI findings. The first experiment was a multiple precognitive protocol involving pairs of percipients who were each asked to independently describe the geographical location where the agent would be 35 minutes in the future. The second experiment involved a series of five long-distance trials in which the percipient was requested to describe the locations where the agent would be, when the targets were an average of 5,000 miles away and 24 hours in the future.

# Experiment One: Multiple Precognitive Remote Viewing

## Method

Seven percipients (two males and five females, ranging in age from 24 to 37) were selected on a volunteer basis and tested in four different pairs. Percipients in each pair knew each other prior to the experiment but were not related either by blood or marriage. The nature and protocol of the experiment were explained to them before the trials began, and they were told that they would have sufficient time to relax, make themselves comfortable, and allow their minds to become as blank as possible. Attempts were made to create an environmental atmosphere of playfulness and congeniality and to avoid placing participants in a state of anxiety or nervous anticipation. They were then instructed to try and visualize where the agent would be between 35 and 50 minutes after the trial began and to describe whatever images or thoughts came to mind during the 15-minute trial period aloud into a tape recorder, as well as to make any sketches of their impressions if they so desired. Percipients were advised not to try to define specifically or identify their impressions but to describe them generally with as much detail as possible, even if the images appeared to make no sense or have no continuity. The time at which the trial was to commence was agreed upon by both percipients and experimenters, and percipients were then separated from each other, with instructions to have no communication between them until after their parts in the trial were over. A total of seven trials were conducted following this protocol. In four trials, the percipients were in the same building but in separate rooms on different floors. There were observers stationed with each percipient in three of these trials. In the remaining three trials, percipients were in different locations, separated by approximately ten miles.

When percipients began generating their descriptions, an experimenter who acted as agent left the area with ten envelopes that had been randomly selected by the second experimenter from a target pool of over 100 locations in the city and suburbs of Chicago. This pool had been previously compiled and sealed by an individual who had no other association with the experiment (the contents of the envelopes were not known by either experimenter or by the percipients). The agent drove continuously for 20 minutes with no particular direction, or until five minutes after the percipients had completed their descriptions. At that time, she blindly selected a number from one to ten from an enclosed container holding ten numbered and folded sheets of paper, selected the envelope corresponding to the chosen number, opened the envelope, and proceeded to the location indicated on the enclosed card, arriving at the target 15 minutes later, or 35 minutes after the percipients had begun recording their descriptions. The agent remained at the target for 15 minutes, photographing the location and making notes as to her impressions of the site, and then returned to the point of origin. (See Table 4.1.) Typed, unedited transcripts were made of percipients' recorded descriptions and attached to any associated drawings which that percipient may have made.

**Table 4.1 Experimental Protocol: Multiple Precognitive Remote Viewing**

| Time | Protocol |
|---|---|
| 10:00 a.m. | Experimenter leaves with ten envelopes containing target locations and begins 20-minute drive; subjects begin descriptions of where experimenter will be between 10:35 and 10:50 |
| 10:15 a.m. | Subjects' responses completed, at which time laboratory part of experiment is over |
| 10:20 a.m. | Experimenter generates random number between one and ten, counts down to associated envelope, and proceeds to target location |
| 10:35 a.m. | Experimenter arrives at target location and remains there for 15 minutes, taking photographs and notes |
| 10:50 a.m. | Experimenter returns to point of origin—experimental trial completed |

Source: Compiled by the authors.

Seven trials were performed, resulting in a set of seven photographs with accompanying notes and 14 transcripts, which were randomly divided into two sets so that each set contained one description for each of the seven targets. The transcript sets were labeled *Group A* and *Group B*. The division into two groups was done for the purpose of simplifying the subsequent judging procedure and enabling us to follow Morris's statistical procedure, which required that the number of descriptions be equal to the number of targets.[5] Six persons, not otherwise affiliated with the experiment, were asked to be judges. Two judges blind rank ordered Group A transcripts against the target photographs and notes; two blind rank ordered Group B transcripts against the targets; and two blind rank ordered Group A transcripts against Group B transcripts. (The purpose of this third matching was to establish reliability of the phenomenon across subjects; it was not an attempt to establish evidence of psi.) In this manner, each judging procedure was independent from the others, avoiding the possibilities of cueing from one set of descriptions to the other or fatigue on the part of the judges, if they were required to match all 14 transcripts.* Each set of rankings was made on a scale of one to seven—one being the best match and seven being the worst. Seven was the lowest possible rank sum for each set, 49 was the highest.

## Results

Statistical analysis of these results was performed according to Morris's method for evaluation of preferentially matched free response material.[6] The sums of the ranks assigned by the two judges matching Group A transcripts against the targets were 15 and 13, with significance of .01 and .005, one-tailed, respectively. The sums of the ranks assigned by the two judges matching Group B transcripts against the targets were 15 in both cases, resulting in a significance level of .01, one-tailed, in each case. The sums of the ranks assigned by the two judges matching Group A and Group B transcripts were 12 and 14, resulting in significance levels of .001 and .005, one-tailed, respectively. Of the total of 42 matches that were made (six judges ranking seven items), there was a total of 17 direct hits (matches ranked as one). (See Tables 4.2 and 4.3.)

**Table 4.2 Ranks Assigned by Judges Matching Subjects' Transcripts against Targets in Precognitive Remote-Viewing Trials**

| | Percipients | | Group A | | Group B | |
| Target | A | B | Judge 1 | Judge 2 | Judge 1 | Judge 2 |
|---|---|---|---|---|---|---|
| Plaza del Lago | $P_4$ | $P_5$ | 1 | 5 | 4 | 2 |
| Wrigley Field | $P_{10}$ | $P_9$ | 1 | 1 | 3 | 2 |
| Techny Mission | $P_4$ | $P_5$ | 3 | 1 | 1 | 3 |
| Lindheimer Observatory | $P_6$ | $P_7$ | 2 | 3 | 1 | 3 |
| Madonna del Strada | $P_5$ | $P_4$ | 3 | 1 | 2 | 2 |
| Northwestern Railroad Station, Glencoe | $P_6$ | $P_8$ | 2 | 1 | 3 | 1 |
| Grant Park Bandshell | $P_7$ | $P_6$ | 3 | 1 | 1 | 2 |
| Sum of ranks | | | 15 | 13 | 15 | 15 |
| Statistical significance | | | p < .01 | p < .005 | p < .01 | p < .01 |

Source: Compiled by the authors.

*Psychological research has repeatedly found that a set of seven judgment categories is optimal over a wide variety of tasks: fewer categories do not make full use of a judge's capacities; more categories tend to overload judges and produce confusion.

**Table 4.3  Ranks Assigned by Judges Matching Transcripts B against Transcripts A in Precognitive Remote-Viewing Trials**

| Transcript | Ranks Assigned | |
|---|---|---|
| | Judge 1 | Judge 2 |
| A.1 (Wrigley Field) | 2 | 2 |
| A.2 (Madonna del Strada Chapel) | 2 | 3 |
| A.3 (Lindheimer Observatory) | 1 | 1 |
| A.4 (Grant Park Bandshell) | 1 | 1 |
| A.5 (Plaza del Lago) | 1 | 1 |
| A.6 (Techny Mission) | 2 | 2 |
| A.7 (Northwestern Railroad Station, Glencoe) | 3 | 4 |
| Sum of ranks | 12 | 14 |
| Statistical significance | $p < .001$ | $p < .005$ |

Source: Compiled by the authors.

An indication of the accuracy of the percipients' descriptions, as well as the variation in individual perception of a single remote target precognitively viewed, can be offered by the following excerpts from the transcripts, selected by the judges as most indicative of the target. The degree of accuracy varied among subjects, as did the specific details of the target.

## Target One: Plaza del Lago Shopping Center

The target was a shopping mall designed like a Spanish courtyard or plaza, with a circular garden area designed around a fountain, having paths leading out in different directions. Two sides of the mall consisted of a series of low brick arches; the third side was a row of low white buildings with awnings flanking a taller structure with a tower. (See Figure 4. 1.)

Group A ($P_4$): "A few trees . . . not really that big . . . there's like a fence around it, maybe a gate . . . cement or something to the left toward the front. . . . There's a lot of white. . . . Everything seems to be very clean and orderly."

Group B ($P_5$):

> Really tall building, some manmade structure of brick or cement. Something rectangular next to it. Is it one building or one next to it? . . . That rectangle is only one story high, I think. The other building is much taller. The tall part might be round, there are lots of parts to it. . . . I see sidewalks, paths go around it. . . . Some trees, other buildings can be seen through the trees. . . . There's a double doorway, double doors with an awning. . . . Maybe the tall building is on top of it, or next to it. . . . There's a circular pathway with grass in front.

**Figure 4.1** Plaza del Lago Shopping Center (target one in multiple precognitive remote-viewing experiment).

## Target Six: Northwestern Railroad Station, Glencoe

The target was a small, dark brick building with a pointed roof and circular turret. There are two sets of tracks in front of the building. During the 15-minute experimental period, two trains passed, one of which stopped. The

**Figure 4.2** Northwestern Railroad Station (target six in multiple precognitive remote-viewing experiment).

experimenter went inside the station for a few minutes, noted wooden floors, benches, and a train schedule posted on one wall. The station was surrounded by trees in a parklike setting. (See Figure 4.2.)

Group A ($P_6$):

> I have an image of looking at the traffic and seeing it go by really fast, speeding cars. . . . I see a train station. . . . I see a train coming . . . older buildings . . . trees. . . . See just the front end of the train station. See a little bit within it, unless they are planks. Wooden planks on the floor. . . . There are posters or something, advertisements or posters on the wall of the train station. . . . I see the benches. . . . I see the tracks.

Group B ($P_8$):

> There are lines pointing in several different directions. . . . There's a roundlike disk . . . it might be the sun on it, might be like a big light. . . . It feels like, looks like, feels that things are blowing, the wind is blowing, and everything is like blowing in the same direction. . . . There's something rising . . . it's sort of blowing upward, maybe things are swirling.

# Experiment Two: Long-Distance Precognitive Remote Viewing

## Method

As a further investigation into the parameters of the precognitive remote-viewing phenomena, a series of five trials were conducted between northern Wisconsin and various sites in Eastern Europe over a consecutive five-day period in August 1976.

Each morning between 8:30 and 8:45 a.m., Central Daylight Time, the percipient in the United States attempted to describe the geographical location where the experimenter would be in Eastern Europe between 3 p.m. and 3:15 p.m. (The targets were of distances up to 5,284 miles away and 24.5 hours in the future.) The descriptions were tape recorded each morning and subsequently transcribed. The experimenter was to spend the 15 minute period between 3 p.m. and 3:15 p.m. (European time) the next day attempting to concentrate on his surroundings and taking a photograph, which could later be compared against the percipient's descriptions. (See Table 4.4.)

**Table 4.4 Experimental Protocol:
Long-Distance Precognitive Remote Viewing**

| Day | Time | Protocol |
| --- | --- | --- |
| First | 8:45 a.m. (CDT) 3:35 p.m. (European) | Percipient in the United States (Mid-west) describes the location where experimenter will be 23.5 hours later in Bratislava, Czechoslovakia or 24.5 hours in the future in Moscow, USSR |
| Second | 3:15 p.m. (European) | Experimenter stops at whatever location he is at for 15 minutes and takes a photograph of target to compare with predicted location |

Source: Compiled by the authors.

Upon his return, the experimenter presented the five photographs and brief descriptions of the five target sites in random order to the percipient for matching in the blind rank ordering procedure followed in previous experiments.[7] The percipient gave the experimenter copies of the transcribed descriptions, also in random order, for the experimenter to match against the targets. In addition, a third person, who had no connection with the experiment, was also asked to blind rank order the photographs against the descriptions.

# Results

These procedures resulted in three independent sets of scores, which were analyzed according to Morris's method for evaluation preferentially matched free response material.[8] The three sets of ranking were significant at .025, one-tailed, in two cases and .05, one-tailed, in one. (See Table 4.5.) Again, two trials have been selected to show the accuracy of the transcripts in prediction.

### Target One: Danube River (Bratislava, Czechoslovakia)

The target was a "flying saucer" restaurant, a circular building raised high into the air on heavy pillars above a bridge near the bank of the Danube River. The percipient described the experimenter as being "near water . . . a very large expanse of water . . . boats . . . vertical lines like poles . . . a circular shape like a merry-go-round or gazebo . . . it seems to have height, maybe with poles . . . a dark fence along a walk . . . at the top of the steps, like a path or walkway . . . a boardwalk, and there's a fence along it." (See Figure 4.3.)

### Target Five: Exhibition of Economic Achievement of USSR (Moscow, USSR)

The target was a huge park with many fountains, flower beds, and buildings. The experimenter stood looking through the entrance, which was a huge archway with a black metal fence. The percipient's transcript reads as follows:

**Table 4.5 Ranks Assigned by Judges Matching Targets to Transcripts in Long-Distance Precognitive Remote Viewing**

| Target | Approximate Distance (miles) | Time in Future (hours) | Experimenter's Ranking | Percipient's Ranking | Independent Judge |
|---|---|---|---|---|---|
| Danube River (Bratislava, Czechoslovakia) | 5,087 | 23.5 | 1 | 1 | 1 |
| St. Michael's Church (Bratislava, Czechoslovakia) | 5,087 | 23.5 | 2 | 2 | 3 |
| Hotel Ukraine (Moscow, USSR) | 5,284 | 24.5 | 1 | 1 | 2 |
| Tretyakov Gallery (Moscow, USSR) | 5,284 | 24.5 | 2 | 3 | 2 |
| Exhibition of economic achievment of USSR (Moscow, USSR) | 5,284 | 24.5 | 2 | 1 | 1 |
| Sum of ranks | | | 8 | 8 | 9 |
| Statistical significance | | | p < .025 | p < .025 | p < .05 |

*Source:* Compiled by the authors.

**Figure 4.3** Danube River, Bratislava, Czechoslovakia (target one in long-distance experiment).

"Lots of different shapes, activity, buildings. . . . Gate or fence . . . made of metal of some sort . . . high for a gate . . . dark metal. . . . People walking. . . . Something round circular . . . light color stone . . . slab on a stand . . . a bench or table . . . something like a row of doorways . . . some sort of fountain in circular shape. . . . Cultivated flowers around in beds." (See Figure 4.4.)

## Discussion

The significant results of these two separate experiments lend further support to the hypothesis that the extrasensory channel of communication and/or

**Figure 4.4** Exhibition of Economic Achievement of the USSR, Moscow, USSR (target five in long-distance experiment).

perception utilized in remote viewing may be a widespread and relatively common faculty that can be exercised without extensive training or experience when the environmental conditions are favorable. Distance and time appear to pose no barriers to its effectiveness.

The findings of Experiment One are in keeping with those of previous studies testing remote viewing in individuals or in group settings,[9] and provide evidence that even the precognitive aspect of this phenomenon operates on an open channel that can be "tuned into" by a variety of "consoles" with differing genetic and cognitive structures. Although there was enough information in each transcript to provide a significant cross correspondence between percipients on the same target, no indication of telepathic communication between percipients can be deduced. The reports of the percipients in each pair differed enough to make it obvious that while both percipients were perceiving the same target, the perceptions reflected individual differences in cognitive processing of information and interpretation. The significant correlation between Group A and Group B is not indicative of a separate channel of communication between the percipients but, rather, suggests that two separate and effective channels appear to have been operating simultaneously between each percipient and target and/or each percipient and agent.

The long-distance precognitive remote-viewing experiment further demonstrated the capability of an individual to extend this ability over extensive spatial, as well as temporal, distances (over 24 hours and 5,000 miles). The results are indicative of a great latitude in the parameters of the remote-viewing experience—parameters that have not previously been tested to these extremes of time and distance.

The principal factor that appears to be operating under the conditions of these experiments is a situation where the everyday modes of perception and communication are inoperable; in this way, internal noise and external stimuli are reduced, permitting the subtler psi signal to be distinguished. Percipients have reported (particularly those who have performed more than one trial) that with experience, they become more capable of screening out the noise, both cognitive and sensory, and perceiving the information being transmitted (within the context of an environment that encourages them to explore their psychic abilities in spite of the apparent logical impossibilities of the task). When psi abilities are the only possible means that can produce results, it seems that percipients are able to construct and function successfully within a belief system where such abilities do exist and are relatively reliable.

The positive results obtained from the various experiments attempted to date indicate that the protocol of this experimental design is a useful and effective one for additional research into the nature of nonordinary information transfer.

## Summary

*Precognitive remote viewing* is a term for an experimental design in which percipients attempt to describe an unknown remote geographical target where an agent will be at a future time before that target has been selected. This is a report of two variations on the design of earlier remote-viewing research in which (1) two percipients at different locations simultaneously attempted to describe where an agent would be 35 minutes later, and (2) one percipient attempted to describe a series of targets over 24 hours in the future at distances of approximately 5,000 miles. In the first experiment, seven trials were carried out with a total of seven inexperienced volunteer percipients, who were tested in pairs to determine their individual abilities to describe a remote geographical location 20 minutes before the target was selected and 35 minutes before the agent arrived at the randomly selected site. Transcripts of the percipients' descriptions were matched against photos of the seven targets and against each other by six independent judges in three separate blind rank ordering procedures. The results of all these matchings were statistically significant. Experiment Two tested a single percipient in five trials where she attempted to describe where the experimenter would be in Eastern Europe 24 hours in the future and at distances of over 5,000 miles. Blind rank ordering procedures yielded statistically significant results. The results of these two experiments provide further evidence of the apparently widespread availability of a perceptual/communication channel in which time and distance appear to pose no barriers and which seems to become accessible when ordinary modes of perception and communication become inoperable. It further appears that this channel can be "tuned into" by individuals with no extraordinary "psychic" ability.

## Notes

1. R. Targ and H. Puthoff, "Information Transfer Under Conditions of Sensory Shielding," *Nature* 252 (October 1974): 602–7; and H. Puthoff and R. Targ, "A Perceptual Channel for Information Transfer Over Kilometer Distances: Historical Perspective and Recent Research," *Proceedings of the IEEE* 64 (March 1976): 329–54.

2. A. Hastings and D. Hurt, "A Confirmatory Remote Viewing in a Group Setting," *Proceedings of the IEEE* 64 (October 1976): 1,544–45; T. Whitson et al., "Preliminary Experiments in Group Remote Viewing," *Proceedings of the IEEE* 64 (October 1976): 1,550–51; and J. Vallee, A. Hastings, and G. Askevold, "Remote Viewing Experiments through Computer Conferencing," *Proceedings of the IEEE* 64 (October 1976): 1,551–52.

3. J. Bisaha and B. Dunne, "Precognitive Remote Viewing in the Chicago Area: A Replication of the Stanford Experiment," in J. Morris, R. Rolls, and R. Morris, eds., *Research in Parapsychology 1976* (Metuchen, N.J.: The Scarecrow Press, 1977), pp. 84–86.

4. R. Targ and H. Puthoff, *Mind-Reach: Scientists Look at Psychic Ability* (New York: Delacorte Press, 1977).

5. R. Morris, "An Exact Method for Evaluating Preferentially Matched Free-Response Material," *Journal of the American Society for Psychical Research* 66 (October 1972): 401.

6. Ibid. B. Dunne and J. Bisaha, "Multiple Channels in Precognitive Remote Viewing," in *Research in Parapsychology 1977* (Metuchen, N.J.: The Scarecrow Press, 1978).

7. Bisaha and Dunne, op. cit.

8. Morris, op. cit.

9. Hastings and Hurt, op. cit.; Whitson et al., op. cit.; and Vallee, Hastings, and Askevold, op. cit.

# Introduction to Chapter 5

A question often asked about psi is, If it is as real and important as it seems to be, why don't we see more of it? The answers starting to emerge from research findings are that psi is probably not as rare as we sometimes think it is and that it probably operates fairly often in an unconscious and unrecognized way.

As to its occurrence, a recent representative poll of the U.S. population indicates that 58 percent of the people questioned believe they have personally experienced telepathy,[1] so while telepathy and other psi phenomena may be para*conceptual*—beyond conventional scientific belief systems—they can hardly be called para*normal* when a majority of the population believes they have personally experienced at least one kind of psi. (This same poll also found that it was the more-educated and better-adjusted people who were more likely to report personal experiences they believed to be psi—an interesting fact in itself.)

With the reality of psi being demonstrated under rigorous laboratory conditions, certain everyday occurrences that might otherwise have been dismissed as "luck" or "coincidence" are being reexamined in the light that they might be possible manifestations of psi, although this does not mean, of course, that everything surprising in life should be attributed to psi.

Further, it is now clear that the manifestation of psi is a complex process of at least two steps, starting with reception of psi information within the person per se and culminating in a conscious experience or overt behavior that expresses the psi-acquired information in a form that lets us realize that psi is involved. One of us has modeled this process in detail elsewhere.[2] Clearly, a person might receive psi information but not necessarily have a conscious experience of it or behave in a way that demonstrated his or her reception.

Can we find some way of detecting this nonconscious reception of psi? The following chapter indicates that physiological responses might serve as an index of psi reception in the absence of any cognition or final expressive step.

This is a relatively new area of research, and while too young to afford any conclusive "proof" of physiological detection of psi reception, it suggests exciting possibilities. For example, we might have biofeedback-amplified psi, where feedback of physiological indicators about a percipient's own physiological state might help him or her decide whether to give extra weight to certain mental processes that might be attributable to psi-conveyed data.

## About the Authors

**Edwin C. May,** Ph.D., is a physicist with research contributions to nuclear and atmospheric physics; he was involved in the first experimental results detecting the unique state of the deuteron as a single "particle." Dr. May has worked on parapsychological problems for several years as a Research Associate in the Division of Parapsychology and Psychophysics of the Maimonides Medical Center in Brooklyn and as a consultant to the Radio Physics Laboratory at SRI. He has organized and designed experiments to test physics mechanisms behind psychic functioning, with special emphasis on the nature of PK.

Biographical material on Dr. May's coauthors of this chapter, **Russell Targ** and **Harold E. Puthoff,** has been presented earlier.

# 5

# EEG Correlates to Remote Light Flashes under Conditions of Sensory Shielding
**Edwin C. May, Russell Targ, and Harold E. Puthoff**

## Introduction

In a number of laboratories, evidence has been obtained indicating the existence of an as-yet-unidentified channel wherein information is coupled from remote electromagnetic stimuli to the human nervous system, as indicated by physiological response, even though overt responses, such as verbalizations or key presses, provide no evidence for such information transfer. Physiological measures have included plethysmographic response[3] and EEG activity.[4] Kamiya, Lindsley, Pribram, Silverman, Walter, and others have suggested that a whole range of EEG responses, such as EPs, spontaneous EEG, and the contingent negative variation (CNV), might be sensitive indicators of the detection of remote stimuli not mediated by usual sensory processes.[5]

A pilot study was therefore undertaken at SRI to determine whether EEG activity could be used as a reliable indicator of information transmission between an isolated subject and a remote stimulus. Following earlier work of others, we assumed that perception could be indicated by such a measure even in the absence of verbal or other overt indicators.

To aid in selecting a stimulus, we noted that Silverman and Buchsbaum attempted, without success, to detect EP changes in a subject in response to a single stroboscopic flash stimulus observed by another subject.[6] Kamiya suggested that because of the unknown temporal characteristics of the information channel, it might be more appropriate to use repetitive bursts of light to increase the probability of detecting information transfer.[7] Therefore, in our study, we chose to use repetitive light bursts as stimuli.[8]

## Pilot Study at SRI

In the design of the study, it was assumed that the application of remote stimuli would result in responses similar to those obtained under conditions of direct stimulation. For example, when normal subjects are stimulated with a flashing light, their EEG typically shows a decrease in the amplitude of the resting rhythm and a driving of the brain waves at the frequency of the flashes.[9] We hypothesized that if we stimulated one subject in this manner (a putative sender), the EEG of another subject in a remote room with no flash present (a receiver) might show changes in alpha (8–13 Hz) activity and, possibly, EEG driving similar to that of the sender, either by means of psi coupling to the sender's EEG or by psi coupling directly to the stimulus.

We informed our subject that at certain times, a light was to be flashed in a sender's eyes in a distant room and if the subject perceived that event, consciously or unconsciously, it might be evident from changes in his or her EEG output. The receiver was seated in a visually opaque, acoustically and electrically shielded double-walled steel room located approximately 7 m from the sender's room.

We initially worked with four female and two male volunteer subjects. These were designated "receivers." The senders were either other subjects or the experimenters. We decided beforehand to run one or two sessions of 36 trials each with each subject in this selection procedure and to do more extensive study with any subject whose results were positive.

A Grass PS-2 photostimulator placed about 1 m in front of the sender was used to present flash trains of ten seconds duration. The receiver's EEG activity from the occipital region (Oz), referenced to linked mastoids, was amplified with a Grass 5P-1 preamplifier and associated driver amplifier with a bandpass of 1 to 120 Hz. The EEG data were recorded on magnetic tape with an Ampex SP 300 recorder.

On each trial, a tone burst of fixed frequency was presented to both sender and receiver and was followed in one second by either a ten-second train of flashes or a null flash interval presented to the sender. Thirty-six such trials were given in an experimental session, consisting of 12 null trails—no flashes following the tone—12 trials of flashes at six flashes per second (fps) and 12 trials of flashes at 16 fps, all randomly intermixed, determined by entries from a table of random numbers. Each of the trials consisted of an 11-second EEG epoch. The last four seconds of the epoch were selected for analysis to minimize the desynchronizing action of the warning cue. This four-second segment was subjected to Fourier analysis on a LINC 8 computer.

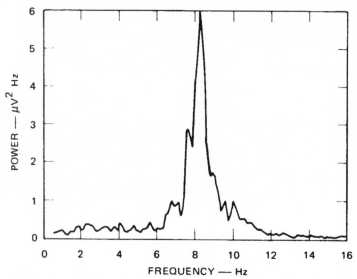

**Figure 5.1** Typical power spectrum averaged over 20 eight-second epochs.

Spectrum analyses gave no evidence of EEG driving in any receiver, although in control runs, the receivers did exhibit driving when physically stimulated with the flashes. However, of the six subjects studied initially, one subject showed a consistent alpha blocking effect. We therefore undertook further study with this subject. Of our six subjects, this one had by far the most monochromatic EEG spectrum. Figure 5.1 shows a typical occipital EEG spectrum of this subject under control (no stimulus) conditions.

Data from seven sets of 36 trials each were collected from this subject on three separate days. This comprised all the data collected to date with this subject under the test conditions described above. The alpha band was identified from average spectra; then, scores of average power and peak power were obtained from individual trials and subjected to statistical analysis. The final analysis showed that power measures were less in the 16 fps case than in the zero fps in *all* seven sets of peak power measures and in six out of seven average power measures.

Siegel's two-tailed t approximation to the nonparametric randomization test was applied to the data from all sets, which included two sessions in which the sender was removed.[10] Average power on trials associated with the occurence of 16 fps was significantly less than when there were no flashes (t = 2.09, df = 118, P < .04, two-tailed). The second measure, peak power, was also significantly less in the 16 fps conditions than in the null condition (t = 2.16, df = 118, P < .03, two-tailed). The average response in the 6 fps condition was in the same direction as that associated with 16 fps, but the effect was not statistically significant.

As part of the experimental protocol, the subject was asked to indicate conscious assessment for each trial as to which stimulus was generated. The guess was registered by the subject via one-way telegraphic communication. An analysis of these guesses has shown them to be at chance, indicating the absence of any conscious awareness, so arousal as evidenced by significant alpha blocking occurred only at the noncognitive level of awareness.

Several control procedures were undertaken to determine if these results were produced by system artifacts or by subtle cueing of the subject. Low-level recordings were made from saline of 12 kilohm resistance in place of the subject, with and without the introduction of 10 Hz, 50 $\mu$ volt (V) signals from a battery-operated generator. The standard experimental protocol was adhered to, and spectral analysis of the results were carried out. There was no evidence in the spectra associated with the flash frequencies, and the 10 Hz signal was not perturbed.

In another control procedure, a five-foot pair of leads was draped across the subject's chair (subject absent). The leads were connected to a Grass P-5 amplifier via its high impedance input probe. The bandwidth was set at .1 Hz to 30 kHz with a minimum gain of 200,000. The output of the amplifier was connected to one input of a CAT 400C "averager." Two-second sweeps, triggered at onset of the tone, were taken once every 13 seconds for approximately two hours, for about 550 samples. No difference in noise level between the foreperiod and the onset of flicker was observed.

## Replication Studies at Langley Porter

The next effort was directed toward replication by an independent laboratory of the original SRI study of EEG response to remote strobe light stimuli. Arrangements for replication were made with the Langley Porter Neuropsychiatric Institute, University of California Medical Center, San Francisco.

As a special precaution against the possibility of system artifacts in the form of electromagnetic pickup from the strobe light discharge or associated electronic equipment (for example, through the power lines), SRI developed an entirely battery-operated package for use as a stimulus generator for the EEG experimentation. It consisted of a battery-driven incandescent lamp, whose continuous light output passed through a mechanical chopper continuously driven by a battery-driven motor, as shown in Figure 5.2. A 10-Hz timing generator (computer triggered) controlled the generation of a one-kHz warning tone two seconds before onset of the experimental period, and it also drove a locking circuit that determined the presence or absence of the ten-second light stimuli, again all battery operated. Thus, everything on the left of the diagram of Figure 5.2 was battery operated and therefore independent of the power line system. Further, replacement of the arc-discharge strobe lamp by an incandescent lamp eliminated the possibility of direct subliminal pickup

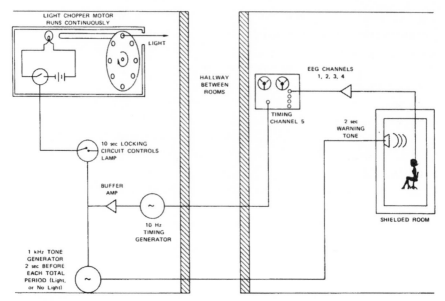

**Figure 5.2** Schematic of the remote-sensing EEG experiment.

of audio or electrical signals from possible transients associated with the arc discharge or associated electronics.

## Description of the EEG Processor

A hardware single-channel power spectrum analyzer was constructed from a commercial bandpass filter with corner frequencies of 9 and 12 Hz and 48 dB down at 8 and 13 Hz. Analog multipliers converted the filter output to a signal proportional to in-band power. To confirm that this system was equivalent to the standard fast-Fourier-transform (FFT) analysis used in the pilot study, the analog data of the pilot study were reanalyzed, and the result was found to be consistent with the earlier analysis.

## Experimental Protocol

Each experimental session consisted of 40 trials, 20 each for the zero (no light) and 16 fps of the remote light stimulus. A trial is defined as a warning tone followed by a ten-second period consisting of a two-second wait and two four-second data collection periods. The trial rate was one trial every 30 + one second. The trial sequence was randomized subject to the following conditions: (1) in each group of ten trials, there were equal numbers of each condition, and (2) no more than three in a row of a single type were allowed. Seven 40 trial sequences were made according to this prescription and recorded separately on audio tape. During the session, trials were generated from one of these tapes; the sequence was unknown to the experimenters, since the sequence tapes were generated one month in advance of the experiments. As in standard EEG protocol and in accordance with preestablished criteria, certain trials were deleted after the session for three reasons only: artifact, logic circuit failure, or abnormal EEG power. If a trial was rejected, a trial of the opposite stimulus condition was rejected at random from the particular set of ten trials in question. If more than ten trials of a given type were rejected from a session, the entire session was deleted. (This occurred twice in each experiment.)

Six channels of EEG and one logic channel taken from the sequence tape were recorded on a multiplexed frequency modulation (FM) analog tape recorder. The logic on the tape differentiated the trials between flashing and nonflashing conditions.

In pretesting the equipment, we ran the experiment using unselected subjects, such as laboratory personnel, in order to test the adequacy of the experiment and to determine whether there were any correlated electronic or mechanical discharges from the apparatus. In 20 sessions of data acquisition of 40 each (800 trials), there were no significant differences between the null and 16 Hz conditions.

## Results

Using the above protocol, two experiments were conducted during a three-month period. In the first experiment, for half of the sessions, the subject was asked to press a button when she felt the light was flashing. For the six sessions (105 trials each for the 0 and 16 fps conditions) when she was *not* asked to overtly indicate her feelings about the light, there was a slight decrease of in-band EEG power measured over the left occipital region of the brain. Similarly, for the six sessions (107 trials each for the 0 and 16 fps conditions) when she *was* asked to respond overtly, there was this time a significant decrease of in-band EEG power ($p < .037$, using an F ratio test derived from a two-way analysis of variance). In considering the experiment as consisting of the combined 212 trials in each stimulus condition regardless of the overt response contingency, we find a statistically significant decrease in in-band EEG power ($p < .011$, one-tailed, using F ratio test as above).

During the second experiment, three months later, a different contingency was added to determine if a "sender" was necessary to produce the effect we had observed earlier. For a given session, a random procedure (with equal trials) was used to determine if a person (called the "sender" person) would be looking at the photo-stimulator. There was no one present with the photo-stimulator otherwise. For the seven nonsender sessions (121 trials each for the 0 and 16 fps conditions), we found a statistically significant *increase* of in-band EEG power measured over the midoccipital region of the brain ($p < .039$, one-tailed, using an F ratio test as above). During the sender sessions (123 trials in each stimulus condition), there was a slight increase of in-band EEG power. All together, there was a statistically significant increase of in-band EEG power when the 244 trials were analyzed regardless of sender condition (p < .008 one-tailed, using an F ratio test as above), and there was no significant difference found between sender/nonsender conditions.

For both experiments, we considered in-band EEG power for the zero- to four-second and four- to eight-second time periods independently to determine if the effects were time dependent. Although some of these isolated subintervals were statistically significant, no systematic relationship emerged. Thus, the effect appears to be cumulative over the eight seconds. The zero- to eight-second results for EEG power are summarized in Table 5.1

**Table 5.1 Summary of Results of Replication Experiments Showing Power Means and Statistical Results for the Various Experimental Conditions**

| | Experiment One | | |
|---|---|---|---|
| Conditions | Guessing Sessions | Nonguessing Sessions | Combined |
| Power: no light flash | 957 | 704 | 832 |
| Power: light flash | 873 | 647 | 761 |
| F ratio | 4.39 | 2.20 | 6.47 |
| $df_1$; $df_2$ | 1; 202 | 1; 198 | 1; 400 |
| p ≤ | .037 | .14 | .011 |

| | Experiment Two | | |
|---|---|---|---|
| Conditions | Sender Sessions | Nonguessing Sessions | Combined |
| Power: no light flash | 854 | 766 | 810 |
| Power: light flash | 860 | 844 | 852 |
| F ratio | .017 | 4.33 | 7.03 |
| $df_1$; $df_2$ | 1; 232 | 1; 228 | 1; 460 |
| p ≤ | .90 | .039 | .0083 |

Source: Compiled by the authors.

## Discussion

Although our pilot experiment and the two replication studies all showed significant changes in EEG production correlated with the presence or absence of a remote light stimulus, the sign of the systematic change in power in the third study was opposite to that of the first two. We therefore undertook a detailed frequency analysis of the EEG data tapes from the last two experiments, since the pilot experiment had already been subjected to FFT analysis. We conjectured that the observed power change in these experiments might be the result of a very small frequency shift, which could become translated into a large amplitude change due to discriminator action of the alpha-band filter. In a chapter on alpha blocking, Kooi, in his *Fundamentals of Electroencephalography* says, for example, that attentiveness is associated with a reduction in amplitude and an increase in average frequency of spontaneous cerebral potentials. . . . The center frequency of the alpha rhythm may be influenced by the type of ongoing mental activity. Shifts in frequency may be highly consistent as two different tasks are performed alternately.[11]

The FFT analysis for the second experiment showed that the average peak EEG power occurred most often near 8 Hz, and thus fell slightly below the hardware summing window (± 3 dB at 8.7–12.4 Hz), enhancing a possible discriminator effect. The FFT analysis further showed that there was an overall increase in frequency of peak power, but the shift was statistically nonsignificant. This slight shift of .11 Hz could possibly account for the observed power increase due to the highly nonlinear discriminator effects. In examining other portions of the spectrum for further effects, we found that systematic amplitude changes are highly dependent upon where in the frequency spectrum the power sum is taken. This is to be expected, since almost all EEG phenomena are known to be strongly frequency dependent.

In the pilot study, the frequency region for analysis was centered about the subject's dominant EEG output frequency, with bandpass determined by the full width 10 percent power points. In the two replication studies, we used hardware filters at this same frequency. FFT analysis showed clearly that if other filter bands had been chosen, significant correlations would not have been found. Thus, although our filter selection was made before the collection of any data, other experimenters might have reasonably chosen other criteria for frequency selection. Therefore, although we have found statistically significant evidence for EEG correlates to remote light flash stimuli, we consider these data to be only suggestive, with a definitive result requiring further experimentation.

## Summary

We have investigated the ability of certain individuals to perceive remote stimuli at a noncognitive level of awareness. To investigate this, we have looked for systematic changes in a subject's brainwave (EEG) production occurring at the same time as light flashes are generated on a random schedule in a remote laboratory. Although we have found in this investigation that significant correlations appear to exist between the times of light flashes and the times of brain wave alternations, we consider these data to be only suggestive, with a definitive result requiring further experimentation.

## Notes

1. A. Greeley, *The Sociology of the Paranormal* (Beverley Hills, Calif.: Sage Publications, 1975).

2. C. Tart, "Models for the Explanation of Extrasensory Perception," *International Journal of Neuropsychiatry* 2 (1966): 488–504; and C. Tart, *Psi: Scientific Studies of the Psychic Realm* (New York: Dutton, 1977).

3. E. D. Dean, *International Journal of Neuropsychiatry* 2 (1966): 439.

4 C. T. Tart, *International Journal of Parapsychology* 5 (1963): 375; and T. D. Duane and T. Behrendt, Science 150 (1965): 367.

5. R. Cavanna, ed., *Psi Favorable States of Consciousness* (New York: Parapsychology Foundation, 1970).

6. J. Silverman and M. S. Buchsbaum, "Perceptual Correlates of Consciousness: A Conceptual Model and its Technical Implications for Psi Research," in Cavanna, ed., op. cit.

7. Cavanna, ed., op. cit., pp. 158–59.

8. R. Targ and H. Puthoff, "Information Transmission Under Conditions of Sensory Shielding," *Nature* 252 (October 1974): 602–7; C. Rebert and A. Turner, "EEG Spectrum Analysis Techniques Applied to the Problem of Psi Phenomena," *Physician's Drug Manual* 5, nos. 9–12 (1974): 82–88; and H. Puthoff and R. Targ, "A Perceptual Channel for Information Transfer Over Kilometer Distances: Historical Perspective and Recent Research," *Proceedings of the IEEE* 64 (March 1976): 329–54.

9. D. Hill and G. Parr, *Electroencephalography: A Symposium on Its Various Aspects* (New York: Macmillan, 1963).

10. S. Siegel, *Nonparametric Statistics for the Behavior Sciences* (New York: McGraw-Hill, 1956), pp. 152–56.

11. A Kooi, *Fundamentals of Electroencephalography* (New York: Harper & Row, 1971).

# Introduction to Chapter 6

One of the difficulties some people have with accepting the reality of psi phenomena, in spite of the large amount of laboratory evidence for it, is that it seems so paraconceptual. The nature of the mechanisms responsible for the phenomena is unknown; the relationship of the phenomena to electromagnetic, quantum, and other bases of present scientific understanding is unknown; at its worst, psi phenomena might appear to the untutored eye to be devoid of lawfulness altogether. This view is not, however, wholly correct. Other chapters have shown that at least some aspects of psi phenomena may not be incompatible with modern physics after all. It also appears that once psi-acquired information has reached the person, further processing of it in consciousness takes place in accordance with lawful psychological principles—for example, disbelievers in psi tend to score below chance expectancy on psi tests, indicating psychological distortion of the psi-acquired information, in accordance with psychological needs to maintain belief systems.[1]

In this chapter, psychologist Charles Tart reports data that strongly suggest another lawful information-processing mechanism involved in psi functioning, one that he calls "trans-temporal inhibition." While it is a perfectly straightforward theory from an information-processing point of view, it is provocative from the point of view of conventional physics in that it requires the mind to operate in an extended or broadened definition of time. As a result, its value as a psychological contribution toward understanding psi may eventually be overshadowed by its value as an impetus in raising questions about the nature of time.

## About the Author

**Charles T. Tart,** Ph.D., is a Professor of Psychology at the Davis campus of the University of California. Over the past 20 years, he has published numerous research studies on the nature of sleep and dreaming, hypnosis, and marijuana intoxication, as well as parapsychological research, and is an internationally recognized authority on altered states of consciousness, as well as parapsychology. He is a past President of the Parapsychological Association, the professional scientific group in the field. His books include *Altered States of Consciousness, On Being Stoned: A Psychological Study of Marijuana Intoxication, Transpersonal Psychologies, States of Consciousness, Learning to Use Extrasensory Perception,* and *Psi: Scientific Studies of the Psychic Realm.*

# 6

## Improving Real-Time ESP by Suppressing the Future: Trans-Temporal Inhibition

### Charles T. Tart

One of the major problems that undermines efficient functional study of the nature of ESP is the unreliability, overall low level of manifestation, and prevalence of decline effects when ESP is studied in the laboratory. In the vast majority of experiments, even when ESP is present to a statistically significant degree, the vast majority of responses made by percipients are simply guesses, and only a very tiny fraction of them are ESP; also, the signal-to-noise ratio is very poor, making study of the characteristics of the signal difficult. As percipients continue to work at ESP tasks, it is very common for them to decline in performance and eventually be reduced to mere chance guessing.[2] Ten years ago, I theorized that this was due to lack of immediate feedback to percipients, so they could not learn to distinguish subtle characteristics of mental events that indicated when they were generally using ESP from mere guessing processes.[3] This theory has recently been elaborated.[4]

Two major studies have now been carried out in my laboratory, one already published[5] and the second in press,[6] which support the hypotheses that the provision of immediate feedback to percipients *with some ESP talent at the start of training* can slow down or eliminate the common decline effect (stabilize performance) and can allow some percipients to learn, and the degree of learning (improving performance) in the feedback situation is directly proportional to the ESP level a given percipient initially brings to the training sessions. These developments suggest that efficient functional studies may soon be possible.

In the course of exploratory post hoc analyses of the first Training Study, some remarkably strong effects produced by *precognition,* ESP cognition of

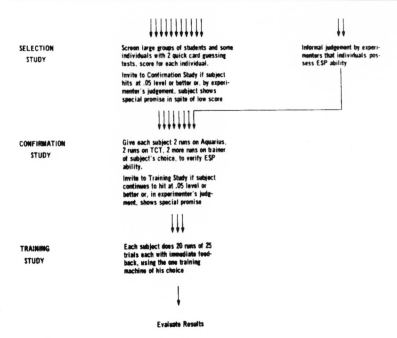

**Figure 6.1** Sequential selection procedure in the two Training Studies.

immediately future events, were discovered; they were confirmed in subsequent analysis of the second Training Study data. These precognitive effects and their theoretical implications for an information-processing mechanism used for enhancing real-time ESP, named *trans-temporal inhibition,* will be the focus of this chapter. The data on learning ESP per se are available elsewhere and will not be discussed further here except when they are relevant to the main focus.[7]

## Overview of the Experimental Procedure

Figure 6.1 provides an overview of the general procedure of each of the two studies. Since the learning theory predicted that percipients had to have some demonstrable ESP to begin with for feedback training to have much effect, it was necessary to start with relatively talented percipients. Since percipients who can demonstrate individually significant number-guessing-type ESP in a short period of testing were assumed to be relatively rare, a two-stage selection procedure proceeded the actual Training Study. In the first stage, teams of experimenters gave quick ESP card-guessing tests to large classes of University of California-Davis students. Students who showed individually significant ESP hitting were selected from these results.

In screening hundreds of students, a certain number were bound to score at least at the .05 level of significance by chance alone, so those selected students who accepted our invitation to participate in the second-stage Confirmation Study were given six individual test runs of 25 trials each. Two were on the ten-choice trainer (TCT) (described below), two were on the Aquarius Model 1000 ESP trainer, a four-choice machine developed by Russell Targ and David Hurt, and two more on whichever of the two machines each student preferred to do two more runs on. Since it would be highly unlikely that a student who made the criterion in the Selection Study by chance alone would also make the criterion of individual significance in the Confirmation Study ([.05] x [.05] = .0025), we assumed that almost all students who

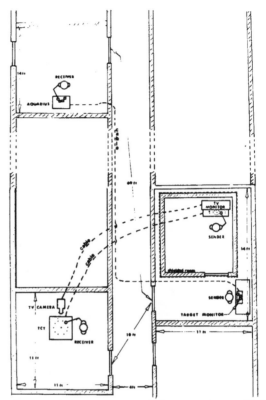

**Figure 6.2** Arrangement of the experimental laboratories.

scored significantly in both studies probably had genuine ESP talent, and they were invited to participate in the Training Study.

A few students went directly into the Confirmation Study without going through the Selection Study because individual experimenters had other reasons to suspect they might have demonstrable ESP ability.

We will deal only with data from the TCT in both the Training Studies in this chapter, as individual trial data were not recorded for the Aquarius four-choice trainer in the first study. Ten student percipients completed the first Training Study, and seven new percipients completed the second Training Study. *Completed* means doing 20 runs of 25 trials each on the TCT, over several sessions, our a priori criterion. Results in this chapter deal with Training Study data.

## The TCT

The TCT consisted of a percipient's and experimenter/sender's console. The two consoles were located in separate rooms, as shown in Figure 6.2. The percipient, or receiver, was alone in the laboratory room shown in the lower

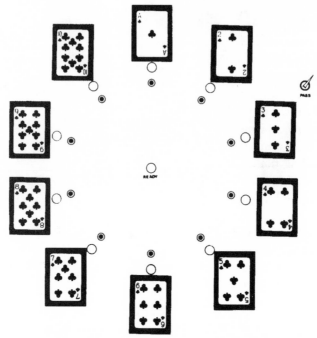

**Figure 6.3** Layout of the percipient's (receiver's) ten-choice trainer console. Target number four is shown as lit, indicating it was the correct target for whatever the percipient's response was.

lefthand corner of Figure 6.2, sitting in front of his or her console. A TV camera was focused on the console. The experimenter/sender was inside a Faraday cage constructed of thin copper sheets soldered together over an otherwise ordinarily constructed room, and this Faraday cage was inside another room, across the hall from the percipient's room. The shielding of the Faraday cage was not intact, however, due to power cables and the TV monitor and TCT interconnecting cables. The laboratory arrangements for the Aquarius four-choice trainer are also shown, although I shall not deal with data from that trainer in this chapter.

Figure 6.3 is a diagram of the arrangement of the percipients' console. It had ten unlit lamps arranged in a circle about 15 inches in diameter, with a miniature playing card glued beside each lamp to numerically identify it. A response push button was located beside each lamp. When the ready lamp in the center of the console came on, the percipient knew that the experimenter/sender had selected (in accordance with the output of a random number generator, to be described later) one of the ten lamps as a target, and was trying to telepathically "send" the identity of that target to him or her.

The percipient could respond quickly or take as much time as he or she wished to make his or her decision. When the percipient had decided on which

**Figure 6.4** Layout of the experimenter sender's console on the ten-choice trainer. Target is number two, and a hit has just been scored, lighting the "hit" lamp on the upper right of console. Experimenter/sender can see receiver's hand movements on the video monitor and thus send "hot" or "cold" thoughts, as well as target number.

number he or she thought the target was, he or she pushed the response button beside it; electrical circuitry immediately scored the percipient's response as a hit or miss and lighted the lamp on the percipient's console that corresponded to the *correct* target, so the percipient had *immediate* feedback on whether he or she was right or wrong. When he or she was right, a chime rang inside his or her console, and the correct light came on.

If, on a given trial, a percipient felt he or she had no idea what the target was, he or she could push the pass switch, signaling to the experimenter/sender that he or she would like a new target. A pass was not counted as a hit or miss, and no feedback on correct target identity was given. Percipients rarely used the pass option. A circuit diagram of the TCT is available elsewhere.[8]

Figure 6.4 is a photograph of the experimenter/sender's console and the TV monitor mounted beside it. Except for operating controls, such as power switches, this console was laid out identically to the percipient's console.

In pilot work with the TCT, my students and I found that many percipients would slowly run their hand around the circle of unlit lamps, trying to get some kind of "impression" as to when they were over the correct lamp. The TCT was designed so no electrical or physical differences of any sort existed[9] so, on the null hypothesis of no ESP, this was an irrelevant procedure. Because of this, however, we had a TV camera focused on the percipient's hand movements, so

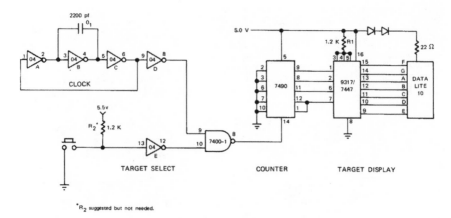

**Figure 6.5** Circuit of the random number generator used to generate targets for the ten-choice trainer. Integrated circuits are Signetics types 7404, 7400, 7447, and 7490. Seven-segment display is a Litronix Data Lite 10. Note that some earlier published versions (C. Tart, *Learning to Use Extrasensory Perception* [Chicago: University of Chicago Press, 1976], and C. Tart, *The Application of Learning Theory to Extrasensory Perception* [New York: Parapsychology Foundation, 1975]) of this circuit were incorrectly drawn.

the sender could tell when the percipient was "hot" or "cold," and so could intensify, diminish, or modify his or her sending effort accordingly.

The experimenter/senders found this full feedback of ongoing process to the sender to be extremely involving, and I think it is quite important, although I have not assessed its effect independently. In terms of training people to use ESP, we were actually training each experimenter/sender and percipient as a *team*, with full feedback to each.

Electrical counters on the TCT automatically recorded the number of trials and the number of hits. Runs were standardized at 25 trials. If, as rarely happened, the pass option was used, additional trials were given so the total of scored trials was 25. On other rare occasions when an experimenter accidentally ran one or two more trials than 25, all data beyond 25 trials were deleted.

## Random Number Generator

Target selection was controlled by an electronic random number generator. This was of the "electronic roulette wheel" type, with a 1-megahertz (MHz) clock cycling a zero to nine counter over and over again. The length of time the clock was connected to the counter was controlled by the exprimenter/sender manually depressing a push button. Since controllable human reaction time is several orders of magnitude slower than the clock speed, which output from zero to nine is selected is a random event. The circuit of the random number generator, designed by Dana Redington, is shown in Figure 6.5

Empirical tests, using a chi-square analysis for equal incidence of individual targets and equal incidence of all 100 possible pairs of target selections, on 1,000 trial test blocks collected before and after the first Training Study, showed satisfactory randomicity. We did not test for even higher-level possible sequential effects (triplets, quadruplets, and so on), as there is no theoretical reason to expect such sequential effects with this type of random number generator.

The TCT was used to gather the data in the first Training Study. We replaced it in the second Training Study with a more sophisticated and somewhat more automated version, the Advanced Decimal Extrasensory Perception Trainer (ADEPT), designed and constructed by Dana Redington, which was similar to the TCT except for the fact that individual trial data were recorded automatically by teletypewriter and the random number generator was internal to the machine, whereas with the TCT, the individual trial data were recorded by hand and the random number generator was external to the machine.* Total trials and total hits were both recorded automatically on both machines.

## Psychological Focus on Real-Time Events

In both Training Studies, neither I, nor my experimenters, nor the percipients had any interest in precognition. Our conception of the experiment was that we were trying to train real-time ESP, either clairvoyance (direct perception of the state of the TCT) or telepathic (perception of the experimenter/sender's knowledge of the correct target) transmission of ESP information. This psychological focus is important to note, in light of later results.

Figure 6.6 illustrates the temporal aspects of target generation. Given that a target had already been generated and the TCT activated (ready light is lighted on the percipient's console) for trial N, a percipient would take a variable period of time, from a second or two to sometimes minutes, to decide on what he or she thought the target was. He or she would then push a response button, giving himself or herself feedback and lighting a target lamp on the experimenter/sender's console, showing what the percipient's response had been. The experimenter/sender recorded the response on his or her record sheet (the target had already been noted), turned off the TCT, and then triggered the random number generator to select the next random number. When this selection had been made, in a second or so, he or she switched on the target lamp for trial N + 1.

---

*Construction of ADEPT was made possible through a grant from the Parapsychology Foundation.

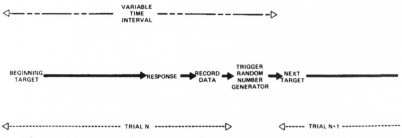

**Figure 6.6** Temporal sequence of target generations.

During the time that a percipient was trying to use ESP to determine what the current, real-time target was, the target for the next trial had not yet come into existence, nor could it be inferred from any knowledge of current events. The random number generator had not yet been activated. Any significant information about the future targets, then, would have to be due to precognition.

## Scoring Responses

For evaluating the presence of ESP and subsequent analysis of learning effects, we were interested in real-time hits, and all scoring was done for such hits. The top third of Figure 6.7 shows data from an actual run from percipient $P_5$. The top row shows the 25 targets that were sequentially generated; the second row shows the percipient's response to each one. Real-time hits are circled. There were six of them for this particular run. This happened to be an individually significant run, as the exact one-tailed binomial probability of six or more hits in 25 trials (with a P of .1) is three in 100.

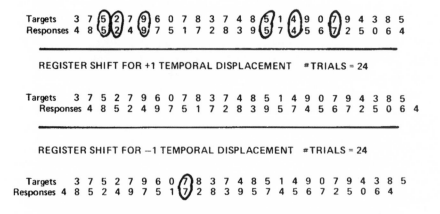

**Figure 6.7** Target and response sequences for percipient ($P_5$), third run, illustrating scoring techniques for real-time hits, +1 precognitive hits, and -1 postcognitive hits.

Although I knew that it was relatively routine in parapsychological experiments to check for possible precognitive effects, I personally had no real interest in them and had not gotten around to such checking until some analyses for another purpose by a colleague in the genetics department, Lila Gatlin, suggested to me that there were important precognitive effects worth looking at. The computer was reprogrammed to do temporal displacement analyses then, in the style shown in the middle and lower thirds of Figure 6.7.

To see if a response given by a percipient at time N was a hit or a miss on the target at trial N +1, the +1 temporal displacement, the response register was uniformly shifted one position forward in time. In the example shown, there were no hits with this procedure. N is reduced to 24 for such a shift, as the last response has no future target to be scored against.

To look at -1 past temporal displacement, as shown in the bottom third of the figure, the response register is shifted uniformly backward one position. In this case, there was one hit by this procedure, with N again reduced to 24. A similar procedure allows looking at any temporal displacement, forward (+1 through +24) or back (-1 through -24).

In looking at possible hits displaced forward in time, any significant deviations from chance expectation must be due to some kind of precognitive ESP, for, as discussed earlier, these targets did not yet exist and could not be predicted from any knowledge (sensory or extrasensory) of current events. In looking at temporal shifts backward, my immediate reaction was to believe these would indicate something about ordinary psychologic processes in the percipient: because of the immediate feedback of results, percipients *knew* what the immediately past target had been (to the extent that they had not forgotten it). The situation may be more complex than that for past displacements, however, as we shall see later.

## ESP Missing

An interesting effect that has been reported in many dozens of published ESP experiments is what is called *ESP-missing* (or *psi-missing*), scoring that is significantly *below* chance expectation.[10] Scoring below chance expectation can indicate as much that ESP is operating as scoring above chance expectation can. If you are guessing whether the cards in an ordinary deck are red or black, for example, getting zero right is just as significant as getting all 52 right.

In terms of a model underlying the process, some *nonconscious* part of the mind must use ESP to *correctly* identify certain targets and then influence *conscious* guessing processes to make sure that these targets are *not* guessed correctly. This has been associated with motivation in a number of parapsychological studies: percipients who have an a priori disbelief in ESP and who are statistically naive, but who (like most of us) think that the worse you score on a test the less you know, have often been shown to score signiflcantly below chance, thus thinking they have validated their belief that there is no such phenomenon as ESP.[11]

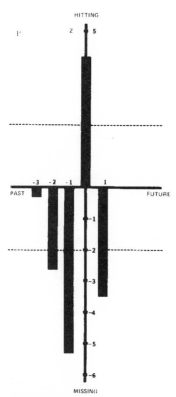

**Figure 6.8** Scoring pattern over all 500 trials (20 runs) of percipient $P_1$ for -3, -2, -1, real-time and +1 temporal displacements. Units of vertical axis are standard normal deviates (Z-scores, $\sigma$).

## ESP Missing in the First Training Study

The ten percipients who completed the first Training Study showed exceptionally significant results in terms of real-time hitting. For their total of 5,000 trials, we would expect 500 hits by chance, but 722 were observed.* The two-tailed probability of such an occurrence, using the normal approximation to the binomial, is $2 \times 10^{-25}$. This corresponded, for the group as a whole, to an average of 3.61 hits per run of 25 rather than the average of 2.50 expected by chance.

There was considerable individual variation, of course, with a few percipients apparently having their overt manifestation of ESP suppressed in terms of real-time hitting and not showing individual significance, a finding often associated with changes in psychological conditions, such as we had in going from the Confirmation to the Training Study.[12] Five of the ten percipients showed exceptionally significant individual scores. The least of these five averaged 3.90 hits per run, for a P of $4 \times 10^{-5}$, two-tailed, and the most significant averaged 6.20 hits per run, for an individual P of $4 \times 10^{-28}$, two-tailed.

In scoring for hits on the +1 future trial, there were 4,790 trials where a hit could have occurred (a few possibilities were lost when an experimenter inadvertently gave only 24 trials in a run, as well as the routine loss of one trial in each run), so 479 hits would be expected by chance. Only 318 hits occurred: this would occur by chance with a two-tailed probability of $8 \times 10^{-15}$. Thus, some part of the percipients' minds was occasionally using precognition to know what the +1 future target was and then affecting the conscious guessing of the real-time target to be sure it was not what the +1 target would be. All other

---

*In the original publication of these ESP learning results (C. Tart, *Learning to Use Extrasensory Perception* [Chicago: University of Chicago Press, 1976]), we worked with total run scores and did not realize that the total number of trials was slightly less than 5,000.

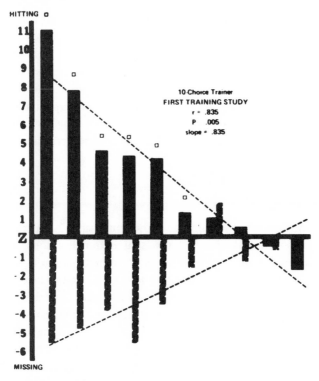

**Figure 6.9** Relationship between real-time hitting and +1 future missing, first Training Study. Solid bars are scoring on real-time targets, and hatched bars are scoring on +1 future targets, paired by percipient.

possible future displacements (+2, +3 . . . +24) were checked but were not of such obvious significance and so will not be reported on in this chapter.

Past temporal displacements were also checked, and a rather regular pattern was found for the -1 and -2 displacements. Figure 6.8 is a bar graph of this for a percipient, $P_1$, whose individual pattern is typical of that of many other percipients. He made 78 real-time hits, when 50 would be expected by chance, $P = 4 \times 10^{-5}$, two-tailed. His avoidance of the immediate +1 future was also extremely significant: $P = 6 \times 10^{-4}$, two-tailed. His avoidance of the immediate -1 past was even greater, $P = 10 \times 10^{-8}$, two-tailed. This avoidance of -1 past targets being greater than the avoidance of the +1 future was the typical pattern for almost all percipients.

---

The current total analysis here retains the convention of 5,000 trials in order to be consistent with the original publication; as this is a conservative error, the data are slightly more significant than the results here calculated.

The past targets at the -2 displacement were also significantly avoided, but by the -3 displacement and for other greater temporal displacements, the group average was generally small, being only nonsignificant variations around chance. This suggests something in accordance with know psychological facts about people's guessing habits, namely that percipients strongly avoid making their guess identical to what the immediately previous target has been; a similar psychological avoidance holds, but is not quite so strong, by two targets back, and is pretty much inoperative by three or more targets back.

## Relationship between Real-Time Hitting and Avoiding the Future

It turns out that this precognitive avoidance of the immediate +1 future in the first Training Study was not an isolated event but was quite strongly and negatively related to the degree of real-time hitting. Figure 6.9 shows the magnitude of the real-time hitting and the +1 missing (hitting in one case) for each individual percipient. The vertical axis is Z or $\sigma$ score, with anything greater than $2\sigma$ conventionally being accepted as statistically significant. I have ordered the real-time hitting scores from the highest on the left down through the greatest degree of missing on the real-time target to the right. The rather good ordering of missing scores on the +1 future target that then results is an indication of the strength of the relationship between these two measures. The dotted lines are fitted regression lines. As can be seen, there is an extremely strong relationship: the more a percipient tends to hit on the real-time target by ESP, the more he or she tends to avoid the +1 future target. The correlation is -.835, P < .005, two-tailed. A rank order correlation, which makes somewhat fewer assumptions about the characteristics of the numerical scaling, gives r = -.89, a slight increase.[13] We shall consider the lower graph, labeled *strategy-boundness,* later.

The small squares beside each individual percipient's data indicate when the real-time hits were significantly different from the +1 future missing by a t-test, applied over the 20 runs of each individual percipient. Six of the ten percipients show such significant differences, including one whose real-time hitting no longer showed individual significance by itself.

As a control test (to be certain that the negative relationship between real-time hitting and +1 future missing in the first Training Study did not result from peculiar numerical properties of the target and response sequences), the target response sequence for each percipient was paired with the response sequence from some other percipient and the same analyses carried out. There were no significant "real-time" hits, no significant +1 missing, and no relationship between the two.

## PK as an Alternative to Precognition?

Because numerous studies have shown that humans can influence the output of electronic random number generators simply by willing some outputs to come up more frequently (PK),[14] and because we could not be sure that some of our percipients might not unconsciously use PK on the random number generator rather than just using ESP to know the state of the machine or the experimenter/sender's mind, we made an a priori decision to test our random number generators for randomness *before* and *after* our Training Studies but not *during* them, when percipients might be "on line," in the sense of being concerned about, and possibly influencing, the random number generators.

As a post hoc exploratory study, we did test the individual target sequences of each percipient for randomicity and found that three of the 17 sequences (both Training Studies combined) did show statistically significant departures from randomicity, as per our hypothesis that our percipients might unconsciously use PK on the random number generators. Two of the nonrandom target sequences were for the two highest-scoring percipients in the first Training Study, $P_3$ and $P_5$. Although the magnitude of these target sequence departures from randomicity was small compared with the magnitude of the ESP effects, suggesting that these percipients occasionally used PK on the random number generator but were mostly using ESP, I did check the correlations between real-time hitting and +1 future missing to see if they would be affected if the data from these two percipients were thrown out. The differences were trivial and can be ignored: for the first Training Study, r = -.81 instead of r = -.84. Further analyses showing that small departures from randomicity are not important in this data have been described elsewhere.[15]

## Replication of Effects in the Second Training Study

The second Training Study was not as successful as the first in terms of magnitude of real-time ESP shown, an unfortunate, but predicted, effect. Our second Selection Study and second Confirmation Study did not give us individual percipients with as high scores as we had in the first Training Study. The group of percipients who entered the first Training Study had Confirmation Study scores ranging from 2.50 to 6.00 hits per run of 25 (chance is 2.50), with a mean group score of 4.78, while the corresponding range was 2.75 to 4.50 (group mean of 3.61 hits/run) for the percipients who completed the second Training Study. The difference was statistically significant (P < .05, two-tailed, by t-test). Ideally, we should have run more students through our Selection Study and Confirmation Study procedure and made the ESP talent level comparable to that of the first Training Study. Time, money, and manpower shortages prohibited this, so we used the percipients we had but predicted that our overall level of ESP would be smaller in the second Training Study. It was.

Seven percipients completed the second Training Study. The overall group mean (2.61) did not differ significantly from chance expectation (P ≈ .40, 2-tailed), although two of the seven percipients showed individually significant results. One of these percipients showed individually significant real-time

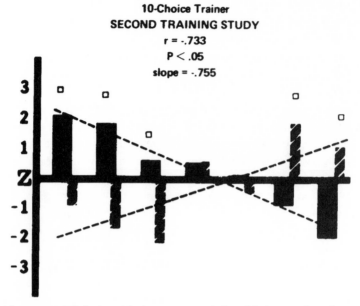

**Figure 6.10** Relationship between real-time hitting and +1 future missing, second Training Study.

hitting (average of 3.20 hits/run, P < .05, 2-tailed); the other showed individually significant real-time missing (average of 1.85 hits/run, P < .05, 2-tailed), so they effectively canceled each other out.

Figure 6.10 shows the individual percipient results for real-time scoring and +1 missing or hitting. My hypothesis that we still had talented ESP percipients but that the increased pressure of the Training Study had probably inhibited their ESP abilities, as in the first Training Study, was confirmed. Five of the seven percipients showed individually significant differences (t-test) between their real-time scores and +1 future scores, again indicated by the small squares above their scores in Figure 6. 10. The negative relationship between real-time hitting and +1 missing was again confirmed, with r = -.733, P < .05, one-tailed. The more conservative rank order correlation gives r = -.79, a slightly stronger effect.

As in the first Training Study, I carried out an exploratory, post hoc analysis for possible nonrandomicity in the percipients' target sequences that might represent a PK effect. One of the seven target sequences, for percipient $P_{10}$, showed too many sevens. Curiously, this percipient scored almost exactly at chance expectation (51 hits versus 50 expected) for real-time hits. Conservatively deleting the data of $P_{10}$, however, again has a negligible effect on the correlation between real-time hitting and +1 future missing: r = -.74, P < .05, one-tailed.

In many ways, the percipients from the second Training Study amounted to a sampling of the lower end of the distribution sampled in the first Training

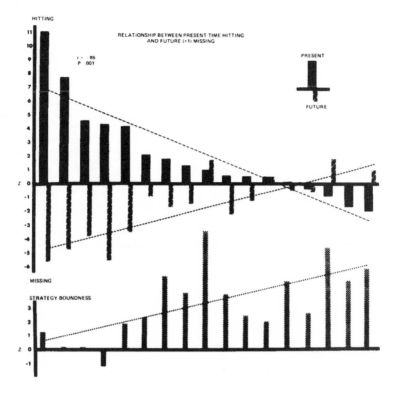

**Figure 6.11** Relationship between real-time hitting, +1 future missing, and strategy boundness, combined data of both Training Studies.

Study, so I combined the results of the two Training Studies, to produce the diagram shown in Figure 6.11. Here, the strong relationship between real-time hitting and +1 missing stands out very clearly (r = -.85, P < .001, two-tailed). The more conservative rank order correlation is also -.85. The highly successful real-time ESP percipients strongly suppressed their calls of the immediate future, while the ones who, under the increased psychological pressure of the Training Study, tended to switch to missing in real time, an incorrect focusing of the ESP effect, showed some tendency to switch to hitting on the immediate future.

If, to be very conservative, the data of the three percipients showing nonrandom target sequences are deleted from the overall correlation, the change is negligible, with r changing from -.84 to -.82, so the data from these three percipients will be left in. More microscopic analyses, aimed at distinguishing these small possible PK effects from ESP effects, will be undertaken in the future.

Such a significant negative relationship between real-time hitting and +1 missing has not, to my knowledge, been previously reported in the experimental

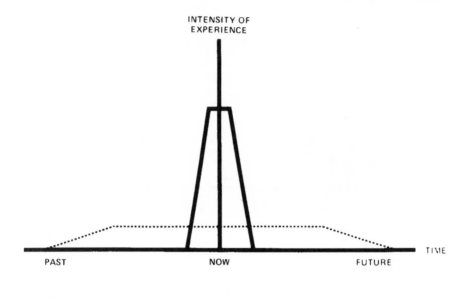

**Figure 6.12** Intensity and duration characteristics of the experienced present for ordinary consciousness (heavy lines) and the extended aspect of the mind that uses ESP (dotted lines).

parapsychological literature.* This may be partly due to the fact that it has not been looked for, but I also suspect it is partially due to a procedural difference. In the present Training Studies, there was a sequential generation of targets "on line," as it were. In most parapsychological studies, until fairly recently, targets have been thoroughly shuffled decks of cards. In precognition studies with cards, the entire sequence of future targets is generated simultaneously when they are thoroughly shuffled at a future time, rather than being generated one by one after each real-time response.

I shall now present the theory I have devised to explain these results. I am deeply indebted to Enoch Callaway, a colleague at the Langley-Porter

---

*Although there are more than 700 published articles showing experimental evidence for the existence of ESP and investigating its mechanisms, they are not generally known to the scientific community, having appeared in specialty journals. The reader interested in getting into this literature should consult the *International Journal of Parapsychology,* the *Journal of Parapsychology,* the *Journal of the American Society for Psychical Research,* the *Journal of the Society for Psychical Research* (London), and the recent *European Journal of Parapsychology.*

Neuropsychiatric Institute, who, after seeing a preliminary analysis of this data, suggested that it resembled a neural inhibitory surround and started the train of thought in me that led to the following theory.

## The Duration of the Present

If you will stop to ask yourself what is "present" to your experience, you will find that your *experienced* present, although very short, definitely seems to have a certain duration. The mathematical *abstraction* of the present being a temporal point of zero width, sandwiched between past and future, is a useful abstraction in a variety of applications but a poor representation of psychological experience. In Figure 6.12, the heavy lines model what we might call, by analogy with filters, the *passband* of the experienced present. For some small duration, centered around the now, all actions and experiences are *now*. The length of this interval is slightly variable, depending on how our attention is focused, and probably is ordinarily somewhere between one-tenth and two-tenths of a second wide. Within this experienced now, the intensity of experience (the vertical axis) is very high. At the edges of the passband, experience drops in intensity and clarity. Dynamically, we should picture this passband as moving along horizontally from past to future. Whether experience within this passband of the experienced now is actually continuous or consists of discrete frames, with awareness of the interframe interval suppressed, is an interesting question.

An old psychological term for this effect was the *specious present*, a term I do not like, as it shows that the mathematical abstraction was being considered more real than actual experience, implying that direct experience was specious. I shall speak of the *experienced present* and its width. By using "outside" time sources, such as a clock, we can say that the experienced present has a definite width, even though, to the mind, this small segment of time is all now.

## Precognition and the Experienced Present

There are dozens of published parapsychological studies indicating that precognition, under laboratory conditions, is a genuine phenomenon.[16] These results are usually conceptualized as the future "influencing" the present or as information flow from the future to the past. Reactions to these data are frequently mixed with "absolute" questions about free will versus determinism or causality, and discussions get phrased in such absolute terms that they lead nowhere.

An alternative way of accounting for the data of precognition is to postulate that there is some other temporal dimension of mental functioning, a temporal dimension in which time "flows at a different rate," or some such thing, with the consequence that the experienced present of the mind in that other temporal dimension has a greater duration, or a wider passband, than our ordinary experienced present. This wider passband is shown in Figure 6.12 as the dotted line. The exact shape of the passband as drawn is not important: it merely represents that, ordinarily, the intensity of experience tapers off to near zero at some point.

I am proposing that the aspect of mind which is activated on those occasions when ESP abilities are used has two properties different from our ordinary consciousness, which seems spatially localized with respect to the brain and temporally localized with respect to the time system's physical processes of brain operation. The first property is that this other dimension of the mind is not so spatially localized and can thus somehow pick up information at spatial locations outside the sensory range of the body/brain/nervous system. The second property is that the center point of the experienced present of this other dimension of the mind can be a different time than the physical time associated with the body/brain/nervous system, and the band width of that other part of the mind's experienced present is wider than the band width of our ordinary consciousness's experienced present. Thus, what is *now* in this other dimension of the mind may include portions of time that, from our ordinary point of view, are past and future, as well as present.

Since consciousness (or basic *awareness,* as I prefer to call it in my systems approach to consciousness) is ordinarily fully identified and preoccupied with body/brain/nervous system functioning, the experienced intensity of the part of mind that operates in this other temporal and spatial dimension is ordinarily quite low, usually below conscious threshold, and is shown accordingly so in Figure 6.12.[17]

When a percipient is asked to use ESP, he or she must disregard ongoing sensory input (the experimental conditions make it irrelevant) and whatever fantasies or strategies he or she has about outguessing the random number generator (since targets are equiprobable and sequentially independent) and try to "contact" or "tune in" to that aspect of mind that exists or is capable of using this broader spatial and temporal dimension. Considering the temporal aspects of it, this creates a problem. If your desire is to obtain real-time information being "sent" by the experimenter/sender in another laboratory, then simply tapping into the wider experiential present of this other dimension is not good enough: it includes information about past and future events, as well as present events. Since your goal is *present* event information, this past and future information is noise, which may interfere with detection of the desired signal.

Given the psychological set of experimenters and percipients in our studies, namely, concentrating on getting the real-time information by ESP, this implicitly defined the temporal boundaries of that real-time information as the immediate -1 past and the immediate +1 future targets/trials. We shall consider effects of altering this psychological definition later.

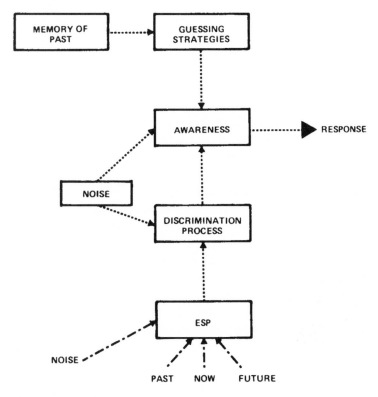

**Figure 6.13** A model of psychological processes used in making a successful ESP response.

Figure 6.13 models what a percipient must do to use ESP successfully, then, to get real-time information. His or her awareness is receiving irrelevant sensory information that must be disregarded. His or her memories of what past targets have been may suggest guessing strategies, but they are irrelevant, since each output of the random number generator is independent of the previous ones. He or she must occasionally tap into that dimension of mind that uses ESP, but since that part of the mind is getting information about the past and future, as well as the present, he or she must further add a *discrimination process* of some kind that will clearly identify the past and future aspects of the ESP information and then actively *suppress* such aspects in order to enhance the detectability of the real-time desired ESP information. The output of the discrimination process, then, consists of some kind of information designed to influence the percipient's conscious guessing processes to correctly guess the present *real-time* target and to inhibit guessing target identities that are the same as the immediate future and the immediate past targets, lest the past or future be confused with the present. The nonconscious ESP and discrimination processes may certainly work intermittently and imperfectly, depending on other factors that could constitute both systematic or random noise at various stages in the total information flow system.

## Trans-Temporal Inhibition

What I am postulating, then, is an *active inhibition* of the precognitively and postcognitively gained information about immediate future and immediate past in order to enhance the detectability of ESP information about real-time events. Since this inhibition extends over time, I have named this phenomenon *trans-temporal inhibition.*

Except for the unusual features of extending over time rather than space, trans-temporal inhibition is analogous to a widely used information-processing strategy in the nervous system called *lateral inhibition.*[18] This is a general phenomenon of a highly stimulated receptor sending out inhibitory impulses to receptor endings laterally/spatially adjacent to it, thus suppressing their initially weaker output, unless they are also strongly stimulated by an appropriate stimulus. It amounts to an edge detection process—to illustrate: if you press on your skin with a sharply pointed object, not only is the touch receptor immediately under the point strongly stimulated, but because of the mechanical deformation of the skin, receptors laterally adjacent to the point are also stimulated, although less intensely. The neural impulses resulting at the first stage of detection, then, would be most intense immediately under the stimulated point, but fairly intense on each side of it, gradually tapering off, producing a neural signal pattern suggesting a blunt, rounded, stimulating object rather than a point. The most stimulated receptor under the point, however, sends out inhibitory impulses suppressing the weaker (less frequent) impulses from the laterally adjacent receptors and so recovering a pattern indicating point stimulation further on in the nervous system. The phenomenon of trans-temporal inhibition, then, suggests that a generally useful information-processing procedure is also operative for ESP.

How well does this theory fit the data?

## Applying the Theory to the Data

In showing the +1, real-time, and -1 score patterns of percipient $P_1$ earlier in Figure 6.8 (we shall ignore the -2 and -3 points from now on, as they are not related to other things), I indicated that the very significant degree of missing on the immediately past -1 target probably reflected maladaptive guessing habits on the percipient's part. The random number generator is so constructed that there are no sequential dependencies, that is, the probability of two sequential targets being a one-one is identical to that of their being a two-two, a three-three, a three-four, a one-nine, and so forth. People, however, have inaccurate conceptions of what random sequences are; they usually believe that the

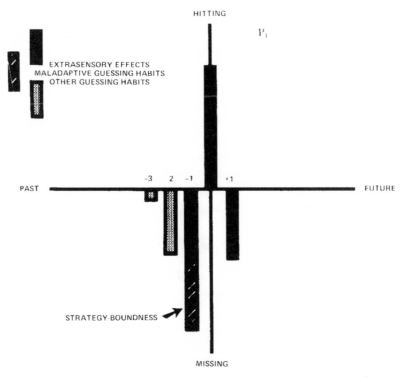

HITTING

$P_1$

EXTRASENSORY EFFECTS
MALADAPTIVE GUESSING HABITS
OTHER GUESSING HABITS

PAST        -3   2  -1      +1        FUTURE

STRATEGY-BOUNDNESS

MISSING

**Figure 6.14** Partialing out the strategy boundness measure from the total missing on the -1 temporal displacement.

probability of the same target occurring twice is considerably less than that of a different target following the original one, that is, that one-one, two-two, and so on are all much less probable than one-two, one-three, two-four, and so forth. Thus, the percipients tend to avoid giving a response that is the same as the previous target, and I suggest that this accounted for the very large degree of the -1 missing. The theory of trans-temporal inhibition, however, assumes that the experienced present of this other dimension of the mind is probably symmetrical in most circumstances; this is an assumption that will be made, paralleling the general assumption that works so well in the physical sciences, namely, that all physical processes are symmetrical.[19] Given this symmetry assumption, I then postulated that the -1 missing could be partialed into two components. One of these would be postcognitive ESP inhibition of the calling of the previous target, and I would further assume that this component would be approximately equal in magnitude to the inhibition of the +1 response for each percipient, treated individually. The rest of the missing on the -1 past displacement would be due to maladaptive guessing strategies, this business of tending not to repeat the immediately past target. I have named this component of the -1 missing *strategy boundness*. Figure 6.14 shows this partialing out applied to the data of percipient $P_1$. For this particular example, about half of the -1 missing would be assumed to be due to trans-temporal inhibition of the postcognitive response to the -1 target and half to maladaptive strategy boundness.

My conception of the optimal way to try to use ESP is that all "rational" processes are irrelevant. A guessing strategy that involves keeping track of what the past targets have been and then trying to outguess the random number generator is not only a waste of time (because of the sequential independence of the random number generator) but it also distracts a percipient from turning his or her awareness toward more relevant mental processes, toward what we might call metaphorically "listening to the still small voice within" that might occasionally give a useful hint about target identity.

## Strategy Boundness and Success in Using ESP

On theoretical grounds, then, we would expect that the more strategy boundness a percipient showed, the less real-time ESP he or she would show. Since trans-temporal inhibition of the future (and by assumption, of the past) target response is adaptive for enhancing real-time ESP, we would also expect that with more strategy boundness, there would be less missing on the +1 future target. The data bear this out quite convincingly.

Because the signs for the straight arithmetical computations of missing, strategy boundness, and so forth require a good deal of attention to follow in terms of their relationships, I have taken the value of strategy boundness, which is inherently negative (missing), and made it positive in order to make the results clearer.

In originally computing the correlations between real-time hitting, +1 future missing, and -1 past missing for percipients in the combined two Training Studies, I found that +1 future missing was significantly correlated with real-time hitting ($r = -.85$, $P < .001$), but the magnitude of -1 past missing did not correlate significantly with either the magnitude of real-time hitting ($r = -.24$, nonsignificant) or with the magnitude of the +1 future missing ($r = +.14$, nonsignificant). After factoring out strategy boundness, as discussed above, it turns out that strategy boundness is significantly correlated with the other two measures. Strategy boundness correlates $r = -.64$, $P < .01$ with present time hitting, and $r = +.83$, $P < .001$, with +1 future missing. Referring back to Figures 6.9 and 6.11, where the degree of individual strategy boundness was plotted for the percipients in the lower part of the graphs, the strength of this relationship is very clear. The more a percipient was caught up in maladaptive strategy boundness, the less likely he or she was to show real-time hitting and the less likely to show trans-temporal inhibition—missing of the +1 future target. Strategy boundness can be conceived of as a failure to direct awareness to that part of the mind which is not so localized in space and time and which thus exercises ESP; instead, awareness is involved with ordinary aspects of the mind, which cannot use ESP.

Applying the symmetry assumption to trans-temporal inhibition theory, then, takes some random data (the absolute magnitude of the -1 past deviations) and partials it into meaningful data. There is, however, a difficulty. When performing these calculations, I was concerned that there might be an artifactual element in this sort of partialing of the -1 deviations that would automatically create a high correlation for numerical reasons alone, whether any correlation existed in reality or not. I checked my procedure with four mathematicians, all of whom assured me that there was no artifact problem. The possibility still nagged at me, however, so I asked a colleague, Eugene Dronek, to do a computer simulation of the process for me; unfortunately, I discovered that you get very high correlations artifactually the majority of the time. Thus, the data presented above cannot prove the concept of strategy boundness, but since the concept makes so much intuitive sense, I present this material nevertheless as a stimulus to thought. How could we assess strategy boundness in a valid way?

## A Further Test of the Theory

As I mentioned earlier, both percipients and experimenters in the two Training Studies were focused on the ordinary present—on the task of picking up real-time information. This implicitly defined the immediate boundaries of the now as the +1 and -1 future and past target events. Since my data only occasionally suggest significant ESP missing on the +2 target (and, by the same sort of operations described above, on the -2 target), this suggests that while the experienced present of this other dimension of the mind was wider than the ordinary experienced present, it was not too much wider. Other studies of precognition, however, have often dealt with events that are much further ahead in the future—minutes, hours, days, and sometimes months.[20] Insofar as the transtemporal inhibition theory is correct, I would predict that if the focus of attention is successfully placed on some *future* event, there ought to be ESP hitting on that event but inhibition of responses to events temporally surrounding that future event. Using our filter analogy, with the experienced present of the dimension of the mind that uses ESP corresponding to the band width of that filter, it should be possible, by means of psychological processes, to shift the center point and/or the band width of the filter and see a corresponding shift of trans-temporal inhibition. I have been able to carry out one test of this prediction to date.

Ingo Swann is a well-known New York artist who possesses a variety of ESP abilities that he has demonstrated under rigorous laboratory conditions in other investigators' laboratories, including SRI and the City College of New York.[21] Swann was present at a small meeting of parapsychological researchers, in October 1976, when I presented the above data and the basic theory about trans-temporal inhibition, although I did not say much about the prediction of the possibility of shifting the center point of the experienced now of this other aspect of mind or its predicted consequences. Swann was very intrigued by my data and made a number of useful comments on it, including his own observation that what he and the SRI researchers R. Targ and H. Puthoff called *analytical overlay* seemed to correspond to my concept of strategy boundness—any kind of "rational" but actually irrelevant activities that diverted one from relevant aspects of the ESP task. He wanted to try my ADEPT training device, and a few days later, he was able to briefly visit my laboratory.

I looked forward to his visit with considerable interest, for he would be the first percipient who, because he had heard about trans-temporal inhibition, would be psychologically set to have some concern with the immediate (+1) future target, as well as the real-time target. I predicted (to myself, not to Swann) he would probably show hitting on the +1 future target but missing on the +2 future target. This is what happened.

Swann did five runs on ADEPT in the course of a little over an hour, for a total of 129 trials (in one run, he inadvertently did 29 trials instead of the usual 25). He made 21 real-time hits in the five runs, where only 12.9 would be expected by chance, $P = 9 \times 10^{-3}$, one-tailed. In terms of +1 future scoring, he made 19 hits, when only 12.4 were expected by chance, $P = .03$, one-tailed. His +1 precognition scores' significance is probably underrepresented by this conventional evaluation, because he tended to have bursts of hitting twice in a row on +1 precognition; a separate evaluation of the probability of the number of doublet precognition hits he showed gives odds of $10^{-6}$.

On +2 precognition hits, he scored only seven hits when 11.9 would be expected by chance, $P = .07$, one-tailed. This is not quite independently significant for below chance scoring by itself, but as predicted, a t-test shows the *difference* between the scoring rate on the +1 and +2 hits is statistically significant ($t = 2.59$, 4 df, $P < .05$, one-tailed).*

I later asked Swann if he was deliberately trying to guess the immediate future target, as well as the real-time target, and he replied that he had not been deliberately trying to do this—*consciously*, he was concentrating on the real-time target. This suggests that the passband of the "wider dimension filter" can be altered without there being full conscious awareness of it.

Figure 6.15 shows Swann's performance on -1, real-time, +1, and +2 temporal displacements. It is also interesting to note the magnitude of his -1 displacement score: it is only slightly larger than the +2 missing displacement, indicating a very low degree of strategy boundness. This is precisely what we would expect for someone with high ESP abilities. Incidentally, we should not overlook the fact that it is a quite amazing performance for Swann to have

---

*Five pairs of data points is a low N for a t-test and pushes the underlying assumption, but I used it to be consistent with earlier analyses.

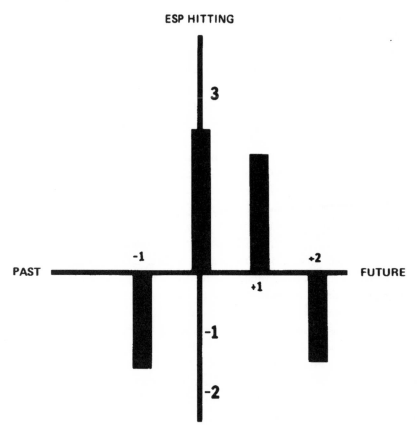

**Figure 6.15** Widened temporal passband for Ingo Swann.

walked in "cold" off the street, as it were, and immediately have shown statistically significant ESP in a new test situation.

Although it is a post hoc speculation, it is of interest to raise the question as to whether the "passbands" of some of the earlier percipients' trans-temporal inhibition processes were shifted in a manner analogous to Swann's. In the first Training Study, percipient $P_{14}$ had Z-scores of -6.69 for -1 temporal missing, +1.04 for real-time hits, +1.83 for +1 future hits, and -2.64 for +2 future missing, and the drop from +1 hitting to +2 missing is significant (t = 3.40 with 19 df, P < .005, one-tailed).* In the second Training Study, percipient $P_4$ had

---

*In comparing scores between real time, +1 temporal displacement, or +2 temporal displacement, we deal with a shortened run length in each case (25, 24, 23), meaning that the expected number of hits by chance would be slightly lower (2.5, 2.4, 2.3), so in doing the t-tests, this was compensated for by testing against the null hypotheses that [real-time hits] = [(+1 hits) + (.1)] and [(+1 hits) + (.1)] = [(+2 hits) + (.2)].

Z-scores of -5.48 for -1 temporal missing, -.89 missing on real-time targets, +1.83 hitting on +1 future displacements, and -.78 on +2 missing. The difference between +1 hitting and +2 missing is significant (t = 2.00 with 19 df, P < .05, one-tailed). The difference between +1 and +2 scoring for a third percipient from the second Training Study, $P_8$, who showed a tendency toward hitting (Z = +1.06) on the +1 future target, is not at all significant (for +2, Z = +.62).

## Persistence of Inhibition

Recall now that the theory of trans-temporal inhibition says that if the psi receptor and appropriate discrimination processes are working on trial N, not only does this positively influence you to call a digit that corresponds to the actual identity of the target at that time but it also inhibits or prejudices you against calling the digit that is the identity of the target on trial N +1 in the immediate future. Now, human psychological processes generally have some degree of "inertia," that is, our immediate past is constantly having some influence on the present. Living totally in the moment is a valued ideal for many, but it is distinguished in reality by its rarity. It follows then that after making a call on trial N, on trial N +1, a problem exists: the percipient is likely to still be carrying some inhibitory bias against calling the digit that corresponds to the identity of the target on trial N +1. Thus, the operation of trans-temporal inhibition is likely to produce a kind of "stuttering" of ESP, a break in its continuity. If you hit by using ESP, you are more likely to miss on the next trial than if you had not hit, an effect we might call *psi stuttering*. In terms of the data available for analysis, we should expect to see fewer hit doublets (two hits in a row) than would be expected if every trial were independent of the previous one.

The appropriate test for this is to use the observed proportion of real-time hits to recalculate the probability of a hit: then, the probability of a real-time hit followed by a real-time hit is simply the square of this empirically obtained proportion, given the assumption that real-time hits are temporally independent of one another. Calculating this, I found that in the first Training Study, there was a deficiency of real-time hits following real-time hits—only 86 when about 106 would be expected. This has a Z-score of -2.07, P = .02, one-tailed. More importantly, the degree of *lack* of real-time hit doublets is strongly and positively correlated with the degree of real-time hitting: r = +.71, P < .025, one-tailed, that is, the more a percipient showed real-time hitting, the more this hitting tended to be broken up and not occur sequentially, as we would expect from the trans-temporal inhibition theory.

This same relationship was found in the data of the second Training Study (r = +.40), but while it is in the right direction, the correlation does not reach significance with the smaller number of percipients and a much more restricted range of ESP. Such a lowering of the range of ESP would automatically lower the estimate of the true population correlation coefficient. If the data from the two Training Studies are combined, r = +.60 between real-time hits and lack of real-time hit doublets, with an associated P < .01, one-tailed.

We would also expect that the degree of *lack* of real-time hit doublets would correlate with our direct measure of trans-temporal inhibition, the degree of *missing* on the +1 precognitive target. It does, although not quite so outstandingly. In the first Training Study, r = +.48, which does not quite reach the .05 level of significance; in the second Training Study r = +.47, also below the level of statistical significance. When the two Training Studies are combined to produce a larger sample size, r = +.47, with an associated probability of P < .05, one-tailed.

Thus, this persistence of inhibition aspect of the theory of trans-temporal inhibition has received good support.

## The Generalized Trans-Temporal Inhibition Test

Given the existence of trans-temporal inhibition, I now believe that a more sensitive test for the presence of ESP in the data of percipients (run under conditions comparable to those of the present studies—where targets are generated one by one) is to look at the *contrast,* the difference between hitting on the target on which ESP is focused and missing on the immediately adjacent (in our case, +1 precognition) targets. If we could always assume that our instructions to a percipient to focus on the real-time target were completely effective, the particular measures to contrast would always be real-time hits versus +1 precognitive hits (and/or -1 postcognitive hits in nonfeedback studies). As Swann's data demonstrated, however, the focus of ESP hitting and the consequent inhibition may be shifted to other than the real-time and +1 targets. After all, when you tell a percipient to use ESP, he or she does not really know just what to do, so he or she tries various mental strategies, and it would not be surprising if he or she occasionally "jiggled" the "temporal focus controls," as well as occasionally managing to activate the "ESP on" control. Indeed, I had suspected such shifts had occurred for at least one of the percipients of the first Training Study and at least one of those of the second Training Study, but for a long while, I had not seen how to objectively test this rather than doing a purely post hoc analysis. I have now devised a more general test for the presence of ESP, assuming trans-temporal inhibition functions, which allows for the fact that a percipient might semiconsistently focus somewhat off from the real-time target and/or have a somewhat wider passband than just the designated target. The test works as follows.

If psi is operating and trans-temporal inhibition is present to some degree but the focus of a percipient's ESP is not necessarily on the real-time target, we will assume that it is nevertheless more likely to be focused *close* to the real-time target than distantly from it. Consider the plot of scoring for all possible temporal displacements shown for a typical significant percipient, $P_1$, in Figure 6.16. Here, we can see the typical high scoring on real-time hits, the significant

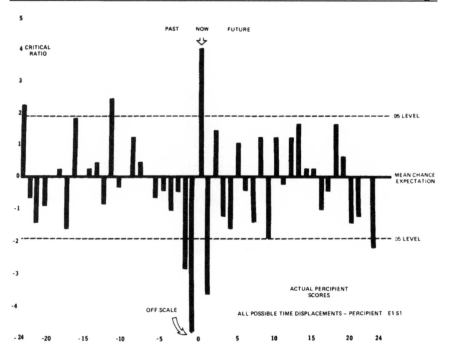

**Figure 6.16** Mean of all possible temporal displacements within a run for percipient $P_1$.

missing on +1 future hits, and the significant avoidance of the -1 and -2 immediately past targets discussed earlier. Since the past displacement registers contain a lot of psychological avoidance of past targets due to people's gross underestimation of the probability of the same target coming up twice in a row, effects there are contaminated by this psychological factor rather than being due to ESP. In general, however, you can see that once you get away from the significant scoring clustered right around real time, you have a random assortment of positive and negative hit scores that are statistically insignificant. Only one distant deviation score on the precognition side reaches the .05 level of significance, for example, which is of no significance given that 24 tests were done on precognitive deviations here. To formally test the focusing of real-time hitting and trans-temporal inhibition around the real-time origin, I took as a contrast measure the first four temporal registers, the real-time, +1, +2, and +3 precognitive scoring registers. Within these four registers, I created a contrast score for each percipient by taking the absolute magnitude of the difference between the highest (usually a hitting) Z-score and the lowest (usually a missing) Z-score. For most percipients, this meant the difference between real-time hits and +1 misses, but for a few, this was the +1 precognitive hits minus the -2 precognitive misses, and so forth. As a control for each percipient, I randomly selected (using my Texas Instrument SR-SIA calculator's random number program) four other precognitive registers from the remaining +4 to +24 precognitive registers of that percipient and computed a control contrast score between the highest and lowest of these four registers. If ESP and trans-temporal inhibition effects are concentrated on or near real time, the desired focus of attention, then the control contrast scores we compute from the registers further away from real time should, in general, be less. The results support this prediction.

In the first Training Study, the mean contrast score, in Z-score units, was 6.90 around the real-time focus, while the control contrast score had a mean of only 1.96. This difference is highly significant: t = 3.13, P < .01, one-tailed. The significance comes from both the high scores per se being above chance expectation (t = 2.80, P < .025, one-tailed), and the low scores per se being below chance expectation (t = 3.09, P < .01, one-tailed). In the second Training Study, the contrast scores are again significant, with a mean contrast score of 2.76 in real-time and adjacent registers, compared with a mean contrast score of 1.76 in the control registers: t = 3.37, P < .01, one-tailed. The significance here is contributed primarily by the high scores in the experimental versus control registers.

We have an interesting result then. The overall data of the second Training Study were not independently significant for real-time hitting (Z = +.85) by conventional scoring, because the data of a strong ESP misser balanced out the data of a strong ESP hitter. This study was statistically significant, however, when evaluated by contrast scores. The real-time ESP misser who wiped out the significance on overall real-time hits was a percipient who may very well have been inadvertently focused on the +1 future target: the difference between +1 hits and +2 misses is independently significant by a post hoc t-test for him. I hope then that this contrast measure may serve to find evidence of ESP in many experiments that were initially considered failures in terms of overall hitting. Insofar as trans-spatial inhibition is real, similar relationships between hitting and missing contrasts should be looked for in existing data: studies using playing cards in the DT mode (cards remain in pack, percipient calls "Down Through"), for example, call for the strong sort of spatial discrimination that might call for trans-spatial inhibition.

## Conclusions

The major mystery about various kinds of ESP is how the information gets from the target to the percipient; once the percipient has "received" or "sensed" the information on some nonconscious level, it generally seems to be processed in psychologically familiar ways.[22] Trans-temporal inhibition is a general information-processing procedure that is psychologically and neurologically familiar: the puzzle is in the precognitive (and postulated postcognitive) acquisition of the information about immediate future (and immediate past) targets.

Further data on these effects would be very desirable. Although emphasis of teaching improved ESP skills in our two studies made the provision of immediate feedback necessary, one clear line of research to follow, once percipients have been brought up to high levels of performance, is elimination of the feedback, so the postulated postcognitive inhibition component can be assessed independently of effects of maladaptive guessing habits. Further work on deliberately shifting the focus of attention, as with Swann, is also needed. If the trans-temporal inhibition effect is validated, it ought to be possible to combine it with an information theory approach to optimize ESP performance. Would long-time intervals between trials, for example, make real-time ESP more successful by reducing interference from future and past targets? Is comparing the contrast between real-time hitting and +1 future missing a better measure of a percipient's *potential* ESP capacity than hitting per se?

I plan considerable more analysis of the microstructure of the already collected data and will, if funds become available, carry out further research along the lines suggested above. I hope others will investigate this fascinating new effect.

## Summary

During exploratory retrospective analyses of the data of a highly successful experiment on teaching real-time ESP ability through the provision of immediate feedback of results, extremely strong, below chance *missing* of the immediately future target was found—a precognitive ESP effect. This avoidance of the future was highly correlated with the magnitude of the real-time ESP used: the more real-time ESP hitting, the more the immediate future was avoided. These results are consistent with a theory of another dimension of the mind, the duration of whose *experienced present* includes times that, to ordinary consciousness, are past and future. Tapping into this other mental dimension is not useful for using real-time ESP per se, for past and future information constitute noise. *Trans-temporal inhibition,* a type of edge detection process extending over time, enhances detection of the desired real-time ESP information by actively suppressing the ESP-derived information about the immediate past and future (postcognition and precognition). An initial experimental test of one of the implications of the theory, shifting of the areas of inhibition by change of psychological focus, further supports the theory. A relatively universal information-sharpening technique thus seems to be employed in using ESP.

## Notes

1. R. Rao, *Experimental Parapsychology* (Springfield, Ill.: Charles C. Thomas, 1966) is an excellent survey of experimental work in parapsychology, although a little dated. The recent *Handbook of Parapsychology,* ed. B. Wolman, L. Dale, G. Schmeidler,

and M. Ullman (New York: Van Nostrand Rheinhold, 1978), is the authoritative review work now. R. White, ed., *Surveys in Parapsychology: Reviews of the Literature, with Updated Bibliographies* (Metuchen, N.J.: Scarecrow Press, 1976) updates the Rao book.

2. J. G. Pratt, "The Meaning of Performance Curves in ESP and PK Test Data," *Journal of Parapsychology* 13 (1949): 9–22; and J. B. Rhine, *The Reach of the Mind* (New York: Sloane, 1947), pp. 189–90.

3. C. Tart, "Card Guessing Tests: Learning Paradigm or Extinction Paradigm?" *Journal of the American Society for Psychical Research* 60 (1966): 46–55.

4. C. Tart, "Conscious Control of Psi through Immediate Feedback Training: Some Considerations of Internal Processes," *Journal of the American Society for Psychical Research* 71 (1977): 375–408.

5. C. Tart, *Learning to Use Extrasensory Perception* (Chicago: University of Chicago Press, 1976). The research reported in this book was generously supported by the Parapsychology Foundation, with administrative assistance from the Institute for the Study of Human Knowledge.

6. This second study by myself, John Palmer, Dana Redington, Henry Bennett, and my students was supported by a generous grant from the est Foundation. C. Tart, J. Palmer, and D. Redington, "Effects of Immediate Feedback on ESP Performance: a Second Study," *Journal of the American Society for Psychical Research* (in press).

7. Tart, *Learning to Use Extrasensory Perception,* op. cit., and work in press by Tart et al., op. cit.

8. Tart, *Learning to Use Extrasensory Perception,* op. cit.

9. Ibid.

10. Rao, op. cit., and White, ed., op. cit.

11. G. Schmeidler, and R. McConnell, *ESP and Personality Patterns* (New Haven, Conn.: Yale University Press, 1958); and J. Palmer, "Scoring in ESP Tests as a Function of Belief in ESP, pt. 1. The Sheep–goat Effect," *Journal of the American Society for Psychical Research* 65 (1971): 373–408. See also J. Palmer, "Scoring in ESP Tests as a Function of Belief in ESP, pt. 2, Beyond the Sheep–goat Effect," *Journal of the American Society for Psychical Research* 66 (1972): 1–26.

12. Rao, op. cit.

13. S. Siegel, *Nonparametric Statistics for the Behavioral Sciences* (New York: McGraw-Hill, 1956).

14. E. André, "Confirmation of PK Action on Electronic Equipment," *Journal of Parapsychology* 36 (1972): 283–93; W. Braud et al., "Psychokinetic Influence on Random Number Generators during the Evocation of 'Analytic' versus 'Nonanalytic' Modes of Information Processing," in *Research in Parapsychology 1975,* ed. J. Morris, W. Roll, and R. Morris (Metuchen, N.J.: Scarecrow Press, 1976), pp. 85–88; C. Honorton and W. Barksdale, "PK Performance with Waking Suggestions for Muscle Tension versus Relaxation," *Journal of the American Society for Psychical Research* 66 (1972): 208–14; F. Matas and L. Pantas, "A PK Experiment Comparing Meditating versus Nonmeditating Subjects," *Proceedings of the Parapsychological Association,* No. 8

(1971): 12–13; B. Millar and R. Broughton, "A Preliminary PK Experiment with a Novel Computer-Linked High Speed Random Number Generator," in Morris, Roll, and Morris, eds., pp. 83–84; H. Schmidt, "A PK Test with Electronic Equipment," *Journal of Parapsychology* 34 (1970): 175–81; H. Schmidt, "PK Tests with a High-Speed Random Number Generator," *Journal of Parapsychology* 37 (1973) 105–18; H. Schmidt, "Observations of Subconscious PK Effects with and without Time Displacement," in *Research in Parapsychology,* ed. J. Morris, W. Roll, and R. Morris (Metuchen, N.J.: Scarecrow Press, 1975), pp. 116–21; H. Schmidt, "PK Experiment with Repeated Time Displaced Feedback," in Morris, Roll, and Morris, eds., op. cit., pp. 107–9; H. Schmidt and L. Pantas, "Psi Tests with Internally Different Machines," *Journal of Parapsychology* 36 (1972): 222–32, R. Stanford and C. Fox, "An Effect of Release of Effort in a Psychokinetic Task," in Morris, Roll, and Morris, eds., op. cit., pp. 61–63; and R. Stanford et al., "Psychokinesis as Psi-Mediated Instrumental Response," *Journal of the American Society for Psychical Research* 69 (1975): 127–34.

15. C. Tart, "Space, Time, and Mind" (Presidential Address, Parapsychological Association, 1977), in *Research in Parapsychology 1977,* ed. W. Roll (Metuchen, N.J.: Scarecrow Press, 1978), pp. 197–250; C. Tart, "Randomicity, Predictability, and Mathematical Inference Strategies in ESP Feedback Training Situations," *Journal of the American Society for Psychical Research* (in press); and C. Tart and E. Dronek, "Trying to Profit from Non-Randomicity in ESP Target Sequences: Initial Explorations with the Probabilistic Predictor Program," submitted for publication.

16. Rao, op. cit.; Wolman et al., eds., op. cit.; and White, ed., op. cit.

17. C. Tart, *States of Consciousness* (New York: Dutton, 1975).

18. G. von Békésy, *Sensory Inhibition* (Princeton, N.J.: Princeton University Press, 1967).

19. Tart, *States of Consciousness,* op. cit.

20. Rao, op. cit.; Wolman et al., eds., op. cit.; and White, ed., op. cit.

21. R. Targ and H. Puthoff, *Mind-Reach: Scientists Look at Psychic Ability* (New York: Delacorte, 1977); and G. Schmeidler, "PK Effects upon Continuously Recorded Temperature," *Journal of the American Society for Psychical Research* 67 (1973): 325–40.

22. C. Tart, *Psi: Scientific Studies of the Psychic* (New York: Dutton, 1977).

# Introduction to Chapter 7

In the field of parapsychology, data pertaining to three general classes of perception are studied. These are telepathy, which is mind-to-mind communication; clairvoyance, which is the real-time direct perception, without the intermediary of another mind, of an object or event hidden from the ordinary senses; and precognition, which is the perception of a future event that could not be known through rational inference. Of these three phenomena, it is possible, surprisingly enough, that contemporary physics will find the least trouble in assimilating precognition. The reason for this has to do with the following: in physics, it is recognized that "causality," the apparent generation of future events out of earlier causes, is a fact observed in our lives or in the laboratory, but it is not necessarily a law of the universe. For example, a lead article in *Science* by Benjamin Gal-Or raised the issue in the following way:

> Is the origin of (time) irreversibility . . . local or cosmological? Is it in the laws or in the boundary conditions? What might be the physical inter-relationships underlying information theory, and the electromagnetic, biological and statistical arrows of time? What is the basic nature of the somewhat mysterious time coordinate system in which the very physical laws are embedded?[1]

The conclusion of Gal-Or, along with a number of others, is that "time irreversibility," the apparently inexorable flow of events from past to future, but not in reverse, appears to be more "factlike" than "lawlike." This is somewhat like recognizing that our planet happens to be 8,000 miles in diameter: a fact, yes; a law governing planetary size, no.

O. Costa de Beauregard agrees with the author of that article in his conclusion that irreversibility appears to be more factlike than lawlike. Therefore, although information is usually observed to propagate from the present to the future, we should not be shaken to our foundations if experiments are devised that show that sometimes information is found to be conveyed in the other direction. Indeed, the equations of physics contain discarded solutions that correspond to just this case and thus suggest models of the type presented here.

For example, Stratton's graduate text, *Electromagnetic Theory*, describes the choice of solutions for the equations of a moving charge as follows.[2] (These equations give two real solutions, one of which is conventionally discarded as not corresponding to any physical observable.)

> The reader has doubtless noted that the choice of the function f (t + r/v) is highly arbitrary, since the field equation admits also a solution f (t - r/v). This function leads obviously to an advanced time, implying that the field can be observed *before* it has been generated by the source. The familiar chain of cause and effect is thus reversed and this alternative solution might be discarded as logically inconceivable. However the application of "logical" causality principles offers very insecure footing in matters such as these and we shall do better to restrict the theory to retarded action solely on the grounds that this solution alone conforms to the present physical data.

In this chapter, Costa de Beauregard addresses such issues. He reminds us of the defining relationship between entropy decrease and information increase—the interplay between biological systems as sources of negative entropy and advanced waves as carriers of information.

In a recent article, Costa de Beauregard summarized his position as follows:

> What would the phenomenology of advanced waves, decreasing probability, and information-as-organizing-power look like? Exactly to what parapsychologists call precognition and/or psychokinesis. Logically these phenomena should show up no less than thermodynamic progressing fluctuations—which indeed they are. Consciousness has two faces symmetric to each other: cognizance and will. Both should show up in the quantal measurement process.[3]

## About the Author

**O. Costa de Beauregard,** Ph.D., is a Professor of Physics and the Director of Research at the National Center for Scientific Research in Paris. His training and research interests have been mainly in special relativity and quantum mechanics, with an interest in the role of consciousness in physics. His books include *Precis of Special Relativity, La Theorie de la Relativite Restreinte, Precis dé Mecánique Quantique Relativiste, La Notion de Temps, Equivalence avec l'Espace,* and *Le Second Principe de la Science du Temps.*

# 7

# Quantum Paradoxes and Aristotle's Twofold Information Concept
## O. Costa de Beauregard

The endeavor to solve the difficult problem of properly interpreting quantum mechanics, which I am presenting in this chapter, has a long personal history behind it—the history of a struggle to understand the relationship between mind and matter, first in the context of the theory of special relativity, then in the context of the theory of probability and statistical mechanics, and finally, in the context of quantum mechanics, mainly in its relativistic expression. This long voyage might well be termed the story of a rational conversion to parapsychology. The central illumination of it consisted in the abrupt awareness that the cybernetic interpretation of *negentropy* as *information,* with the two symmetrical procedures of gaining knowledge by decoding a message (that is, an ordered structure) *and* of emitting a message (that is, producing order) by means of one's *information,* was merely a technical restatement of what Aristotle had said long ago. Information is a two-faced medal: *cognitive awareness* on one side, *volitive awareness* on the other.

The point is, of course, that these two faces of conscious awareness—or should we say *and also,* with quite a few philosophers and biologists, of *subconscious* awareness—are coupled to matter. *Information* is *negentropy; entropy* is the logarithm of a *probability;* thus, probability is neither objective nor

This chapter was first published in *Quantum Physics and Parapsychology,* published in 1975 by the Parapsychology Foundation, Inc., and is reprinted here by permission of the author and the copyright owner, the Parapsychology Foundation, Inc.

subjective: it is *indissolubly objective and subjective, being the hinge around which mind and matter are interacting.*

Thus, the intrinsic symmetry between the two facets of Aristotle's information—*cognition* and *volition,* in a broad sense—is tightly bound to corresponding symmetries in the real world. Gain in knowledge is coupled to a production of external entropy, that is also, as we shall see, coupled to the emission of retarded waves. Symmetrically, an ordering or volitive act is coupled to a destruction of external entropy, which is also coupled to an absorption of advanced waves. Such statements receive a very clear formulation in that highly specific blending of wave theory and of probability theory that quantum mechanics truly is. In this way, the otherwise abstract association of causality with gain in knowledge on one side and of finality with volition on the other finds itself dressed in lively attire. We can imagine with Leibniz (but *not* in deterministic style) of the universe as containing myriads of (conscious or subconscious) monads exchanging *information* by means of quantized waves.

Having come to these views some time ago, I was keeping them for myself, only letting the interested reader guess all about it by reading between the written lines, as we say in French. Then suddenly, the old Einstein-Podolsky-Rosen (EPR) paradox[4]—which is also the Einstein,[5] Schrödinger,[6] and Renninger[7] paradox—suddenly came to the center of the quantum speculations, mainly by the efforts of Bohm,[8] Bell,[9] Shimony,[10] d'Espagna,[11] and others. Resolving this paradox, together with one or two other ones, Schrödinger's cat paradox,[12] and Wigner's friend paradox,[13] became an international nightmare. At this point, I decided I had something to say and that I should dive right into the froggy pool. I have by now dived in it quite a few times, with the result that—thanks to the seemingly unsolvable EPR paradox—I was not "thrown out, as I would have been only five years ago," as a U.S. physicist put it. Another one said, "If your intention was to show that all the well-known quantum paradoxes can be reduced to one, then certainly you have succeeded." According to a British physicist, my thesis is "very logical," this perhaps implying (I really do not know) that it is schizophrenic.

So let us proceed.

My starting point along this line of thought occurred in 1951 when I suddenly said to myself: If *you* truly believe in Minkowski's space-time—and *you* know you have to—then you *must* think of the relationship between mind and matter not at one universal or Newtonian instant but *in space-time.* If, by the very necessity of relativistic covariance, matter is time extended as it is space extended, then, again by necessity, awareness in a broad sense must also be time extended.

Of course, we know that our conscious awareness is tightly bound to the present. Bergson is very interesting when analyzing this fact. But then, and with Bergson, it is only natural to conceive consciousness as somewhat similar to the focalization of a *subconsciousness* that is time extended, toward the past of course, but *why not also toward the future?* Then it suddenly flashed in my mind that precognition, flashing into consciousness out of subconsciousness, but seemingly floating like a mirage above the horizon, without a solid connection to the general landscape, was not something irrational. Quite the contrary, it was something that should be expected according to the relativistic concept of space-time. Precognition, in this context, should look very much like the intuitions one occasionally gets when leisurely probing into a logically constructed treatise beyond the point reached by one's methodical and attentive study. This again is very Bergsonian, as for Bergson, *consciousness* is *attention to life.*

That consciousness goes ahead through space-time, like one's methodical study goes ahead through the thickness of a written book, is of course commonplace in relativity theory. But one is entitled to ask *why* consciousness, or attention to life, is in fact bound to thus proceed. Boltzmann, in his famous "Treatise on Statistical Mechanics," here makes a striking guess.[14] He argues that according to Loschmidt's and Zermelo's well-known paradoxes, there may well be in the universe just as many entropy-decreasing as there are entropy-increasing evolutions.[15] Such a statement obviously implies that all physical evolutions are conceived as time extended, as in relativity theory. Let us denote these two classes by $F$ and $C$, respectively. Boltzmann's guess is that both in the $F$ and the $C$ class, the biological time of living entities is bound to go up and not down the entropy curve. Therefore, these two collections of living beings are exploring the time dimension in opposite directions. It is hard to conceive how they could exchange information.[16] Of course, as the physical arrows of increasing entropy and of retarded waves are one and the same, retarded waves are opposite to each other in the $F$ and the $C$ regions.

In its original form, the Boltzmann apologue is hardly reconcilable with what we presently know of the universe, but the essence of the argument retains its flagrancy. We just have to think of two time-symmetrical points with respect to the "initial" cusp of the evolutionary curve of an expanding universe or else of two points near opposite ends of an arc of the curve of an oscillating universe.

Finally, as information theory tells us that knowledge must be gained at the expense of a preexisting negentropy, if we just postulate that on the whole, knowing awareness prevails over willing awareness, we conclude that the biological arrow is de facto (if perhaps not de jure) directed along, rather than against, the arrow of entropy increase and of wave retardation.[17]

The next step of my rational pilgrimage through physics toward parapsychology was as follows.

All recent analyses of physical irreversibility by many physicists and/or philosophers of science, including me, have shown that the irreversibility principle is of the nature of a boundary condition rather than of an elementary law of motion.[18] It states in the realm of either statistical mechanics or the theory of waves that *on the macroscopic level,* one is de facto (if not de jure) allowed only to integrate the equations (the so-called master equation, or the wave equation) by using an initial condition; it is forbidden to do so by using a final condition. Well-known facts are expressed in this way. Nobody relies on shuffling cards to put a deck of cards in order, or by dipping a pipette into a glassful of mixed water and ink, one should not hope to have thus induced the ink to concentrate at the right point, so that the pipette could suck it. Such is the familiar situation prevailing inside a causalistic, or Carnot-style, universe, whereas, of course, the reverse would occur in a finalistic, or anti-Carnot universe. To see how things would look in the paradoxical, anti-Carnot universe, one has just to run backward any movie film. The result is, in almost every respect, fantastic.

To speak, as we have done, of a causalistic or of a finalistic universe is facile but not quite right. As previously said, we should rather speak of the causalistic *versus* the finalistic *direction* along which our awareness is exploring space-time. To this, we will come back at length.

Now I stress the logical connection existing between the two arrows of entropy increase and of wave retardation. For instance, if, between time instants $t_1$ and $t_2$, a physicist moves a piston in the wall of a vessel containing a gas in equilibrium, Maxwell's velocity distribution will be disturbed after time $t_2$, not before time $t_1$. Moreover, the disturbance is emitted as a retarded pressure wave, not absorbed as an advanced pressure wave.

It is in the realm of quantum mechanics—a theory where concepts of both probability and waves are inherent—that the connection is concisely expressible. A mere rewording of von Neumann's celebrated proof of the irreversibility of the measurement process (implying his ensembles and his definition of entropy) shows that entropy increase and integration by retarded waves go hand in hand.[19] In a more literary form, the statement is as follows: while, as is well known, retarded waves are used in quantum mechanics for statistical prediction, symmetrically, as stated by Fock and by Watanabe, advanced waves should be used for statistical retrodiction.[20] Thus, to say that *macroscopically speaking,* blind statistical retrodiction is forbidden or that advanced waves are nonexistent is merely two different wordings for one and the same statement.

Let us now come back to information. Decoding a message is a *learning transition,* where knowledge $I$ is extracted from a preexisting negentropy, or macroscopic order N, according to the scheme

$$N \rightarrow I$$

where de facto (if not de jure)

$$N \geq I.$$

This is one face of Aristotle's information as rediscovered by cybernetics, and it is an extremely trivial one.[21] One buys a newspaper to get *information* from it. And one need not buy it for the advertisements, which go straight into the wastebasket. Retarded waves and entropy-increasing evolutions are cascading everywhere, and most of them are not even used as information sources. This is a cybernetical rewording of Carnot's and Clausius' irreversibility principle.

The other face of Artistotle's information is far more recondite. It is in fact in private use by those few philosophers interested in will and in finality. It shows itself in the ordering or willing transition, where a preexisting conceptual scheme is used for producing macroscopic order, for instance, for sending a message, according to the scheme

$$I \rightarrow N$$

where, de facto (if not de jure)

$$I \geq N.$$

Why this second facet of Aristotle's information has fallen into general oblivion is a corollary of the de facto situation we are living in, where retarded waves outweigh by far advanced waves, or, in other words, where more probable complexions are coming out of less probable ones rather than the reverse. Looking at things from the subjectivistic side, we thus see that the willing transition $I \rightarrow N$ is as rare and hard to obtain as the learning transition $N \rightarrow I$ is common and easy. The social cost of the process is reflected in the high wages of workmanship or technical competence.

But perhaps the more subtle aspect of the reason for generally overlooking the second Aristotelian aspect of information is the following one. As we have said, increasing probabilities and causality go hand in hand, and so do causality and learning awareness. All this is the general trend around us. Trying to understand and analyze finality when looking from this side is simply hopeless, precisely because finality is as obvious to willing awareness as causality is to learning awareness. Practically, this means that if we are to uncover the rare and recondite instances of anti-Carnot processes, we must by necessity have recourse to an antipassive observational approach.

It is the duty of fundamental research to explore the consequences of the de jure symmetries existing in the mathematical formalism, which may well be hidden by large factlike asymmetries. A famous example of this is the experimental discovery of the positron by Anderson in 1932. The positron was mathematically present in the formalism of the Dirac equation—in exact symmetry to the electron. It turned out that though extremely rare (at least in the part of the universe we are living in), the positron really exists nevertheless. It is a member of a whole family of antiparticles, each mathematically implied by the corresponding particle.

Could it not be that advanced wave processes,[22] that is, probability-decreasing processes,[23] which mathematically duplicate the trivial retarded waves and probability-increasing processes, though de facto very rare, or at least not trivially producible, nevertheless exist around us? Putting the question is begging the answer. *Of course,* they do exist; they must be at work in the very heart of biological phylogenesis and ontogenesis, not to speak of human activity. Of course, it is well known that those scientists more inclined toward operational reasoning than toward fundamental thinking have pointed out long ago, and are presently developing as an elaborate formalism, the de facto true idea that the order-producing evolutions are growing like parasites on the universal order-destroying evolution, from which they are sucking their information. This is an excellent remark—provided one does not stay at it, because, then the big question remains: "Whence does the initial information come out of which the universal negentropy is cascading?" So let us not brush the dust under the rug, and let us face the fundamental question.

At this point, quantum mechanics has something significant to say.

In classical statistical mechanics, the occurrence of stochastic events was postulated without much discussion. In quantum mechanics, however, the mathematical formalism is so tight that it leaves no room for letting in the stochastic event without a very specific assumption. As emphasized by von Neumann and by London and Bauer one hardly sees any other possible issue than postulating that the stochastic event, or *quantal transition,* or *collapse of the wave function* is induced by an act of consciousness on the observer's part.[24] This is a very explicit statement concerning the subjective *and* objective character of the sort of probability that is involved.

This entails two important consequences that have not been stated up to now. The first one pertains to the coupling existing between different observers of the same quantal transition. If all of these observers are equally entitled to collapse the wave function, then all of them are bound together through the act of observation. *They must either cooperate or compete for producing the result.* Thus, even the learning transition is not so passive as it might have seemed at first; it may very well contain an active connotation. This is not surprising, since an *individual* stochastic event does not distinguish between retarded and advanced waves and it is entirely describable by means of (relativistically covariant) propagators.

The second consequence is tightly bound to the preceding one. It states that acts of will are de jure symmetrical to acts of cognizance, that is, that under appropriate circumstances, information as an organizing power should act as a sink of advanced waves, just as information as a gain of knowledge acts as a source of retarded waves.

It remains, finally, to be shown that PK and telepathy are implied in the above statements.

In the Schrödinger cat paradox, the cat is in a box and will be either killed or left alive according to whether the decay electron of a radionuclide goes, or does not go, through a Geiger counter.[25] The amplifying device is of the usual sort, and the choice of the lethal weapon is left to the reader.

In ordinary statistical mechanics, the cat is already either dead (*D* state) or alive (*L* state) when the experimental biologist opens the box. In quantum mechanics, things are not so simple, if it is believed that it is the awareness of the observer, when opening the box, that collapses the wave function. Should we then say, according to the well-known rules of quantum mechanics, that after the atom has decayed but before the observer takes a look, the cat is in a superposition, or interference, state, of the form *aD* + *bL,* with $|a|^2$ and $|b|^2$ denoting the respective probabilities that the electron does or does not trigger the counter? This certainly looks very much like a student's joke.

The point is, however, that the first informed observer—and the one that is primarily interested in the issue—is the cat himself. *He* must be the principal collapser of the wave function. One guesses, moreover, that a normal cat will be in favor of the *L* issue, so that, using Aristotle's information in its recondite aspect, that is, calling from the past the appropriate advanced wave, he will incline the decay electron beside, rather than through, the Geiger counter. This is *blind statistical retrodiction* and a *probability-decreasing* process.

I need not say here that *precisely that* sort of experiment has been done many times by parapsychologists, not in the crude form of a death-or-life dilemma but in the more sadistic form of a punishment-or-reward experiment. H. Schmidt (see Chapter 9) has built to this end a random outcome generator governed by radioactivity, and he has found, with quite a few other experimentalists, that not only cats but also rats, and perhaps cockroaches, definitely favor rewards rather than punishment.[26]

*No better direct proof of the existence of anti-Carnot, or finality, processes could be given.*

Having thus solved, by a theoretical explanation that is experimentally verified, the main core of Schrödinger's paradox, we immediately face another paradox. What if no cat is inside the box? Will not the radionuclide decay according to the laws of probability?

As we have decided from the outset that *every* stochastic event requires an act of consciousness in a broad sense, we are essentially left with two possibilities. The first one is that the wave function is collapsed by the first macroscopic observer taking cognizance of what has happened, maybe ten years later, even if there is a clock registering at what time the nuclide has decayed. This is perhaps pushing one's faith in the existence of advanced waves too far.

The second way out of the problem is to postulate, with Leibniz, Bergson, and quite a few other thinkers, the existence of very many monads, or rudimentary psyches, inside the universe. If no cat is inside the box, one or the other of these many "monads" will collapse the wave function, according to the

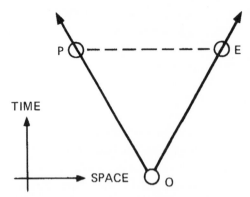

**Figure 7.1** The Einstein–Podolsky–Rosen paradox.

usual rules of blind statistical prediction, because they are not vitally concerned with the issue.

There remains, however, the possibility that the human experimentalist's consciousness does contribute to collapsing the wave function. This brings into the problem some sort of telepathy between the cat and his tormentor. This is the very sort of problem that is at stake in the EPR paradox we are considering now.

The EPR paradox was initially expressed in terms of nonrelativistic quantum mechanics;[27] however, it is in the framework of relativistic quantum mechanics that it assumes its full significance.

Let us, for instance, consider a positronium atom decaying around time $t = 0$ near the point $x = y = z = 0$, and suppose it is in a spin-0 state. Then, the decay electron and positron, which fly apart with opposite velocities, must have, according to the conservation law for angular momentum, opposite spins if their velocities are collinear. This statement makes no problem in classical statistical mechanics, where both spins are ordinary vectors, more precisely, *pseudo*vectors, but (as we shall see), it raises a serious problem in quantum mechanics.

One important point, however, needs to be made in the context of classical statistical mechanics. Suppose that observer $E$, observing the electron $e$, finds that its spin (which has been produced by a random event $O$ occurring near $x = y = z = t = 0$) is represented by the vector S. He is then sure that if another observer $P$, which may be operating far way from $E$, measures the spin of the decay positron $p$, he is bound to find that its value is -S. This is because of the conservation law *and* the information $E$ has pertaining to the initial event.

The question is, How is the inference drawn—or how is the information telegraphed—between $E$ and $P$? Is it directly along the (four-dimensional) vector $EP$, which may be taken to be spacelike and extremely large? This would violate Einstein's prohibition to telegraph outside the light cone.

The very mathematical formalism, however, shows that the inference is drawn not directly along $EP$ but along the two timelike vectors $EO$ and $OP$, forming a sort of Feynman zigzag. (See Figure 7.1.) By this statement, we are now violating Einstein's prohibition to telegraph into the past, but this prohibition is much less stringent than the former one, being of a factlike rather than a lawlike character. It does not hold at the level of a single random outcome, where quite the contrary, it is the de jure time symmetry of wave propagators that is enforced.

When leaving classical statistical mechanics and entering quantum mechanics, the sting of the EPR paradox becomes painful. Now, any two orthogonal components of the spin vector are no more simultaneously measurable, and both observers $E$ and $P$ are entitled to wait until the very last moment before deciding which component they will measure. In such circumstances, the quantum measurement is said to contribute in producing the answer, so that between observers $E$ and $P$, we do not have only *telediction* as before but also *teleaction*. The latter conclusion is the one that Einstein, Podolsky, and Rosen were ruling out as obviously absurd. But it is the one I must accept as the only one consistent with my overall philosophy. Moreover, it is a conclusion that can be experimentally tested in the form of parapsychological experiments.

Interest in the EPR paradox has now come to a climax due to the thinking of Bohm, Bell, and Shimony.[28] It has, of course, been known for a long time that the classical and the quantal stochastic formalisms, though similar in many respects, display some very specific differences that can in principle be tested. Bell has deduced the existence of such a testable difference in the case of spin measurements (or of polarization measurements for photons) in the EPR context. Quite a few recent experiments of this sort have been, or are being, done, the results of which are presently not consistent with each other.[29] So we must wait and see.

However, in a parapsychology colloquium, the most attractive suggestion is to undertake the EPR type of experiments with, as agents $E$ and $P$, not only impartial observers (as has been the case up to now) but also psychokinetic agents. Quite a few different combinations could then be tried.

Another famous quantal paradox is the paradox of Wigner's friend.[30] I will not delve into it here, because it borrows traits from both the preceding ones and, also, because the sort of experimentation one could do with it is not too obvious. Now let us conclude.

It is of the very nature of waves to produce distant correlations in space-time. The scientific analysis of these correlations has already uncovered two major discoveries: Einstein's relativity theory in 1905 and de Broglie's and Schrödinger's wave mechanics in 1925. I am submitting today that a third scientific revolution of comparable importance is implicit in the physics of waves.

It has been said that the relativity theory has lost the subject of the verb *to undulate*. If so, quantum mechanics, the legal heir of wave mechanics, has recovered it, and in a very unexpected form indeed. What is undulating through space-time is no longer the lost *ether*. It is the amplitude of a set of associated probabilities. Loosely speaking, it is *information*.

Now, according to Aristotle (the promoter of the concept) and to modern cyberneticists, *information* is a two-faced medal: one side is gain in knowledge, the other is power of organization, that is, will. Thus, information is the very hinge around which mind and matter are interacting.

As the quantized waves are information waves, they are potentially propagating through space-time Aristotle's de jure symmetry between cognition and will in the form of the de jure symmetry between retarded and advanced waves, which is also, as we have seen, of entropy-increasing and entropy-decreasing processes, of causality and of finality.

I need not say that if this is the true state of affairs, relativistic quantum mechanics is a conceptual scheme where phenomena such as PK or telepathy, far from being irrational, should, on the contrary, be expected as *very rational.* My thesis is that they are postulated by the very symmetries of the mathematical formalism and should be predicted for reasons completely akin to those that led Einstein to enunciate the principle of special relativity, de Broglie to produce the concept of matter waves, and Dirac to (almost) predict the positron.

Was it not Schrödinger who exposed witchcraft in the quantum paradoxes?

## Notes

1. B. Gal-Or, "The Crisis about the Origin of Irreversibility and Time Anisotropy," *Science* 176 (1972): 11–17.

2. J. Stratton, *Electromagnetic Theory* (New York: McGraw-Hill, 1941).

3. O. Costa de Beauregard, "S-Matrix, Feynman Zigzag, and Einstein Correlation," *Physics Letters* 67A (1978): 171–74.

4. A. Einstein, B. Podolsky, and N. Rosen, "Can Quantum-Mechanical Description of Physical Reality be Considered Complete?," *Physics Review* 47 (1935): 777.

5. A. Einstein, "Rapports et discussions de 5º Conseil SOLVAY," mimeographed (Paris: Gauthier Villars, 1928), pp. 253–56.

6. E. Schrödinger, *Naturwiss.* 23 (1935): 807, 823, 844.

7. M. Benninger, *Physiche Zeitschrift* 136 (1963): 251.

8. D. Bohm, *Quantum Theory* (Englewood Cliffs, N.J.: Prentice-Hall, 1951), chap. 22.

9. S. Bell, *Physics* 1 (1965): 195.

10. A. Shimony, in *Foundations of Quantum Mechanics,* ed. B. d'Espagnat (New York: Academic Press, 1971), pp. 182–94.

11. B. d'Espagnat, in d'Espagnat, ed., op. cit. pp. 84–96.

12. Schrödinger, op. cit.

13. E. P. Wigner, in d'Espagnat, ed., op. cit., pp. 1–19, especially pp. 14–19.

14. L. Boltzmann, *Vorlesungen Uber Gastheorie* (Leipzig: Barth, 1896), 2: 257–58.

15. J. Loschmidt, *Weiner Ber.* 73 (1896): 139, and 75 (1877): 67; and E. Zermelo, *Annals of Physics* 57 (1896): 585, and 59 (1896): 793.

16. N. Wiener, *Cybernetics* (Paris: Hermann, 1958), p. 45.

17. O. Costa de Beauregard, *Actes du Congrès Bergson* (Paris: Armand Colin, 1959), pp. 77–80.

18. The fundamental remark has been more or less implicitly made a very long time ago: it pertains to the use of Bayes' conditional probability formula in problems of retrodiction. See, for instance, J. W. Gibbs, *Elementary Principles of Statistical Mechanics* (New Haven, Conn.: Yale University Press, 1914), p. 150, or E. Borel, Le Hasard (Paris: Alcan, 1914), chap. 4. The first explicit statement that the statistical interpretation of the Second Law of Thermodynamics is a (temporally asymmetrical) application of Bayes' principle is by J. D. van der Waals, *Physik. Z.* 12 (1911): 547.

Very thorough discussions of the overall problem, stressing different aspects of it, and all compatible with each other (except possibly for minor points), have been made by E. N. Adams, W. Büchel, A. Grünbaum, G. N. Lewis, G. Ludwig, J. A. McLennan, H. Mehlberg, P. Penrose and I. C. Percival, H. Reichenbach, E. Schrödinger, J. P. Terletsky, S. Watanabe, C. von Weiszäcker, Y. Wu and D. Rivier, M. M. Yanase, and this writer. Most of these references are given in O. Costa de Beauregard, *Studium Generale* 24 (1971): 10.

19. von Neumann, *Mathematical Foundations of Quantum Mechanics* (Princeton, N.J.: Princeton University, 1955).

20. V. Fock, *Dokl. Akad. Nauk SSSR* 60 (1948): 1157; and S. Watanabe, *Rev. Mod. Phys.* 27 (1955): 179.

21. O. Costa de Beauregard, *Dialectica* 22 (1968): 187.

22. L. Fantappie, *Teoria Unitaria del Mondo Fisico e Biologico* (Rome: Humanitas Nova, 1944).

23. H. Bergson, *Creative Evolution* (New York: Random House, 1944), chap. 3.

24. von Neumann, op. cit.; and F. London and E. Bauer, *La Théorie de l'Observation en Mécanique Quantique* (Paris: Hermann, 1939).

25. Schrödinger, op. cit.

26. For the state of the art as it stood in 1971, see Shimony, op. cit. More recent experiments that have been done, or are in progress, are those of S. J. Freedman, Ph.D. diss., University of California-Berkeley, 1972 (unpublished) (see also S. J. Freedman and J. F. Clauser, "Experimental Test of Local Hidden Variables," *Physical Review Letters* 14 [April 1972]: 938); R. A. Holt, Ph. D. diss., Harvard University, 1973 (unpublished); G. Faraci et al., *Nuovo Cimento Lett.* 9 (1974): 607.

27. Einstein, Podolsky, and Rosen, op. cit.

28. Bohm, op. cit.; Bell, op. cit.; and Shimony, op. cit.

29. See Shimony, op. cit.; Freedman, op. cit; Freedman and Clauser, op. cit.; Holt, op. cit.; and Faraci et al., op. cit.

30. Wigner, op. cit.

# Introduction to Chapter 8

One of the common objections to the existence of psi functioning is that it would seem to be in conflict with our present scientific understanding of how the universe works. There are, however, a growing number of physicists who hold a contrary view, namely, that in all probability, psi data will be accounted for either within the framework of physics as presently understood or within the framework of extrapolations that have been proposed to account for other (nonpsi) data. If this viewpoint turns out to be correct, we could anticipate that not only would present scientific knowledge contribute to an understanding of psi phenomena but that the psi data base would, in return, contribute to the solution of some of the current problems in physics, for example, with regard to the foundations of quantum theory or the nature of time (see Chapter 7).

Although one might be tempted to consider that such a rapprochement between physics and psi would "explain away" psi phenomena, it is more likely that the expansion of present-day scientific concepts to include what is now paraconceptual will simply lead to a more mature science. This is the goal toward which the scientific pursuit of psi strives. If that goal is reached, the observations of psi will have been assimilated into an expanded scientific world view, and our understanding of both psi and science will have been increased accordingly. It is by this time-honored route that the observations of astrology and alchemy led to the science of astronomy and chemistry.

One hypothesis that has been put forward by Michael Persinger and others is that some instances of apparent psi phenomena may be mediated by ELF electromagnetic waves, a proposal that does not seem to be ruled out by any obvious physical or biological facts. In some cases, ELF radiation would seem to provide a carrier mechanism for information transfer; in other cases, ELF radiation might act as a source of triggered correlations between the mentations of individuals isolated from each other. While psi phenomena en masse would seem to defy an explanation in conventional electromagnetic terms, in

this chapter, Persinger addresses those areas that may well yield to such an interpretation. His proposals are especially interesting in light of the developing evidence for a variety of physical and mental effects on humans and animals
caused by low-level electromagnetic radiation.

## About the Author

**Michael A. Persinger,** Ph.D., is an Associate Professor of Psychology at
Laurentian University in Ontario, Canada. Dr. Persinger has published numerous technical articles in scientific journals on the subjects of physiological psychology, neurobiology, anatomy, biometeorology, psychopharmacology, and
the experimental analysis of behavior, as well as parapsychology. His books
include *ELF and VLF Electromagnetic Field Effects, The Paranormal, Part I:
Patterns, The Paranormal, Part II: Mechanisms and Models,* and (with Gyslaine
Lafreniere) *Space-Time Transients and Unusual Events.* His primary research
interests in addition to the paranormal involve the behavioral and biological
effects of electromagnetic fields and waves.

# 8

# ELF Field Mediation in Spontaneous Psi Events: Direct Information Transfer or Conditioned Elicitation?

Michael A. Persinger

An essential problem for parapsychologists concerned with telepathy–clairvoyance (T–C) is the isolation and experimental simulation of the mechanism by which information traverses some point A to some point B without using conventional sense modes or stimulus sources. One approach to this problem assumes natural physical mechanisms are involved and that the apparent operations of T–C only appear to violate bioenvironmental principles because of inadequate data availability or failure to clearly describe the phenomenon in an objective manner. Since alleged T–C involves long distances and opaque boundaries between the putative agent and percipient, the basic natural mechanisms that satisfy the conditions of a T–C mediator candidate are limited.[1] Several experimenters [2, 5, 7, 10, 17] have suggested naturally produced ELF electric and magnetic fields as one means by which T–C information could be generated;[2] other geophysical sources would be included conceptually within this format.[3]

## General ELF Electromagnetic Characteristics

ELF electromagnetic field waves and impulses occupy the frequency band between 3 Hz and 3 kHz, while ultra low frequency (ULF) electromagnetic phenomena (< 3Hz) occupy adjacent wave bands.[4] Persinger, Ludwig, and Ossenkopp suggest that the ELF range should include time-varying electric, magnetic, or electromagnetic phenomena ranging between .01 Hz and 100 Hz, since this range overlaps with major time-varying electromagnetic-chemical processes in living systems.[5] There are myriad forms of natural ELF electromagnetic events. Some general forms of ELF electromagnetic phenomena are shown in Figure 8.1; other examples have been published elsewhere.[6]

Complex ELF electromagnetic field-wave patterns are generated by, or associated with, a large variety of geophysical and meteorological events. Geomagnetic storms may produce prolonged periods or trains of ELF oscillations, called *pearls, hydromagnetic emissions,* or *PC 1 variations,*[7] with amplitudes rarely more than $10^{-9}$ Tesla (T) or 1 $\gamma$. These oscillations are associated with perturbations in the geomagnetic flux lines and may involve large areas in the order of $10^6$ km². However, almost identical signals can occur simultaneously at stations with conjugate locations involving much larger distances. More diffuse agitations can occur globally during geomagnetic storms.

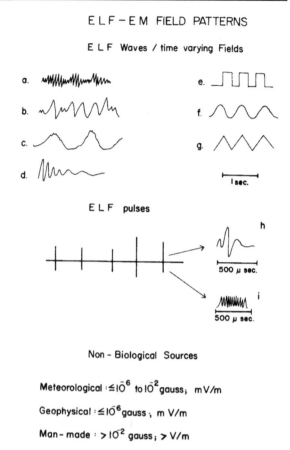

Figure 8.1 A few examples of different extremely low frequency (ELF) electromagnetic field patterns. Forms a to d represent natural patterns according to Konig (H. L. Konig, "Physical Characteristics of ELF and VLF Signals," in *ELF and VLF Electromagnetic Field Effects,* ed. M. A. Persinger [New York: Plenum Press, 1974], pp. 8–34), while forms e to g indicate typical manmade productions. Type h illustrates higher frequency carriers of ELF pulses.

ELF electric and magnetic field fluctuations are associated with local (in the order of $10^3$ to $10^4$ km²) weather conditions as well. According to Konig, peak wave modes occur around 3 to 6 Hz and .5 Hz with strong harmonic contents.[8] The temporal processes of these waves are usually irregular, with durations lasting often more than one hour. Values of over 10 V/m are frequently recorded during active periods, although 100 mV/m and $10^{-6}$T (in the air)

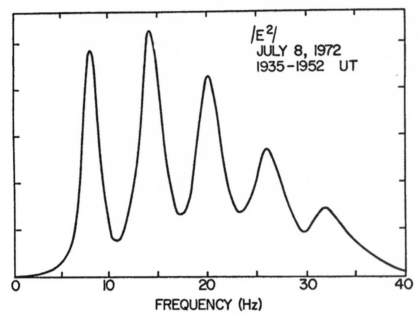

$$|E^2|$$
JULY 8, 1972
1935–1952  UT

FREQUENCY (Hz)

**Figure 8.2** Sample power spectra for Schumann resonance frequencies (from H. L. Konig, "Physical Characteristics of ELF and VLF Signals," in *ELF and VLF Electromagnetic Field Effects,* ed. M. A. Persinger [New York: Plenum Press, 1974], pp. 8–34).

amplitudes are median values. These waves could be recorded at all times with no obvious day-night differences. Conditions of low-lying clouds appear to favor these ELF signals, at least in the Bavarian region.

One special form of ELF waves has been called the *Schumann resonances,* which may be explained in terms of "standing waves" that occur in the earth-ionosphere cavity as a result of extremely low attenuation at ELF frequencies. A sample power spectra is shown in Figure 8.2. The basic Schumann frequency occurs around 7 to 8 Hz with $10^{-9}$T and .1 mV/m (distant field) components. Harmonies around 14.1, 20.3, 26.4, and 32.5 Hz are displayed as well,[9] although resonances above the 20 Hz band are usually obscured by noise, including manmade sources (for example, telephone-ringing systems and railway systems in Germany).[10] The low attenuation of these ELF waves, between .5 db/1,000 km to .8 db/km (depending upon the calculation), and the high penetrability of typical housing structures used by human organisms are attractive features of this T–C mediator candidate.[11] Frequencies propagated within the spherical wave guide may travel Mm without appreciable attenuation.

VLF or higher-frequency electromagnetic waves may display pulses within the ELF range. These pulses may occur for very short times in the order of $10^{-4}$ seconds and may achieve very complex EP-like patterns. These pulses, which include the "atmospherics," as well as local field fluctuation categories, still maintain their low attenuation rates in air. Atmospherics, which are associated with many atmospheric electrical disturbances, demonstrate low attenuation and temporal shifts in wave shapes as a function of propagation distance. Their amplitudes, in the order of $10^{-9}$T and 1 mV/m demonstrate a directional preference for propagation. Manmade ELF signals are typically highly localized (< 1 km$^2$) time-varying fields. Proposed communication antennae would allow ELF wave propagation over global distances.

## ELF Phenomena and Organismic Responses

Many organismic electromagnetic-chemical processes display time variations that overlap the ELF waveband. The human heart (< 1 to 4 Hz), brain (< 1 to 30 Hz), and musculature (1 Hz to 1 kHz) display major power spectra within the ELF region. Several of the EEG wave patterns are remarkably similar in shape and order of amplitude (magnetic and electric components) to those associated with weather-related ELF electromagnetic signals.[12] Such similarities suggest that biogenic-environmental ELF interactions could occur through resonancelike[13] or lock-and-key mechanisms.[14] Resonance interaction would allow, theoretically at least, information transfer between the organism and distant environment; however, the quantitative values for such exchange have not been specified. Other possible mechanisms have been proposed and more typically reflect differences in level of discourse rather than fundamental differences of principle.[15]

If ELF waves are involved with T–C phenomena, then organismic conditions that facilitate response to (reception of) these fields should increase the probability of T–C experiences.[16] Assuming a resonancelike mechanism of interaction, organismic conditions in which biogenic ELF patterns predominate should enhance environmental ELF signal detection and T–C reports. If T–C information is associated with Schumann resonances, then periods with predominant alpha rhythm in the EEG profile and organismic conditions displaying "split" EEG power spectra, typified by 7 to 8 Hz and beta (14 Hz, 20 Hz) frequencies (for example, some classifications of schizophrenia, geriatric progression, and thyroid and related endocrine alterations) should probabilistically enhance T–C reporting. Spontaneous cases superficially support these contentions. Frequently, the alleged percipient is engaging in daydreaming, relaxation, or some ritualistic motor task (washing dishes or driving a car) in which alpha rhythms would predominate. More specific statements could be made by comparing the technical literature on EEG behavioral correlates with natural ELF electromagnetic records.

## ELF Interactions with Agent and Percipient

The conceptual relationships between the agent or object (A), the percipient or reporter (P), and the geophysical mediator (G) are shown in Figure 8.3. A Type 1 interaction would be a simple A–G–P relationship, by which information from

**Type 1**

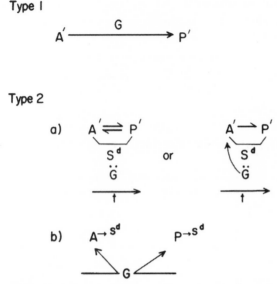

**Type 2**

A modifies or is coded onto G and influences P some time and distance later. A Type 2 interaction would be another example of a "third-factor theory," whereby G would influence A and P separately at about the same time. Since G would not be apparent to either A or P, the conclusion of a direct A–P interaction would be likely but inaccurate.

## The A–G–P Theory: Type 1

This theory requires that information from the target or agent modifies the ELF wave-field, especially if one assumes that no previous association between some wave form of G and A has been learned by P. In other words, the percipient must directly respond to the modification of the ELF signal correlated

**Figure 8.3** Representation of two types of mechanisms by which some G factor (geophysical-meteorological ELF fields) might mediate spontaneous T–C events. Type 1 involves direct information transfer from the putative agent (A′) to the putative percipient (P′). The Type 2 (a) model requires the role of previous learning, whereby the G factor becomes a conditioned stimulus or discriminative stimulus ($S^d$) for particular behaviors shared by A′ and P′. Later presentation of the G (b), when A′ and P′ are separated by significant distances but still within G range, would elicit the $S^d$ = related behaviors in both A and P independently.

with the agent's organismic condition.

Initial evaluation suggests that in principle, information could be received from ELF waves. Using generous assumptions, elementary information theory indicates that ELF waves would have low information-carrying capacity, in the order of $10^{-2}$ bits/s. These values are compatible with experimental data for some laboratory T–C experiments, according to Puthoff and Targ,[17] who calculated the transmission rate of a 15-digit number (49.8 bits) through paranormal means to be $2.9 \times 10^{-4}$ bit/s.[18] In Kogan's experiments, an apparent distance dependence of information transfer occurred, ranging from .1 bit/s for A–P distances of < 1 km to .005 bit/s for A–P distances of 1,000 km.[19]

If T–C were mediated by ELF waves, then the information transfer process would be small in terms of bits and or very long in terms of detection.

Estimated maximum information capacity for spoken English is 50 bits/s, assuming a 150,000-word vocabulary and a speaking rate of 300 words per minute.[20] A simple word passage involves about 100 bits of information, while a simple geometric object can be described in macroscopic terms with about 60 bits of information.[21] Presumably, more complicated objects, such as images of human beings or technical geometries (buildings and room furnishings) would require much larger amounts of information.

This difficulty can be obviated by increasing the ELF exposure duration or through "closure effects" displayed by P. If a subject was capable of receiving and storing .01 bit/s for 100 minutes, then 60 bits of information could be accumulated. Assuming more experimentally palatable periods of ten minutes, ELF information could vary from .01 to 1 bit. Although the percipient could be exposed to the ELF signal for hours before sufficient information influenced appropriate response systems (awareness behaviors), more critical features would be the increment of time that the agent could maintain ELF "coding" and P's neural capability for "understanding" the signals.

Closure effects would allow the susceptible subject to "fill in the gaps" after receiving only a small portion of the transmitted information. Such phenomena are well documented with visual information, where partial stimuli (for example, four right angles) presented for threshold durations are interpreted by the perceiver as a total object (for example, a square). Closure would attenuate the difficulties of large information requirements or exposure times for ELF-associated T–C.

However, there is still a problem of the mechanism by which the agent influences adjacent ELF waves, since they would require modification or modulation by the object-body locus. Although not impossible theoretically, since the body can be considered an influential medium, the operation does not appear highly feasible. Any ELF modification within a small volume (for example, the human body, in the order of 1 m³) without some additional change in adjacent field-waves would require extremely precise directional localization of the percipient, even if A and P occupied conjugate loci. An as yet unspecified mechanism must exist to allow large lateral dispersions of the A-related information. There is another option.

## The G as a Third-Factor Theory: Type 2

Much of paranormal behavior is associated with the implicit assumption that A and P are the primary and causal conditions of the T–C event. Within this context, something happening to A is somehow transmitted to P; the direction of the interaction is relevant only to the model employed. Other options are not invoked, since it is further assumed that the stimulus events occurring around A, such as death or crisis, are specific only to the time and place of the *single* episode rather than to some more general pattern.

The Type 2 option in Figure 8.3 indicates that some third factor, G, initiates changes independently in both A and P. In this situation, the environmental (geophysical-meteorological) factor G would initiate both the alleged "transmitted" information in A and the "paranormal" responses in P. Clearly, such a relationship would require shared reinforcement histories (shared experiences) between A and P in the presence of G. The basic operation would involve elementary learning principles, such that the G factor becomes a conditioned stimulus (CS) or discriminative stimulus ($S^d$).

One simple application of this theory (Figure 8.3, Type 2 [a], first option) would require the display of behaviors by either A′ (the person who would later be called the agent) and P′ (the person who would later be called the percipient) during the presence of G at least once. Emotional behaviors, such as response sequences associated with death, crises, and sex (or related) autonomic stimuli would be more effective for recall and would require fewer pairings with G. Later presentation of G (Figure 8.3, Type 2 [a]), when A′ and P′ are separated by significant distances, would elicit independently in both A and P the display of responses associated with the initial learning situation. The conclusion of direct A–P communication would be an artifact of describing the event without including G.

For example, suppose A′ and P′ share a given response sequence, such as watching an emotional movie, while some specific G factor is present. The initial presence of the G factor would be quite accidental and behaviorally "neutral." However, since G was contiguous with the learning situation, it would also acquire reinforcing capacities. Later, A′ and P′ become separated by a significant distance that still includes the space of a potential G (with ELF G factors, distances in the order of $10^3$ km would not be prohibitive). The occurrence of the specific G at that time would initiate responses (such as memories) about the shared experience (the emotional movie) in both the A and P independently. Shortly thereafter, A might telephone P and relate the "sudden and intense remembering of the movie for no apparent reason," as well as the image of P (a significant reinforcer present during the initial learning situation). P might report a similar experience that occurred about the same time, plus or minus 30 minutes. The couple might conclude, erroneously, that some type of "personal exchange" had taken place.

A more complex application of the model (Figure 8.3, Type 2 [a], second option) would involve the G as an unconditioned stimulus (UCS) or related powerful stimulus (first-order CS) that would actually initiate A′ behaviors leading to typical T–C events (accidents and death). In this situation, the G would have elicited specific responses in A′, for example, depression, proneness to accidents, or agitation while in the presence of P′. As a result, the G would become an $S^d$ to P to emit responses (memories) about A displaying the specific responses. If the display of the responses by A was aversive to P, then a conditioned suppression situation would arise. The G factor would be a cue to the later presentation of aversive stimuli (the behaviors of A′). During G presentation, P would display typical conditioned suppression paradigm behaviors like anxiety, foreboding of something bad about to happen, or general feelings of unspecified negative anticipation. Quite likely, P would report difficulty in thinking during the G presentation period, except for thoughts directly paired with A′.

For example, suppose a potential A′ responds with irritable depression to some specific ELF component of a geomagnetic storm, $G_x$. Since geomagnetic storms are quite persistent in time, one would expect that A′ would be exposed to $G_x$ or stimuli that fall within the stimulus generalization gradient many times during adulthood. Members of the family would learn to anticipate, through incidental learning, that the irritable depression of A′ was displayed during $G_x$. Incidental learning is a key feature here, since isolation of or specification of G by P′ would not be required for learning to occur, that is, covert conditioning.[22] The decreasing involvement of immediate family, peripheral family, friends, and acquaintances, a common gradient found in spontaneous psi accounts,[23] would reflect the probability of being present for the pairing of $G_x$ presentation and display of irritable depression by A′.

Time after time, the appropriate geomagnetic storm patterns are presented. During one of these periods, A′ is separated from P′ by a considerable distance, but still within the storm inclusion area. This particular time, the storm is stronger than usual, and the agent, driving alone, shows an increased susceptibility to depressive agitation. The probability of an accident increases, and the accident occurs. During this time, the same geomagnetic stimulus is presented to potential P′s and, in the most susceptible P′ displays, the behaviors associated with $G_x$. Since $G_x$ has been associated with the display of undesirable/aversive behaviors by A′, the geomagnetic storm acts as a CS to produce anxiety, vague feelings of anticipation, and related diffuse, autonomic displays. As the period of $G_x$ presentation continues, P becomes more anxious, and the autonomic activity increases. Since the particular sequence has been associated with A, the P begins to experience images about A in context of the anxiety. These contents would reflect the most recent aspects of the A (for example, clothes or driving a car).

That geomagnetic perturbations can demonstrate UCS-like characteristics has been suggested by several authors. Freidman, Becker, and Bachman have shown that geomagnetic perturbations are associated with increased agitation in psychiatric populations.[24] Other correlational data have linked geomagnetic perturbations with disturbances in "mood" and proneness to self-destructive behaviors. Geomagnetic disturbances are correlated also with cardiovascular and autonomic variations, which could contribute to the undesirable behaviors in the susceptible A′. These weak correlations in conjunction with laboratory human data suggest that ELF G factors have the *potential* to be involved with operations depicted by this model. The experimental demonstration is another matter.

Traditionally, in spontaneous T–C cases, the A displays the apparent target behaviors first, while the P responds to these stimuli at the same time or some time later, in the order of minutes to hours. If the person designated as P displays a psi response before the alleged event occurs to the designated A, then the conclusion of precognition might be made. It would appear that the P somehow "knew" the information before it happened to A.

In this model, the designation of who was the A and who was the P would be arbitrary. Since the G factor initiated responses independently in both persons, the use of the traditional A and P labels would be spurious. A or P capacity would reflect merely the response latency of the organism to G; if the male of the couple was displaying behaviors more favorable to the display of the conditioned responses in the presence of G before the female, then the male might be called A. On the other hand, if the female had been displaying behaviors that increased her susceptibility to G, then she might be called the A.

If G maintained the reinforcing potencies to initiate specific behaviors that lead to a crisis event in one of the two organisms, then the response of the other organism to G first might result in the conclusion of precognition. In this situation, the G factor would initiate its $S^d$ characteristics to the P′ first because of his/her increased susceptibility (shorter response latency) to the presence of G. Later, the person to be affected, A′, would enter a behavioral condition allowing G to initiate $S^d$-related responses (for example, depression or agitation), thus increasing the probability that a related event (for example, an accident) would occur. The conclusion of precognition would be inaccurate; rather, the P′ would have responded to a stimulus (G) that had been presented more or less simultaneously to both A′ and P′ for a significant duration.

The occurrence of $S^d$ effects from the G factor would be compatible with some puzzling aspects of spontaneous precognition and T–C events. These phenomena display similar-shaped cumulative response curves over time.[25] Typical temporal delays of .01 to three days exist between the precognitive experience and the occurrence of the event or the event and the T–C experience. Within the context of this model, these values would reflect the periods of time by which the typical G factor was presented independently to both the A′ and P′.

## Difficulties with the ELF Electromagnetic Theory and Conclusions

A major limitation of ELF electromagnetic involvement in the Type 1 G-factor theory discussed in this chapter involves the number of ELF electromagnetic incremental characteristics—amplitude, frequency, rise time, peak time, superimposed ripples, or wave trains—that the P can discriminate as different. As mentioned previously, organismic discrimination is important here—not "awareness" of the presence or absence of ELF fields. Although the discrimination of required information loads within complex wave forms now appears unlikely, sufficient information might be gleaned by using 0,1 ELF signal modes. Assuming reaction time differences to be a model for discrimination, experimental data and interpretations by Konig indicate that human subjects display significantly altered reaction times to the presence or absence of weak (4 Hz or 10 Hz) electric fields and frequency shifts of only 1 Hz at field strengths of 2 mV/50cm.[26] However, a 0,1-like detection mechanism would necessitate an organismic capacity to distinguish temporal patterns. The maximum time increment within which a specific sequence of 0,1 ELF signals can be maintained (short-term memory), compared and discriminated from other sequences, appears biologically prohibitive.

The Type 2 G-factor theory has less of a requirement for large numbers of discriminable ELF electromagnetic characteristics, since the majority of information is already within P as memory; the ELF signal is only a trigger. This operation is analogous to the presentation of a single four-letter curse word, which involves very little stimulus energy, to a person with the appropriate conditioning history. Massive autonomic and verbal sequences, at energy level orders of magnitude above the stimulus strength, would be evoked in a cascading manner. The important requirement for the Type 2 model is that the organism merely can respond to the ELF field. Massive or diverse information capacity of the ELF field is not required, since this factor would reflect the diverse learning histories of As and Ps. In fact, the same ELF wave pattern that had become an $S^d$ for hundreds of different A–P pairs could evoke the display of hundreds of different specific responses.

At present, the greatest weakness of the ELF theory in spontaneous T–C cases is the lack of experimental detection data. A few nonhuman animal studies have suggested that ELF electromagnetic (and sonic) fields may effectively enter the learning paradigm—predominantly respondent-conditioning formats.[27] Quite frankly, the experimental data for human subjects have not demonstrated sufficient information properties of ELF fields. Frequency or amplitude-dependent changes in reaction time are important first steps. However, what must be established clearly, in order to substantiate the ELF hypothesis as a viable T–C model, is the capacity for these fields to become reliable CSs or $S^d$s for specific responses within highly controlled experimental psi-simulating situations.

## Summary

The possible mechanisms by which ELF electromagnetic fields generated in the geophysical-meteorological environment could mediate spontaneous T–C behaviors are discussed. One model involves direct information transfer by ELF fields between the putative agent and percipient; however, this option is limited by the necessity for wide area modification of the ELF signal by the agent's condition and by the low bit rate of ELF fields. The second model involves ELF fields as a third factor that evokes behaviors in both the "agent" and "percipient" independently. Due to their incidental presence during the display of particular shared behaviors by person A and person B, ELF fields would become CSs or S[d]s. The later presentation of these ELF stimuli, when A and B are separated by significant distances, would evoke independently in A and B the display of those or related behaviors. In this model, traditional designation of "agent" or "percipient" would be irrelevant, since temporal relationships (including apparent precognitive patterns) reflect only response latencies to the field's presence. Predictions, advantages, limitations, and experimental verification of these mechanisms are discussed.

## Notes

1. M. A. Persinger, "Geophysical Models for Parapsychological Experiences," *Psychoenergetic Systems* 1 (1975): 63–74.

2. I. Bentov, *Stalking the Wild Pendulum* (New York: E. P. Dutton, 1977), p. 142; W. Franklin, "Metal Fracture Physics Using Scanning Electron Microscopy and the Theory of Teleneural Interactions," in *The Geller Papers,* ed. C. Panati (Boston: Houghton Mifflin, 1976), pp. 83–106; I. M. Kogan, "Information Theory Analysis of Telepathic Communication Experiments," *Radio Engineering* 23 (1968): 122–30; M. A. Persinger, *The Paranorinal, Part II: Mechanisms and Models* (New York: M.S.S. Information, 1974); and H. Puthoff and R. Targ, "A Perceptual Channel for Information Transfer Over Kilometer Distances: Historical Perspective and Recent Research," *Proceedings of the IEEE* 64 (March 1976): 329–54.

3. Persinger, "Geophysical Models for Parapsychological Experiences," op. cit.

4. W. H. Campbell, "Geomagnetic Pulsations," in *Physics of Geomagnetic Phenomena,* ed. S. Hatsushita and W. H. Campbell (New York: Academic Press, 1967), pp. 821–909.

5. M. A. Persinger, H. W. Ludwig, and K-P. Ossenkopp, "Psychophysiological Effects of Extremely Low Frequency Electromagnetic Fields: A Review," *Perceptual and Motor Skills* 36 (1973): 1131–59.

6. H. L. Konig, "Physical Characteristics of ELF and VLF Signals," in *ELF and VLF Electromagnetic Field Effects,* ed. M. A. Persinger (New York: Plenum Press, 1974), pp. 8–34; and Y. L. Al'pert and D. S. Fligel, *Propagation of ELF and VLF Waves Near Earth* (New York: Consultants Bureau, 1970).

7. Campbell, op. cit.

8. Konig, op. cit.

9. Campbell, op. cit.

10. Konig, op. cit.

11. H. W. Ludwig, "Electric and Magnetic Field Strengths in the Open and in Shielded Rooms in the ULF- to LF-Zone," in Campbell, ed., op. cit., pp. 35–80.

12. Konig, op. cit.

13. Persinger, Ludwig, and Ossenkopp, op. cit.

14. M. A. Persinger, "Effects of Magnetic Fields on Animal Behavior," in *Progress in Biometeorology: Animal Biometeorology,* ed. H. D. Johnson (Amsterdam: Swets and Zeitlinger, 1976), pp. 177–82.

15. M. A. Persinger, "ELF Electric and Magnetic Field Effects: The Patterns and the Problems," in Persinger, ed., op. cit., pp. 275–310; and Persinger, Ludwig, and Ossenkopp, op. cit.

16. Persinger, "Geophysical Models for Parapsychological Experiences," op. cit.

17. Putboff and Targ, op. cit.

18. M. A. Persinger, "The Problems of Human Verbal Behavior: The Final Reference for Measuring Ostensible Psi Phenomena," *The Journal of Research in PSI Phenomena* 1 (1976): 72–90.

19. Kogan, op. cit.

20. J. F. Corso, *The Experimental Psychology of Sensory Behavior* (New York: Holt, Rinehart and Winston, 1967), pp. 487–507.

21. Franklin, op. cit.

22. M. A. Persinger, "Behavioristic Descriptions of Paranormal Behaviors," *Psychoenergetic Systems* (in press).

23. Persinger, *The Paranormal, Part II: Mechanisms and Models,* op. cit.

24. H. Friedman, R. O. Becker, and C. H. Bachman, "Geomagnetic Parameters and Psychiatric Hospital Admissions," *Nature* 200 (1963): 122–30.

25. Persinger, *The Paranormal, Part II: Mechanisms and Models,* op. cit.

26. Konig, op. cit.

27. Persinger, "ELF Electric and Magnetic Field Effects: The Patterns and the Problems," op. cit.

# Introduction to Chapter 9

Most of the chapters in this book have dealt with the acquisition of *information* by parapsychological means (various forms of ESP). But psi is not limited to ESP; it includes the converse of perception, namely, motor output. The psi version of this is PK.

Although it began with the spectacular but often questionable "physical phenomena" of the nineteenth-century seance room, experimental study of PK became more standardized and consistent in this century with the development of dice-throwing tests by J. B. Rhine and his colleagues in the 1930s. In these tests, machines threw various numbers of dice, while subjects willed either that a particular die face would come up more often than expected by chance or that the dice would come to rest on designated target areas of the table. Much evidence for the reality of PK was laboriously collected in this way.

Helmut Schmidt was one of the pioneers in creating a new computerized era of PK research, where the PK action was not on macroscopic events, such as the throwing of dice, but on electronic or quantum mechanical events in electronic random number generators. In these experiments, electronic noise derived either from a diode noise source or from radioactive decay is monitored while a subject attempts to alter the statistical properties of the noise distribution. The usual protocol involves providing visual and audio feedback signals, proportional to various statistical parameters, to a subject, who is asked to concentrate on the feedback signals and to alter them in a prescribed way. To date, there have been 54 such experiments reported in the literature,[1] of which 35 report statistically significant effects, while none of these studies shows similar departures from randomness during control runs. That the mind can directly influence such basic physical processes is of enormous significance, not only in understanding human nature but in formulating an adequate picture of the physical universe.

## About the Author

**Helmut Schmidt,** Ph.D., is a Senior Research Associate at the Mind Science Foundation in San Antonio, Texas, having previously served as the Director of the Institute for Parapsychology in Durham, North Carolina. While working as a physicist at Boeing Scientific Research Laboratories in Seattle, Dr. Schmidt became interested in both extrasensory and psychokinetic abilities and studied both with sophisticated testing machines. He has been a major contributor to the experimental literature on ESP and PK for the past decade and has proposed a mathematical theory for working with parapsychological events.[2] His other research interests include the foundations of quantum theory and solid state theory, as well as the relationship of parapsychology to modern physics.

# 9

# Evidence for Direct Interaction between the Human Mind and External Quantum Processes

Helmut Schmidt

## Introduction

In 1894, Sir Oliver Lodge demonstrated the usefulness of radio waves for information transmission, but ten years earlier, he had already participated in experiments where messages were transmitted telepathically over large distances from one person, the "sender," to another person, the "receiver."[3]

Today, more than 80 years later, we understand radio waves well—we have a theory in the form of Maxwell's equations, and we have efficient electronic senders and receivers to make radio waves useful. The telepathy mechanism, however, is still obscure; we do not have a satisfactory theory, and we have no electronic transmitters and receivers of telepathic signals. Nevertheless, the study of telepathy has already led to a series of quite unexpected discoveries. It now appears that telepathy was just the tip of the iceberg—that it is closely related to a large family of psychic phenomena, or "psi effects," which challenge a basic tenet of our everyday and scientific thinking, the axiom of causality.

The first indication that telepathy implies more than a "mental radio" came from the clairvoyance experiments of Charles Richet, the famous physiologist.[4] Richet shocked his colleagues by demonstrating that the "telepathy mechanism" also worked without a human sender. In these experiments, a human receiver could successfully identify randomly selected distant pictures and playing cards that were not known to anyone.

There were more surprising developments to come. Richet had already wondered whether clairvoyance could perhaps reach into the future, and later, J. B. Rhine reported that in large-scale laboratory experiments, test subjects had indeed successfully predicted the order in which the cards in a deck would appear after shuffling.[5]

Richet based his discussion of precognition on a deterministic world model in which the future could, in principle, be calculated from the present. Modern quantum theory, on the other hand, suggests that the future is not completely determined by the past and that there are processes, the quantum jumps, which are, in principle, unpredictable. Therefore, the physicist's most basic question with regard to precognition is whether human subjects can predict the outcome of quantum processes, like radioactive decays. In the next section, I will report some experiments in this direction.

## Precognition of Quantum Processes

For these experiments, I used a quantum mechanical random number generator, which utilized the random timing of radioactive decay as its basic source of randomness.[6] A weak source of strontium 90 was placed near a Geiger tube, so that decay particles were registered at random time intervals at an average rate of ten events per second. Connected to this system, was an electronic modulo-4 counter, which was incremented by a clock at the rate of $10^6$ steps per second. An arrangement was made so that the counter could be stopped at the time when the Geiger tube registered the next signal. Then, each of the four possible stopping positions of the counter was practically equally likely. This is the modulo-4 random number generator.

In the detailed design of this random number generator, proper precautions were taken so that the expected variations in component characteristics could not effect the randomness. Furthermore, frequent randomness tests were alternated with the precognition test sessions.[7] These randomness tests, comprising approximately 5 million generated numbers, evaluated the frequency of each number and of each possible pair of successive numbers. No permanent or temporary deviation from randomness was found.

During a precognition test, the subject sat in front of a panel with four colored lamps, four corresponding push buttons, and two electric counters (a trial counter and a hit counter). Before a button was pressed, the lamps were dark, and the internal modulo-4 counter advanced at the megacycle rate. If any button was pressed, nothing happened until the next decay particle reached the Geiger tube. At this moment, the modulo-4 counter was stopped, and the random stopping position 1, 2, 3, or 4 was indicated by the lighting of a corresponding lamp.

The subject tried repeatedly to guess which lamp would light next, and he or she registered his or her guess by pressing the corresponding button. If the predicted lamp did light, a hit was scored. Thus, the subject could operate at his or her preferred speed and receive immediate feedback on the correctness of his or her predictions. A punch tape recorder registered automatically the sequences of guesses and random events, so that the scores given by the display counters could be independently checked by a computer. The whole equipment was transportable, so that the subjects could be tested at their own homes under seemingly casual conditions.

The first exploratory experiments done in 1969 with about 100 subjects produced mainly chance scoring. Only one subject, a physicist who reported frequent precognitive dreams, produced surprisingly high results. In a follow-up test, this man obtained, in 7,600 trials, an average success rate of 33.7 percent, where the chance expectancy is 25 percent. The odds against chance producing such a high or higher score are about $10^5:1$. Soon afterward, I found several further promising performers among a group of professional and amateur psychics, who tried systematically to develop certain "psychic abilities." With these preselected subjects, I did two experiments aimed only at confirming the existence of abnormal scoring under rigorously controlled but psychologically favorable conditions. For these experiments, I specified the total number of trials to be made in advance, but I left the subjects the freedom to work on the machine whenever they wanted (I did visit them on a moment's notice) and only as long as they felt confident. Thus, the total data were gathered in many short test sessions, comprising sometimes as few as 100 trials. Note that for establishing the existence of the effect, it was quite irrelevant how many different subjects contributed to the total number of trials and how frequently breaks were taken during the whole experiment.

Three subjects participated in the first confirmatory experiment: Mr. K. R. and Mrs. J. B. were professional psychics, and Mr. O. C. was a truck driver and an amateur psychic. These subjects completed a total of approximately 63,000 trials at an average scoring rate of 26.1 percent. Even though this scoring rate is only slightly above the chance expectancy of 25 percent, the high number of trials makes this difference statistically highly significant. The odds against chance producing such a high or a higher score are about 500 million to one.

For the second confirmatory experiment, K. R. was no longer available and was replaced by S. C., the 16-year-old daughter of O. C. In this experiment, the subjects had the option to aim for either a large or small number of hits. In the latter case, they tried to push a button corresponding to any lamp that would *not* light next. This choice was made before the beginning of a test session, and the two types of tests were recorded in different codes such that the evaluating computer could distinguish between them. Among the total number of 20,000 trials made, 10,672 trials aiming for a high score gave 26.8 percent hits, and the remaining trials, aiming for a low hit rate, produced only 22.7 percent hits. The odds against obtaining this or a better score by pure chance are more than 10 billion to one ($10^{10}:1$). Figure 9.1, giving the increase of the scores with the number of trials, indicates that the subjects performed rather consistently.

Other researchers could confirm the existence of the effect with the same or a similar test machine.[8]

## The Problem of Interpretation

The reported experiments showed some not yet understood correlation between the subject's prediction and the later random event, the lighting of a lamp. This correlation might be interpreted in terms of a precognition

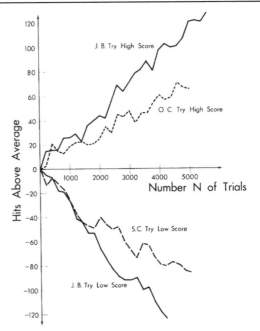

**Figure 9.1** Increase of the total scores with the number of trails in the second confirmatory precognition test. The numbers of hits above chance expectancy are plotted after each block of 200 trials.

mechanism, which permits the subject to look into the future. Experiments to be reported later, however, indicate that there exists another possible mechanism, PK, which could have enabled the subjects to affect the outcome of the random process such as to agree with the prediction.

In an attempt to suppress a PK mechanism, I replaced the indeterministic random number generator by a punch tape (hidden in a paper tape reader), which contained the numbers 1, 2, 3, 4 in a random sequence derived from the RAND tables. The order of the lamps to be lit was now determined by this hidden number sequence. Again, significantly high scores were obtained.[9] But even though PK seemed to be excluded, the experiment did not isolate a precognition mechanism. Rather than foreseeing the lamp to be lit directly, the subject might have, in this case, used some "clairvoyance mechanism" to read the hidden paper tape.

Further experimental and theoretical work has suggested that there may exist only one universal "psi mechanism" and that it may not be conceptually meaningful to subdivide psi into separate submechanisms.[10] If I label the experiments to be reported next as PK experiments, I want to characterize only a specific test arrangement rather than a particular mechanism.

# PK Experiments

The first systematic experiments which suggested that the human mind could affect external random events were conducted by Rhine.[11] In these experiments, people tried to influence mentally the outcome of die throws. An attempt to use quantum processes—radioactive decays—as targets in PK experiments was made by Beloff and Evans, but no PK effects were observed.[12] Later, however, Chauvin and Genthon reported significant results from tests in which subjects had tried to increase the counting rate of a Geiger tube exposed to a radioactive source.[13]

In the following experiments, I wanted to confirm the existence of a PK effect on quantum processes.[14] Instead of the described four-choice random number generator, I used a binary random generator built on the same principle. This "electronic coin flipper" could automatically produce a random sequence of "heads" and "tails" at a typical rate of one event per second. This sequence was recorded on paper punch tape, and the numbers of generated heads and tails were indicated by counters. A display panel, showing nine lamps in a circle, was connected to the generator in such a way that one lamp was always lit and that a generated head or tail made the light jump one step in the clockwise or counterclockwise direction, respectively. Thus, the light, moving at the rate of typically one jump per second, performed a random walk around the nine lamps.

In a standard test run, the light started at the top of the circle, and the generator was set to produce a sequence of 128 binary events, which took approximately two minutes. The subjects sat in front of the panel and tried mentally to enforce an overall clockwise motion of the light. This task was equivalent to forcing the generator into producing more heads than tails, but usually the subjects directed their exclusive attention to the display panel.

A pilot study with the most easily available subjects showed a negative scoring tendency: if the subjects tried to superimpose an overall clockwise motion on the random walk of the light, then the light tended to move in a counterclockwise direction. In order to confirm this unexpected effect, I selected 15 of the most negative scorers to do a total of 64 sessions, each session comprising four runs of 128 trials. During the test session, the subject sat next to the display panel, and the generator was stationed in another room, approximately 6 m away from the subject. In an attempt to preserve or even amplify the negative scoring tendency of the subjects, I avoided giving them any encouragement toward successful performance and even asked some subjects to associate feelings of failure and pessimism with the test.

In the total $32,768 = 2^{15}$ trials, the light moved in only 49.1 percent of the jumps in the desired direction. This deviation from the 50 percent chance level is significant with odds against chance of 1,000:1. To guard against any bias caused by a potential malfunction of the generator, I took two precautions. First, I let the machine run unattended and confirmed the absence of a systematic bias when there was no human subject present. Second, after each test run, I interchanged the two output lines from the generator to the display panel such that even a constant bias of the generator could not have led to a systematic bias toward clockwise or counterclockwise motion of the light.

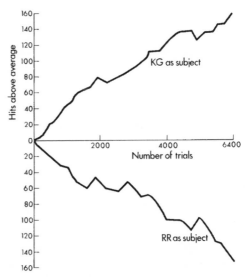

The second confirmation of the PK effect was effected shortly afterward when two unusual subjects happened to visit the laboratory: K. G., an outgoing girl who was believed to possess a variety of psychic abilities, and R. R., a quiet, methodical parapsychology researcher who was believed to have the power of "mental heal-

**Figure 9.2** Increase of the total scores with the number of trials for the PK test with two Subjects, K. G. and R. R. The cumulative numbers of hits above chance are plotted after each section of 256 trials.

ing." In preliminary tests, K. G. and R. R. scored exceptionally high and low, respectively, and I proceeded immediately to a confirmatory test in which each subject completed 50 runs of 128 trials each.

Throughout this experiment, the subjects maintained their scoring pattern, as shown by Figure 9.2.

When K. G. concentrated on the panel, the lights showed a preference for the desired clockwise motion at an average success rate of 52.5 percent in the 6,400 trials. When R. R. tried to affect the lights however, they moved generally against his wish. Only 47.75 percent of the 6,400 light jumps went in the desired clockwise direction. The odds against obtaining by chance such a large or a larger difference between the scores of the two subjects are more than 10 million to one. Thus, chance as an explanation of the results can well be ruled out.

Other experimenters could confirm the existence of the PK effect with the same or similar equipment.[15]

## PK Tests with a High Speed Random Number Generator

The collection of data in the reported experiments was unfortunately very slow and laborious. Even after promising subjects had been found, the tests could not be conducted in a routine manner because successful scoring seemed to require exceptional mental efforts. Thus, test sessions aiming for positive scores were held only if the subjects felt eager to perform, and a session was adjourned whenever a subject showed loss of interest or signs of fatigue.

In an attempt to increase the efficiency of PK experimenting, I introduced a high-speed generator, which could produce binary random events at rates of up to 1,000 per second.[16] The generator worked like the aforementioned electronic coin flipper—the only difference was that the source of randomness was electronic noise rather than radioactive decay. This change was made because no sufficiently strong radioactive source was available to provide the desired high counting rate.

Tests were done at two generation speeds, a "low" speed of 30 events per second and a "high" speed of 300 per second. The number of trials made per test run in these two cases were 100 and 1,000, respectively, so that each run lasted approximately three seconds. Two electronic counters on top of the generator accumulated the heads and tails produced in each run, and the detailed binary sequence was recorded on magnetic tape so that the manually recorded counter readings could be checked by a computer.

During a test run, the subjects received immediate feedback on their momentary performance by an auditory or a visual display. The auditory feedback was provided by a pair of headphones, which presented each generated head or tail as a click in the right or left ear, respectively. For obtaining more heads than tails, the subject was instructed to concentrate on the right ear, trying to receive there an increased number of clicks. The volume of the clicks was usually kept very low, and the subjects would often close their eyes and listen to the clicks in the target ear as one would listen to a distant voice in a relaxed but alert state. The visual feedback was given by the needle of a pen chart recorder, which was connected so that each generated head or tail moved the needle by a small step to the right or left, respectively. The subject concentrated on the statistically fluctuating needle, trying to move it to the right.

The confirmatory stage in this experiment was conducted with ten subjects, who contributed a total of 40,000 trials (400 runs) at the low speed and 400,000 trials (400 runs) at the high speed. The results with the visual and auditory feedback were not significantly different, and Table 9.1 gives only the combined results.

#### Table 9.1  PK Results for Generator Speeds of 30 and 300 Targets per Second

| Trial Speed (per second) | Number of Trials | Hit Rate (percent) | Odds against Chance |
|:---:|:---:|:---:|:---:|
| 30 | 40,000 | 51.6 | $7 \times 10^9 : 1$ |
| 300 | 400,000 | 50.37 | $4 \times 10^5 : 1$ |

Source: Compiled by the author.

We see that at both speeds, PK effects were produced rather efficiently insofar as a high statistical significance was obtained within a "pure test time" of only 400 x three seconds = 20 minutes. The finding that the lower generation rate (30 per second) led to considerably higher scoring on the individual trials appears plausible, since there, the subject had more time to concentrate on the individual events.

One might hope that a high-speed PK test arrangement where the subject would receive immediate feedback on his or her momentary performance could help in training PK abilities. It should be kept in mind, however, that PK performance may depend more than most other skills on subtle psychological factors, like the subject's motivation and confidence. Thus, the main goal of any PK training program should be the cultivation of a favorable mental attitude in the subject.

## Complexity Independence of PK

After we have seen that PK can affect the operation of electronic random generators, it appears most natural to ask whether there are some random generators that are more sensitive to PK efforts than others. A study of this question should help us to get a better understanding of the basic PK mechanism. The following experiment compares the PK action on two very different random generators, a "simple" and a "complex" generator.[17] The complex generator obtains one binary decision by first generating a sequence of 100 binary random events and then taking the majority vote (in the case of a tie, no decision is made, and the test proceeds to the next trial). The individual decisions come from the described fast generator operating at the rate of 30 events per second, so that the decision process takes about three seconds. The generator is mounted inside a closed box, which displays only the majority decision, whereas the information on the detailed outcome of the individual trials is lost. The simple generator, like the electronic coin flipper from the first PK experiment, obtains a binary decision in a single step by the random stopping of a fast modulo-2 counter. In order to make the two generators behave similarly, the simple generator is combined inside a closed box with a delay mechanism, so that the binary decision appears also about three seconds after the system is activated.

In order to obtain information about the basic PK mechanism, it was important to test the subjects with the two generators under the same psychological conditions. Therefore, an arrangement was made that neither the subject nor the experimenter knew whether the next trial would be made with one or the other generator. This decision was provided by a paper tape containing a long binary random sequence, which was advanced after every trial to the next number.

The subject was seated in a comfortable chair in front of a red and a green lamp. For each trial, the subject had to press a button that triggered the generator selected for this trial. Three seconds later, the decision of this generator was displayed by the lighting of the red or the green lamp. The subject was instructed first to visualize vividly a specified color (green or red), then to press the button, and finally to make an intense three-second effort to have the specified lamp lit. The random generators were stationed in a room 15 m apart from the subject's room, and all decisions of the two generators were recorded on paper punch tape.

After some exploratory tests with this arrangement, 35 subjects made a total of approximately 1,600 trials on each of the two generators. Table 9.2 shows that the scores obtained with both generators are statistically significant and that there is no statistically significant difference between the scoring rates on the two generators, even though the scores with the simple generator turned out slightly higher.

### Table 9.2 Comparison of PK Scoring Rates on Simple and Complex Random Generators

| Generator | Number of Trials | Scoring Rate (percent) | Odds against Chance |
|-----------|------------------|------------------------|---------------------|
| Simple    | 1,695            | 55.3                   | 90,000 : 1          |
| Complex   | 1,606            | 53.8                   | 700 : 1             |

Source: Compiled by the author.

The similarity of the scores obtained with the two different generators suggests that under identical psychological conditions, PK might perhaps affect *any* two random generators in the same manner. Let me formulate such an "equivalence hypothesis" more rigorously, as follows.

Consider two binary random generators whose decisions are based on indeterministic quantum processes. Let each generator be mounted inside a "black box," with one trigger input and two output lines carrying the binary decisions. Assume that the two systems behave alike, so that they are, for the physicist, indistinguishable from the outside. Then, the equivalence hypothesis states that the two systems are also indistinguishable by PK experiments, that is, that they are affected by PK efforts in the same manner.

In the following, we will explore this equivalence hypothesis further by studying one of its far-reaching implications, namely, the noncausality of the psi mechanism.

## Noncausality of the PK Mechanism

Compare the following two black box random generators. The first black box contains our electronic coin flipper, which is activated once per second by a timer, so that two output jacks receive binary random signals at this rate. The other black box contains an identical coin flipper activated at the same rate.

The generated signals, however, are not sent directly to the output jacks but rather are stored on an endless magnetic tape from which they are, 24 hours later, played back to the output jacks. Then, each of the signals that emerges from this generator at the rate of one per second was internally generated 24 hours earlier.

These two black box generators are, from the outside, indistinguishable, and if we take the equivalence hypothesis seriously, then they should work equally well in any PK experiment. Note, however, that if the subject succeeds in a test session with the second system and if the subject obtains significantly more heads than tails, this requires that the internal electronic coin flipper developed a bias for heads 24 hours before the subject made his PK effort. Thus, it appears that the familiar time sequence of cause and effect was inverted. Let me next specify what I mean by *causality* through the following operational definition.

I will call the world *causal* if, for any measurement on a system, the outcome depends, apart from pure chance, only on how the system was prepared, that is, on what the experimenter did with the system before the measurement. But if there should exist systems for which the outcome of a measurement depends on what the experimenter will do with the system later, after the measurement, then I would call the world *noncausal*.

In my first exploratory PK experiment to study the causality question, a binary random number sequence was first recorded in the absence of the subject and the experimenter; later, this sequence was played back to the subject while he or she made his or her PK effort.[18] This experiment was done in the following steps:

*Step 1.* A fast binary random generator was set to produce runs of 201 events at the generation rate of 20 events per second. A large number of such ten-second runs was automatically generated, and the resulting sequences of heads and tails were recorded on the two channels of cassette tapes. Twelve cassette tapes holding an average of 140 test runs each were prepared in this manner. No one was present during the recording, and at this stage, no one knew what was recorded on the tapes.

*Step 2.* With the help of a random sequence from the RAND tables, six of the 12 tapes were selected as PK test tapes, whereas the other six tapes were set aside as control tapes. The RAND sequence had been previously selected but was unknown to the experimenter at the time the tapes were recorded.

*Step 3.* Several days later, the PK test tapes with the recorded sequences of heads and tails were played back to a subject through some display device while the subject tried to enforce the appearance of more signals corresponding to heads than to tails. For three of the tapes, the heads and tails were displayed as weak and strong clicks, respectively, while the subject tried to get more weak clicks. For the other three tapes, the display was given by an instrument needle that was shifted by a head or tail, 1 mm to the right or left, respectively, and the subject tried to make the needle go to the right. After each run, a short break was taken. The whole experiment was spread out over many days.

*Step 4.* After the subject had worked on all six PK test tapes, these tapes, as well as the control tapes, were computer evaluated. Calling a run with an excess of heads or tails a hit run or a miss run, respectively, the six tapes contained a total of 454 hit runs and 378 miss runs (54.6 percent success on the 832 runs). This result is statistically significant with odds against chance of more than 200 : 1. The control tapes, on the other hand, showed no significant deviation from chance scoring: 409 hit runs and 425 miss runs.

Remember that the two sets of six tapes were prepared under the same conditions. These tapes recorded the output of the random generator at a time when the experimenter did not yet know which tapes would serve as test tapes or control tapes. The only difference between the two sets of tapes was that *later*, one set was only evaluated by a computer, whereas the other tapes were played back to the subject while he or she made a PK effort. Thus, the output of the random generator at the recording time was dependent on what later happened to the tapes. Therefore, according to our operational definition, we appear to live in a noncausal world.

Two later experiments have confirmed the existence of the effect and suggest that the PK mechanism works to about the same degree, no matter whether the PK effort is being made while the random generator is running or at some later time.[19]

It seems certainly very surprising that such a basic effect as the violation of causality should have escaped all observations in the physics laboratory. On the other hand, it might be noncausality that is the earmark of psychic phenomena and which makes this phenomena, from our causal viewpoint, appear so mysterious and elusive.

One might wonder whether noncausality as stated in our operational definition need not lead to a logically inconsistent world picture. That is not the case, however, because one can give specific world models that contain noncausal effects similar to the described ones and are nevertheless logically fully consistent.[20] Thus, there are no compelling logical reasons against noncausal psi effects.

In the experiments done so far, the prerecorded random events sequence was not inspected by anybody before the subject made his or her PK effort. As a first interesting modification, one could change this and let somebody else, with or without PK abilities of his or her own, look at the data before the subject comes into play. By this and similar modifications of the initial experiments, in connection with available theoretical models, we should be able to learn in the future more details about the relationship between cause and effect in the presence of psi processes.

## Summary

The reported experiments use electronic equipment to investigate some psychic phenomena that have been reported by many researchers during the last 100 years. In these experiments, human test subjects try either to predict the outcome of quantum jumps, which according to current theory should be unpredictable, or they try mentally to affect the outcome of these quantum processes. The experiments confirm the existence of an anomalous interaction between the human mind and external quantum events and draw attention to some of the unusual features of this interaction.

## Notes

1. C. Honorton, "Replicability, Experimenter Influence, and Parapsychology: An Empirical Context for the Study of Mind" (Paper delivered at meeting of American Association for the Advancement of Science, Washington, D.C., 1978).

2. H. Schmidt, "Toward a Mathematical Theory of Psi," *Journal of the American Society for Psychical Research* 69 (1975): 301.

3. W. P. Jolly and Sir Oliver Lodge (London: Constable, 1974).

4. Charles Richet, *Proceedings of the Society for Psychical Research* (1888); and Charles Richet, *Our Sixth Sense* (London: Rider, 1930).

5. J. B. Rhine, *The Reach of the Mind* (New York: Sloane, 1947).

6. H. Schmidt, "Quantum Mechanical Random Number Generator," *Journal of Applied Physics* 41 (1970): 462.

7. H. Schmidt, "New Correlation between a Human Subject and a Quantum Mechanical Random Number Generator," mimeographed (Boeing Scientific Research Laboratories Document DI-82-1684) (November 1967); and H. Schmidt, "Quantum Processes Predicted?," *New Scientist* (October 1969): 114.

8. E. Haraldsson, "Subject Selection in a Machine Precognition Test," *Journal of Parapsychology* 34 (1970): 182; and E. F. Kelly and B. K. Kanthamani, "A Subject's Effort toward Voluntary Control," *Journal of Parapsychology* 36 (1972): 185.

9. H. Schmidt, "Clairvoyance Tests with a Machine," *Journal of Parapsychology* 33 (1969): 299.

10. Schmidt, "Toward a Mathematical Theory of Psi," op. cit.

11. Rhine, op. cit.

12. J. Beloff and L. Evans, "A Radioactivity Test of PK," *Journal of the Society for Psychical Research* 41 (1961): 41.

13. R. Chauvin and J. Genthon, "Eine Untersuchung über die Möglichkeit psychokinetischer Experimente mit Uranium und Geigerzähler," *Zeitschrift für Parapsychologie und Grenzgebiete der Psychologie* 8 (1965).

14. H. Schmidt, "Mental Influence on Random Events," *New Scientist* (June 1971): 757.

15. E. André, "Confirmation of PK Action on Electronic Equipment," *Journal of Parapsychology* 36 (1972): 283; C. Honorton and W. Barksdale, "PK Performance with

Waking Suggestions for Muscle Tension vs. Relaxation," *Journal of the American Society for Psychical Research* 66 (1972): 208; and R. Stanford et al., "Psychokinesis as Psi Mediated Instrumental Response," *Journal of the American Society for Psychical Research* 69 (1975): 127.

16. H. Schmidt, "PK Tests with a High Speed Random Number Generator," *Journal of Parapsychology* 37 (1973): 105.

17. H. Schmidt, "Comparison of PK Action on Two Different Random Number Generators," *Journal of Parapsychology* 38 (1974): 477.

18. H. Schmidt, "PK Effect of Pre-recorded Targets," *Journal of the American Society for Psychical Research* 70 (1976): 267.

19. Ibid.

20. Schmidt, "Toward a Mathematical Theory of Psi," op. cit.

# Introduction to Chapter 10

In parapsychology, as in music or athletics, it is the human being who is the source of the phenomenon under observation. Therefore, in the scientific pursuit of the paranormal, perhaps more than in any other science, one must take into account the human component in the equation. It is the individual labeled *subject* to whom we must turn if we are to obtain a proper perspective of what is going on.

Ingo Swann, widely known as an artist and an author, is one such individual. Having demonstrated his psychic abilities in a number of laboratories around the world, Swann is known not only for his consistently reliable performance as a subject but, also, for his tough-minded approach to research. Unlike many subjects who leap on any unusual event in their environment and claim it as proof of their paranormal ability, Swann is often the first to discount an apparent success, pointing out some potential loophole in a protocol or possible misinterpretation of the data.

Swann's forte, however, lies in his creative input to the field in the form of research concepts. Often brilliant, always provocative, he cuts across established definitions of what constitutes useful laboratory tests of telepathy, clairvoyance, and precognition to suggest large-scale laboratory investigation of the remote-viewing phenomenon; rejecting the concept of subject-as-guinea-pig, he insisted that it is the viewing of natural target sites of relevance and interest rather than the dull, boring, repetitive viewing of contrived targets that prevents trivialization and extinction of a great human ability.

Swann offers here his views "from the inside" of such factors as the subject–experimenter relationship and the psychic personality.

## About the Author

**Ingo Swann** is a well-known author and artist whose psychic aptitudes have been studied extensively (more than half a million ESP trials) in several laboratories. Starting with an educational background in both Fine Arts and Biology, Mr. Swann has studied various areas relating to the nature of consciousness and psychic functioning. He has contributed substantially to our understanding of these areas, not only as a psychic subject, but also as a creative and insightful colleague. His paintings have been exhibited in many galleries, including the Smithsonian, and his major books include an autobiography, *To Kiss Earth Good-bye* (Hawthorne, 1975), a work, which he edited, on the relation of art to human potentials, *Cosmic Art* (Hawthorne, 1976), and a novel on the social implications of psychic functioning, *Star Fire* (Dell, 1978).

# 10

## On the Subjective Nature of Psychic Research, the Subject–Experimenter Relationship, and the Psychic Type of Personality

Ingo Swann

## Introduction

The following brief chapter represents not so much a critical assessment of certain areas of parapsychology as a tentative description of some work to be done in the future. It is based partly on the author's extensive participation as a parapsychology research subject in some 17 separate research situations over the past six-year period and partly on studies of official and unofficial parapsychological literature.

Essentially, up to the present, parapsychology in the United States exhibits characteristics associated with a closed intrasociety. New members find entrance into it difficult; it possesses a hierarchy of influence; it has a low toleration for unusual and extraordinary hypotheses; and it tends to depersonalize its topic—psychic abilities—from human attribute to impersonal empiricism. It possesses a literature in the form of journals (hereafter referred to as "official"). There exists also a vast amount of "unofficial" literature, in the form of biographies, records of unusual "psychic" material, and anthologies of mixed official and unofficial content.

It has been the experience of the author that psychic subjects are confined to unofficial status and are seldom, if ever, invited into, or obtain membership within, the official community. This condition is, of course, not unusual in the mental sciences, but presently, it is showing some signs of change. In the past, though, this political divisiveness has led to many impasses in the emergent understanding of paranormal aptitudes, and many of these impasses are perpetuated by the dominant attitudes and personalities of official status.

The official community can be criticized, as has already been done in many instances, of failing in achievement, and this criticism is likely to increase as the advances of the Soviets continue to come to light presently. The author believes that this criticism is justified in some part, but failure of parapsychologists is not total, nor does it originate totally within the official parapsychological community itself. The official parapsychological community suffers from strong constraints that originate within the disbelief systems of the broader scientific community. The scientific community, as a suprasocial order, has a very low tolerance for the parapsychological community, since the base hypotheses of the two are in extreme disagreement.

## The Unofficial Parapsychological Community as an Untapped Source of Advancement

The unofficial community, therefore, has no direct route into scientific consideration, since it is not incorporated into official status, which, in turn, is rejected for the most part by the suprasocial order. Because of this, the unofficial sources might be thought of as an uninspected source of advancement for the future, and the author feels that the granting of renewed interest in a novel cooperation of the official and unofficial parapsychological communities is now in order, especially in view of the emerging clues concerning Soviet advances in psychotronics.

## Three Major Areas Where Official and Unofficial Status Can and Do Meld

There appear to be three major areas (at least) where official and unofficial characteristics either meld or conflict, depending upon the individuals involved. Of these three, the extraordinary difficulties found in the subject–experimenter relationship is the most obvious, as well as the most documented. Second, the official community, it might be assumed, would be interested in identifying the psychic type of personality, but interest in this topic has been sporadic; it was stronger some 20 years ago than it is at the present. The identification of the psychic type of personality would necessitate larger and increased inputs by those personalities themselves, creating a bridge (if even tentative) between official methodologies and unofficial content. Third, there exists a vast and unexplored area of subjective or qualitative information that has hardly ever been solicited by the official community from its psychic subjects, nor, frankly, tolerated by the majority of its present or historical personalities. The present author views this situation as unfortunate in the extreme, since the United States has possessed many gifted and creative psychics.

These three areas might be seen by contemporary parapsychologists and future comers to be of high interest, if not of high priority, and each area possibly represents a discrete area of inquiry concerning the nature of psychic potential.

## The Subject–Experimenter Relationship

It has been apparent in psychical research for quite some time that psychic subject relationships with experimenters constitute a special field of inqiry in parapsychology—and, perhaps, a special problem to science in general.

It is understood, in science as a whole, that subject–experimenter relationships often suffer from standard pitfalls and experimenter effects.[1] In parapsychology, however, this situation takes on extraordinary importance. In sociology and psychology, for example, subject–experimenter relationships may suffer merely from bias originating in the experimenters school of thought or from within the experimenter's hypothesis that he or she is testing. When this is so, the experimenter may eventually overcome the difficulties if and when he or she is willing to go beyond his or her schooling and favorite hypothesis. In psychic research, however, accumulating evidence indicates that the subject–experimenter relationship is of extraordinary, if not basic, importance and that the subject–experimenter relationship is possessed of problems that involve the experimenter's own psychic potential and, hence, are amazing in their complexity and stunning for their magnitude.

At this present stage in psychic research, the situation is cogently identified by what appears to be a paradox: some experimenters seem to achieve confirmative results in their experimentation, while others do not, and in fact, seem to disrupt chance expectation in their experiments toward an unexpected, unexplained negative statistic. In some cases, failure of the experiment can be explained by lack of psychic ability in the subject, experiment incompatibility, experiment deficiency, and standard experimenter bias and ineptitude. Often, however, when these factors are corrected, the subject–experimenter relationship still fails to produce results. Past inspection of this situation suggests that there are several factors not usually found in other disciplines that enter into parapsychological experimentation. An understanding of these factors seems paramount if psychical research achievement is to be seriously envisioned.

As early as 1938, it was discovered that in independent research projects whose conditions and goals were closely parallel, highly significant results were obtained in one case, while in another, only chance results were found. It was felt then that the possible cause of this discrepancy was due to differences in the experimental approach and the handling of the subjects. A joint experiment was made to determine if such was the case, and it was concluded that "failure to find evidence of ESP in card tests may be due to an unfavorable experimenter–subject relationship."[2]

During 1943 to 1945, it was confirmed that an individual's personal belief system concerning the existence of, and possibilities in, ESP influenced not only successful results in subjects but also the experimenter's attitude and approach to ESP experiments.[3] A negative belief depressed results, while a positive belief contributed to successful experimental outcomes. Schmeidler labeled the nonbelievers "goats" and the believers "sheep."

Schmeidler's discovery of the sheep–goat effect probably constitutes one of parapsychology's most basic phenomenologies, indicating that one person's psychic gestalt (composed of learning, attitudes, preferences, bias, tolerance, and expectations) somehow interacts with the psychic gestalt of others. In 1966, confirmatory sheep–goat experiments showed a highly significant relationship between belief and scoring in ESP tests.[4] Thus, the basic opinion and psychological attitudes of the experimenter interact at some communal sub-awareness level with those of the subject and tend to influence the visibility of ESP in the subject. In parapsychology, therefore, the peculiar psychology of the experimenter becomes of as great an interest as is the psychology of the psychic subject.

A survey of the parapsychological literature, however, indicates a deficit of inquiry concerning the psychologies of parapsychologists, and no reports are available revealing the psychological profiles of experimenters who have obtained positive results and experimenters who have obtained negative results. It seems obvious, therefore, that in the future, methodologies that isolate a more exact image of the ideal experimenter in his or her own psychic poise will take on as much importance as probing into the insights and talents of psychic subjects. A recent assessment of this situation deliberates this situation and establishes the probable truth that a psychic experiment can no longer be considered apart from its overall context, environment, participants, and sociological expectations.[5]

## Is There a Psychic Type of Personality?

There has been, within the official literature, some effort to determine the characteristics of the psychic type of personality. For the most part, this effort has been sporadic, falling victim to the exclusion principles operating in the official community. Identification of the psychic type certainly has not received overwhelming attention, nor does this category of parapsychological work appear to have other than a low priority.

Evidence exists, however, that there is a psychic type of personality, or at least a type of subject personality that is most likely to be successful in experiments. It is to be understood that this type might be very elusive in the experimental situation, since the experimental situation appears to respond and be influenced by other than subject willingness and abilities, as mentioned above.

It might be expected that positive platforms involving incentives, vital interests, attitudes and expectations would contribute to successful outcomes in parapsychological testing, since these categories are seen to contribute to other areas of human endeavor. In 1943, it was found that experiments with incentives yielded significantly higher scores than tests without incentives.[6] A moderate improvement in scoring was obtained merely by informing the subject of his or her result, while a significantly higher improvement accompanied the giving of a reward for high scores.

Effect of attitudes was demonstrated in 1960,[7] while, similarly, a high significance between interest of the subject in the task and his or her scoring was established in 1967.[8] In 1975 and 1976, it was found that those who expected psi hitting scored significantly higher above chance than those who expected not to be successful.[9] This latter type of report echoes the implications of the sheep–goat phenomenon.

In 1945 and 1948, attempts were made to discover if ESP and IQ were possibly related, but it was found that if any, there was only a small correlation between ESP performance and IQ.[10] In 1965, it was established that the separation of ESP scores on the basis of IQ showed no relationship between intelligence and ESP,[11] and, in 1950, evidence was offered that mental health analysis did not prove to be a reliable basis for selecting good ESP subjects.[12] In terms of IQ and mental health, therefore, psi performance is not necessarily predictable, any more than is genius or inventiveness predictable or measurable by IQ.[13]

A search of the official parapsychological literature reveals that it may be possible to isolate successful psi subjects on the basis of extroversion, expansiveness, and world view. In 1946, it was found that high and low scores in ESP drawing tests were separable on the basis of the expansive or compressive quality of subjects' drawings.[14] Subjects who did well in ESP tests tended to make expansive drawings, while those who scored below chance expectations tended to produce compressive drawings. It was also found that given the Maslow Security–Insecurity Test, high ESP scores were obtained by the secure subjects and low scores by the insecure subjects. This particular indicator of good ESP performance expectation was confirmed in 1973, where expansive subjects scored significantly higher in ESP than compressive subjects ($p < .05$), these results being indicative of an interaction between extroversion and expansiveness.[15] A consistency between high-scoring subjects and extrovert–introvert ratings was found in 1951, where 74 percent of extroverts gave high ESP scores and 1 percent of the introverts gave lower scores than the expected average.[16] The relationship of extroversion to ESP scoring was seen again in 1952, when, in telepathy tests, extrovert receivers scored positively, while introvert receivers scored negatively.[17] It was found in 1971 that the difference between extroverts and introverts was significant in every case and that positive and negative characteristics could be established based upon extroversion and introversion.[18] Extroversion and ESP, thus, may be taken as a positive correlation.[19]

In 1954, it was found that subjects who turned their aggression outward scored low in ESP tests, as contrasted with subjects who did not, who scored significantly above chance,[20] while it was shown in 1967 that subjects who had a high degree of anxiety as measured by the Defense Mechanism Test scored below chance and those who had a low level of anxiety tended to score well above chance.[21] In 1968, it was established that those who tended to perceive the external world in a holistic manner showed more evidence of ESP than those who tended to perceive the world in an analytical manner.[22]

The psychic type of personality, therefore, is probably not isolable by IQ determinants and is divergent from standard mental testing processes; therefore, in these contexts, it is generally unknown. In his or her subjective qualities, however, the psychic type of personality can be seen as a nonaggressive extrovert who tends toward holistic world views and is capable of high interest, both subjectively and empirically, in psi processes. (Holistic world views are composed partly of empirical associations and experience, but there is a good deal of evidence suggesting that a world view may be composed of additional factors not associable to external realities, as we presently understand them. These factors, which, so far, are to be considered as subjective in their nature, gather increasing importance as evidence for them accumulates.)

## The Subjective Nature of Psychic Research

A tentative assessment of the future of psychic research (but an assessment that the author does not feel is too hasty or unwarranted) indicates that a great deal of future parapsychological achievement in research will rely upon revealing the subjective determinants of both subject and researcher alike. As noted before, the official literature carries no reports on the mental makeup or subjective realities of experimenters. The subjective realities of subjects, when written up, exist in the unofficial literature, which is diverse, cloudy, and of a massiveness that is prohibitive to organized investigation, save in the presence of a large staff, adequate funding, and computer storage and retrieval systems. This chapter, in fact, constitutes a preliminary proposal for a project to collect, categorize, test, and evaluate the subjective realities of subjects and experimenters alike.

The evidence in the official literature has led inexorably toward the elusive, intangible areas of the subjective, but this trend has been engaged in only tentatively and only by select researchers. This type of research—into the subjective—would necessarily begin with the disadvantage that the mental sciences hold the subjective to be at least irrelevant, if not irrational, and characteristic of the "lunatic fringe." Notwithstanding, it seems appropriate that based upon the limited but clear evidence given here and found in the official literature, increasing excursions into the subjective seem recommended.

In the author's opinion, the subjective realities of psi subjects possess at least three tangible qualities that cannot be avoided. First, the verifiable data that emerge out of a subjective attempt to view distant locations are seen to be remarkably accurate.[23] There is hardly any other interpretation for this phenomenon, except to hypothesize that there exist additional forms of human perception at the subjective levels, forms that have not yet been isolated fully and whose structure is unknown at this point. But that that structure must exist, there can hardly be any doubt. Second, creative individuals, psi subjects, and parapsychological experimenters alike are seen to interact within hitherto unelaborated subjective constraints. Third, successful ESP subjects appear to depend almost as heavily upon their subjective realities as they do upon objective experience. This allows them to create or participate in operant modes of consciousness that are alien to objective science alone and which are, for lack of a better term, almost solely subjective in their nature. There may be a fourth reason for engaging heavily in subjective research of the psychic. This chapter is being prepared before the author can have sufficient access to information coming out of the Soviet Union as a result of the Toth detainment. What information is available, however, seriously substantiates that Soviet parapsychologists have intruded deeply into the subjective possibilities of psychic potential, have isolated a certain amount of structure, and are expediting development of psi-mediated communication channels and lines of perception and influence at a distance.

## Conclusion

It is the author's opinion that the subjective aspects of psychic research can no longer be avoided. It has been his experience in active and extended parapsychological research that successful outcomes of experimentation depend almost totally upon commensurate subjective flexibilities, both in the subject and in the experimenter alike. This might also be extended to include individuals not directly associated with the experiment.

It seems apparent that the individual's subjective qualities might be static or frozen in many instances but that the subjective qualities are nonetheless capable of swift flux, association, and psychic concretizing. These subjective qualities might exist either as a gestalt or holistic psychological platform, but upon occasion, they can be convened with a precision capable of perceiving, identifying, and communicating bits of information that flow into the analytical capabilities of gifted psychics. These subjective qualities can, and do, interact with the psi fields of others and are influenced accordingly, depending upon the confidence and goals of the individuals involved.

The tips of these subjective qualities can be seen in the official literature by the subject–experimenter paradox and in the personality characteristics (limited as they may so far have been established) of the psychic type. The overall subjective implications can be seen, if one's belief system is permissive of novel and unique information, in the unofficial literature and, quite possibly, in the Soviet approach to parapsychology and psychotronics.

# Summary

Successful psychic research subjects are seldom asked to estimate or elaborate upon their personal contact with psychic abilities. The emergent field of parapsychology is thereby weighted heavily with the opinions, hypotheses, and selective areas of interest of researchers. Therefore, the field is deficient in information that might lead to the establishment of novel hypotheses incorporating subjective inputs from psychic subjects. This condition has probably not been favorable to the establishment of a holistic view of parapsychological potential. It has created an unreal formal division between psychic abilities and experimenter, perpetuated difficulties in the subject–experimenter relationship, and delayed an understanding of the psychic type of personality. These difficulties are real and are reflected in the literature, which is reviewed.

# Notes

1. T. X. Barber, "Pitfalls in Research: Nine Investigator and Experimental Effects," in *Second Handbook of Research and Teaching,* ed. R. M. W. Travers (Chicago: Rand McNally, 1973), pp. 296–309.

2. J. G. Pratt and Margaret M. Price, "The Experimenter–Subject Relationship in Tests for ESP," *Journal of Parapsychology* 2 (June 1938): 84–94.

3. G. R. Schmeidler, "Predicting Good and Bad Scores in a Clairvoyance Experiment: A Preliminary Report," *Journal of the American Society for Psychical Research* 37 (1943): 103–10; G. R. Schmeidler, "Predicting Good and Bad Scores in a Clairvoyance Experiment: A Final Report," *Journal of the American Society for Psychical Research* 39 (October 1945): 210–21.

4. B. H. Bhadra, "The Relationship of Test Scores to Belief in ESP," *Journal of Parapsychology* 30 (March 1966): 1–17.

5. Rhea A. White, "The Limits of Experimenter Influence of Psi Test Results: Can Any Be Set?," *Journal of the American Society for Psychical Research* 70 (October 1976): 339–69.

6. J. L. Woodruff and Gardner Murphy, "Effect of Incentives on ESP Visual Perception," *Journal of Parapsychology* 7 (September 1943): 144–57.

7. Carroll B. Nash, "The Effect of Subject–Experimenter Attitudes on Clairvoyance Scores," *Journal of Parapsychology* 24 (September 1960): 189–98.

8. Dallas E. Buzby, "Subject Attitude and Score Variance in ESP Tests," *Journal of Parapsychology* 31 (March 1967): 43–50.

9. Judith L. Taddonio, "Attitudes and Expectancies in ESP Scoring," *Journal of Parapsychology* 39 (December 1975): 289–96; and Judith L. Taddonio, "The Relationship of Experimenter Expectancy to Performance on ESP Tasks," *Journal of Parapsychology* (June 1976): 107–14.

10. Betty M. Humphrey, "ESP and Intelligence," *Journal of Parapsychology* 9 (March 1945): 7–16; and Betty M. Humphrey, "A Further Study of ESP and Intelligence," *Journal of Parapsychology* 12 (September 1948).

11. M. Eason, Jean Clare, and Boleslaw A. Wysocki, "Extrasensory Perception and Intelligence," *Journal of Parapsychology* 29 (June 1965): 109–14.

12. Olivia B. Rivers, "An Exploratory Study of the Mental Health and Intelligence of ESP Subjects," *Journal of Parapsychology* (December 1950): 267–77.

13. Silvano Arieti, *Creativity, the Magic Synthesis* (New York: Basic Books, 1976); and John H. Douglas, "The Genius of Everyman" (1), "Discovering Creativity," *Science News* 111 (April 1977).

14. Burke M. Smith and Betty M. Humphrey, "Some Personality Characteristics Related to ESP Performances," *Journal of Parapsychology* 10 (December 1946): 169–89.

15. B. K. Kanthamani and Ramakrishna Rao, "Personality Characteristics of ESP Subjects," pt. 5, "Graphic Expansiveness and ESP," *Journal of Parapsychology* (June 1973): 119–29.

16. Betty M. Humphrey, "Introversion–Extroversion Ratings in Relation to Scores in ESP Tests," *Journal of Parapsychology* 15 (December 1951): 252–62.

17. George W. Casper, "Effect of the Receiver's Attitude Toward the Sender in ESP Tests," *Journal of Parapsychology* 16 (September 1952): 212–18.

18. B. K. Kanthamani and Ramakrishna Rao, "Personality Characteristics of ESP Subjects," pt. 1, "Primary Personality Characteristics and ESP," *Journal of Parapsychology* 35 (September 1971): 189–207.

19. B. K. Kanthamani and Ramakrishna Rao, "Personality Characteristics of ESP Subjects," pt. 3, "Extraversion and ESP," *Journal of Parapsychology* 36 (September 1972): 198–212.

20. G. R. Schmeidler, "Picture-Frustration Ratings and ESP Scores for Subjects Who Showed Moderate Annoyance at the ESP Task," *Journal of Parapsychology* 18 (September 1954): 137–52.

21. Martin Johnson and B. K. Kanthamani, "The Defense Mechanism Test as a Predictor of ESP Scoring Direction," *Journal of Parapsychology* 31 (January 1967): 99–110.

22. Dallas E. Buzby, "Precognition and Psychological Variables," *Journal of Parapsychology* 32 (March 1968): 39–46.

23. H. E. Puthoff and R. Targ, "A Perceptual Channel for Information Transfer Over Kilometer Distances: Historical Perspective and Recent Research," *Proceedings of the IEEE* 64 (March 1976): 329–54.

# Introduction to Chapter 11

While science is often viewed as an abstract intellectual enterprise, it actually goes on in a social, political, and economic context that has important consequences for both the direction of research and the applications developed from research discoveries. The following chapter, as well as other sources, establishes that there is a very significant research effort on psi phenomena in the Soviet Union—research that appears to be supported at least 20 and perhaps 100 times the level of support in the United States.[1] The importance of psi research in the Soviet Union has been underlined by the Soviet Psychological Association, who called on the Soviet Academy of Sciences to step up efforts in this area.[2] They recommended that the newly formed Psychological Institute within the Soviet Academy of Sciences and the Psychological Institute of the Academy of Pedagological Sciences review the area and consider the creation of a new laboratory within one of the institutes to study persons with unusual abilities. They also recommended a comprehensive evaluation of experiments and theory by the Academy of Science's Institute of Biophysics and Institute for the Problems of Information Transmission. With regard to wide-scale screening for psi abilities among the Soviet population, the depth of the search can be inferred from a 1974 article in *Leninskoye Znamya* ("Lenin's Banner"), an official organ of the Moscow Communist Party.[3] In that article was an interview with a leading scientist and information theorist, I. M. Kogan. Kogan discussed a number of recent developments in the field of psi research, including some of his own experiments, and estimated that the number of well-developed psychics in the general population was on the order of one in 100,000.

Aside from the overall importance given psi research in the Soviet Union, the content of Soviet psi research has an emphasis that is characteristically Soviet, since Marxist philosophy strongly affects the kinds of research questions that are considered valid and socially useful. Special emphasis, for example, is placed on finding "materialistic" explanations for psi. Further, as contrasted with the predominantly academic stance of Western parapsychology, analysts observe that Soviet political factors influence research on potential applications of psi toward, for example, military applications. The ability to hypnotize people at a distance by psi, which has been studied extensively in the Soviet Union, is obviously of interest to police and military organizations, although such research would be ethically questionable in the West. While these ideas are not pleasant to consider, they need to be realistically assessed, so this chapter by Edward Wortz and his collaborators is of considerable interest.

## About the Authors

**Edward C. Wortz,** Ph.D., received his Ph.D. in psychology from the University of Texas, at Austin, in 1957. At AiResearch he directed and managed research, in the Life Sciences, for 15 years. He has published more than 50 papers and patents. Currently, Dr. Wortz has a private practice in psychotherapy and biofeedback therapy in Pasadena, California. He was president of the Biofeedback Society of California and a director of the Biofeedback Society of America. He is a member of the American Psychological Association, the Society for Psychophysiological Research, and the American Association for the Advancement of Science, and is an "Associate Fellow" of the Aerospace Medical Association.

**A. S. Bauer,** B.S., received his B.S. in Physics from the University of Minnesota in 1952. He is Senior Program Specialist in the Laser Systems Department at AiResearch, where he directs R&D programs on laser systems.

**R. F. Blackwelder,** Ph.D., received his Ph.D. in Fluid Mechanics from Johns Hopkins University in 1970. He is currently Assistant Professor, department of Aerospace Engineering, at UCLA. He has published numerous papers and patents on heat transfer and aerodynamics.

**J. W. Eerkens,** Ph.D., received his Ph.D. in Engineering Science from the University of California, Berkeley, in 1960. His principle interests have been laser systems. At AiResearch he was Staff Scientist and author of the Air Force document, "Rocket Radiation Handbook." He is currently the president of Liscom Corp. in Lawndale, California. He has numerous publications, patents, and honors.

**A. J. Saur,** Ph.D., received his Ph.D. in Physics from the University of Illinois in 1951. He is currently Engineering Specialist at AiResearch, where he is in charge of engineering and fabrication of electronic special test equipment. He has extensive experience in engineering R&D.

# 11

# An Investigation of Soviet Psychical Research

Edward C. Wortz, A. S. Bauer, R. F. Blackwelder,
J. W. Eerkens, and A. J. Saur

Historically, parapsychological research in the United States and the Soviet Union has been markedly different in approach. The Soviets have generally proceeded from the perspectives of a psychophysiology that is Pavlovian in origin and the physical and mathematical sciences, whereas parapsychological research in the United States has been largely influenced by early approaches in England and has dealt with attempts to convince others that such processes exist. In the recent past, typical research in the United States has attempted to reveal the legitimacy of parapsychology by statistically oriented experimentation based on association theory or by exploration of experimental paradigms that might be more demonstrative, such as exploring telepathy via dreams, sheep versus goat experimental designs, children versus adults, receiver characteristics, transmitter characteristics, psi characteristics, and so forth. Recently, investigators in the United States have become gradually influenced by the apparent successes of their Soviet counterparts and, in general, seem to be commencing to emulate their approach.

On reviewing the Soviet literature, research in novel biophysical information transfer (NBIT) was emphasized. The Soviet literature almost invariably shows interest in the physical and physiological mechanisms. An example is the interest in psychoenergetics, bioplasma, and psychotronics. The term *psychotronics* was coined by a French journalist after the analogy with electronics, bionics, nucleonics, and so forth. The Soviets have devised their own term— *psychoenergetics*. These new names were chosen to give the field of study an air of scientific or technological respectability.

A fundamental question remains: Does the name imply a basic difference in the approach, and if so, what effects can be expected from it? Judging from the available literature, the name does imply a difference in the approach of the Soviet and Czech investigators from that of most Western parapsychologists. Some of the differences are outlined below.

1. The Soviets do not undertake studies like those of J. B. Rhine, in which remote card reading or other simple telepathic tasks are carried out repeatedly to gather statistical evidence. The Soviets assume the reality of thought transference. Their best experiments are designed to elucidate the physical basis of these NBIT mechanisms.

2. Many of the Soviet researchers that publish in open literature in this field pursue their studies on their own time and at their own personal expense. They lack the resources to carry out well-designed or long statistical studies.

3. Many Westerners remain convinced that parapsychology will never be explained in terms of physics. They cling to an undertone of a religiouslike belief in transcendent mechanisms. The Soviets, in contrast, reject such an approach; being doctrinaire materialists, everything has a physical, scientific explanation. Again, this line of reasoning reinforces the trend toward eliciting the physical mechanisms of NBIT.

In reviewing Soviet and Western work on NBIT phenomena, it seems reasonable to suppose that serious interdisciplinary research and development is being carried on. Furthermore, it seems that the Soviets have organized laboratories for just such programs. On the other hand, it is obvious that many Soviet workers in this field pursue their research as an extracurricular activity, with little or no funding. Thus, there are hints of secret work, as well as indications that parapsychological research may be in disfavor. It may be that high-quality systematic research is officially approved, well funded, and well organized, whereas research in this field from "nonofficial" laboratories may be allowed to flounder without funds, thus providing a smoke screen of poor-quality work. If the Soviets did indeed establish laboratories for a systematic approach to this problem, in our opinion, they are certainly capable of making good progress.

The literature surveyed varies widely in degree of sophistication. Most experimental papers give rather vague descriptions and insufficient data to assess the accuracy and importance of claimed results. Upon completion of the review, the bulk of what was considered to be creditable work was found to be centered around, but not limited to, the activities of three principal individuals—Kogan, Viktor Adamenko, and G. A. Sergeyev. Of the theoretical papers, those by Kogan are undoubtedly the best and reflect the good thinking of an experienced physicist. Using physically acceptable arguments,

Kogan demonstrates the possibility that ELF and very low frequency (VLF) carrier waves might be part of NBIT mechanisms and initiates an information theory approach to the study of NBIT. His ideas are much like those of Persinger (see Chapter 8).

The work by Adamenko, on the other hand, is spotty with respect to knowledge of modern physics and physiology. He utilizes a number of poorly defined and unquantifiable concepts, such as *bioplasma, psi energy,* and so forth. Nevertheless, significant contributions are made by him—particularly his study and explanation of telekinesis in terms of electrostatics. The work of Sergeyev shows the effectiveness of a radar signature expert analyzing electrophysiological events. He shows some interesting new possibilities, taking into account that the noise in the signals not only contains statistical random variations but that the carriers also may have nonstationary drifts. His work also seems to suffer from the lack of an interdisciplinary approach. Furthermore, he is probably responsible for the development of at least one (and perhaps two) remote physiological sensor.

## Application of Statistical Theories to NBIT Mechanisms

In the field of theoretical statistics, the Soviets are usually considered to be ahead of the Western countries. Kolmogorov and his contemporaries did a considerable amount of work in the 1920 to 1945 era, developed many new theories, and applied them to some classical problems, such as Kolmogorov's theory of isotropic turbulence. Directly before and during World War II, Rice, Shannon, and others in the West developed more advanced ideas, which are now embedded within information theory and communication theory. However, the Soviets were the first to apply these ideas and techniques to the field of parapsychology. Kogan seems to have been the leader in this venture, and the known papers by him are good in that he demonstrates a knowledge of these advanced fields, correctly applies the techniques, and reaches some justifiable and creditable conclusions. Kogan seems to have started working on these ideas in the early 1960s. Milan Ryzl states that the bioinformation section of the Scientific Technical Society of Radiotechnique and Electrocommunication was founded in 1965 and that Kogan was its first director, indicating that Kogan's ideas were viewed favorably at the time.[4] Ryzl further reports that the bioinformation section seemed to flourish under Kogan. It organized meetings, seminars, and discussions; he embarked upon a publicity campaign in newspapers and magazines and was concerned with the use of parapsychology as a military weapon. Kogan also headed the section as it undertook some successful experiments involving transmission of images over short ranges.

Kogan seems to have been at his peak when he visited the United States in 1969 and gave a presentation at University of California-Los Angeles on the application of information theory to the problem of telepathy.[5] That paper summarized his work and represents the most advanced work on this topic by anyone. Then, publication of his work inexplicably stopped. Judging from the papers reviewed, no one else in the USSR has reported on this line of endeavor.

Although this work may have been completely stopped, it hardly seems likely. Considering that Kogan had successfully started to apply these new concepts to parapsychology and had obtained some new information, it is more plausible that this work did not abruptly stop but is continuing secretly. Ryzl indirectly lends credence to this idea by discussing the military work done at Kogan's institute.[6]

It is significant that the Soviets pursued the application of nonstationary analysis to parapsychology, especially in the study of EEG signals. Sergeyev has been the leader in this effort; he has used both correlation functions and spectral analysis.[7] Under the more common assumption of stationariness, these statistical quantities are independent of time. Since parapsychological events are quite intermittent and occur rather randomly, their statistical functions, such as correlation, spectra, and so forth may vary dramatically in time.

Sergeyev thus defines a nonstationary autocorrelation function as

$$R(t, \tau) = \frac{1}{T} \int_{t}^{t+T} [X(S) - \overline{X}(S)][X(S + \tau)$$
$$- \overline{X}(S + \tau)] \, dS$$

where X is the stochastic variable, $\overline{X}$ is the average value of X (presumably over time T), $\tau$ is a time delay, and T is the averaging time. He does not specify the averaging time T, but T must be of the same order of magnitude as the time scale of the event being studied.

Since $R(t, \tau)$ is a function of the time delay $\tau$, Sergeyev suggests characterizing this correlation function by several time scales, which he defines as

$$\tau^{(n)}(t) = \int_{0}^{T} [R(t, \tau)]^{n} \, d\tau.$$

Thus, $\tau^{(n)}$ are random functions of time, and Sergeyev claims that $\tau^{(1)}/\tau^{(2)}$ is a measure of the nonlinear modulation by the stimuli received through extrasensory channels. He does not justify nor substantiate this conclusion.

Sergeyev has applied this type of analysis in at least two different modes. First, he compares the ratio $\tau^{(1)}/\tau^{(2)}$ from a "bioplasmagram" to that obtained from signals external to the body, such as the fluctuations in the earth's magnetic field.[8] He claims to have obtained a well-defined relation between these two signals; however, the data shown in his paper do not support the statement that is given in the text. In spite of this discrepancy, Sergeyev's ideas are sound, and in view of the intermittent nature of parapsychological phenomena, it seems reasonable to explore nonstationary analysis of the recorded data. Ryzl claims that Sergeyev can detect an incoming telepathic stimulus by analyzing EEG records.[9]

Second, Sergeyev has applied these ideas in studying changes in the bioplasmagram during emotional stress.[10] He used digital analysis and retained the high-frequency content (that is, up to 30 kHz) of the EEG. It is obvious after studying the data in his previous paper that he also retained the high-frequency content there as well.[11] Although it is not obvious what type of information is obtained in these higher frequencies, Sergeyev does believe that they are important in the dynamic functioning of the brain; it is conceivable that frequencies higher than the normal beta wave frequency may be present and would be instructive to study. Also, if a VLF carrier wave is important in the parapsychological communication channel, a study of these frequencies would be beneficial.

It is purely speculative to guess what type of work the Soviets are now doing in this area. Obviously, they have a great interest in parapsychology. Mutshall says that they have opened seven new laboratories to study these phenomena since 1960.[12] Kogan had just started to apply information theory to these problems and seems to have developed this technique to the point of usefulness before publication of his work ceased. Although information theory cannot explain the physical mechanism of the NBIT communication channel, it is a very useful tool to analyze the data quantitatively. Kogan had already used this to yield new information (for example, the information rate dropped as distance traversed increased). More advances from this avenue of approach can be expected, such as qualifying the information to be transferred, designing experiments more amenable to analysis, and studying coding and encoding techniques.

Sergeyev's published work suggests that he is possibly continuing his study of nonstationary analysis of NBIT phenomena. In particular, it seems strange that he did not publish or even mention the use of his techniques for cross correlations or cross spectra. Since he almost always was comparing two different signals (EEG and the earth's magnetic field), a nonstationary analysis of the cross correlation between these signals seems more appropriate than the single-channel analysis he published.

It also could be expected that Sergeyev has pursued nonlinear analysis and modeling of NBIT events. He reported that he found a modulation of the EEG at a frequency $f_1$–$f_2$ when lights were flashing at frequencies $f_1$ and $f_2$.[13] If only linear mechanisms were involved, there would be no energy or modulation of the spectra at a frequency of $f_1-f_2$, thus suggesting that nonlinear mechanisms may be responsible for this behavior. This phenomenon should be verified and explained, if possible.

The Soviets should have a vested interest in remote viewing, which, interestingly, is never mentioned in the available literature. Based upon the experience of Puthoff and Targ (see Chapters 2 and 3), it is not too difficult to set up an experiment in this area, and it seems reasonable to assume that the Soviets have probably successfully done so.[14] The next step is obviously to improve the efficiency of the transmission process. Here, the ideas from information and communication theory become important tools because they can be used to determine the amount of information transferred, and thus represent a quantitative measure of success or failure. This tool can then be used to measure the effect of different variables, such as distance (which Kogan has already done), directivity, shielding, and the type of information transferred. Mutshall says Kogan has studied this also. It is more reasonable to assume that this work has continued than that it was terminated at this level of development.

## Electrostatics of Telekinesis

According to the published reports, there are several investigations of telekinesis (that is, moving material objects without touching them) that have occurred at various times and places in Communist bloc countries. In work done in Leningrad by Vasiliev and his associates, Nina Kulagina (also called Nelja Mihailova) exhibited remarkable psychokinetic ability. Benson Herbert, Ryzl, Zdenek Rejdak, and Adamenko, among others, have discussed or commented on Kulagina's feats. In Moscow, Adamenko worked with another subject, Alla Vinogradova, who is more skilled in telekinesis than Nina Kulagina. Herbert and others also have reported some of the work of Julius Kremessky of Bratislava, who moves hanging mobiles. As telekinetic subjects, the women seem to be superior to the men; Vinogradova and Kulagina are said to be able to move objects weighing as much as 100 grams (gm) on a table top.

Adamenko has advanced an explanation for observed phenomena of telekinesis that is more interesting psychologically than physically. In the article "Some Problems of Biological Electrodynamics and Psychoenergetics," he theorizes that the physical force causing the objects to move is due to static electric charges on the objects and electrical fields generated by the subject.[15] It can be shown (as discussed subsequently) that electrostatic forces can indeed be strong enough to produce some of the effects reported. Anyone living in dry climates is quite familiar with electrostatic forces, for example, static electricity discharges from the finger when one walks across the room to the light switch and articles of clothing sticking together and crackling with corona discharge when removed from the gas clothes drier.

Adamenko's descriptions of the observed phenomena are easier to deal with

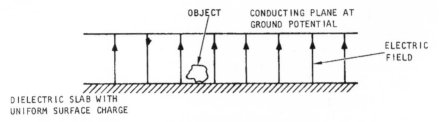

**Figure 11.1** Electric field between parallel plates.

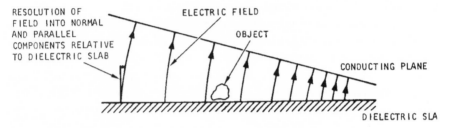

**Figure 11.2** Electric field between nonparallel plates.

than his theoretical expositions. An example is his 1973 article in *The A.R.E. Journal.*[16] In the work with Vinogradova and others in a Moscow, Adamenko used a dielectric cube, 50 cm edge to edge, as a table. Various small objects were placed on the upper surface of the cube. Vinogradova was able to induce an electric charge on the cube, after which she could then move small objects on its surface. With biofeedback training, other subjects were able to duplicate Vinogradova's feats. There must have been some effect that reduced the coefficient of friction between the moved object and the cube, since Adamenko writes at some length about the reduced friction and theorizes that the electric field of the cube polarizes the air molecules and reduces their number of degrees of freedom from six to two. In addition, Adamenko states that the field is inhomogenous and produces a net flow of the air molecules, which tends to buoy up the objects on the cube. Elsewhere, he states that the electric field is as great as 10,000 V/cm. This value is approximately the maximum electric field that can exist in dry air because of corona discharge and ionization of the air molecules at higher field strengths. The explanation of air molecules providing the buoyant force to overcome sliding friction is necessary because electrostatic forces alone could not, in the situation described by Adamenko, levitate objects weighing more than a gram or so and because the coefficient of sliding friction is in the range of .1 to .3 for nonlubricated surfaces.

The concept of a conductor at ground potential near a charged dielectric surface as the mechanism for generating an electric field whose direction and magnitude can be altered is illustrated in simplified form in Figures 11.1 and 11.2. In Figure 11.1, a plane conducting surface is placed parallel to the dielectric. The resulting electric field is uniform and normal to the two parallel surfaces. If the extent of each surface is much larger than the distance between them, the field is not changed by moving the plates closer together or farther apart. In Figure 11.2, the plates are not parallel. In this case, the electric field is nonuniform and has a component parallel to the dielectric slab.

In the case illustrated in Figure 11.1, the object experiences no force parallel to the surface of the slab. In the case shown in Figure 11.2, the electric field is not normal to the slab. Hence, if the object has an electrostatic charge, it will experience a force that tends to move it parallel to the plate, either toward or away from the region of closest approach between the dielectric slab and the conducting plate. It will experience a force in the same direction (but it will be weaker if the effect is due to polarization of the object rather than an unbalanced charge).

The human body is a conductor. According to Adamenko, the conductivity can be varied at will to affect the field. He does not try to explain in detail the physiological mechanism involved. Even with constant conductivity, the human subject can vary the field near the dielectric surface by positioning his or her body, arms, hands, and so forth.

There are two possible mechanisms whereby a small object on the dielectric surface can be moved by the electric field—particularly a nonuniform field. The first mechanism is that the small object is itself electrostatically charged. The second is that it is electrically neutral but can be polarized. An electric dipole in a nonuniform electric field experiences a force in the direction of the field.

The work reported by Adamenko on telekinesis appears to be genuine information. The experimental arrangement he describes can be analyzed on the basis of electrostatic theory, with predicted results in substantial agreement with the results reported. Adamenko's theoretical explanation appears to be a mishmash of classical electrostatics and parapsychology. It appears probable that Adamenko himself is a believer in the psi field because he tries to incorporate it into his theoretical framework.

In terms of application to the transmission of intelligence, the telekinetic work of Adamenko does not seem to lead anywhere. However, it does point up the ability of certain individuals to develop an ability to influence the ambient electrical field, apparently by violitional control over phsyical and physiological processes (for example, electrical conductivity of the skin). In addition, we must not overlook the possibility that the psychophysiology of this phenomenon may have relevance to transducer mechanisms.

## Remote Physiological Sensors

A remote sensor is an instrument for measuring a physiological response of the human body without the use of electrodes or other means of contacting the body. In the literature reviewed, there are references to one or more remote sensors developed by Gennadij Aleksandrovic Sergeyev.* It is claimed that one of these instruments will measure the EEG of a person at a distance of 5 m. The instrument is classified, and no credible description of it is available—there is only allusions to its existence. One must keep in mind that there is reason to doubt the Soviet claim. It the instrument is to register the EEG, it must remotely sense the electromagnetic field associated with the EEG potentials. These potentials are typically of the order of tens of microvolts. U.S. investigators have measured EEG signals with electrodes placed a few centimeters from the head. These electrodes sensed the electric field generated by the brain. Cohen has measured the magnetic field associated with the EEG by means of a search coil several centimeters from the head.[17] At larger distances from the head, the electric and magnetic EEG fields become drowned in noise. The following discussion is a speculative attempt to guess the operating principles of the instrument.

It is possible that a sensitive electric or magnetic sensor or some combination of the two would detect electrical signals from a human body at a distance of 5 m. Although it is unlikely that the output of such an instrument would be a direct measure of the EEG, it would provide information of interest to a police interrogator, such as the strength and rate of the heart beat, the tensing and relaxation of muscles, the depth and rate of breathing, and, perhaps, the electrical properties of the skin. The uses to which the instrument would be put are reasons enough for official secrecy about its operating principles. Moreover, the story that a remote sensor is a remote EEG sensor would be a natural way of trying to hide the real purpose of Sergeyev's invention. Some support to the speculation that the invention is a remote lie detector is provided by the statement by Ostrander and Schroeder that Sergeyev is a mathematician at the Uktomskij Laboratory run by the Soviet military.[18]

In reviewing the available literature, five references have been found that may help shed some light on the Sergeyev invention(s). First, Ostrander and Schroeder report Sergeyev's assertion that Kulagina, who reportedly exhibits remarkable telekinetic ability, generates a pulsating magnetic field whose amplitude is not much weaker than the magnetic field of the earth, according to measurements made with his remote sensor.[19] Second, the reporter Anatolij Kongro discusses work by Sergeyev and his students in measuring emotional-states of a subject by a remote sensor.[20] No description of the instrument is given in the article. In another reference, there is a description of a remote sensor. The sensor consists of a metal disc suspended in a vessel of water. The disc is coated with a semiconductor and appears to be electrically connected to an EEG recorder. The patient is connected to the other (ground) input of the recorder.

---

*Sergeyev is also referred to as Sergeev in the literature.

The fourth article contains the intriguing statement that the sensitivity of the bioplasmagram detectors is increased by placing them in water. A doubling of the output is claimed. Although it is claimed that these detectors respond to electromagnetic radiation, we are unfamiliar with any simple detector whose sensitivity would be enhanced by immersing it in water, except possibly a proton resonance detector for the magnetic field. A small acoustic detector (such as a hydrophone), consisting of a piezoelectric or magnetostrictive material with appropriate electrical connections, might exhibit greater sensitivities to sound when immersed in water. The greater sensitivity would be achieved because of the improved match of acoustic impedances between water and detector, as compared with the poor match between air and detector. In addition, the physical size and shape of the water container might provide a larger sensitive area for detecting sound than the detector alone.

A speculative conclusion from the previously cited literature, together with the known fact that Sergeyev is a mathematician who has published articles on the application of information theory to parapsychology (see, for example, an article he published on some methodological problems of parapsychology[21]), is that the Sergeyev remote sensor does exist and is an instrument for measuring electric and magnetic fields generated by a human subject at a distance of a few meters. Because of background noise, sophisticated analysis of the signal generated by the instrument is required to extract useful information. The instrument is probably a research tool and apparently has been used with some success on subjects that generate strong electric or magnetic fields (for example, Kulagina). The coated disc in a vessel of water is probably mostly a Soviet fairy tale if we discount the possibility of an acoustic sensor; however, the mention of water suggests that possibly magnetic fields are detected with a proton resonance magnetometer. Certainly, water would be a poor medium for detecting electric fields because of its high dielectric constant. The instrument probably comprises several sets of electric and magnetic field detectors arranged such that the noise due to extraneous fields can be reduced by signal extraction techniques.

In the fifth article, a set of noncontacting electrodes used to measure changes in the dielectric properties of the patient is described.[22] It may well be that this instrument is completely different from the Sergeyev remote sensor. On the other hand, these noncontacting electrodes may, in fact, be the Sergeyev sensor, and the other published information may be a complete fabrication.

If it is assumed that the described sensor is different from the Sergeyev remote sensor, it can be concluded that the instrument comprises noncontacting electrodes arranged electrically to sense small changes in the dielectric constant of the human body. The electrodes are silver, probably formed by depositing silver on plates of barium titanate. They are built into a rubber covering that insulates them electrically from the body and holds them in a fixed geometric configuration with respect to a portion of the body. The two terminals of a high-voltage supply (for example, a battery) are connected to the two silver electrodes, with a large resistance in series with one electrode. A change in the dielectric constant of the body causes a change in the capacitance between the electrodes. The resulting flow of charge either to or from the electrodes produces a measurable potential difference across the resistance. This potential difference is amplified and constitutes the output of the instrument.

The resistance or other details of the signal conditioning and amplifying system are not explicitly mentioned in the article. Instead, the theory of the instrument based on the bioplasma hypothesis is described, as is the notion that there are maser effects in living organisms which lead to the emission of free electrons and protons and, thereby, to changes in the electrical properties of the surrounding air. An analysis also is presented to show that the observed signal is not due merely to the piezoelectric effect in barium titanate.

The fact that barium titanate is used to support the silver electrodes is irrelevant to the operation of the sensor but relevant to the evaluation of the paucity of the report. It is likely that silver-plated barium titanate slabs happened to be available to the investigators. Because of its piezoelectric properties, barium titanate has a variety of uses in military weapons and instruments, such as hydrophones for underwater sound detection and shock-actuated detonators for explosive devices. As previously noted, Sergeyev works in a military research and development laboratory, where barium titanate would be available. It has been previously reported that much of the Soviet parapsychological work to which we have access is done as an avocation by the investigators (without official support or sanction). In such circumstances, the use of silver-plated barium titanate as an inexpensive and available substitute for solid silver electrodes is understandable.

Other types of remote sensors mentioned in the available literature seem quite simple and conventional. For example, V. Puskin (Pushkin) wrote about a sensor used to demonstrate that the power shown by Vinogradova to move objects without touching them was due to the electrostatic charges induced on the objects.[23] The sensor in this case was a simple neon glow lamp. When the object was discharged by means of the neon lamp, it could no longer be moved.

A broader question regarding remote sensors is to determine or predict types of sensors that logically would have been or would be developed in the course of following the indicated lines of investigation. Perhaps the Soviets have, in fact, developed such instruments; perhaps they are going to do so. Perhaps they have tried and have not been successful. Possible sensor developments discussed in the following paragraphs are not meant to be exhaustive; rather, they are speculative and offered as examples of what may or might be.

A tunable antenna for detecting low-frequency, VLF, or ELF electromagnetic radiation could be used. The Soviets believe both in mental telepathy and in a prosaic physical mechanism for it. The most probable mechanism is electromagnetic radiation. A tunable antenna could be used in two types of experiment: trying to detect the radiation from the telepathic agent and trying to generate radiation of the right frequency to interfere with telepathic reception.

A neutrino detector may be used. Both the Soviet J. Parnov and the American Ruderfer have suggested neutrinos as the means of transmitting thought from one mind to another.[24] One of the collaborators for this chapter, J. Eerkens, has a plausible hypothesis about the production and detection of neutrinos that could be experimentally tested by relatively modest expenditures for equipment and labor. A magnetic field or field gradient detector could be used. The Soviets and other Eastern Europeans are greatly interested in dowsing, or finding groundwater. A currently popular theory of dowsing is that the human body is sensitive to small changes (temporal or spatial) in the magnetic field of the earth, such as might be produced by water near the surface of the ground. If the human body can generate, as well as sense, magnetic fields, such human magnetism might be the basis of some form of thought transference or PK. It is reported that Kulagina warms up her psychokinetic powers by causing a compass needle to move; as previously mentioned. Sergeyev claims that Kulagina generates a pulsating magnetic field not much weaker than the magnetic field of the earth, according to measurements made with his remote sensor.

A noncontacting temperature detector may be used. Adamenko and others have shown interest in the properties of human skin in three separate lines of investigation. First, Adamenko ascribes some electrostatic properties to the skin to support his theories about telekinesis. Second, he has developed a tobioscope for investigating the electrical properties of the acupuncture points on the skin. Third, he has written joint articles with the Kirlians about photographing the skin with the Kirlian apparatus.

It seems natural that eventually, he or other workers in the USSR, will be curious about other properties of skin, such as temperature. Two U.S. investigators, Barrett and Myers, have recently reported a technique of subcutaneous temperature measurement by measuring microwave radiation from the skin.[25] One might expect the Soviets to develop remote temperature monitors, either on their own or by copying the U.S. techniques. Such a monitor would be a useful adjunct to a remote lie detector, and its development would probably be supported by the military or the secret police.

In addition to work on the development or application of remote sensors, one can expect the Soviets to try to develop data-processing equipment to handle the signals from an assembly of several sensors. In their published work, the Soviets have shown interest in various types of correlation analysis. For example, Sergeyev has published an article dealing with nonstationary random functions and their application to parapsychological phenomena.[26] It would be natural for Sergeyev (or others) to attempt to mechanize his methods of statistical analysis by a special purpose electronic signal processor. The difficulty may be that the Soviets are not very advanced in electronics and would hesitate to develop such a piece of equipment. Nevertheless, it would seem to be a logical next step.

## Sensitivity of Human Subjects to Magnetic Fields

An interesting facet of this study is the fascination of Soviet and Czechoslovakian parapsychologists with the effects of magnetic fields on human beings, as well as the presumed ability of human subjects to generate magnetic fields. Presman presents a survey of the effects of weak magnetic and electric fields on living organisms, such as the ability of birds to use the earth's magnetic field as a cue in navigation.[27] There is, in fact, a respectable body of experimental evidence in reports published both in Iron Curtain countries and in the West on the effects of magnetic fields on the growth of plants, the orientation of simple animals, and the like. Presman is mainly interested in the possibility that electric and magnetic fields can be used by complex animals for information transfer. He theorizes that humans have largely lost this ability through evolutionary disuse following the development of speech, a much more efficient method of communication. Those few individuals who have the ability to communicate by electromagnetic signaling are, in Presman's view, evolutionary throwbacks.

There is some evidence that human subjects can detect small changes in a magnetic field. Z. V. Harvalik, a Czech-American, reports that about 80 percent of subjects tested were sensitive to magnetic field changes in tests where the field was generated by an ac or dc current passing through damp ground.[28] Harvalik proposes that dowsers are able to sense changes in the earth's magnetic field due to moisture in the ground. The sensing organs are the muscles of the forearms. The dowsing rod is an amplifying and indicating device for the slight twitching of the muscles responding to the changes in magnetic field strength. Native Czech writers also are fascinated with dowsing, as evidenced by reports by the following authors cited in the "Annotated Bibliography": Boleslav and Boleslav, Brada, Drbal and Rejdak, and Kaderavek.[29] It appears that the articles present actual experimental data. Actual data on the sensitivity of humans to weak magnetic fields are scarce, a situation that should be remedied by research.

A related question to magnetic field sensitivity is the ability of a human subject to generate a detectable magnetic field. Adamenko alleges that a Soviet psychic (Kulagina) generates a pulsating magnetic field when she is demonstrating telekinesis. Belief in the existence of such an ability is speculative at present. However, the concept of volitional human generation of a magnetic field is consistent with present knowledge of physics and biology.

## Biophysical Information Carrier Mechanisms

In several articles, Kogan reports experiments and hypotheses concerning telepathic information, and describes information theory aspects of the observed phenomenon; he developed a rationale for transmission mechanisms. Essentially, his thesis is that the energy required is about $10^{-8}$ to $10^{-20}$ joules. He hypothesizes that the transfer of information is advanced by ultra-long electromagnetic waves in the spherical wave guides formed by the surface of the earth and the ionosphere. In our opinion, the work of Kogan is creditable and the best thought out of any of the work reviewed.

Observing that experienced physicists, such as Kogan, took serious notice of parapsychology from 1966 to 1969 and that almost nothing profound has appeared on the subject in the Soviet literature in the last five years suggests that further theoretical and experimental developments along the lines outlined by Kogan are continuing underground in the Soviet Union. Kogan posed too many interesting and challenging questions for himself and his colleagues not to have delved into them further. Based on the well-known predilection of Soviet physicists to solve difficult and challenging problems and their excellent training in modern physics, the possibility that a team of Soviet physicists is at work to systematically uncover and learn the physical mechanisms of parapsychological events is highly probable. Had Kogan not presented such a clear and sound proposal six years ago, one might have wondered if Soviet physicists had any interest at all in NBIT mechanisms. Clearly, if one could find out where Kogan is working and what he is doing, this question would be answered.

Assuming that the USSR started a special NBIT program some time in 1970, by now, they should have developed some sensitive instruments to detect, monitor, and analyze VLF and ELF radiations for possible information content, as Kogan suggested should be done. Also, they must have been instrumental in developing sensors to monitor fluctuations in the human body's electric and magnetic fields, and they may have a team of scientists studying the properties of bio-organic molecules and their response to electromagnetic ELF/VLF radiation. The Soviets may now be implementing the next logical step, namely, to reinforce, enhance, or aid NBIT in certain trained or gifted individuals after having discovered the basic communication carriers.

If experiments that generate special ELF/VLF waves are being conducted, it may be possible to intercept and analyze them because they will travel across the world. However, as discussed subsequently, these manipulated VLF and ELF frequencies may be very monochromatic and undetectable by the usual relatively broad-band radio frequency detectors. For example, it would be like finding the red emission line of the 1 milliwatt (mw) helium–neon laser emitted from a satellite to the earth and observed against a background full of bright direct sunlight. With the proper narrow-band filter, such a line can be observed, of course, but the frequency must be known.

It is rational to assume that the Soviets pursued the investigation of various physical methods that might serve as NBIT mechanisms. Whether or not ELF/VLF mechanisms explain parapsychological events may be a moot question if these mechanisms can be utilized for human information transfer. A review of possible NBIT transmission mechanisms that are compatible with current modern physics yields three schemes.

1. VLF and ELF electromagnetic waves

2. Neutrinos, based on the photon theory of neutrinos

3. Quantum-mechanical ($\psi$) waves, based on the schizophysical interpretation of basic quantum mechanical theory

Presently, most U.S. and Soviet experiments on psychic phenomena, as well as the use of the law of parsimony, would point to ELF/VLF mechanisms, but the other two possibilities cannot be ruled out.

## Miscellaneous Observations

The bulk of the Soviet published work on parapsychological events and NBIT demonstrates not only a poor understanding of physics but also generally fails to deal with psychological and physiological processes that may underly NBIT. No interdisciplinary approach that would help alleviate these difficulties is described in the literature reviewed. For example, Sergeyev measures the bioplasmagram (presumably, the electrical or electrostatic field) associated with heart action and the bioplasmagram associated with breathing. He states that under certain conditions, the heart action and breathing can interfere with one another, apparently by inductive interference. Our guess is that he may not know exactly what he is measuring and probably does not understand the interaction of breathing rate and heart rate. From his background in signal analysis, he does know how to analyze the bioplasmagram.

### Performance Training and Volitional Control

In the more creditable parameters reviewed in this study, the Soviets indicate an interest in volitional control of the phenomena observed. For example, Adamenko indicates that subjects are trained by hypnosis or by using biofeedback procedures to control the conductance between acupuncture points in the skin. In another case, he refers to the use of self-induction, self-suggestion, and bioelectric induction to achieve the electromagnetic changes associated with psychic phenomena.

His model for training in telekinesis is volitional effort that leads to changes in skin conductivity which are simultaneous with telekinesis. During training, the subjects learn by volitional effort to charge a battery of condensors; the charge is roughly proportional to volitional effort. Once trained, the subjects can use a similar volitional effort to electrostatically charge an object at a distance. In describing what may be a current Soviet position in training,

Adamenko further states that "production of special states of consciousness and psychic training at the level of psychoenergetics using modern devices has just as great significance as the investigation of the psychic field of physically talented individuals."[30]

Another method of training in the literature reviewed on telepathy is described by Ryzl.[31] Ryzl claims that approximately 10 percent of the 500 subjects he trained demonstrated some ability as a consequence of the training. The six principal stages of Ryzl training procedure are outlined below:

1. Orient subject and improve his or her motivation

2. Training in hypnosis—increase confidence of the subject, increase suggestibility

3. Attempts to induce visual hallucination—close off subjects to incoming stimuli other than hypnotist's words; perfect mastery and consistency of visual hallucination and inhibit spontaneous mental processes

4. Induction of extraordinary perception; simple assignments (simple discriminations); suggestion is to be able to see, with eyes closed, objects in front of subject—objects may be described in detail to facilitate hallucination

5. Training, including elaboration of procedures, removal of errors, training in use of skills, and development of sense to discriminate between correct and erroneous psychics

6. Autoinduction of the essential state of mind; on the razor's edge between sleep and wakefulness

Ryzl goes to great lengths to prevent the occurrence of errors that are perceived by the subject as a mistake that has been made. For example, when the subject reads a license plate of a car, "if the subject reads OE–6333 instead of CF–6888, we interpret the result as successful and strengthen the subject's compliance."[32]

The training then may be characterized as "shaped" reinforcement learning, utilizing hypnosis and the development of a special state of consciousness. The training is extremely extensive and time consuming (three-hour sessions three times a week over a period of months). If nothing else, the training can be conceived to be an elaborate screening process during which subjects with insufficient talent and motivation are weeded out.

Ryzl's "essential state of mind" appears to be a semihypnogogic state usually accompanying low-frequency $\alpha$ and high-frequency $\theta$ brain rhythms of 7 to 5 Hz. Such a subject state could be more quickly developed utilizing biofeedback techniques.

In view of the high-reward frequency no/failures allowed aspects of the training procedure, it is surprising that Ryzl only claims that 10 percent of his subject population demonstrates psychic ability as a consequence of the training. Due to the dual Soviet interest in both hypnosis and NBIT, the Soviets have probably done a thorough evaluation of Ryzl's procedure.

## Hypnotizing Machines

The Soviet interest in hypnosis has led to many attempts at automating hypnosis. Typical techniques are tape recordings, rotating discs in the visual field, and application of pulsating electrical current through the head. The latest Soviet attempt in this area is "LIDA" (apparently, an acronym for remote control therapeuti apparatus); a U.S. patent (no. 3,773,049, November 1973) by Rabichev et al. has been issued for apparently the same device.[33]

This device, described by Belenkig, Rabichev et al., and Bragen and Petrov is essentially different embodiments of an apparatus that subjects a patient to pulsating light, heat, sound, or VHF electromagnetic radiation simultaneously or individually.[34] The pulse repetition rates (PRR) are programmable. It is uncertain to the authors whether the pulse repetition rates suggested in the patent, 10 to 100 Hz, can be achieved for thermal sensations. At the correct PRR, the device may be effective, at least in neuropsychiatric disorders.

D. Nowlis has demonstrated that certain EEG biofeedback devices with PRRlike visual feedback causes alpha entrainment and enhancement, while L. Fehmi has demonstrated the same for auditory EEG biofeedback. EEG entrainment caused by strobe light sources is, of course, a well-known phenomenon. The range of PRR of the apparatus is 10 to 100 Hz. Apparently, the inputs made to the subject in each sensory modality are synchronous and directed to the recipient's head or face. The subjective consequences of the apparatus are difficult to imagine, especially for VHF electromagnetic radiation and thermal stimulation. The selection of appropriate stimulus intensities and PRR is not described. However, apparently the training of the subjects involves gradually lowering the PRR.

The Soviets claim numerous therapeutic advantages of the LIDA apparatus as a consequence of "inducing the desired biorhythm." The desired biorhythm is unfortunately not described in the literature available to us.

An alternative use of LIDA may be in changing the subjective psychological state of the subjects. For example, it is well-known to biofeedback therapists in this country that EEG biofeedback promotes feelings of well-being, openness, and transference to the therapist. One model for the use of LIDA to achieve these effects without monitoring the patient would be to gradually reduce the pulse repetition rates from 15 to 6 Hz over the course of one hour, thus entraining the individual's α at some frequency and shaping it to some lower frequency. The Soviets claim that the effectiveness of LIDA improves with use (that is, training) of the subject. Being familiar with the subjective effects of biofeedback, it is still difficult to imagine the subjective consequence of pulsed VHF electromagnetic radiation either separately or in synchronous combination with the other modulation.

In summary, the device is considered veridical with probable unique subjective consequences. At lower PRRs, the subjective experiences may correlate to those of EEG biofeedback.

## The Radio Frequency Electromagnetic Radiation Hypothesis

Vasiliev describes Soviet attempts, starting in the 1930s, to replicate the work of F. Cazamalli, an Italian researcher of the 1920 to 1930 period.[35] Cazamalli essentially assumed that the human brain produced electromagnetic radiation in the radio frequency spectrum and claimed to have measured the same. Vasiliev claims that the Soviets conducted a systematic attempt to replicate Cazamalli's work, but to no avail. In the rest of the article (approximately 170 pages), he puts down the radio frequency electromagnetic radiation hypothesis.[36] In reviewing Cazamalli's book, *El Cervanto Radiante,* not much was achieved in the way of enlightenment if the report is accepted from Cazamalli's perspective. His idea was essentially that people doing parapsychological tricks would produce novel and systematic radio frequency electromagnetic radiation. If this hypothesis is ignored and the consequences of the behavior of his subjects are examined, there is some indication that he might have been actually getting something of which he was not aware. For example, he indicates surprise that he received signals of greater amplitude when his subjects did not try. He also indicates that when there were three to four people in the shielded room with the subject, there were no signals detected. Another observation that he frequently made was that physical activity of the subjects reduced or eliminated the signals. Furthermore, he reported that when "emoactive" tension was discharged through motor, vascular, and glandular expression (passionate reactions, flushing of the face, cries, and wails), the phenomenon of radiation stopped abruptly.

Based on Cazamalli's behavioral description of his subject, there may have been a negative correlation between the level of cortical arousal of his subject and the occurrence of whatever he was measuring with his primitive radio frequency antenna and receivers. If this is indeed the case, his primitive apparatus may have, in some way, detected the higher cortical voltage of his resting subjects or changes in their electromyographic levels. Consequently, Vasiliev's effort to discredit Cazamalli could possibly have been due to disinformation, although such a position would be difficult to defend.

## Psychotronics

At this writing, the only available source of information about psychotronics is the "Annotated Bibliography."[37] The introduction to the "Annotated Bibliography" states merely that the terms *psychotronics, psychoenergetics,* and *parapsychology* are used to denote the same field of investigation by the Czechs, the Soviets, and the Western scientists, respectively. It is reported that in Czechoslovakia, psychotronics is an officially recognized branch of science. There is a conflict between the emphasis suggested by the word itself and the brief descriptions presented in the "Annotated Bibliography."

The term itself suggests a blend of the concepts embraced by psychology and electronics. In many portmanteau words of this type, the suffix *tronics* suggests electrical or electronic instrumentation techniques applied to experimental investigations in the field. One might conclude from the form of the word alone that the field of psychotronics is visualized as comprising elements of psychology combined with sophisticated instrumentation techniques to discover new and useful properties of the human mind and central nervous system.

The "Annotated Bibliography" presents a somewhat different view. The introduction, as noted above, states that *psychotronics* is the Czech word for parapsychology. An abstract on page 66 states that psychotronics embraces telepathy, telegnosis, rhabdomancy, PK, cosmic biology, and biological radiation.

Perhaps there is some truth in both views. The Czechs have published serious papers on dowsing, or finding water by means of a divining rod. For example, Branda presented a paper in Prague in 1973 relating dowsing to electromagnetism, myotransfer, electromyography, and the effect and influence of the seasons on these paranormal phenomena.[38] Drbal and Rejdak have written a paper on "Divining, Dowsing, and Readiesthesia."[39]

Perhaps the most informative abstract on the theory of dowsing is that on the work of Harvalik.[40] Harvalik points out that the human body can respond to minute changes in the magnetic field. It is suggested that groundwater distorts the local terrestrial magnetic field and that successful dowsers exploit this effect. The dowsing rod, held loosely in the hands, is merely a mechanical amplifier of a slight reaction of the forearm muscles to the changing magnetic field. There is also an abstract on Kaderavek's work on dowsing rod reactions.[41]

There appears to be a bias in the "Annotated Bibliography" toward the occult and paranormal view of psychotronics and away from the physical and instrumental view. Short shrift is given in the abstracts to articles that describe reasonably good experiments. The work reported by Harvalik occupies about a third of a page. The paper of Kaderavek rates only a few lines. However, a paper by Miloslav Loucka about a model of telepathic communication, which looks like pure fantasy, rates about one and two-thirds pages. The compilers of the "Annotated Bibliography" seem to want to believe in the occult, the mysterious, and the unexplainable. Experimental attempts to provide rational explanations for certain phenomena classified as parapsychological receive little space. The work by Loucka reveals the attitude of many Czech scientists about psychotronics. Loucka postulates the existence of an information field as the carrier of telepathic information. Loucka considers that the same field provides the explanation of telekinesis; this is in contrast to the work of Adamenko and other Soviets, who claim that telekinesis is a manifestation of the electrostatic field.

To summarize the field of psychotronics from the point of view of its practitioners, the following can be postulated:

1. Mental telepathy, clairvoyance, telekinesis, and telegnosis are real. There is a lack of unambiguous experimental evidence concerning these phenomena; this lack must be remedied.

2. These phenomena do not conflict with physics and other sciences. Insofar as possible, physical explanations will be sought for these phenomena.

3. Existing theories of physics are not adequate to explain all psychotronic phenomena. Therefore, there must exist some new physical principles to be discovered or elucidated.

In short, the theoretical basis of psychotronics is substantially the same as that advanced for parapsychology in this country.

## Bioplasma

The appropriate starting point for this discussion is to try to define or explain what is meant by the term *bioplasma*. In origin, the concept seems to be analogous to the *aura* of the Western parapsychologists. The Western concept is an old one, dating from the prescientific age (the Age of Faith) when the soul, or spiritual body of a human being, was thought to be as real as the physical body. The aura was an emanation or radiation from the spiritual body. Saints in old paintings are depicted with halos or auras. Modern Western psychics still believe in the aura and in the ability of gifted individuals to see it.

However, the Eastern (bloc) term *bioplasma,* although used in a confusing fashion, appears to be frequently a generic term for all radiant phenomena associated with a living body (for example, thermal, electrical, magnetic, and electrostatic). Adamenko has used the bioplasma concept as supported by theoretical and empirical considerations. However, in his later published work, he does not mention *bioplasma* but instead writes about the psi field, the biological electric field, and so forth. The strongest theoretical arguments for bioplasma seem to come from Sergeyev.[42] For Sergeyev, the bioplasmagram is a low-frequency electrostatic field.

The Soviets assert correctly that plasma is a fourth state (or phase) of matter. Confusingly, Sergeyev and other Soviet parapsychologists aver that living organisms generate a plasma that surrounds them. They get around the physical difficulties of maintaining a plasma at temperature and pressure conditions compatible with life by the hypothesis that living matter obeys physical laws different from those for inanimate matter.

The classical physical objections to the bioplasma concept are summarized below. A plasma is a state of matter similar to a gas, in which a large fraction of the molecules or atoms are ionized. A plasma can exist at high temperatures or at very low densities. At high temperatures, the individual particles have enough kinetic energy that ionization can result from collisions; the plasma is maintained by virtue of the high rate of production of ions, which balances the recombination rate. At low pressures or densities, the rate of ionization need not be high because the recombination rate, which depends on the rate of collision of ions with each other, is low. A physical plasma consists of approximately equal numbers of positive and negative ions. Electrostatic attraction between the bodies of positively and negatively charged matter holds the plasma together, in a sense. The plasma can absorb and lose energy by electromagnetic radiation. A means of detecting the presence or absence of plasma is to look for the characteristic emission or absorption of radiation. If the Soviets take the bioplasma concept seriously, they will probably try to detect it by virtue of these radiation characteristics. At temperature and pressure conditions consistent with the maintenance of life, a classical plasma cannot exist.

The Soviets must have done significant work in plasma physics as part of their program of developing nuclear weapons. This technology would be applied to a study of bioplasma. For several reasons, such studies probably would have been done secretly. First, the Soviets might not wish to reveal their full capabilities in plasma physics. Second, not every Soviet scientist is a parapsychologist and would not want to experience the expected ridicule for such a frivolous use of plasma physics terminology. Thus, in the available published reports on Soviet parapsychology, the theory of bioplasma remains vague and unclear and at best is an attempt to employ analogous terminology from physics to NBIT.

## Speculation of the Nature of Soviet Laboratories Investigating NBIT

Available published reports are contradictory or inconclusive regarding whether (and to what extent) the Soviet government actively supports investigative or speculative work in the field of NBIT, parapsychology, or psychoenergetics. It appears that some of the older work in the field, before the middle 1960s, was sponsored by the government. More recently, there is conflicting evidence as to whether the field has fallen into official disfavor, with the result that most published work has been done without specific funding or authorization. In the USSR, scientific research work is done mostly in institutes. Each institute is presided over by a senior scientist or academician. Apparently, in the Soviet system, the presiding scientist of an institute has a great deal of freedom and independence from bureaucratic dictation as to the kind of work undertaken. We have seen nothing about the organization of scientific work conducted by Soviet military organizations. One must presume that the organization parallels the civilian institute, with a military officer in charge, assisted by a chief scientist.

Parapsychological investigations in the Soviet Union are probably conducted in two types of circumstances: first, work that is not officially sanctioned or funded by the Soviet government, and second, work that is officially supported and is conducted in a military research laboratory or in a laboratory that is an adjunct to another institution. In the first type, the investigators themselves are employed in research institutes to do other types of work. Their work on parapsychology is conducted on the side, perhaps on their own time. Where possible, they employ the facilities of the institutes in which they work. For example, a shielded room used for testing electronic apparatus also may be used for subjects and investigators in mental telepathy experiments. Special test equipment has to be borrowed or bootlegged from other projects in the institute, built on their own time, or purchased with money contributed by the investigators themselves. The results of such work seem to be published in the unclassified literature. Apparently, official government disapproval of such work does not preclude publication of results. As an indication of this condition (as previously mentioned), barium titanate slabs coated with silver may have been used as electrodes because pure silver was not readily available.

In the second type, government approval of the work seems to imply the intent to use the results to the advantage of the military or the secret police. The officially sanctioned work, if there is any, seems to be classified. The laboratory itself would be camouflaged. It would probably be part of another organization, such as a military research laboratory or a psychiatric hospital. In any event, the camouflage would be fairly difficult to penetrate, since a parapsychological laboratory would not have unusual requirements for electrical power, material supplies, or test equipment. The staff would probably consist of psychologists, biologists, physicists, electrical engineers, mathematicians, technicians, and some "gifted" subjects.

Much of the work of Vasiliev was conducted with subjects who had psychological or psychiatric problems. It would thus be logical to locate the secret parapsychological laboratory in a mental hospital. It is reported that the Soviets tend to sentence political deviates to mental hospitals rather than prisons. It might be possible to learn from interviewing political deviates and other patients who have been released from Soviet mental hospitals if such work is being done there.

## Conclusions

From the review of essentially open Soviet literature, the following conclusions are made:

1. The Soviets have done significant work on signal extraction and statistical and information theory approaches to NBIT mechanisms.

2. The Soviets have done creditable work on the electrostatics of telekinesis and have probably now turned their attention to the psychophysiological aspects of the phenomenon.

3. The Soviets have an interest in remote physiological monitors, have developed one or two new instruments, and are probably involved in research and development in this area.

4. The Soviets had and probably still have an interest in the physics of NBIT transmission mechanisms and are probably doing research in this area.

5. There is a developing interest in the Soviet bloc to apply psychophysiological training methods (similar to biofeedback) to develop control over NBIT mechanisms.

6. All the Soviet research that has been reviewed suffers from the lack of an interdisciplinary approach.

7. The Soviets are investigating the psychophysiology of multimodal programmed stimulation as a method to entrain physiological rhythms and produce changes in states of consciousness.

8. A systematic, interdisciplinary approach to NBIT by the Soviets would require only a modest commitment of resources. A small number of key personnel with an adequate supporting staff of engineers and technicians could make substantial headway in this area. At this stage, in our opinion, no unique technological breakthrough is required—only careful investigation. In addition, no unique features, such as physical plant, facilities, services, or equipment, would specifically identify an NBIT research and development laboratory from other types of laboratories.

These conclusions are drawn in spite of the fact that most of the published material we have reviewed is confusing, inaccurate, and of little value from a scientific point of view. In this respect, the review team may have erred in the direction of trying to make too much sense from a small data base.

## Summary

This chapter presents the results of an analysis of Soviet research on the biophysics of parapsychological processes. The study covered Soviet application of statistical theories, research done on electrostatics, the development of remote sensors, hypothesized carrier mechanisms, human sensitivity to magnetic fields, and training to improve performance of subjects. Speculations are made with regard to Soviet research organization and as to the direction of future research and development. For example, it appears that parapsychological investigations in the Soviet Union are conducted under two types of circumstances: first, work that is not officially sanctioned or supported by the Soviet government, and second, work that is officially supported and is conducted in a military research laboratory or in a laboratory that is an adjunct to another institution. Finally, some conclusions are drawn concerning Soviet progress in understanding and employing what are considered NBIT mechanisms.

## Notes

1. C. Tart, "A Survey of Expert Opinion on Potentially Negative Uses of Psi: U.S. Government Interest in Psi, and the Level of Research Funding of the Field," *Psi News* 1, no. 2 (1978): 2.

2. W. P. Zinchenko et al., "Parapsychology: Fiction or Reality?," *Questions of Philosophy* 9 (1973): 128–36.

3. N. E. Bauman, "Unsolved Riddles: Phenomena amongst Us," *Leninskoye Znamya* (April 1974): 4.

4. Milan Ryzl, "Parapsychology in Communist Countries of Europe," *International Journal of Parapsychology* 10 (1965): 263.

5. I. M. Kogan, "The Information Theory Input of Telepathy" (Paper delivered at University of California-Los Angeles symposium, "A New Look at ESP," 1969).

6. G. A. Sergeyev, "Principles of Spectral Analysis of Bioplasmagrams During Emotional Stress," *Kontrol Sostoyaniya Cheloveka-Operator* (1970): 18.

7. Ibid., and G. A. Sergeyev, "Some Methodological Problems in Parapsy," *Telepatie a Jasnovidnost* (1970): 79.

8. Sergeyev, "Some Methodological Problems in Parapsy," op. cit.

9. Ryzl, op. cit.

10. Sergeyev, "Principles of Spectral Analysis of Bioplasmagrams During Emotional Stress," op. cit.

11. Sergeyev, "Some Methodological Problems in Parapsy," op. cit.

12. Vladimir Mutshall, "The Present State of Research in Telepathy in the Soviet Union."

13. Sergeyev, "Some Methodological Problems in Parapsy," op. cit.

14. R. Targ and H. Puthoff, "Information Transmission Under Conditions of Sensory Shielding," *Nature* 251 (October 1974): 602–7.

15. V. G. Adamenko, "Some Problems of Biological Electrodynamics and Psychoenergeties," *Nekotoryve Vop Biol Eleki Psikh* (Moscow), pp. 27–29; and V. G. Adamenko, "Some Problems of Biological Electrodynamics and Psychoenergetics," *Certain Problems of Biological Electrodynamics and Psychoenergetics* (Moscow), pp. 22–29.

16. V. G. Adamenko, *The A.R.E. Journal* 8 (March 1973): 76–77, cited in S. M. Fullah, "Selective Psychoenergetic Activities—Annotated Bibliography," mimeographed

(prepared for Department of the Army, Contract DAAKO273-M-4729, MRU, Task no. 106 [July 1973]), p. 4.

17. D. Cohen, *Science* 161: 784–86.

18. S. Ostrander and L. Schroeder, *Psychic Discoveries Behind the Iron Curtain* (Englewood Cliffs, N.J.: Prentice-Hall, 1970), p. 20.

19. Ibid., pp. 73–74.

20. A. Kongro, "Emotion Detector Experiments," *Znaniye Sila* (Moscow), no. 7 (1972): 29–36.

21. G. A. Sergeyev, "Some Methodological Problems of Parapsychology," *Telepatie a Jasnovidnost* (Prague: 1970): 79–87; also in *Translations on Czechoslovakia* (GVO no. 772, JPRS L/4922) (U.S. Joint Publications Research Service, June 1974), pp. 1–13.

22. G. A. Sergeyev; G. D. Shuskov; and E. G. Griasnuhin, "A New Detector for Registering the Physiological Functions of the Organism," *Bioenergetics Questions* (Proceedings of the Scientific Methodological Seminar in Alma-Ata, California), ed. B. A. Dombrovsky, G. A. Sergeyev, and B. M. Inyushin (Southern California Society for Psychical Research, 1972), pp. 18.1–18.2.

23. V. N. Puskin, "Knowledge–Strength," *Znaniye Sila* (1972): 4–49.

24. J. Parnov, *Nauka i Religiya* (1965): 48–49; and Martin Ruderfer, "Neutrino Theory of Extrasensory Perception," in *Abstracts: 1st International Conference on Psychotronics* (Prague: 1973): 2: 9–13.

25. Barrett and Myers, *Science* 190 (November 1975): 669–71.

26. G. A. Sergeyev, in *Telepatie a Jasnovidnost,* op. cit., pp. 79–87.

27. A. S. Presman, "Electromagnetic Signaling in Animate Nature" (Moscow: 1974) (JPSR 62434) (U.S. Joint Publications Research Service, July 10, 1974).

28. Z. V. Harvalik, "A Biophysical Magnetometer–Gradiometer," *Virginia Journal of Science* 21 (1970): 59–60.

29. Boleslav and Boleslav, Brada, Drbal and Rejdak, and M. Kaderavek, in S. M. Fullah, op. cit., pp. 13, 14, 19, and 36.

30. Adamenko, "Some Problems of Biological Electrodynamics and Psychoenergetics," op. cit.

31. M. Ryzl, "Training the Psi Faculty by Hypnosis," *Journal of the Society for Psychical Research* 41 (1962): 234–52.

32. Ibid.

33. L. Y. Rabichev et al., "Apparatus for the Treatment of Neuropsychic and Somatic Diseases with Heat, Light, Sound, and VHF Electromagnetic Radiation," U.S. Patent no. 3,773,049, November 20, 1973.

34. B. Belenkig, "LIDA Apparatus for Biorhythmological Studies," *Sovetskaya Moldaviya* (USSR) (December 1973): 4; Rabichev et al., op. cit.; and V. Bragen and P. Petrov, "Hypnotizing Machines," *Nauka i Religiya* (1974): 34–35.

35. L. L. Vasiliev, *Experimental Studies of Mental Suggestion* (JPRS 59, 163) (Joint Publications Research Service, May 1973) (U.S. edition from Dutton & Co., New York, 1978).

36. See, for example, ibid., pp. 110, 160–71.

37. Fullah, op. cit.

38. Brada, in S. M. Fullah, op. cit., p. 14.

39. Drbal and Rejdak, "Divining, Dowsing, and Readiesthesia," in Fullah, op. cit., p. 19.

40. Z. V. Harvalik, in S. M. Fullah, op. cit., pp. 25–26.

41. Kaderavek, op. cit.

42. G. A. Sergeyev and V. V. Kulagin, "The Interaction of Bioplasmic Fields of Living Organisms with Light Photon Sources," in Dombrovsky, Sergeyev, and Inyushin, eds., op. cit., pp. 14.1–14.2.

# Appendix
## The Persistent Paradox of Psychic Phenomena: An Engineering Perspective
Robert G. Jahn

*Invited Paper*

*Abstract*—Although a variety of so-called psychic phenomena have attracted man's attention throughout recorded history, organized scholarly effort to comprehend such effects is just one century old, and systematic academic research roughly half that age. Over recent years, a sizeable spectrum of evidence has been brought forth from reputable laboratories in several disciplines to suggest that at times human consciousness can acquire information inaccessible by any known physical mechanism (ESP), and can influence the behavior of physical systems or processes (PK), but even the most rigorous and sophisticated of these studies display a characteristic dilemma: The experimental results are rarely replicable in the strict scientific sense, but the anomalous yields are well beyond chance expectations and a number of common features thread through the broad range of reported effects. Various attempts at theoretical modeling have so far

Manuscript received July 15, 1981; revised October 26, 1981. This work was supported in part by the McDonnell Foundation, Inc., and by the John E. Fetzer Foundation, Inc., The Explorers Club, the Institute of Noetic Sciences, and the Little River Foundation.

The author is Dean of the School of Engineering/Applied Science, Princeton University, Princeton, NJ 08544.

shown little functional value in explicating experimental results, but have served to stimulate fundamental re-examination of the role of consciousness in the determination of physics reality. Further careful study of this formidable field seems justified, but only within the context of very well conceived and technically impeccable experiments of large data-base capability, with disciplined attention to the pertinent aesthetic factors, and with more constructive involvement of the critical community.

## Prologue

The world of psychic phenomena might be likened to a vast, fog-shrouded swamp, wherein are reported to dwell a bewildering array of bizarre phenomenological creatures, all foreign to our normal perceptual and analytical catalogs. Some scholars who have explored this clouded domain have returned to announce categorically that all such life is illusory—mere sunken stumps and swirling subsurface shadows, inviting misperception by the gullible and misrepresentation by the purveyors. But others of comparable conviction have described in minute detail their observations of a variety of extraordinary beings of awesome dimensions and capability. Some of these are claimed to appear unexpectedly, erupting from the roily depths to flash momentarily in the sunlight of human experience, only to disappear again before any systematic calibration of their characteristics can be taken. Others are reportedly enticed to more replicable and controlled behavior, but only by persons of special talent or extensive training. Much invalid, even fraudulent evidence of such activity has been touted by exploiters of these mysteries, thereby casting deep suspicion on all other testimony. When fully sifted, only a very few legitimate specimens seem to have been captured, by tediously deliberate trolling of the brackish domain, or by more incisive invasion of its turbid interior, and even these have proven so incomprehensible and so delicate to exposure, and the imposed criteria for their credibility have been so severe, that they have not been fully persuasive. Yet the goal remains alluring, and the search continues.

## Introduction

With this unlikely bit of allegorical musing, I venture to begin the most extraordinary writing task I have yet attempted: to respond to the request of the Editors of this journal for a critical review of the status and prognosis of scientific research into so-called psychic phenomena. I do so with some trepidation, first because the topic is far from my principal line of scholarship and my involvement with it has been brief and tightly circumscribed, and second, because of the intensity of reactions any commentary on this subject tends to call forth from many quarters.

For these reasons, it may be well at the outset to specify my perspective on the field and the purpose that I hope this article will serve. My formal training is that of an engineer and applied physicist, and the bulk of my research has concerned a sequence of topics in the broad domain of the aerospace sciences: Fluid mechanics, ionized gases, plasmadynamics, and electric propulsion. In my present position as Dean of the School of Engineering and Applied Science of Princeton University, I have occasion to be involved with an even broader selection of topics selected for undergraduate independent projects, and it was in that context some four years ago that I was requested by one of our very best students to supervise a study of psychic phenomena. More specifically, this young lady proposed to bring her talents and background in electrical engineering and computer science to bear on some experiments in controlled, low-level psychokinesis. Although I had no previous experience, professional or personal, with this subject, for a variety of pedagogical reasons I agreed, and together we mapped a tentative scholarly path, involving a literature search, visits to appropriate laboratories and professional meetings, and the design, construction, and operation of simple experiments. My initial oversight role in this project led to a degree of personal involvement with it, and that to a growing intellectual bemusement, to the extent that by the time this student graduated, I was persuaded that this was a legitimate field for a high technologist to study and that I would enjoy continuing to do so.

I have since assembled a small professional staff, secured the requisite funding from a few private sources, and undertaken a modest experimental program in selected aspects of the field that could ultimately have some engineering implications. I should emphasize that my fractional involvement with this program remains quite minor in comparison to my other responsibilities, and that the work is still very preliminary and tentative, but it provides the base of cognizance for my broader observations on the field as a whole.

The intention of this article is to provide some balanced perspective on the modern status of this conceptually and logistically difficult subject. Certainly no field of scholarly endeavor has proven more frustrating, nor has been more abused and misunderstood, than the study of psychic phenomena. Dealing as it does as much with impressionistic and aesthetic evidence as with analytical substance, and carrying by its nature strongly subjective and numenistic overtones, it has been incessantly prostituted by charlatans, lunatics, and sensationalists, categorically rejected by most of the scientific establishment, and widely misunderstood by the public at large. Interspersed with this, and greatly encumbered by it, a pattern of legitimate effort to comprehend and utilize the purported phenomena has evolved to a point where some dispassionate assessment of its accomplishments can be attempted. The questions addressed by this review are whether, once the overburdens of illegitimate activity and irresponsible criticism are removed, there remains sufficient residue of valid evidence to justify continued research and, if so, how this research might most effectively be styled, facilitated, and evaluated.

Before addressing these issues directly, it may be helpful to review briefly the historical evolution of the field, its contemporary nomenclature and conceptual organization, and the dimensions of current activity. This can then be followed by a general overview and critique of the modern research, and that in turn by more detailed description of a few specific efforts, drawn primarily from our own work. Toward the close, we shall attempt to survey several theoretical approaches to modeling of psychic processes and comment briefly on potential implications and applications of the phenomena. In all of this, no tone of advocacy is intended, other than for objective assessment of the evidence in hand.

## History

In a sense, the study of psychic phenomena is one of the oldest of human endeavors [1]–[7]. As far back as can be traced, mortal man has pondered the supernatural in one form or another. Cave drawings at Lascaux and Altamira, circa 20,000 B.C., reflect this preoccupation, and the religious rites of early societies of both the eastern and western worlds were heavily loaded with psychic formalisms. The classic civilizations of Egypt, Greece, and Rome dealt extensively in psychic process. The Delphic Oracle was politically important from the earliest Hellenic times to the age of Alexander the Great, and was consulted on problems as diverse as the proper measures to stop a plague, the constitutions of Greek city-states, and the best locations for new colonies. Even Aristotle, one of the most empirical of the classical philosophers, examined the causal links in prophetic dreams.

Virtually every form of organized religion practiced by man has been thoroughly laced with various forms of psychic mechanism. The Bible, like most other basic theological texts, treats psychic process as a central ingredient, in a tone so matter-of-fact that one is inclined to believe that people of those times accepted such events rather routinely. Indeed, the Bible is an excellent catalog of psychic phenomena; virtually every category of effect identified today is illustrated there in one form or another.

Christian writers and philosophers, from Augustine to the Reformation, recount many purported instances of psychic phenomena, usually attributed to visitations of divine grace or demonic posession. Secular medieval writing also abounds with supernatural and mystical reference, and even in the Renaissance period it is still difficult to separate psychic allusion from religious dogma, although both were then translated into more organized forms in art and literature. Early in the 16th century the celebrated Swiss physician and philosopher Paracelsus wrote extensively on psychic capabilities and potentialities. In his words:

The mind of man is the microcosmic counterpart of the universal mind. . . . One man may communicate his thoughts to another with whom he is in sympathy, at any distance however great it may be, or he may act upon the spirit of another person in such a manner as to influence his actions. . . . [8].

Perhaps the first major scientific commentaries on the topic were offered near the turn of the 17th century by Sir Francis Bacon, widely regarded as the originator of the scientific method. In *The Advancement of Learning* he suggested that "superstitions and the like" should not be excluded from scientific study, and in his posthumous book, *Sylva Sylvarum,* he proposed deliberate investigation of telepathic dreams, psychic healing, and the influence of "imagination" on the casting of dice [9]. Some years later, a group of British intellectuals including Henry More and Joseph Glanvill met regularly to discuss paranormal topics, and in 1681 Glanvill published the substance of these studies in a book entitled *Saducismus Triumphatus* [10].

Meanwhile, some four centuries of public and church hysteria over sorcery and witchcraft, as manifested in a sequence of trials, tortures, and executions, had begun to subside, and by the mid-18th century, the Roman Church authorized Prospero Lambertini, who later became Pope Benedict XIV, to carry out a scholarly investigation of reports of psychic events. His conclusions, recorded in *De Canonizatione* [11], were surprisingly unecclesiastical: namely, that 1) psychic experiences were not necessarily divine miracles, but could occur to "fools, idiots, melancholy persons, and brute beasts"; 2) apparitions had little to do with sanctity or demonic entities; 3) prophesy occurs more often in sleep than in waking; 4) it is difficult for a prophet to distinguish his own thoughts from extrasensory messages; and 5) predictions frequently take symbolic forms. In all of these, he presaged to some degree modern thoughts on these topics.

At roughly the same time, Anton Mesmer's discovery of hypnosis opened an alternative route to demonstration and study of unconscious psychic process that has continued to this day. Early reports of hypnotized subjects performing telepathic or clairvoyant tasks were common [12], [13], and although much of this evidence might now be discounted on the basis of inadequate experimental control, interest in hypnosis specifically, and in various altered states of consciousness generally, as facilitators of psychic experience persists into some of the modern experimentation.

Also in this mid-18th century period, a spiritualist movement focused on extrasensory contact with the dead, possibly influenced by the work of Emanuel Swedenborg [14], [15], germinated in this country as well as in England, and by the 19th century had reached the dimensions of an organized religion. Symbolic of the popular preoccupation with the topic, Mary Todd Lincoln was reported to have held séances in the White House in the early 1860s [16]. A classic two-volume work by F. W. H. Myers, entitled *Human Personality and Its Survival of*

*Bodily Death* [17], brought the topic to its acme of sophistication, but eventually the fanaticism the movement attracted and its fraudulent exploitation created a negative attitude in the scholarly community which prevails yet today.

Despite these millennia of human concern with the paranormal, orderly and organized scholarly search for verification and understanding of psychic phenomena began only a century ago, with the establishment in London in 1882 of the Society for Psychical Research, in whose Proceedings appeared the first formal publication of controlled experiments in telepathy and clairvoyance [13], [18], [19]. Three years later the counterpart organization in this country, the American Society for Psychical Research, was founded in Boston by several distinguished scientists and philosophers. Because of financial difficulty, this shortly merged with the British group, but reemerged in 1905 as a separate entity with its own professional journal, and has continued as such to the present [20].

Although the SPR attracted a barrage of criticism from the scientific and intellectual communities, it also attracted significant participation of eminent scholars from established fields. Numbered among its presidents are three Nobel Laureates, ten Fellows of the Royal Society, one Prime Minister, and a substantial list of physicists and philosophers, including Henry Sidgwick, Frederic W. H. Myers, Lord Rayleigh, Sir J. J. Thomson, William McDougall, Edmund Gurney, Sir William Crookes, Sir William Barrett, Henri Bergson, Arthur, Earl of Balfour, Gardner Murphy, G. N. M. Tyrell, Charles Richet, Gilbert Murray, and one of the most articulate contributors to the evolution of critical thought on this topic in this period, the Harvard psychologist and philosopher, William James. One of the founders of the ASPR, James wrote extensively and eloquently on behalf of objective and disciplined study of psychic phenomena [21]–[25]:

> Any one with a healthy sense for evidence, a sense not methodically blunted by the sectarianism of 'science,' ought now, it seems to me, to feel that exalted sensibilities and memories, veridical phantasms, haunted houses, trances with supernormal faculty, and even experimental thought-transference, are natural kinds of (phenomena) which ought, just like other natural events, to be followed up with scientific curiosity [25].

Entering the 20th century, a new perspective on psychic phenomena was provided by the emergence of psychology as a scholarly discipline, and especially by the early efforts in clinical psychology and psychoanalytic therapy. The patriarch of this evolution, Sigmund Freud, was a member of the SPR and contributed, albeit somewhat reluctantly, to its publications [26], [27]. His recognition and exploration of the unconscious mind and of the function of dreams prompted Myers to suggest a possible explication of various psychic effects which is still of theoretical value [17]. Freud's interest in parapsychology increased toward the end of his life, and he is reported to have conceded informally that were he to begin his career anew, he would focus on this topic.

Freud's former protegé, Carl Jung, who had written his Ph.D. thesis on the psychology of occult phenomena, pursued exploration of the unconscious to deeper dimensions of paranormal experience, publishing widely on such subjects as telepathy, mediumship, synchronicity, the collective unconscious, and theoretical models of psychic process [28]–[30]. In *Memories, Dreams, Reflections,* he stated:

> . . . the relationship between doctor and patient, especially when a transference on the part of the patient occurs, or a more or less unconscious identification of doctor and patient, can lead to parapsychological phenomena. I have frequently run into this [30].

Jung's collaboration with the eminent physicist Wolfgang Pauli on the topic of synchronicity clearly influenced the subsequent evolution of both careers and of fundamental concepts in both disciplines [31]. Although much of the established psychological community has since rejected parapsychology as a valid discipline, some interest has been retained by a few clinical practitioners, presumably because of the demonstrated concomitance and similarities of apparent psychic experiences with certain psychological processes [32], [33].

It was also early in this century that the first organized academic studies of psychic phenomena were mounted. One of the more visible of these devolved from gifts and a bequest from Thomas W. Stanford, brother of the founder of Stanford University, to endow psychic research at that institution, and to this day the university provides support of a "psychic research fellow" and retains a collection of so-called "apports" indicative of the donor's long personal involvement with the field. Modest research programs were also undertaken at Harvard and a few European universities in the first decades of this century, as evidenced by occasional publications in various established journals.

The benchmark academic effort, however, germinated at Duke University in the late 1920s, when William McDougall, who had been James' successor at Harvard, arrived to chair the department of psychology and appointed J. B. Rhine and Louisa Rhine, "to study the claims to scientific value of the field known as psychical research." Their early tentative efforts in the study of postmortem survival gradually evolved into a laboratory for controlled research in "extrasensory perception," as they first termed the process. In this laboratory were established many of the basic concepts and protocols of modern psychic research, as well as the first extensive and systematic data bases of several types of psychic experimentation. The professional and personal history of the Rhines and their laboratory is a fascinating saga in its own right, but would take us too far afield here [34]–[37]. A few excerpts from a 1967 address of J. B. Rhine to the American Psychological Association, in which he attempted to summarize his first two decades of intensive study, give hint of the inherent attractions and frustrations of this field, and of the man's optimistic vision:

> The phenomena that were being studied began to show lawful interrelations and even a degree of unity. One by one the major claims, based originally only upon spontaneous human experiences, were subjected to laboratory test and experimentally verified. . . . Certain general characteristics of the psi process became clear during this period. The most revealing of these is the subject's lack of conscious control over any type of psi ability, a characteristic which accounts for its elusive nature. It was new methodological ground, even for psychology. . . . Also, we were surprised to find that psi ability is widespread, probably even a specific human capacity rather than a capability possessed by a few rare individuals as had been the popular belief. Evidence that psi is not linked with illness or abnormality was another welcome advance. . . . By 1951 . . . a healthy young science was emerging [38].

In 1937, the Rhines began publication of the *Journal of Parapsychology*, which remains a leading journal in the field today. A professional organization calling itself the Parapsychological Association was formed in 1957, and in 1969 was accepted as an affiliate by the American Association for the Advancement of Science.

At the present time, there are eight English language publications covering this field [39], supplemented by numerous less formal magazines and countless books of widely varying quality and relevance. Research activity is reported from some twenty U.S. universities and colleges and at least as many institutions in Western Europe [40], but in most cases it is of very small scale. There are very few academic programs of study, although some fifty M.A. and Ph.D. theses have been accepted on psychic topics at reputable universities over the past forty years [41]. Some ten research institutes and private corporations in the United States have also authorized publications and reports in the field [42]. The extent of Eastern Bloc and Oriental efforts [43]–[54] and of classified research in this country are matters of considerable speculation on which I cannot comment with authority.

Further review of contemporary programs will be attempted in subsequent sections, following an outline of modern nomenclature and conceptual organization of the topic. In closing this historical overview, we might simply observe that in many respects the growth pattern of this field resembles that of the natural sciences in their earliest days, or perhaps even more the incubation of classical psychology, in terms of the absence of replicable basic experiments and useful theoretical models, the low level of financial support and internal professional coordination, and the low credibility in the academic establishment and public sectors. Also like those fields, the survival and early growth of psychic research can largely be attributed to the efforts of a few scholars of sufficient conviction, stature, and courage to withstand the rejection of the orthodox communities.

## Nomenclature and Conceptual Organization

Before turning to an assessment of contemporary research, it may be useful to specify some notation and delineation of the field, to an extent consistent with the present limited comprehension of the phenomena. First, let us agree to a global definition of "psychic phenomena" (frequently denoted by "psi" or "ψ") to include all processes of information and/or energy exchange which involve animate consciousness in a manner not currently explicable in terms of known science. Similarly, let "psychic research" imply any scholarly study of such phenomena employing scientific methodology, as opposed to any dogmatic, ritualistic, or theological approaches. Within these definitions, the field may then be roughly divided into two major categories: extrasensory perception (ESP) and psychokinesis (PK).

ESP refers generally to the acquisition of information from sources blocked from ordinary perception. Under this category are included such subdivisions as telepathy, which refers to detection of another person's thoughts; clairvoyance, which refers to contemporary perception of remote physical objects or events; precognition and retrocognition, which refer to perception of future events and events in the past not accessible by normal recollection; and animal ESP, which encompasses a variety of seemingly inexplicable capabilities, such as homing, psi-trailing, collective behavior, communication, etc.

PK (occasionally termed telekinesis, or psychoenergetics) refers to a palpable influence of consciousness on a physical or biological system. The interaction may be deliberate or spontaneous, and the energy transfer involved may range from microscopic disturbance of atomic-level processes, through macroscopic distortion or levitation of objects, up to some very drastic "poltergeist" effects. Psychic healing and man-plant interactions would be two examples of PK in biological systems.

Note that in its major subdivision into ESP and PK, the field conforms to two of the main categories of present-day science and high technology, i.e., that encompassing the extraction, conversion, transmission, storage, and utilization of information, and that comprising the same sequence of processing of energy. Other domains of psychic research can be identified which do not fit into these major categories of ESP and PK and with which we shall not be further concerned in this article. Examples would include research into survival of death, and the family of "out-of-body experiences (OBE)," including astral projection, autoscopy, and bilocation. The following table attempts to summarize the subdivisions in a concise form.

### Categories of Psychic Phenomena

    I.  Extrasensory Perception (ESP)
        A. Telepathy
        B. Clairvoyance
        C. Precognition/Retrocognition
        D. Animal ESP
    II.  Psychokinesis (PK)
        A. Physical Systems
        B. Biological Systems
    III.  Survival
        A. Reincarnation
        B. Apparitions
        C. Mediumship
    IV.  Out-of-Body Experiences (OBE).

Clearly this particular arrangement is neither unique nor orthogonal. Elements of one category frequently appear in the context of another, e.g., precognitive clairvoyance; telepathic healing, etc., and occasionally an assignment is ambiguous, e.g., a particular effect may be regarded as precipitated by PK, or simply to be forecast by precognition. Notwithstanding, the table may aid in keeping the subsequent illustrations in some order.

# Pattern of Contemporary Research

By its nature and heritage, modern psychic research remains rather diffuse and lightly structured, making any attempt to catalog the work by institution or laboratory, or by tracing developments of given lines of effort, rather ineffective and premature. Instead, it may be more useful to comment on the pattern of attention to this field by academic disciplines, noting the variations in emphasis, methodology, representation, and interpretation brought to bear, using specific projects only as illustrations with no implications of hierarchy or attempt at completeness. Even in this format, no recitation of specific research results or conclusions will be attempted, since these can be misleading or incomprehensible when extracted from the detailed context of their experimental arrangements and protocols. In later sections, an effort will be made to follow a few sample experiments through to their particular results and conclusions.

By far the most sustained and broadcast attention to this field has been given by a cadre of scholars with professional backgrounds in classical psychology, comprising a controversial subdiscipline termed "parapsychology." This group has tended to approach the field with the traditional psychological protocols and vocabulary, and to interpret results in the context of their clinical, cognitive, and behavioral psychological heritages, with the natural consequence that they have concentrated mainly on the ESP category of psychic tasks, although some PK work dots their recent literature. Perhaps the most extensive class of parapsychological research has attempted to correlate psychic performance with personality variables. The age, sex, creativity, openness, hostility, extroversion, motivation, and intelligence of the participants as indices of ability to perform ESP tasks have been explored at length, and some significant correlations, most notably with positive *a priori* attitudes toward the tasks and with outgoing, creative personalities, have been reported from several laboratories. Other studies have searched for connections between psychic performance and dream recall, learning and response strategies, memory, and feedback [55]–[61].

A more aggressive style of parapsychological research has invoked a variety of altered states of consciousness in attempts to enhance psychic process. These have included various natural and traditional practices, such as sleep, meditation, and progressive relaxation [62]–[67]; more mechanical sensory inhibition strategies such as hypnosis, isolation and "ganzfeld" [66], [68]–[70]; and a few controversial efforts with drug-induced states [71]. Physiological correlates have also been sought, using conventional EEG, GSR, and plethysmographic equipment to monitor neurological, cardiovascular, and muscular response to psychic effort [35], [72]–[75]. The difficulty of obtaining successful replications of previously positive results and an observed common tendency of participant performance to deteriorate over time ("decline effect") have led to systematic study of the role of the experimenter in eliciting results, i.e., to consideration of the possible influence of the experimenter's personal attitudes, expectations, and style of interaction with his subjects, as well as the overall environmental ambience of his laboratory, on the experimental yield [76]–[81].

Despite its present recalcitrance toward more systematic study of psychic phenomena, the richly diverse, rapidly maturing parent field of psychology continues to offer an expanding array of modern methodologies and models which could be brought to bear on increasingly sophisticated study of this subject. Computer-assisted linguistic analyses; psychoneurological studies of attention, perception, and concept formation; social learning theory and similar approaches to human interactions; and the emerging formulations of transpersonal and humanistic aspects of human consciousness, all bear possible relevance to comprehension of various aspects of this ultra-difficult stepchild, but at the moment, the low level of financial support, and negative professional peer pressures have discouraged such enterprise.

The involvement of physicists in psychic research, while considerably less extensive, has been no less dedicated and no less controversial. Since the days of Sir Francis Bacon, a number of noted physicists have made excursions into this field, usually to the bemusement and ridicule of their colleagues of the day. One of the most notable of these was Sir William Crookes, discoverer of the element thallium and pioneer in the physics of low pressure discharges, whose broadside professional and personal battles with the scientific establishment over this issue make entertaining, and possibly enlightening, reading [82]. Sir Isaac Newton was intensely involved in the study of alchemy, including some of its more metaphysical aspects [83], and as already mentioned, Lord Rayleigh and J. J. Thomson were active members of the S.P.R.

In more recent years the attention of physicists has influenced development of the field in at least three ways. First, their interests have focused more on the PK category of problems, i.e., the interaction of human consciousness with physical systems, to balance the predominant ESP interests of the parapsychologists. Second, more sophisticated experimental equipment than has typically been available to the psychological community has been brought to bear on the identification and correlation of very low-level physical effects. Third, the traditional theoretical physics formalisms have been directed to the proposition of various models of psychic phenomena, from whence has arisen some hope of establishing the traditional dialogue between critical experimentation and theoretical hypothesis essential to any ultimate comprehension and application of such phenomena.

Typical of the modern physicist's specific contributions to the field have been the development and application of a variety of electronic random event generators (REG) for the purpose of identifying and correlating PK abilities in human subjects [84]–[93], and similar application of magnetometers [94], torsional pendula [95], lasers [96], interferometers [97], and electronic strain gauges [98], [99] to a variety of other PK tasks. On the theoretical side, a number of applications of quantum mechanics, statistical thermodynamics, electromagnetic theory, and other formalisms to the representation of psychic process have been proposed [100]–[113], and attempts at some philosophical correlation of the phenomena with other previously or presently obscure physical processes have been suggested [114]. Again, despite the open identification of a few distinguished personalities with such efforts, a more broadly held categorical rejection of the field has inhibited much collaborative or systematic attention to it.

Up to this time, the involvement of engineers with psychic research has been very recent, very sparse, and very much along the lines of the experimental physicists. Beyond our own program, which will be outlined in some detail below, I am aware of only a very few engineering laboratories addressing any aspects of the field in any substantial and deliberate way [115]. These have so far tended to concentrate on applied physics types of experimentation and on aspects of information processing, rather than on more empirical technological applications.

Another community of scholars to influence the pattern of psychic research comprises the statisticians and other applied mathematicians and logicians who have been concerned with the proper evaluation and interpretation of the research data. In the absence of any experiments displaying rigid causal replicability, all of the inferences and hypotheses about psychic phenomena have necessarily been based on either anecdotal or statistical evidence. The former defy any systematic representation; the latter are vulnerable to alternative interpretations and hence to impressionistic bias and argument.

Early in the emergence of mathematical statistics as an integral discipline, S. S. Wilks found himself involved in a controversy over the validity of the statistical procedures of early psychic researchers, and published some recommendations for methods that could be applied to telepathy experiments [116]. Since that time, much of the commentary from the critical community has addressed perceived flaws in the statistical methodology underlying the experimental evidence [117], [118], and the advocate community has reacted by paying disproportionate attention to this aspect of their logic. Most of the encyclopaedic references in the field contain substantial components on the statistical methods [119], and the leading journals regularly display intense dialogues on specific statistical issues [120]–[124]. At least one of these journals routinely refers all articles submitted for publication to a consultant statistician as a part of their review process. A few illustrations of the statistical questions that can arise in psychic experiments appear in the detailed examples presented below.

A number of other disciplines have played roles in the evolution of the study of psychic process and continue to contribute, albeit somewhat more peripherally. A succession of philosophers, from Aristotle through James and Bergson to C. D. Broad in the present era, have mused on these topics [21]–[25], [125]–[129]. The intersections of the field with anthropology, theology, and history have been approached from many perspectives ranging from aesthetic to analytic, and from dogmatic to scholarly [130]–[134]. Its relevance to the study and practice of medicine has been an enduring and intense debate, focusing in the present day on the propriety and efficacy of holistic health strategies and psychic healing. Isolated instances of interest on the part of chemists, biologists, geologists, and archaeologists can be found, and the application of psychic techniques in criminology and law enforcement, while less rigorous than most of the academic efforts, contributes further anecdotal evidence to the overall data base. In the arts and humanities, the topic continues to provide stimuli for a variety of creative compositions.

Still other areas could be cited, but these become progressively more satellite than central to the task of this paper. Rather than pursuing this disciplinary survey further, it seems preferable next to focus in greater detail on a few contemporary studies that can serve to illustrate more specifically the bizarre phenomena, the awkward and tedious protocols, and the unconventional theoretical concepts that arise in this class of research. Although these will provide a better sense of the status of the field than any attempt to summarize results from the diffuse multidisciplinary pattern of effort sketched above, one general assessment may be useful at this point. Namely, throughout all of the work just skimmed, and that sharpened somewhat below, I am aware of no reputable investigator who has claimed, let alone demonstrated, any psychic experiment approaching classical scientific replicability. What have been put forward are a varied assortment of observations, currently inexplicable in terms of established science, which display certain common phenomenological and psychological features, and which could have substantial implications for basic physical theory and ultimate practical applications. The following examples are presented in that spirit.

## Psychokinesis

The first group of experiments selected as more detailed illustrations of contemporary psychic research are drawn from the general subdomain of PK. As defined above, this broad category of purported psychic phenomena encompasses the possible influence of human consciousness on the behavior of physical or biological systems or processes, and comprises several loosely related classes of effect characterized by different scales of energy, forms of manifestation, replicability, and statistical behavior. Confining attention to interactions with physical objects or systems, the most popularly publicized class features the deformation, levitation, or other macroscopic disturbance of objects, as commonly propounded by professional performers, mediums, and various Eastern practitioners [135]–[137]. Although a number of serious efforts have been made to submit such demonstrations to rigorous scientific testing, these have tended to yield only equivocal confirmations, fodder for the critical community, and some embarrassment and frustration to the investigators.

Of a yet more bizarre nature are the family of very rare and spectacular "poltergeist" effects, more technically termed "recurrent spontaneous psychokinesis" (RSPK), wherein are reported specific major events of levitation, vibration, teleportation, and breakage of a wide range of objects, a variety of acoustical and electromagnetic phenomena, and various optical aberrations [138], [139]. For years these phenomena were naively attributed to manifestations of the spirit world, or return of the dead to "haunted" houses, and inspired countless horror movies and pulp-magazine articles. Recently, some order has been brought to this weird business by systematic surveys of documented poltergeist cases undertaken by A. R. G. Owen, W. G. Roll, J. G. Pratt, and others [138]–[142]. In one of these surveys, 116 cases of reported poltergeist activity, ranging back to the year 1612, were re-examined. Of these, 92 were found to be associated with particular individuals living in the affected dwelling, most of whom were adolescents, and most of whom were affected by some neurological/emotional ailment, most commonly epilepsy. Often a precipitating traumatic event could be identified which seemed to initiate the activity, after which the general pattern involved a period of relatively mild precursor events, a sequence of major disturbances, and a period of "after shocks," extending as much as several weeks beyond the main events. Controlled experimentation on poltergeist phenomena has proven virtually impossible because of their infrequent and unpredictable occurrence pattern and because of the delicate physiological and emotional situations prevailing in most cases, which have taken precedence over the technical investigations. Nevertheless, these processes have retained some fascination because of the magnitude of the energy transfer involved and because of their apparent correlation with specific types of individuals and neurological disorders.

The most systematic and persuasive studies of PK, however, have dealt with much more modest scales of physical disturbance, in some cases reaching down to the atomic level. This somewhat more viable domain has been addressed by numerous investigators in various ways, but basically one of two strategies is followed. In one approach, relatively simple physical systems are employed—mechanical, electrical, optical, thermal, etc.—each of which involves a particular component or process that is ultra-sensitive to disturbance. The experiment is arranged to signify such disturbance by a relatively large change in some display which provides feedback indication to the operator, much in the spirit of a biofeedback instrument, and simultaneously to provide some form of permanent data record. Examples of this class of experiment would include the use of magnetometers, torsional pendula, optical interferometers, electronic strain gauges, glow discharges [143], and sensitive thermistors [144].

In the second approach, attempt is made to distort the normal statistical patterns of various random physical processes on either a microscopic or macroscopic scale. In a sense, these experiments deal with energy rearrangement within the systems, i.e., with their information content or entropy, rather than with energy transfer to the system *per se*. The earliest versions of this class employed dice, or other simple mechanical implements of well-known statistical behavior [37], [92], [145]–[148], but more recent studies have tended to employ more sophisticated apparatus, such as electronic REGs like those described in detail below.

Although the first two categories of PK feature more dramatic effects and thus have enjoyed greater popular attention, the smaller scale phenomena seem more amenable to controlled experimentation and theoretical interpretation, and the remainder of this section deals only with such. Perhaps the most efficient means of elaborating on this type of research would be to review briefly the spectrum of such experiments in progress in our own laboratory, and then to display and attempt to interpret data from one of them. In so doing, we intend no neglect of other work noted in the references, but simply deal from greater familiarity.

As examples of the first class of low-level PK experiment mentioned above, we have in operation a Fabry-Perot optical interferometer, a dual-thermistor bridge, and a photoelastic strain detector. In the interferometer experiment, shown in the photograph and schematic of Fig. 1, a Coherent Optics

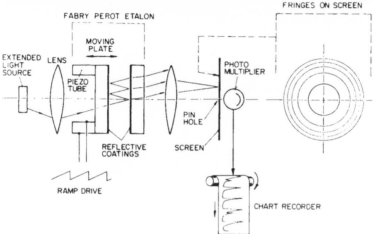

**Fig. 1.** Photograph and schematic of Fabry–Perot interferometer.

Instrument #360–370, using a diffuse sodium lamp as source, is adjusted to produce circular fringes on a screen visible to the operator (Fig. 2). Small changes in the separation of the interferometer plates cause the fringes to migrate radially inward or outward. By visual observation of the fringe movement, plate motions of less than 0.1 wavelength can be readily detected. Via a pinhole in the screen, the brightness of the central fringe is recorded by a photomultiplier/chart recorder system at an order of magnitude higher sensitivity, thereby preserving quantitative output data while the operator simultaneously sees an attractive optical display of his progress for use as feedback.

The task of the operator is to elicit significant migration of the fringe pattern in a stated direction relative to the normal baseline drift of the instrument. The protocols involve rigid control and monitoring of the environment of the instrument and surrounding laboratory, and the interspersing of baseline responses with active PK efforts obtained under otherwise identical conditions,

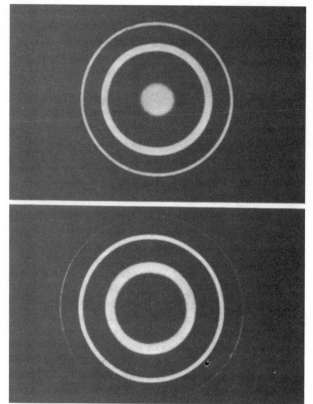

**Fig. 2.** Interferometer fringe patterns.

including the position of the operator and any other personnel relative to the instrument. In pilot studies with this device, a variety of fractional-fringe responses were observed, using several different operators and various initial interferometer settings. A more formal procedure has since been developed which provides more precise conditions for an ongoing series of trials. In this protocol, the central fringe is set initially on a maximum gradient position between a bright and dark fringe, and its progress monitored for subsequent periods of baseline or PK effort. Encouragingly replicable data have been obtained from a number of different operators, in the form of chart recordings of 5-min PK trials with interspersed 5-min baseline drifts of the instrument. Using computerized graphic, regression, and spectral analyses of the data, it is possible to discern characteristics in the hierarchy of trace derivatives and the Fourier spectra which, while not definitive, display certain recurrent features [97]. No physical interpretation has been attempted other than to acknowledge that the observed fringe migrations could also be indicative of slight changes in the index of retraction of the air in the plate gap or in the wavelength of the light source, as well as of a displacement of the plates.

The dual-thermistor experiment comprises a much more sensitive version of a multiple-thermistor arrangement on which PK influence was originally reported by Schmeidler [144]. As shown in Fig. 3, two Omega Engineering thermistors, Model UVA 3254, each with its own electronic bridge and voltage source, are connected differentially to a Tektronix 1A7A oscilloscope preamplifier and to a visual feedback display. With suitable ground planes and cable shielding, sensitivities greater than 0.001 K are obtainable, and by subtracting the two output signals the major portion of spurious electrical and mechanical interference is eliminated. The effects of ambient thermal variations in the laboratory are essentially excluded by enclosing each of the thermistors in identical Pyrex flasks immersed in a large liquid reservoir, in which configuration the undisturbed system exhibits stable baselines over long periods of time. Using the same interspersed baseline protocol as in the interferome-

**Fig. 3.** Dual-thermistor apparatus.

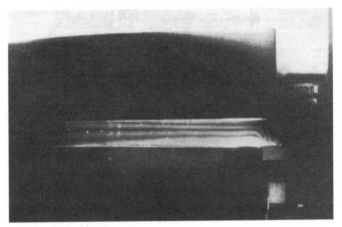

**Fig. 4.** Photoelastic stress pattern.

ter experiment, the task of the operator is to achieve an increase in the reading of one thermistor with respect to the other or in some more subtle fashion to alter the PK response relative to the baseline. Some such effects have indeed been observed, but little systematic data have so far been accumulated on this experiment.

Also in a preliminary stage is an experiment to monitor internal strain in a solid specimen via photoelastic optical techniques. Several studies have been reported on the PK deformation of solids, but most of these have employed conventional engineering strain gauges or microacoustic sensors as detectors [98], [99], [135], [149], [150], both of which require substantial interface electronics before a feedback signal reaches the operator, leaving unclear the role of the sensor in any possible PK influence. Although less sensitive than the electronic methods, photoelastic techniques have the advantage of relating the

"NORMAL" DISTRIBUTION          DISTORTED DISTRIBUTION

**Fig. 5.** Gaussian analog device and distributions.

operator more directly to the sensitive element of the experiment via an attractive optical fringe pattern much like that of the interferometer (Fig. 4). This equipment and technique may also be applied to a sensitive levitation experiment wherein the object is suspended on a photoelastic lever arm of suitable dimensions.

Within the second category of low-level PK experiment, we are employing or are now constructing several devices based on random physical processes, some macroscopic in scale, others deriving from atomic-scale processes. The largest of these involves a 6 x 10 ft apparatus, shown in Fig. 5, which drops some 10,000 3/4 in spheres through a "quincunx" array of 336 nylon pegs in about 12 min. As a consequence of the multitudinous collisions with the pegs and with each other, the spheres are dispersed into a good approximation of a Gaussian distribution as they fall into 19 collecting compartments at the bottom. The goal of the operator is to distort the distribution in some prescribed fashion to a significant degree compared to empirical baseline experience. Photodiode counters mounted in funnels at the entrance to each bin provide real-time digital displays of the bin populations to supplement the more qualitative feedback of the growing ball stacks seen by the operator and to provide quantitative data for on-line statistical analysis. Fig. 5 shows a typical baseline distribution for this device and a distorted distribution obtained in a particular PK effort. Full statistical analysis of the significance of any particular achieved pattern is a challenging problem in its own right, since it must deal with a combination of

19 bin populations, each of which has its own empirical baseline mean and standard deviation, all constrained by total ball count.

A somewhat similar experiment, not yet refined, employs a device which allows small metallic or dielectric spheres to bounce on an optically flat, precisely horizontal circular plate of glass, which is oscillated by a vibration coil at frequencies from 10 Hz to 20,000 Hz. In the absence of any external disturbance, a sphere started at the center of the plate executes a random walk toward the outside edge, arriving with equal probability at any azimuth. Since the sphere may make as many as $10^5$

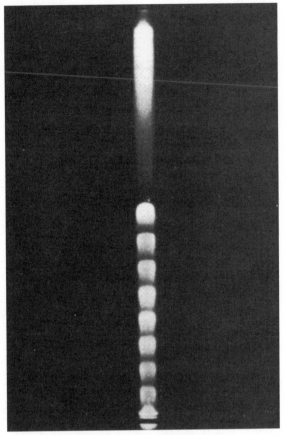

**Fig. 6.** Glow discharge experiment.

collisions in the process, it is vulnerable to statistical distortion of its trajectory and consequent terminus. The task of the operator is preferentially to direct the sphere to a prescribed terminal quadrant.

In an attempt to intervene with a random physical process at the atomic level, we have constructed a large glow-discharge device whose luminous patterns are indicative of the mean free path of the current-carrying electrons against inelastic excitation collisions with the background gas. This device, shown in Fig. 6, presents a 36-in x 2-in diam cylindrical glow marked by a sequence of bright and dark zones along its positive column typical of dc discharges in a given range of gas pressure and terminal voltage. The number and locations of these striations are sensitive to the electron inelastic mean free path, which in turn depends on the gas type and density, the electron temperature, and the local electric field. Striation position is monitored by photoelectric detectors, and the goal of the operator is to expand or contract the pattern on demand, to a significant extent compared to the normal background jitter and drift. Protocols are much the same, output data take the same general form, and are analyzed by the same algorithms as in the interferometer and photoe-lastic experiments.

A number of other atomic-scale random system PK experiments are under consideration, design, or construction, involving such processes as information storage on a microelectronic chip, the spontaneous decay of phosphorescent surfaces, laminar to turbulent transition in a fluid stream, atomic and molecu-lar resonators, and resonant acoustical or electrical cavities, but none of these is far enough advanced to merit description here. Rather, we shall concentrate for the remainder of this section on a more detailed presentation of our most serv-iceable experiment, and the one on which we have the largest data base, the electronic REG.

## Random Event Generator Experiments

REGs have been the most widely used and most productive facilities for experimentation with low-level PK. Although a broad variety of such devices exist, most involve four conceptually and functionally separable components: an electronic noise source; a sampling system which examines the noise at pre-scribed intervals and prepares an output pulse train corresponding to the sam-ples thus obtained; a system which analyzes the pulse train in accordance with preset instructions and prepares suitable output for a feedback system; and the feedback display itself, which informs the operator of the results of the sam-pling process.

The particular version we have employed utilizes a packaged commercial noise source module based on a solid-state junction and precision preamplifier (Elgenco Model 3602A15124), but modules employing radioactive decay units or glow discharges can be readily substituted. This source produces a random noise spectrum up to several megahertz, which our logic circuit first filters to a flat spectrum from 50 to 20,000 Hz, then amplifies and clips to the flat-topped profile shown in Figs. 7 and 8. This is then sampled by a regular train of gate pulses, yielding a corresponding random succession of positive and negative

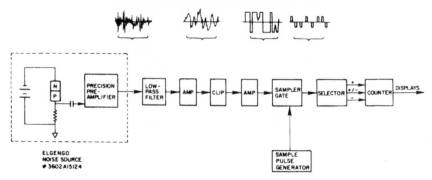

**Fig. 7.** Functional diagram of REG.

output pulses indicative of the sign of the noise at the time of sampling, and these are then counted. Since the average time between zero crossings of the clipped noise waveform is about 30 µs, sampling rates to about 15,000/s can be tolerated with statistical independence.

The full functional array is sketched in Fig. 9, and a photograph of the boxed units in Fig. 10. By panel setting the sampler may be instructed to take "trials" of 100, 200, or 2000 samples, at a frequency

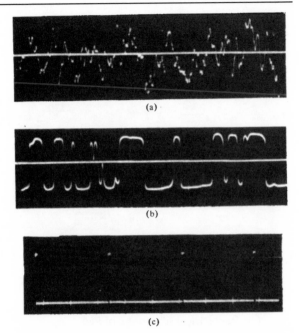

(a)

(b)

(c)

**Fig. 8.** REG waveforms: (a) Filtered noise. (b) Clipped noise. (c) Sampling pulses.

of 1, 10, 100, 1000, or 10,000/s. The counting system may be set to count only positive pulses, only negative pulses, or to alternate positive and negative counting on successive samples. The alternating positive/negative mode effectively factors out any systematic bias in the noise source, and is the mode employed in all the experiments reported here. The counting results are displayed by LED arrays tracking both the running count of each trial and the concurrent mean relative to a preset origin and are permanently recorded on a strip printer. For most of the experiments described below, an AIM-65 microprocessor interface is also utilized to insert the trial-count data on-line into processing routines supported by a TERAK Model 8510 used as a terminal and PDP 11/45 and VAX 750 employing a UNIX operating system programmed in C language. All of the sampling, counting, and display functions can be simply checked by referring them to an internal or external calibrated pulse train generator.

The device also has a manual/automatic option, whereby it will either collect its trial samples only when a panel switch or parallel remote switch is pushed, or it will repeat that process for 50 trials automatically once activated by the switch. The operator thus has the option of triggering each trial or of initiating a repetitive flow of 50 such trials with no further intervention.

The experiments reported here were performed by a single operator, seated in front of the device with the remote initiation switch in hand and the LED

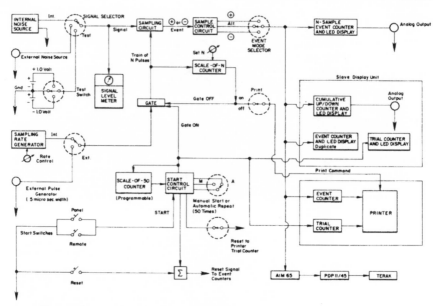

**Fig. 9.** Electrical schematic of REG.

**Fig. 10.** REG arrangement.

count indicators and TERAK terminal display visible. This operator attempted, on instruction or volition, to distort the trial counts either toward higher or lower values. The several options of sampling number, sampling frequency, +/- polarity, and manual/automatic sequencing were variously determined by random instruction, operator preference, or experimental practicality, and recorded before the beginning of each trial. Clearly, the full matrix of such possibilities could not be explored, and for our first sequence of experiments only 200-sample trials were used, at 100 or 1000 counts/s, all counted in the +/- alternating mode. The automatic/manual and high/low options were more thoroughly tested, in both the volitional and instructed choice modes.

Fifty trials of the 200-sample units comprised a test run, and data from these were processed individually and in many concatenations via a statistics package in the UNIX system developed specifically for this task. Calculated were the mean, standard deviation, range, kurtosis, skew coefficient, $z$-score, $t$-score, $\chi^2$ goodness-of-fit with both 8 and 16 degrees of freedom, and the corresponding one-tailed probabilities against chance of the last four measures. Applied to earlier and ongoing baseline data, this analysis confirmed that in undisturbed operation this REG conforms very well to a Gaussian approximation to the appropriate full binary statistics.

The major portion of the results listed below comprised three separate experimental series, extending over fifteen months, labeled REG I, REG II, and REG III, respectively. All other data acquired under slightly less formal conditions of protocol during this period, included for completeness, are grouped under two other series, labeled REG Ia and IIa, respectively. Details of these series protocols, calibration tests, and their individual results are available in the reference [93]. All told, over 25,000 active PK trials were obtained, corresponding to more than 5,000,000 binary events.

## Table I REG 200-Sample Data Summary

| Series | Instr. | No. Trials | Mean | Std. Dev. | $t$-score | $P_t$ | $n_+/n_-$ |
|--------|--------|-----------|------|-----------|-----------|-------|-----------|
| REG I | B.L. | 12,000 | 100.009 | 6.994 | 0.144 | 0.443 | 5678/5611 |
| | PK$^+$ | 4,550 | 100.264 | 7.037 | 2.528 | 0.006 | 2230/2056 |
| | PK$^-$ | 3,850 | 99.509 | 7.063 | -4.313 | $10^{-5}$ | 1716/1926 |
| | $\Delta$ PK | 8,400 | | | 4.890 | $5 \times 10^{-7}$ | |
| REG II | B.L. | 2,500 | 100.033 | 6.875 | 0.239 | 0.406 | 1188/1179 |
| | PK$^+$ | 1,950 | 100.247 | 6.849 | 1.590 | 0.056 | 916/919 |
| | PK$^-$ | 1,800 | 99.597 | 6.775 | -2.526 | 0.006 | 797/902 |
| | $\Delta$ PK | 3,750 | | | 2.920 | 0.002 | |
| REG III | B.L. | 3,500 | 99.977 | 7.013 | -0.193 | 0.424 | 1658/1655 |
| | PK$^+$ | 2,400 | 100.227 | 6.821 | 1.634 | 0.051 | 1150/1086 |
| | PK$^-$ | 2,600 | 99.736 | 7.026 | -1.918 | 0.028 | 1192/1270 |
| | $\Delta$ PK | 5,000 | | | 2.507 | 0.006 | |
| $\Sigma$ REG I | B.L. | 18,000 | 100.006 | 6.981 | 0.115 | 0.454 | 8524/8445 |
| II | PK$^+$ | 8,900 | 100.250 | 6.938 | 3.403 | $3 \times 10^{-4}$ | 4296/4061 |

| | | | | | | | |
|---|---|---|---|---|---|---|---|
| III | PK⁻ | 8,250 | 99.600 | 6.989 | -5.203 | $10^{-7}$ | 3705/4098 |
| | Δ PK | 17,150 | | | 6.107 | $5 \times 10^{-10}$ | |
| REG Ia | no B.L. | | | | | | |
| | PK⁺ | 2,150 | 100.206 | 7.091 | 1.340 | 0.088 | 1059/993 |
| | PK⁻ | 2,100 | 99.945 | 6.937 | -0.365 | 0.358 | 954/1019 |
| | Δ PK | 4,250 | | | 1.213 | 0.113 | |
| REG IIa | B.L. | 5,000 | 100.186 | 6.974 | 1.882 | 0.030 | 2367/2337 |
| | PK⁺ | 2,000 | 100.117 | 7.041 | 0.746 | 0.228 | 955/950 |
| | PK⁻ | 1,750 | 99.941 | 6.898 | -0.360 | 0.359 | 803/839 |
| | Δ PK | 3,750 | | | 0.772 | 0.220 | |
| Σ REG I Ia II IIa | B.L. | 23,000 | 100.045 | 6.980 | 0.978 | 0.164 | 10891/10782 |
| | PK⁺ | 13,050 | 100.223 | 6.979 | 3.644 | $10^{-4}$ | 6310/6004 |
| III | PK⁻ | 12,100 | 99.709 | 6.968 | -4.596 | $2 \times 10^{-6}$ | 5462/5956 |
| | Δ PK | 25,150 | | | 5.828 | $3 \times 10^{-9}$ | |

Table I summarizes all of the baseline and PK data acquired during these five experimental series. A total of 23,000 baseline trials were taken under a variety of conditions before, during, and after the active PK trials. Their overall mean was 100.045, and their standard deviation 6.980, compared with the values of 100.000 and 7.071 predicted by the theoretical Gaussian approximation to the appropriate binary statistical distribution. As shown in Fig. 11, the frequency of count distribution conformed very well with the theoretical curve.

The results of the PK trials are also presented in Table I and in Figs. 12 and 13. Briefly, the 13,050 high-instruction trials, denoted PK⁺, yielded a mean of 100.23 and a standard deviation of 6.979; the 12,100 low-instruction trials, denoted PK⁻, yielded a mean of 99.704 and a standard deviation of 6.968. The one-tailed probability of chance occurrence of the former, computed from $t$-score, is about $10^{-4}$; of the latter, about $2 \times 10^{-6}$. The combined probability of the split, i.e., of this total "direction-of-effort" success, denoted ΔPK, is about $3 \times 10^{-9}$. (A number of more elaborate statistical measures have been applied to these data; the results are not qualitatively changed thereby.)

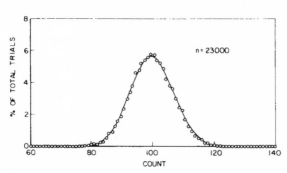

**Fig. 11.** REG 200-sample baseline data on theory.

As is evident from Figs. 12 and 13, and as is verified by the more detailed statistical tests performed, no significant distortion of the frequency-of-count distributions other than the shifting of the means has occurred. In other words, the observed effect is to shift the total distributions intact, rather than to distort any of their higher moments significantly. This result clearly has felicitous implications for this class of experimentation, since it allows much simpler and faster data collection and analysis than might otherwise have been anticipated.

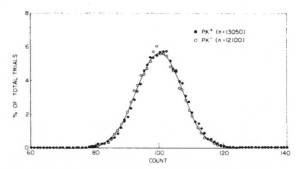

**Fig. 12.** REG PK+ and PK- 200-sample data on theory.

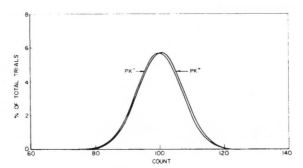

**Fig. 13.** REG PK+ and PK- 200-sample data fitted curves.

It is illustrative to exhibit the overall data behavior via graphs of the cumulative deviation of the trial score means versus the accumulated data base. Fig. 14 shows such a representation for the total data pool plotting PK+, PK-, and baseline data

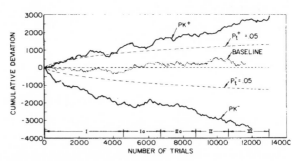

**Fig. 14.** REG cumulative deviations of PK+ and PK- 200-sample data.

with reference to cumulative 0.05 confidence levels. Fig. 15 uses a similar representation for compounding the PK+ and PK- data in a "direction of effort" cumulative deviation. (Had REG Ia and IIa been excluded from these data, the overall slopes would have been slightly more severe and uniform.)

Alternatively, the cumulative data may be presented in terms of the progressions of the average deviations from the theoretical mean, as shown in Fig. 16, where the stochastic variations of the small data bases are seen to damp out to well-defined terminal values after several thousand trials.

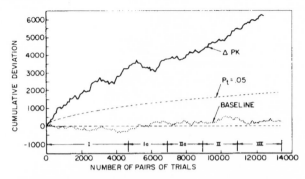

**Fig. 15.** REG cumulative deviations in direction of effort of all 200-sample data.

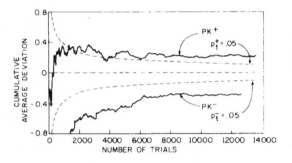

**Fig. 16.** REG cumulative average deviations of PK⁺ and PK⁻ 200-sample data.

The PK⁺ and PK⁻ effects also manifest themselves in terms of the number of trial means recorded above and below the theoretical value. As displayed in Table I, PK⁺ efforts were generally characterized by an excess of trial means above 100.00 and PK⁻ efforts by an excess below. The total concatenations in these terms are significant at a level of 0.003 for PK⁺ and 3 x $10^{-5}$ for PK⁻.

The ensemble of results acquired in these experiments display certain instructive general features:

1) The importance of accumulating very large data bases when dealing with such marginal phenoma is emphasized by the relative scales of the statistical vagaries and the broader systematic trends in Figs. 14–16. Although the trends are established early in the data collection sequence, unambiguous departures from the accumulated vagaries of chance behavior occur only well into the total 25,000 trial, 5,000,000 bit, sequence.

2) Over this large a data base, there arises some quantitative statistical regularity in the PK process, epitomized by the mean slopes of the cumulative deviations in Figs. 14 and 15 and by the terminal values of the average deviations in Fig. 16. Traced back to the elemental binary samples, these values imply directed inversions from chance behavior of about one or one and a half bits in every one thousand or, alternatively, of 0.2 or 0.3 bits per trial.

3) The differences between the somewhat larger values for the PK⁻ deviation and the lesser values for PK⁺ are only marginally significant on this data base, but prevail rather uniformly throughout all the test series. The suspicion that these reflect some subtle bias in the REG itself is not supported by the baseline data, which concatenate to a grand mean very slightly above the theoretical value.

One of the primary goals of such controlled PK studies at this early phase in the understanding of the phenomena is to develop experiments of sufficient yield and replicability that various parametric correlations may be systematically explored, thereby hopefully separating the consequential from the inconsequential factors. The experiments outlined above hold some promise of serviceability for this purpose, but a great deal of data will need be accumulated to establish any such correlations. Four classes of parameters could be considered: those associated with the experimental equipment; those associated with the operator's physiological and emotional characteristics; those associated with the operator's technique; and various environmental factors not directly associated with either. So far we have accumulated only small amounts of data from other operators, and given the general indication #1 above regarding the importance of large data bases, we can make no statement about the generality or peculiarity of our principal operator's performance. Similarly, we have attempted no systematic variation of external environmental factors, and although test times, dates, durations, and laboratory temperature, pressure, and humidity have been routinely recorded, we cannot comment on the importance of this category of parameter.

On the matter of operator technique, it should first be reemphasized that the sole formal difference between the PK⁺ and PK⁻ trials is the specified intention of the operator to influence the device to generate numbers in the assigned direction. No other variation in protocol is permitted, save those subjective differences in psychological attitude the operator chooses to invoke. Although no records of such aspects were kept, this operator, who claimed no special talent for this or any other psychic task, reported that any conscious variations in psychological strategy, such as focus of visual attention, or intensity of concentration or desire, did not appear to have any evident effect on the yield. Similarly, differences in the laboratory ambience, such as the lighting level, background noise, or peripheral presence of other persons, did not seem to influence this operator's performance. When queried about any impressionistic sense of the interaction process, the operator alluded to a "resonance or identification with the system, leading to a loss of self-awareness similar to that experienced in a game, a movie, or some creative occupation." Clearly this class of parameter will be the most difficult to specify and correlate, and we are far from any definition of its mechanisms.

With respect to experimental options on the equipment parameters, we can make very limited explorations with the acquired data base. Briefly, binary correlations of the data for the 100/1000 counting rate option, for the volitional/instructed direction of effort, and for automatic/manual sampling give little indication of importance of such factors in the overall performance. Each category shows clear and significant separation of the means for the PK⁺ and PK⁻ efforts, with little to choose between the $t$-scores for the various categories. Thus, at least for the data base at hand, the process seems insensitive to these particular experimental parameters.

We have also attempted correlation in terms of the trial-number sequence. With cognizance of the ubiquitous "decline effect" which is reported over a broad range of psychic experimentation, we have prepared an algorithm which cross-concatenates from the data base all scores achieved on the first trials of the experimental run, all achieved on the second trials, etc., up to the fiftieth, and arrays those fifty means in a graphical form. The results show little systematic profile of yield versus trial number. A similar exercise has been performed to cross-concatenate the data by run-number over the various series to search for a decline effect on that larger scale, but again no significant correlation is found within this data base.

The most extensive parametric exploration attempted to date was motivated by the apparently fundamental question implicit in general conclusion 2) above, i.e., whether the magnitude of the observed effect correlates with the total number of bits processed, or with the number of trials. To explore this aspect, the same operator has performed a second ensemble of experimental series totaling 25,000 trials, all consisting of 2000-sample bits rather than 200. As before, various combinations of the automatic/manual and volitional/ instructed modes were employed, but to speed data acquisition and reduce the operator's tedium, only the 1000/s counting rate was used. This, coupled with the more elegant data processing capabilities that had evolved over the preceding experiments, allowed this sequence to be completed in less than six months.

The results of this effort, as presented in Table II and Figs. 17 and 18, are curiously ambivalent. As before, there is clear and significant separation of the means of the PK⁺ and PK⁻ efforts, and the baseline is well behaved. As could be anticipated from the larger standard deviation of the 2000-bit data, the cumulative traces display larger statistical fluctuations and require a larger number of trials to settle toward well-defined terminal values. To the quantitative precision allowed by this data base, these terminal values appear not to endorse any simple bit-level hypothesis in that they fail by a factor of 6 or 7 to achieve the one or one and one-half bits per thousand inversion accomplished in the 200-bit trials. However, the new values are larger on a per-trial basis by a factor of about 1.7, which is not negligible in this context. Again, much more data of this sort will be required to come to grips with this class of correlation.

### Table II Summary of REG 2000-Sample Data

| Instr. | No. Trials | Mean | Std. Dev. | t-score | $P_t$ | $n_+/n_-$ |
|--------|-----------|----------|-----------|---------|-------|-----------|
| B.L. | 12,500 | 1000.016 | 21.879 | 0.079 | 0.468 | 6157/6088 |
| PK⁺ | 12,200 | 1000.380 | 21.906 | 1.914 | 0.028 | 6092/5897 |
| PK⁻ | 12,800 | 999.569 | 22.005 | -2.216 | 0.013 | 6218/6351 |
| Δ PK | 25,000 | – | – | 2.920 | 0.002 | |

In addition to continuing study of this sample-size parameter, our next generation of experiments employs a number of other operators to explore the variation of yield with operator type and technique, and a number of alternate noise sources, including pseudo-random sources, in an attempt to localize the effect somewhat and thereby to narrow the range of future experiments and models.

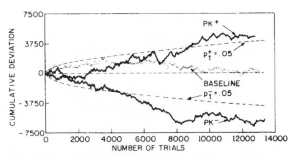

**Fig. 17.** REG cumulative deviations of PK⁺ and PK⁻ 2000-sample data.

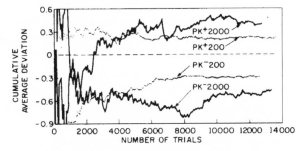

**Fig. 18.** REG cumulative average deviations of PK⁺ and PK⁻ 2000-sample data compared to 200-sample data.

The results outlined above are by no means the only consequential REG data available for contemplation. Of particular interest are a variety of experiments reported by Schmidt, some employing pseudo-random as well as physically random sources, and others using taped source outputs recorded well in advance of their presentation to the operator [87]–[90]. In another approach, May has recently reported an REG study using electronic gear specifically designed to preclude very subtle artifacts that might confound the effects of interest, and includes in his paper a thorough search of the modern REG literature [91].

In addition, considerable research in the parapsychological community has been performed using REG devices as drivers for various forced-choice video games employed in both the PK and clairvoyance modes [151]. Many of these claim significant yields, but rarely are the data-bases sufficiently large to present quantitative trends, or to allow much parameteric correlation.

Regardless of their particular implementation, any potential vulnerability of random electronic noise sources to incidental or intentional distortion by the means under study here would seem to be of some interest to a number of engineering communities, given the proliferate application of such devices in various functional and computational capacities.

# Remote Perception

As a second example of contemporary psychic research that has displayed some substantial yield and interlaboratory replicability, we select a topic which has come to be called "remote perception" or "remote viewing." The basic concept of this process is far from new; in the early 16th century, Paracelsus stated it unequivocally:

> Man also possesses a power by which he may see his friends and the circumstances by which they are surrounded, although such persons may be a thousand miles away from him at that time [8].

In its modern form, the experimental protocol requires a "percipient" to describe, by free-response oral or written narrative or drawing, a remote, unknown target location at which is stationed an "agent," with whom there is no normal sensory mode of communication during the course of the experiment. The targets are usually selected by some prescribed random process from a previously prepared pool of targets, which is unknown to any of the active participants. The quality of the perception is assessed by various impressionistic or analytical judging methods described below.

Historically, this experiment has evolved from several generations of free-response clairvoyance and telepathy experiments, which were found to have certain advantages over the more traditional "forced-choice" ESP tasks, such as the Xener card identifications of the early Rhine laboratory [34]–[37], in displaying less tendency for percipient stagnation and "decline-effects" over extended testing, and in maintaining some of the spontaneity of anecdotal clairvoyance experiences. One of the earliest detailed reports of such free-response studies appears as a book by Upton Sinclair entitled *Mental Radio,* which features an equivocal foreword by Albert Einstein [152]. More modern work of this class was performed at the Maimonides Medical Center by Ullman and Krippner in the 1960s, and reported in their book *Dream Telepathy* [64]. From this work emerged the so-called "ganzfeld" or sensory inhibition perception studies of Honorton and many others which propounded the desirability of emotionally stimulating tasks to which the subjects could relate in a personal and spontaneous fashion [66], [67].

The contemporary version of the remote perception protocol was introduced in a sequence of publications by Targ and Puthoff [94], [153]–[156], which prompted a substantial number of attempted replications [157]–[174], and considerable critical comment. The most extensive of the replications, conducted by Dunne and Bisaha in the Chicago area over the period 1976 to 1979 comprised 40 formal trials to which were applied 157 independent transcript judgings, 84 of which assigned first-place rank to the proper targets [161], [162].

The type of data which can be acquired in such studies is illustrated in the sequence of Figs. 19–22. In each case is shown a photograph of a particular target, selected by some random process, which was visited by an agent on the date and time indicated. Below each figure is a portion of the corresponding percipient transcript, with the time and location of the perception effort also noted. The examples shown are drawn from a variety of experimental series conducted under somewhat different protocols, but serve to display some of the characteristics which commonly appear in the more successful efforts:

**Fig. 19.** Remote perception target: Picnic area, Feathered Pipe Ranch near Helena, MT; 12:00 N MDT, Sept. 5, 1978.

Percipient transcript: Princeton, NJ; 8:30 A EDT, Sept. 5, 1978:

"Outdoors ... open landscapeælarge areas of trees—pines? interspersed with open fields. Single road. High overcast, cool, breezy. (Agent) in dark jacket talking to someone near road—possibly turnout area or picnic area. Assembly of stones—possibly pylon or marker or wall. Large sign somewhere."

1) The overall ambience of the scene is accurately perceived.

2) Certain details are accurately identified; others are misconstrued or totally ignored.

3) A feature which is impressive to the agent is not necessarily so to the percipient, and vice versa.

4) The composition of the scene may be distorted by errors in scale, relative positions of key objects, or total right-left inversions.

5) The aesthetic aspects, such as colors, general shapes, degree of activity, noise level, climate, and other ambient features tend to be more accurately perceived than more analytical details such as number, size, or relative positions.

6) The perception is not necessarily centered on the defined target, and may even provide accurate information on adjacent areas external to the target, unnoticed by the agent.

7) The fidelity of the perception seems to be independent of the remoteness of the target, up to distances of several thousand miles.

8) The time of the perception effort need not coincide with the time the agent is at the target. Perceptions obtained several hours, or even days, prior to the agent's visit to the target, or even prior to selection of the target, display at least as high a yield as those performed in real time.

**Fig. 20.** Remote perception target: Woodrow Wilson School, Princeton, NJ; 2:15 P EDT, Aug. 28, 1980.
Percipient transcript: Princeton, NJ; 12:15 P EDT, Aug. 28, 1980:

"Some kind of courtyard, enclosed by buildings on two sides. Paths or walks around periphery, a statue or monument of some kind in the middle surrounded by grass. Could be a fountain; I have the feeling of water. Trees or tall hedges on one side. Fairly quiet, but some people walking around. Not sure of sound, the idea of a fountain suggests sound of water but I'm not sure I really hear it or not."

The philosophical and practical implications of items 7 and 8 are clearly substantial. If the data are valid, the most parsimonious explications would require access of the percipient's consciousness to other portions of the space-time grid than that in which it is currently immersed, or that it can reach by normal processes of communication or memory. These same items also seriously delimit the potential physical mechanisms for such access.

Rigorous evaluation of the data from experiments such as these is confounded by the psychological components of the process, by the impressionistic nature of the information involved, and by the inevitable subjective biases of all those participating in the experiment. Doubtless the earliest and most primitive assessments were informal *a posteriori* exchanges of impressions about the target between agent and percipient which, although possibly informative and stimulating to them, lacked any quantitative basis and held little scientific credibility. In a somewhat less vulnerable strategy invoked more recently, the percipient, after completing his transcript, visited several possible targets drawn from the pool and attempted to identify the one he perceived, or to rank-order each of them in terms of conformity to his earlier perception. Statistical arguments

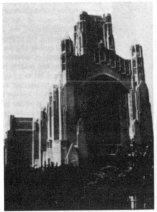

**Fig. 21.** Remote perception target: Rockefeller Chapel, Chicago, IL; 2:15 P CDT, June 10, 1977.

Percipient transcript: Mundelein College, Chicago, IL; 1:00 P CDT, June 10, 1977:

"I'm seeing a heavy wooden door with a black bolt on it rounded at the top in a dome fashion. I have a feeling of opening the doors and looking in and it's dark inside. My feeling at the moment is that it's a building like a church. And I can see the pews. There is some light but I feel basically a kind of darkness in there and a quietness. I'm seeing little turrets, very elaborate-looking little turrets, a whole series of them like across the entire top of the building and there's a straight line and then up to a triangle. I have a definite image of an angel-type of statue, marble, flowing robes. I see the door again and I see some stairs. I think it's very high. I'm getting some stained-glass windows that are arch shape and they would look to be dark blue. Whatever the architecture of it the ornamentation on the building is quite elaborate and it looks like there's a section on the top with the turrets and then below that there are some other kinds of designs but more linear designs.

"I again have a vision of the doors and then maybe a ledged area or an area of the building that protrudes with some kind of a design and there maybe even be a couple of those before you get to the top part which is either triangular or rounded. There is filigree work, little filigree turrets or something. And within the building there is a sort of a continuation of arches, but possibly they meet columns or something like that, but whatever the decoration is where walls join or separations, it looks like it's arched.

could then be applied to these ranks to estimate the likelihood that information about the target had been acquired by means other than chance [175]–[177].

In an attempt to separate the possible ESP functioning of the percipient during the visitation and ranking process from his original perception effort, the protocol subsequently evolved to invoke independent judges who were provided copies of the various transcripts and taken to the target sites to perform their preferential rankings. Even in this form, the technique has been criticized for possible sensory cuing of the judges [178] and has tended in turn to be replaced by a protocol wherein the judges perform their ranking on the basis of photographs of the targets, usually taken by the agent at the time of the trial. In one such version, the judges, who have not been involved in any earlier portion of the experiment, are asked to compare a single percipient transcript with agent-generated descriptions and photographs of a number of alternative targets, including the proper target, and to rate or rank-order them by some prescribed criteria. Again, statistical assessment of the significance of the rankings follows.

The bulk of the remote perception data reported in the literature has been evaluated by some form of these independent judging processes, and displays sufficiently high yield to encourage further refinement of the protocol and analysis before attempting categorical judgment on the validity and viability of the phenomena. Beyond minor tightening of the target selection, agent maneuver, and perception acquisition and recording phases of the experiment, the major potential improvements would still seem to pertain to the judging process, which remains potentially vulnerable to subtle cues in the transcripts, to vagaries in the judges' capability, to their subjective biases toward the individual experiments and to the topic as a whole, and to possible psychic input of their own [161], [162].

In an effort to improve the judging process further, our laboratory has explored the applications of various information theoretic methods to the quantification of the data, and an analytic technique has been devised which is based on a limited binary alphabet of target/perception descriptors [179]. While less sensitive to the Gestalt impressionism and symbolic representations which a human judge might capture, this method does provide a rudimentary framework for evaluation of

**Fig. 22.** Remote perception target: Danube River, Bratislava, Czechoslovakia; 3:00 P European Standard Time, Aug. 24, 1976.

Percipient transcript: Minoqua, WI; 8:30 A CDT, Aug. 23, 1976:

"I have the feeling that the agent is somewhere near water. I seem to have the sensation of a very large expanse of water. There might be boats. Several vertical lines, sort of like poles. They're narrow, not heavy. Maybe lamp posts or flag poles. Some kind of circular shape. It's round on its side, like a disc, it's like a round thing flat on the ground, but it seems to have height as well. Maybe with poles. Could possibly come to a point on top. Seeing vertical lines again. Seems to be a strong impression, these vertical lines. Predominant colors seem to be blue and green. Water again. Some very quick impression of a fence, a low fence. The steps seem to go up to some kind of fence. It's a dark fence and it's along like a walk sort of at the top of the steps. The steps sort of lead up to like a path or walkway. Like a boardwalk. And there's a fence along it. There's people walking along it, and there's vertical lines along that walkway."

signal-to-noise ratio in the information transfer, and an assessment standardization less dependent on subjective interpretation. In essence, the strategy is to replace impressionistic assessment of the quality of a perception by the identification of specified elements of information therein, after which a mechanical scoring and ranking procedure takes over. In the hope of conveying a bit more substantive flavor of the data acquired in remote perception experiments and the processing thereof, permit us to describe this analysis in a little detail.

The heart of the method is the establishment of a code, or alphabet, of simple descriptive queries which may be addressed to all targets and all perceptions, responses to which serve to distinguish them and to permit quantification of the information acquired in the perception process. In one version, these "descriptors," thirty in number, are posed in binary form and range over a spectrum from quite factual discriminations, e.g., whether the scene is indoors or outdoors, whether trees are present, or whether there are automobiles, to much more impressionistic aspects, such as whether the ambience is noisy or quiet, confined or expansive, hectic or tranquil. The particular ensemble of descriptors has evolved in part through personal experience and intuition, and in part through trial-and-error application to various pilot data. The goal has been a balanced alphabet whose elements are a) relatively unambiguous; b) commonly perceived by a broad selection of percipients; c) individually instructive in defining the scene; d) complementary to one another; and e) sufficient in number to permit reasonable synthesis of the scene, but not so numerous to burden the data collection or computation excessively.

Given this descriptor alphabet, each target in the pool is then represented in terms of 30 binary bits, corresponding to the appropriate YES/NO responses to the queries. This encoding is normally performed by the agent at the time of target visitation, although reference may be made to the target selector's judgment or to photographs of the target for verification. Each perception is similarly tendered into a corresponding sequence of binary digits, but only after the percipient has been allowed to form a free-response impression of the target. Various scoring recipes are then invoked for quantitative comparison of the perceptions with the targets, using for computation the UNIX operating system of a PDP 11/45 or VAX 750.

The simplest recipe merely counts the number of correct responses to the 30 descriptors, i.e., the positive correlations between the target and descriptor matrices. This does not normally provide a particularly accurate index of the quality of the individual perceptions, since the *a priori* probabilities of the various descriptors are widely different. For example, a given pool may have more outdoor than indoor targets, and hence a correct identification of an indoor context should be given higher credit than identification of an outdoor context. To facilitate such weighting, a step is included in the computational program to provide the *a priori* probabilities of all descriptors in the prevailing target pool, on the basis of which more elaborate scoring recipes may be invoked.

Since the various targets have substantially different characteristics and hence different capacities for achieved scores, a variety of normalization procedures also have been developed, using as denominators the total number of descriptors, the perfect score, i.e., the score that would be achieved for a given target if all descriptors were identified correctly, and various "chance" scores for the target, defined by some random or arbitrary process of descriptor response. A "selective" scoring/normalization process has also been applied which effectively allows the percipient to reject any descriptor on which he feels unqualified to comment, and thence to be scored only on the reduced descriptor set.

The statistical significances of these various normalized perception scores are assessed by a collective ranking process reminiscent of the traditional human judging techniques, but having the advantages that the ranking proceeds on a much more standardized and analytical basis, and that many more alternative targets can be ranked by the machine than by a human judge. Specifically, the program scores each transcript not only against its proper target, but against every other target in the pool, and then ranks these targets in order of descending score and specifies the rank of the match with the proper target. This process is repeated for every scoring method, and the results displayed in corresponding matrix arrays.

Table III displays typical results of these analytical ranking procedures as applied to a group of 24 perceptions of 24 targets in the Chicago area. Tabulated are the ranks of the proper targets compared with all other targets for each of the perception efforts, as computed by five of the scoring methods we have found to be most instructive, namely, A) number of correct descriptors/total number of descriptors; B) weighted full descriptor score/perfect score; C) weighted full descriptor score/number of descriptors; D) weighted selective descriptor score/perfect score; and E) weighted selective descriptor score/chance score. Also included in the table are the mean ranks assigned by independent human judges subjectively comparing these perceptions with a much smaller number of alternative targets. Although the bases of comparison are quite different, it appears that in the majority of these cases the analytical and impressionistic evaluations concur at least roughly in their estimate of the quality of the perceptions, particularly for those which consistently obtain low rank assignments. If the analytical computation is carried through using as target pool only those alternative targets available to the human judges, the agreement in mean ranks is found to be somewhat closer, perhaps fortuitously so, given the categorically different bases of assessment implicit in the two methods.

To this analytically scored and ranked data it is possible to apply a variety of statistical assessments of widely ranging sophistication and complexity. Consistent with the rather broad mesh of the descriptor code and the elementary scoring recipes invoked in this version of the concept, we confine ourselves to correspondingly simple statistical measures which provide at least semi-quantitative indication of the yield beyond chance. Specifically, we address only

### Table III  Precognitive Remote Perception
### 24 x 24 "Chicago" Series Proper Target Ranks

| Perception No. | Scoring Method[a] | | | | | | Avg./ 24 | Human Judges Mean Rank[b] |
|---|---|---|---|---|---|---|---|---|
| | A | B | C | D | E | Avg. | | |
| 1 | 3/4 | 7 | 7 | 9 | 2 | 5.9 | 0.25 | 2.7/8 = 0.34 |
| 2 | 1/2 | 2 | 4 | 1 | 1 | 1.9 | 0.08 | 1.0/8 = 0.13 |
| 3 | 1 | 1 | 1 | 1 | 1 | 1.0 | 0.04 | 1.5/8 = 0.19 |
| 4 | 2/8 | 7/2 | 2/2 | 4/2 | 2/2 | 4.5 | 0.19 | 2.7/8 = 0.34 |
| 5 | 7/3 | 9 | 11 | 4 | 8 | 8.0 | 0.33 | 1.7/8 = 0.21 |
| 6 | 9/5 | 12/2 | 7/2 | 16/2 | 7/2 | 11.0 | 0.46 | 3.5/8 = 0.44 |
| 7 | 13/2 | 11 | 14 | 10 | 13 | 12.3 | 0.51 | 2.3/8 = 0.29 |
| 8 | 20/3 | 22 | 20 | 14 | 19 | 19.2 | 0.80 | 1.8/8 = 0.23 |
| 9 | 4/2 | 4 | 8 | 1 | 5 | 4.5 | 0.19 | 2.6/7 = 0.37 |
| 10 | 10/7 | 13 | 13 | 9 | 5 | 10.6 | 0.44 | 1.4/7 = 0.20 |
| 11 | 9/4 | 9 | 11 | 6 | 12 | 9.7 | 0.40 | 3.6/7 = 0.51 |
| 12 | 1/3 | 2 | 2 | 2 | 5 | 2.6 | 0.11 | 1.8/7 = 0.26 |
| 13 | 1/3 | 1 | 3 | 1 | 3 | 2.0 | 0.08 | 2.2/7 = 0.31 |
| 14 | 1 | 2 | 2 | 1 | 1 | 1.4 | 0.06 | 1.4/7 = 0.20 |
| 15 | 1/2 | 2 | 2 | 1 | 1 | 1.5 | 0.06 | 1.0/7 = 0.14 |
| 16 | 2 | 2 | 2 | 1 | 2 | 1.8 | 0.08 | 1.0/10 = 0.10 |
| 17 | 1/4 | 9 | 1 | 9 | 1 | 4.5 | 0.19 | 1.0/5 = 0.20 |
| 18 | 2/2 | 10 | 5 | 1 | 2 | 4.1 | 0.17 | 1.0/5 = 0.20 |
| 19 | 14/3 | 14 | 14 | 19 | 17 | 15.8 | 0.66 | unjudged |
| 20 | 7/6 | 11 | 11 | 8 | 10 | 9.9 | 0.41 | 5.0/6 = 0.83 |
| 21 | 1/2 | 2 | 3 | 4 | 1 | 2.3 | 0.10 | 2.0/6 = 0.33 |
| 22 | 5/6 | 7 | 12 | 2 | 7 | 7.1 | 0.30 | 3.0/6 = 0.50 |
| 23 | 16/4 | 23 | 11 | 15 | 9 | 15.1 | 0.63 | 3.0/6 = 0.50 |
| 24 | 3 | 3 | 4 | 3 | 4 | 3.4 | 0.14 | 2.0/6 = 0.33 |
| Mean | 6.73 | 7.75 | 7.13 | 5.96 | 5.79 | 6.67 | 0.28 | 0.31 |

[a]Computed rank/number of ties for that rank.

[b]Assigned rank/number of possible ranks.

the distribution of *proper* target ranks achieved in the series of perceptions, such as summarized in columns 2–6 of Table III. Using the common $z$-score method for a discrete distribution, the probability of achieving the mean rank of any of these columns by chance may be directly computed. Table IV displays the results of such calculation for the same 24 x 24 "Chicago" series. Note that, whereas all of the methods suggest significant departures of the computed mean ranks from chance, there is relatively little disparity among them, indicating that the specific method of scoring and normalization is not a sensitive element in the overall evaluation of the perception series.

## Table IV Precognitive Remote Perception
### 24 x 24 "Chicago" Series Score Summary

| Method[a] | Mean Rank | No. 1st (2nd) Ranks | No. Ranks Below Mean | z | $P_z$ | $\chi^2(4)$ | $P_\chi$ |
|---|---|---|---|---|---|---|---|
| Chance expectation | 12.5 | 1.0 (1.0) | 12 | | | | |
| A | 6.73 | 4.4 (4.0) | 19 | -4.08 | $2 \times 10^{-5}$ | 18.5 | <0.005 |
| B | 7.75 | 2.0 (6.0) | 20 | -3.36 | $4 \times 10^{-4}$ | 11.8 | <0.01 |
| C | 7.13 | 2.0 (4.5) | 20 | -3.80 | $7 \times 10^{-5}$ | 19.6 | <0.001 |
| D | 5.96 | 8.0 (2.0) | 20 | -4.63 | $2 \times 10^{-6}$ | 24.0 | <0.001 |
| E | 5.79 | 6.0 (3.5) | 21 | -4.75 | $1 \times 10^{-6}$ | 27.6 | <0.001 |

[a]As described in text:  A) Number of correct descriptors/total number of descriptors.
B) Weighted full descriptor score/perfect score.
C) Weighted full descriptor score/number of descriptors.
D) Weighted selective descriptor score/perfect score.
E) Weighted selective descriptor score/chance score.

The departure of the shape of the proper target rank distribution from chance is also displayed in Table IV in terms of the number of perceptions achieving first-place ranks, the number ranked better than the chance mean, and a simple $\chi^2$ test with its associated probability.

The method is not restricted to square arrays, i.e., to equal numbers of targets and perceptions in one-to-one correspondence. Table V displays the results of a recent "Ocean" series in which six perceptions were ranked against 24 targets in the pool from which the six actual targets were drawn. (The percipient for this series was at the time sailing alone across the North Atlantic Ocean.)

## Table V Precognitive Remote Perception
### 6 x 24 "Ocean" Series Score Summary

| Method[a] | Mean Rank | No. 1st (2nd) Ranks | No. Ranks Below Mean | z | $P_z$ |
|---|---|---|---|---|---|
| Chance expectation | 12.5 | 0.25 (0.25) | 3 | | |
| A | 4.5 | 1.0 (1.1) | 6 | -2.83 | 0.002 |
| B | 4.2 | 2.0 (0.0) | 6 | -2.95 | 0.002 |
| C | 5.0 | 1.0 (1.0) | 6 | -2.65 | 0.004 |
| D | 5.2 | 1.0 (0.5) | 6 | -2.59 | 0.005 |
| E | 5.3 | 1.0 (1.0) | 6 | -2.54 | 0.006 |

[a]As described in text:

A) Number of correct descriptors/total number of descriptors.
B) Weighted full descriptor score/perfect score.
C) Weighted full descriptor score/number of descriptors.
D) Weighted selective -descriptor score/perfect score.
E) Weighted selective descriptor score/chance score.

Because of its particularly severe protocol, we also include as illustration the results of a "European" series judged by this method. In this series, the agent was traveling in eastern Europe, and on five successive days, at 3:00 P.M. local time, utilized whatever location he happened to occupy as the target. The perceptions of these targets were recorded by a single percipient in northern Wisconsin at approximately 8:30 A.M. local time of the preceding day, i.e., each perception was roughly 24 h precognitive. (Fig. 22 depicts a target and perception from this series.) Table VI displays the analytically judged results of this series, and compares them with the results of previous human judging. Although the data base is small, the consistency of yield is striking.

**Table VI  Precognitive Remote Perception
5 x 5 "European" Series Score Summary**

| Method[a] | Mean Rank | No. 1st (2nd) Ranks | No. Ranks Below Mean | z | $P_z$ |
|---|---|---|---|---|---|
| Chance expectation | 3.0 | 1.0 (1.0) | 3 | | |
| A | 1.2 | 4.3 (0.3) | 5 | -2.85 | 0.002 |
| B | 1.4 | 4.0 (0.0) | 5 | -2.53 | 0.006 |
| C | 1.4 | 3.0 (2.0) | 5 | -2.53 | 0.005 |
| D | 1.8 | 4.0 (0.0) | 4 | -1.90 | 0.029 |
| E | 1.6 | 3.0 (1.0) | 5 | -2.21 | 0.013 |
| Seven human judges (avg.) | 1.9 | 2.1 (1.6) | 4.6 | | |

[a]As described in text:

A) Number of correct descriptors/total number of descriptors.
B) Weighted full descriptor score/perfect score.
C) Weighted full descriptor score/number of descriptors.
D) Weighted selective descriptor score/perfect score.
E) Weighted selective descriptor score/chance score.

To obviate the possibility that this method of analysis may somehow process even random inputs to apparently significant scores, artificial target data matrices and artificial perception data matrices have been constructed from the output of an REG, and the computational schemes applied to various combinations of these with each other and with true data. The pattern of results conforms to chance expectations. An alternative form of control is provided by application of the method to discernibly unsuccessful test series, which yields appropriately insignificant results.

The project outlined in the last few paragraphs is described in greater detail, with many other experimental examples, both successful and unsuccessful, in reference [179]. We have since developed the capability of employing ternary rather than binary responses to the descriptors, in order to convey more shaded information about the aspects queried. A given feature may thereby be specified as a) present and dominant; b) present but secondary; or c) absent. Or alternatively, the feature may be described as a) definitely present; b) ambiguous or unspecified; or c) definitely absent. While these approaches clearly provide more specific target and perception data, the scoring thereof becomes more complex, especially in the definition of certain of the normalization denominators.

We have also been exploring a modification of this analytical judging procedure which would bypass the ranking steps altogether and move directly to compute individual statistical scores for each transcript. The key to this variation is the definition and utilization of a generalized target pool composed of over 200 targets, local, national, and international, assembled for a broad range of earlier and ongoing experimental series, from which correspondingly generalized *a priori* descriptor probabilities may be calculated. Evaluation of the transcript scores on the basis of these generalized probabilities, rather than those calculated for the specific series target pools, has been found to alter only slightly the relative ranks of the perceptions determined by any of the five methods used above and provides the desired common basis for evaluating the individual statistical significance of those scores.

To pursue this, the program next assembles a set of empirical chance distribution functions, one for each scoring method, by concatenating all mismatched perception scores assigned by that method, i.e., all off-diagonal elements of that perception-target matrix. With reference to Gaussian fits to these empirical chance distributions, the proper perception-target scores can then be assigned z-values and corresponding probabilities against "chance." As one example of this approach, Fig. 23 shows the empirical distribution of scores compounded from some 1400 mismatched targets and transcripts by method E, on which are superimposed the scores achieved by the 24 proper target perceptions of the "Chicago" series. The corresponding z-values and probabilities against chance are listed in Table VII.

These individual significance values can subsequently be compounded into an overall significance level for the entire series by various standard procedures [180]. The latter result should agree with that derived from the original ranking method, to the order of approximation implicit in each form of this analysis. In this case, the series value is about $10^{-8}$, compared to $10^{-6}$ for the ranking method.

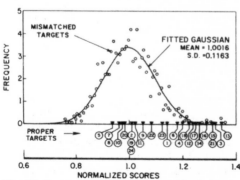

**Fig. 23.** Remote perception empirical chance distribution (method E).

**Table VII  Precognitive Remote Perception Individual Statistical Scores (Method E) 24 x 24 "Chicago" Series**

| Perception No. | z-score | $P_z$ |
|---|---|---|
| 1 | 1.210 | 0.113 |
| 2 | 0.089 | 0.465 |
| 3 | 2.737 | 0.003 |
| 4 | 1.700 | 0.045 |
| 5 | -0.553 | 0.709 |
| 6 | 1.533 | 0.063 |
| 7 | -0.315 | 0.623 |
| 8 | -0.315 | 0.623 |
| 9 | 0.451 | 0.326 |
| 10 | -0.197 | 0.578 |
| 11 | 0.191 | 0.424 |
| 12 | 2.037 | 0.021 |
| 13 | 2.948 | 0.002 |
| 14 | 2.244 | 0.012 |
| 15 | 2.661 | 0.004 |
| 16 | 2.478 | 0.007 |
| 17 | 2.180 | 0.017 |
| 18 | 1.904 | 0.028 |
| 19 | 0.083 | 0.467 |
| 20 | -0.152 | 0.560 |
| 21 | 2.679 | 0.004 |
| 22 | 0.701 | 0.241 |
| 23 | 1.057 | 0.145 |
| 24 | 0.113 | 0.455 |

The specific results shown in Tables III–VII represent some of the most successful data we have acquired; many less successful examples could also be displayed. To summarize our total experience with over two hundred remote perception efforts, all performed with volunteer percipients claiming no special abilities, we might note that the data tend to fall into one of four categories, in roughly comparable quantity:

1) the target is accurately represented in detail and composition;

2) particular features of the target are accurately perceived, but the context is incorrect;

3) the ambience of the target is perceived, but the details are inaccurate;

4) the perception seems unrelated to the target in context or detail.

Survey of the pertinent literature indicates a comparable pattern of yield across the experience of others involved in similar experiments.

To date there has been little progress in correlating the degree of success of such efforts with the prevailing experimental conditions or with the personality traits or attitudes of the participants. A certain body of lore has compounded from the testimony of the more successful percipients, such as the desirability of a personal rapport between the agent and percipient, the value of a lighthearted attitude, the importance of excluding any associative or constructive logic, etc., but much of this is still too vague and inconsistent to provide any basis for experimental refinement or theoretical modeling. At present, the only fair statement would be that empirical evidence for this class of phenomena continues to accumulate, but with frustrating irregularity and little basic comprehension. Notwithstanding, the present and potential applications of the process in a variety of arenas, combined with the relatively simple and inexpensive nature of the experiment, keep this type of study active.

## Theoretical Concepts

No remotely satisfactory physical theory of psychic phenomena yet exists. Indeed, next to the evasiveness of the effects under controlled experimentation, the second greatest frustration in the study of psychic processes has been the absence of viable theoretical models with which to begin the traditional dialogue between theory and experiment on which all scientific progress eventually depends. This may, of course, be indicative of an illegitimacy of the phenomena themselves, or at least of an evanescence that fundamentally precludes any analytical representation. On the other hand, it may be an indication that modern physical theory, elaborate and sophisticated as it is, has not yet evolved to a stage where it can properly acknowledge and deal with the role of consciousness in the physical world [181], and that this should be one of its new frontiers. Before pouncing toward either extreme, it may be worthwhile to play through some of the more canonical attempts that have been made to deal with this domain, both from a formalistic and philosophical point of view.

Efforts toward theoretical explication of psychic phenomena over the past century have proceeded from various levels of presumption as to the fundamentality of the effects observed. Some have insisted that the effects are totally illusory, i.e., artifacts of poor experimentation or data processing, or that they are the chance results of random processes. Others have assigned the effects to known physical and physiological mechanisms associated with, but not deliberately precipitated by the participants, e.g., electromagnetic radiation from brain circuitry or intercardial potentials, or heat transfer, vibration, or aerochemical changes in the experimental environment caused by human presence or exertion. More ambitious efforts have contended that no such conservative models can suffice, and that it will be necessary to identify new forms of energy or information transfer to retain the established physical formalisms, or possibly even necessary to expand the physical laws themselves, as was required in the generalization from classical mechanics to quantum mechanics or to special and general relativity, with the present forms becoming subsumed under more comprehensive statements. Still others have concluded that the scientific paradigm in general is inadequate and that basic revision in the representation of the process of conscious observation of physical events will be required.

Beyond the uncertainty as to the fundamentality of the model required, these modeling efforts have labored under the confusion of whether the purported phenomena are most basically psychological, physiological, physical, or some inextricable combination thereof, and hence which class of concepts should dominate the model and which should be secondary. Virtually all permutations have been explored to some degree, under labels of "psychophysiological," "biophysical," "psychophysical," etc., but none of these can claim more than suggestive analogies or philosophical stimulation. This author is unqualified to assess any models based in the psychological or physiological domains, other than to note that those most frequently discussed tend to acknowledge the role of random processes, information ordering, and statistical, rather than directly causal mechanisms [182]–[187], all of which have their counterparts in several of the more physically oriented modes which have been proposed. Confining ourselves to such physical theories, the history of credible analytic effort is conveniently short and, in my view, more instructive in its philosophical than in its functional characteristics.

## Electromagnetic and Geophysical Models

For perhaps naive reasons, the earliest physical models tended to presume wavelike propagation of psychic effects, usually in the electromagnetic modes [188]. Doubtless the concurrent emergence of radio technology with its revolutionary wireless capabilities influenced the concepts and nomenclature of these versions, and frequent reference to psychic "transmitters," "receivers," "antennas," "tuning," and "static" are found in them. Upton Sinclair's book, *Mental Radio,* mentioned earlier, is one example of such an analogy [152].

More modern models of this genre, appearing predominantly in the Russian literature [43], [50], [100], [189], [190], have focused on very low frequency bands, of the order of 10 Hz, characteristic of various physiological frequencies, especially the brain wave spectra. Some variations of these have invoked modulation of the earth's magnetic field or of the electrostatic fields of the atmosphere. Wave models involving other than electromagnetic environmental media have also been proposed, such as infrasonic atmospheric waves, geoseismic waves, and barometric fluctuations, possibly stimulated by contemporary attention to the inexplicable homing capabilities of birds, fish, and animals, and the hive or swarm behavior of certain insects [101], [102], [132].

As suggested by the pre-occupation with screen-rooms in the early days of the electromagnetic concept, and by more recent long-distance remote perception experiments, some of the obvious validation/disqualification tests examining attenuation diffraction, interference, and polarization effects have indeed been attempted, but the very large dimensions involved for these wavelengths leave the studies less than conclusive. Some contemporary workers retain support for this category of model, claiming that the necessary electromagnetic signal levels required for influence on the brain circuitry are so small that no coarse-grained tests can properly discriminate against them. More problematic, in my own view, are the absence of any demonstrated velocity of propagation of psychic effects and the large body of precognition evidence which, if accepted, cannot be accommodated by any reasonable advanced wave characteristics.

However, setting aside for the moment the quantitative functional difficulties with the electromagnetic approach to psychic phenomena, certain broader philosophical analogies in the conceptual and experimental aspects of the two topics may be worth noting. In electromagnetism, beyond the bald empiricism of the definition of the fields themselves as representations of "action-at-a-distance," there are many features which to a naive or primitive observer would, and indeed historically did, appear as "paranormal," or at least anomalous: the noncolinear aspects of Ampere's and Biot-Savart's laws and of the Faraday effect; induction effects and switching transients; the Maxwell displacement current; the propagation of waves in a vacuum, with a specified finite velocity—each of these in some sense digressed from contemporary "normal" experience, was conceptually difficult in its time, and required certain leaps of empiricisin to get on with the formalism.

To the extent that we just now hold a similarly naive and primitive view of psychic phenomena, it may be necessary to tolerate similarly empirical representations until a more comprehensive model can knit itself into a more fundamental representation. For this purpose, there may be some merit in looking to just such electromagnetic effects for analogies. As one example, the pervasive "decline effect" in psychic experimentation, wherein the performance on psychic tasks is widely reported to be highest immediately after initiation, to decrease over protracted testing periods, and then to improve again just before termination, is somewhat reminiscent of the induced signatures of certain electromagnetic processes. The decline effect has been commonly ascribed to a psychological boredom or reduction in the emotional intensity of the operator performing the task; just possibly it may be a more fundamental characteristic of the phenomenological domain.

In a similar vein, many psychic effects are reported to be intrinsically transient, e.g., the "fleeting impression"; the "sudden vision"; the "unexpected effect." One of the favored techniques of some remote perception percipients is to "sweep through" their image of the target repeatedly until it is clarified.

Many PK effects are reported to be achieved just at the first effort or immediately after the effort is terminated. Such "beginner's luck" evidence might be construed to indicate that psychic processes are invalidated by prolonged and careful examination; alternatively, it may be a hint that they are inherently "inductive," in the electromagnetic sense, i.e., that they are intrinsically unsteady phenomena wherein the time derivatives influence the magnitudes of the effects.

Yet another characteristic that psychic effects share with certain electromagnetic processes is their tendency to be indirect, tangential, or peripheral: direct effort on one PK task fails, but a secondary effect is noted on another component or device; central elements of a remote perception target are ignored by the percipient, but minor or peripheral aspects are identified with precision; the pattern of physical disturbance in a poltergeist event is reported to be vortical rather than radial, all of which call to mind cross-product and vector curl effects in the electromagnetic domain.

The point in suggesting such analogies is not to endorse direct physical correspondence between electromagnetic and psychic processes, but rather to speculate whether the human mind may tend to perceive and assess phenomena in the two domains in certain similar fundamental ways.

## Entropy and the Random Process

A second, more recently opened class of psychic model addresses the interaction of consciousness with natural random processes [95], [187], [191]. A common aspect of the established physical formalisms of kinetic theory, thermodynamics, statistical mechanics, and information theory is the role of randomicity as the reference plane for information and energy exchange. By whatever representation, the second law of thermodynamics, expressing the tendency of isolated physical systems to drive irreversibly toward configurations of minimum order and information content, stands starkly asymmetric in the time coordinate, thereby raising profound philosophical issues in virtually every domain from biophysics to cosmology.

Some of the most controlled and replicable experiments in PK, such as the REG studies outlined earlier, could be construed to challenge the second law, or at least to suggest modifications of the concept of an isolated physical system. Namely, under the circumstances of those experiments, human consciousness could be postulated to be inserting order, albeit to a small degree, into a random physical process.

This possibility can be extended conceptually to the anomalous acquisition of information in remote perception experiments, to psychic healing, and to animal and plant PK, but to my knowledge, no attempts at formulation have yet specified any details of the ordering capability, e.g., its physical or physiological source, its propagation modes, or its manner of interaction. Pending these, one can again only proceed with high empiricism to attempt to represent the observed correlations in a useful fashion, a strategy which has sustained many other observational fields in their primitive phases. Notwithstanding, this class of psychic model poses a profound question: The long-accepted essence of consciousness is its ability to extract information from its environment; may the reverse also be possible? May consciousness have the ability to insert information into its environment?

One extreme variation of this model escalates the question even one step further, to ask whether it is possibly an indigenous property of extremely elaborate and complex systems that they may embody inherent functional consciousness of their own—that somehow out of their very complexity, the interlockings of their systems, they derive not only abilities to learn, to reproduce themselves, to adapt to their environment, but also to exert an entropy reversing form of "consciousness" on themselves [192], [193].

## Hyperspace Representations

A few attempts have been made to represent paranormal effects by recasting the basic laws of physics in more than the four coordinates of normal human experience and applying the consequent new terms to the representation of paranormal effects [104], [105], [194]. For example, one such approach adds an imaginary component to each of the spatial and temporal coordinates, i.e., invokes complex space and time, somewhat in the spirit of ac circuit theory or exponential wave mechanics [195]. The imaginary components and their "cross-talk" with the traditional real ones thereby permit representation of anomalous effects within the framework of established physical laws. To date, no convincing fundamental definition of these new dimensions has been offered, thereby reducing such models to an heuristic or empirical level. In this sense, the approach bears some similarity to the "hidden variable" aspect of quantum mechanics, mentioned below.

One may speculate that if such models are to address the interaction of consciousness with physical process, the requisite new coordinates or components must relate to, or in some way define or localize, the processes of consciousness. In other words, to the normal "hard" coordinates, whereby events are conventionally specified in the physical world, it may be necessary to add certain "soft" coordinates to specify the conscious processes by which those events are perceived and possibly influenced. Clearly, the coordinate frame in which one chooses to observe and represent any physical process is intimately linked to the perception of that process. Two common examples would be the perceptions of kinematic and dynamic effects in a rotating frame of reference, such as a merry-go-round or an orbiting spacecraft, or the even more bizarre appearances of physical processes in rapidly accelerating frames, à la general relativity.

To compound this interdependence of perception and reference frame by including "consciousness coordinates" in the specification of the latter is an awesome proposition, but an intriguing one. And the consequences need not be restricted to the mechanical behavior of physical systems, but may also influence their perceived substance. The noted British astronomer Sir Arthur Eddington, some fifty years ago, presaged this concept most boldly and heretically [196], [197], [203]:

> The whole of those laws of nature . . . have their origin, not in any special mechanisms of nature, but in the workings of the mind. . . .
>
> All through the physical world runs that unknown content which must surely be the stuff of our consciousness. . . .
>
> Where science has progressed the farthest, the mind has regained from nature that which the mind has put into nature. . . .
>
> We may look forward with undiminished enthusiasm to learning in the coming years what lies in the atomic nucleus—even though we suspect that it is hidden there by ourselves. . . .
>
> The stuff of the world in mind-stuff.

## Transform Models

Another rather extreme approach proposed recently has come to be referred to as the "holographic" or "transform" model [198]–[200]. Essentially what is suggested here, as I understand it, is that the information of the universe is arrayed, not in terms of position and time as we have come to perceive it, but rather as frequency and amplitude information, and that the human consciousness essentially performs "Fourier transforms" on this to order that information into the more familiar form. In the sense that the space and time coordinates are thereby downgraded from the fundamental coordinates of experience to useful ordering parameters, one could interpret such models to imply that consciousness may, by this mechanism, access any portion of space and time to acquire information, and then interpret it in some characteristic form.

The physicist David Bohm, in conjunction with the psychologist Karl Pribram, has elaborated such concepts to a considerable degree of generality, proposing a so-called "implicate order" or "enfolded order" of fundamental reality from which the more familiar "explicate order," i.e., the commonly manifest perceptions are assembled in accordance with the prevailing circumstances of their observation [201], [202].

## Quantum Mechanical Models

Probably the most exercised category of contemporary model attempts to apply the concepts and formalisms of quantum mechanics to represent some of the paranormal effects presented in the psychic domain. Of all the forms of physical analysis, quantum mechanics invokes the largest array of empirical postulates that are at variance with conventional rationality, and yields in their implementation a corresponding array of results which contradict common impressions of reality. The quantization process itself, which limits measurable properties to discrete values; the representation of particulate systems by wave functions; the role of observation in collapsing the wave functions to a single state vector; the uncertainty principle; the exclusion principle; the indistinguishability principle; and most drastic of all, the commitment to totally probabilistic mechanical behaviors—all, in some sense concede a degree of paradox in human perception of physical processes. The familiar conundrums of "Schrödinger's Cat," "Wigner's Friend," or the "Einstein–Podolsky–Rosen Paradox," all suggest that the laws of quantum mechanics are not so much statements of fundamental physical reality, as of our ability to acquire information about that reality. Quantum mechanics, in other words, does not so much describe the state of a physical system as it describes our *knowledge* of the state of that system.

It is somewhat in this spirit that a number of authors have aspired to model psychic process in quantum mechanical terms. Some have attempted to invoke the so-called "hidden" or unused variables of the formalism to involve conscious process more explicitly in the behavior of physical systems [107], [204]–[208]. Others have endeavored to draw analogies between the synaptic processes in the brain and quantum mechanical "tunneling" [209].

Given the primitive state of the phenomenological data base, much of this effort may be prematurely elaborate and complex. Our own approach to quantum mechanical modeling has been far more superficial and generic, attempting only to explore possible analogies between the paradoxical consequences of the formalism, and the paranormal evidence of certain psychic experiments. Again with the indulgence of the reader, we might sketch a bit of this argument, for the purpose of illustrating this class of approach with the example closest to hand.

One conventional interpretation of the application of quantum mechanical formalism to the observable behavior of physical systems is to associate appropriate mathematical operators with a corresponding measurement process. When applied to the prevailing wave function of the system, these operators call out the observable values of the property in question as eigenvalues of an equation of the form

$$M\psi_i = m_i \psi_i$$

where $M$ is the measurement operator, $m_i$ are the observable values of the measured property, and $\psi_i$ the corresponding eigenstates of the wave function. Our approach is to generalize this representation to include conscious systems as well as conventional physical ones, and to allow the measurement operator concept to include specification of psychological as well as physical properties.

Thus, we denote a particular individual consciousness by a "state function" $\psi_i$, and represent a situation to which it is exposed by an operator $S$. Application of the situation operator to the consciousness wave function then yields the possible psychological responses, $s_i$, as eigenvalues:

$$S\psi_i = s_i\,\psi_i.$$

We then invoke certain aspects of quantum mechanical interaction theory to develop the capacity for "paranormal" behavior of both physical and conscious systems. For example, in the traditional theory of the covalent chemical bond between two hydrogen atoms, one constructs from the separate atomic functions, $\psi^a$ and $\psi^b$ using arguments of symmetry and indistinguishability, a composite molecular wave function $\psi^{ab}$, which yields expectation values for the molecular energy levels substantially different from simple linear superposition of the atomic energy eigenvalues, i.e.,

$$e_i^{ab} = e_i^a + e_i^b + \Delta e_i^{ab}$$

where $e_i^a$ and $e_i^b$ are the energy eigenvalues of the atomic systems, and $\Delta e_i^{ab}$ embodies an "exchange energy" term which is classically inexplicable, but devolves formally from the postulate that the electrons are indistinguishable in the bonded configuration. Stated more bluntly, surrendering information about the identity of the atomic electrons in the molecular configuration leads directly to a significant and observable component of the binding energy, thus posing an equivalence between information and energy far more stark than that implicit in the second law of thermodynamics.

Using similar formalism, we may represent the state function of two interacting individuals, or of an interacting individual and physical system, by a composite state function $\psi^{ab}$ whose behavior characteristics also differ significantly from those of the separated systems, i.e.,

$$s_i^{ab} = s_i^a + s_i^b + \Delta s_i^{ab} + \Delta s_i^{ba}$$

where $s_i^a$ denotes the "normal" response of the first individual to the prevailing situation, and $s_i^b$ that of the second individual or of the physical system, and $\Delta s_i^{ab}$ and $\Delta s_i^{ba}$ denote modifications of those behaviors arising because the two systems are strongly interacting during the observed situation.

As a specific example, to apply this approach to remote perception experiments we could denote the percipient by $\psi^p$, the agent by $\psi^a$, and the experimental protocol by the mathematical operator $P$. In the absence of interaction between the percipient and agent, each would have certain "normal" reactions to the experimental situation, $p_i^p$, $p_i^a$ derived from the eigenvalue relations:

$$P \, \psi_i^p = p_i^p \, \psi_i^p$$
$$P \, \psi_i^a = p_i^a \, \psi_i^a$$

i.e., the percipient would perceive nothing about the target that was not accessible to his normal perceptual modes, and the agent would react to the target under no influence from the percipient.

However, if the percipient and agent are strongly enough interacting to require a new "molecular" wave function, $\psi^{pa}$, "paranorrnal" terms will appear in their response patterns:

$$p_i^{pa} = p_i^p + p_i^a + \Delta p_i^{pa} + \Delta p_i^{ap}$$

where in $\Delta p_i^{pa}$ we may accommodate the anomalous acquisition of information about the target, and in $\Delta p_i^{ap}$ the commonly reported experience of the agent of having his attention attracted to specific details he would "normally" have ignored.

Application of this formalism to a PK experiment proceeds in a similar fashion. Here we might represent the experimental operator (person) by $\psi^o$, and the experimental device by $\psi^d$. Again the experimental protocol is represented by a mathematical operator, $K$. In the absence of major interaction, the device behaves "normally":

$$K \, \psi_i^d = k_i^d \, \psi_i^d$$

and the operator has the "normal" psychological experiences:

$$K \, \psi_i^o = k_i^o \, \psi_i^o$$

But if the operator and the device are in some state of resonance, $\psi^{do}$, each behaves somewhat differently, i.e.,

$$k_i^{do} = k_i^d + k_i^o + \Delta k_i^{do} + \Delta k_i^{od}.$$

The anomalous modification in the behavior of the system $\Delta k_i^{do}$ is termed PK; $\Delta k_i^{od}$ accomodates any paranormal psychological reactions of the operator.

Development of further illustrations of this general method here would be inappropriate and would require more detailed specification of the nature of the consciousness wave functions, their functional form, their proper "soft" coordinates, and the interpretation of their quantum numbers. Some of this has been attempted, along with various other applications to the psychic domain, and is available in a reference [210]. The point of exposition here is largely a philosophical one: namely, the "paranormal" effects emerge as a consequence of the comparison of the behavior of an interacting system with that of its separated components.

Quantum mechanics may have quite another analytical precedent to contribute to the representation of psychic phenomenology. Clearly, much of the psychic research data will continue to be acquired and processed in statistical form, using established statistical methods. Yet, all statistical models ultimately trace back to certain fundamental probability rules for the elemental systems involved. For the statistical models to be viable, these probability rules must a) exist; b) be known; and c) be analytically tractable. At present, virtually all processing of psychic research data presumes the applicability of classical statistics, yet the basic probability rules for the elemental processes are, in point of fact, unknown [211], [212].

It may fortuitously be the case that much of psychic process can be adequately treated as marginal deviation from classical chance behavior. In some cases, however, it may be necessary to invoke categorically different statistics, tracing back to fundamentally different probability rules, to deal with the effects. The quantum mechanical precedents of relevance, of course, are the two systems of quantum statistics, i.e., the Fermi–Dirac and Bose–Einstein systems, which are based upon the phase-space population rules for half-integer and integer spin particles as imposed by the Pauli principle, i.e., the wave function symmetry requirements. For most common physical systems, these quantum statistics conveniently degenerate into the classical form, but for certain special situations, e.g., the specific heats of metals and certain radiation properties, their full application is essential.

By analogy, one could postulate that physical reality, as perceived and influenced by human consciousness, actually plays by more elaborate probability rules than commonly attributed to it, and hence strictly requires a more complex statistical mechanics. Thus, in this view, the processes commonly regarded as "normal" would be those for which the "classical" approximation to this more complex system is adequate; small-scale psychic effects would then comprise those displays of minor deviations of the complex statistics from the "classical" limit; the more drastic phenomena—poltergeists, levitations, metal bending, etc.—would presumably become explicable only in terms of the full statistical formulation.

## Holistic Models

Yet more extreme in conceptual difficulty is a body of contention that psychic processes are inseparably holistic, and that no model rooted in any sector of established science can adequately represent them [213]. In particular, the suggestion is offered that psychic processes are manifestations of the interdiffusion of the analytical, scientific world with the creative aesthetic world, and thus to represent them effectively it will be necessary to combine the philosophical perspectives and techniques of both domains. To resort to metaphor for illustration once again, one could ponder such analogies from the common physical world as the interface regions between the sea and land, where the diffuse patterns of the ocean wave structure meet the solid promontories and sloping beaches of the coast to produce the crashing breakers and hissing foam of seashore phenomena, or the overrunning of a warm, moist atmosphere by a cold-front of drier, cooler air to initiate the striking electrical and acoustical phenomena of the summer thunderstorm.

By whatever analogy it may be illustrated, theoretical representation of the interpenetration of causal physical mechanics with creative conscious process must be a formidable undertaking, yet not totally without precedent or allied effort. For examples, interest is just now growing in the humanistic psychology community in the analytical study of human creativity [214]–[216], and, on the other side of the interface, a few physicists are beginning to muse openly about the role of aesthetics in subnuclear and cosmological physical behavior [217]–[220]. In yet a different arena, certain futurists are now examining the interplay of aesthetic and functional human needs and values in the evolution of social and political structure [221]. To be sure, none of these has produced much in the way of analytical formalism, but the peculiarity, magnitude, and significance of the interpenetration effects are being acknowledged.

Any summary assessment of the status of physical models of psychic phenomena should properly begin with reiteration of the opening statement: none of the approaches outlined above has yielded anything approaching a functional theoretical basis. Yet, the ensemble of empirical experimental experience seems to suggest that certain of the conceptual and perceptual characteristics underlying those formalisms may be relevant to ultimate representation of such processes. Specifically, they suggest that the following rather general hypotheses may be worthy of more detailed examination:

1) The phenomena may be inherently statistical, rather than directly causal, and we may be observing them "on the margin." That is, the observed phenomena may represent marginal changes from normal behavior on a very grand scale and with fluctuation times which tax human observational capability. It also may be necessary to deal with more complex statistical mechanics, appropriate to more involved basic probability rules, to represent the most drastic effects.

2) Just as human consciousness has the ability to extract information from an external system, e.g., by observing it, that consciousness may also have the ability to project information into it, e.g., by ordering random processes.

3) Quantum mechanics may be more than a system of physical mechanics; it may be a more fundamental representation of human consciousness and perception processes, and the empirical pillars of this formalism, such as the uncertainty principle, the exclusion principle, the indistinguishability principle, and the wave/particle dualities may be as much laws of consciousness as laws of physics.

4) Psychic processes may be inherently holistic, and thus the ultimate model may need to integrate both the scientific and the aesthetic aspects in order to identify the sources of the phenomena. That is, psychic processes may

be manifestations of the intersection of the analytical, scientific world with the creative, aesthetic world, and thus, to represent them effectively, it may be necessary to integrate both perspectives without sacrificing the integrity of either.

Clearly, any of these intuitions will have to be developed in far more philosophical and analytical detail before a trenchant theoretical model can emerge, but at this primitive stage it is probably stimulating to consider a few such radical possibilities, along with more prosaic explications. Changes of this magnitude in representation of human perceptual reality inevitably, and properly, would be attended by much philosophical recalcitrance and agony, but the broader personal and collective insights that could derive from legitimate efforts to bridge the analytical/aesthetic interface could be of at least corresponding benefit.

## The Negative Side

Contemporary criticism of psychic research and rejection of the phenomena it purports to demonstrate tend to focus on a number of specific objections, each of which has some degree of validity and merits some thought in any balanced assessment of the topic [118], [178], [222]–[224]. The most commonly cited concerns include:

1) demonstrable fraud;

2) naivete of technique, including inadequate controls, faulty equipment, sensory cuing of participants, other experimenter biases, selective treatment of data, improper statistical methods, and general experimental and theoretical incompetence;

3) little improvement in comprehension over many years of study;

4) absence of adequate theoretical models;

5) suppression of negative results;

6) poor experimental replicability;

7) elusiveness of effects under close scrutiny;

8) sensitivity of results to participants, attitudes, and laboratory ambience;

9) tendency for many results to be only marginally significant compared to chance expectation;

10) inconsistency with prevailing "scientific world view";

11) contradictory to personal psychology, philosophy, theology, or "common sense."

Obviously this list runs a gamut from rather technical and procedural objections, through phenomenological inconsistencies, to rather categorical and subjective rejections, and only a few of these issues can be constructively addressed here.

Unfortunately, but undeniably, one or the other of the first two judgments may legitimately be applied to a large body of the propounded results. By its nature, the field is immensely vulnerable to fraudulent exploitation and naive gullibility, and such have indeed occurred to a distressing degree. It is also true that the topic has attracted a disproportionate share of less than fully competent researchers, and that it presents extraordinary pitfalls for even the most disciplined scholars. Yet despite the substantial validity of these claims, and the suspicion they inevitably cast on all other results, it does not seem that they should predicate categorical rejection of the entire field. Rather, the vulnerable cases should be patiently ferreted out using obvious scholarly criteria, and only those efforts surviving such scrutiny used for scientific insight and judgment.

The lack of definitive progress toward comprehension of the phenomena and the absence of viable theoretical models have already been acknowledged in the foregoing text, and although these assessments should perhaps be qualified by the relatively minute integrated investment of resources made in this field in comparison to many of the more favored areas of science, they nonetheless constitute legitimate concerns about the ultimate tractability of the field. It should perhaps also be noted that, despite the prolonged effort, it is only very recently that more sensitive and powerful experimental equipment and data processing techniques have been brought to bear, and equally recently that more sophisticated physical formalisms have been invoked, and that these have had a much briefer opportunity to render the phenomena into comprehensible terms.

The subsequent five objections, 5)–9), are more specific and substantive, and merit examination from two orthogonal points of view. Namely, to what extent do such characteristics indeed invalidate the results, and conversely, to what extent might they illuminate the basic nature of the phenomena? With respect to suppression of unfavorable results, there has undoubtedly been some tendency in this field, as in most others, to advance positive or definitive findings more enthusiastically than negative or equivocal ones. Indeed, this paper has been guilty of the same bias. In an effort to provide concise representation of the style and substance of psychic research and of the nature of the effects it can produce, we have tended to invoke as illustrations some of the more successful and familiar pieces of work without balancing the presentation with comparable examples of the negative or equivocal results that are regularly acquired in these efforts.

To the credit of the psychic research community, it has officially encouraged thorough and objective reporting of negative data, and much of these indeed appear regularly in its established journals [225]–[228], with a number of consequent benefits. First, beyond adding credibility to the body of positive results, such data compound to provide some quantitative index of the ratio of positive to negative yields in a given class of experiment, thereby contributing to a broader sense of the grand statistics of the phenomena. In addition, documentation of the specific conditions prevailing in unsuccessful experiments may be helpful in excluding irrelevant parameters from further consideration, and in identifying and reducing counterproductive influences. Perhaps most pointedly, however, the body of negative and equivocal data emphasize that psychic phenomena, if real, are highly irregular and sensitive to intangible influences well beyond current scientific control, and, if their study is to be pursued, this caveat must be accepted *ab initio,* at least for the present.

A similar interpretation also applies to the irreplicability complaint, and to the three following it. Without question, the dominant experimental frustration in this field is the inability to replicate on demand previously observed paranormal effects, not only at other laboratories, but even in the original facility, using the original participants, under apparently identical experimental circumstances [172], [173], [229]–[231]. This ubiquitous characteristic has precipitated major philosophical excursions which are well beyond our capacity to review here. Only briefly, four possible categorical interpretations have been advocated:

a) The phenomena are illusory.

b) The phenomena are rare and bizarre chance occurrences, beyond any hope of regularization.

c) The phenomena are precipitated, at least in part, by psychological and/or physiological factors which are presently beyond experimental control, but which if fully comprehended would conform to established scientific paradigm.

d) The phenomena are inherently statistical; and possibly quantum mechanical, on a macroscopic scale, thus manifesting themselves with finite but fractional probability on any given occasion.

The latter pair of options are not necessarily mutually exclusive, particularly if one takes a rather generous doubly statistical point of view, namely that the human population embodies a range of capability for engendering such effects and that beyond that, any individual may display a variable range of personal capacity, depending on a variety of environmental, physiological, and psychological factors prevailing at the time.

The evasiveness of the phenomena under carefully controlled and observed study may be the most damning criticism of all, or it may also constitute a valid and illuminating phenomenological characteristic. The tendency of a given preliminary or anecdotal effect to disappear or diminish when the experiment is tightened, or when it is displayed to a skeptical jury of observers, obviously casts major doubt on the scientific integrity of the process. Yet it also brings to mind at least two other processes which, while superficially dissimilar, may not be totally irrelevant, namely artistic creativity, and quantum mechanical measurement as limited by the uncertainty principle. In the former, there should be little quarrel that the creative processes of artistic, musical, or literary composition, or of lofty philosophical thought in general, are not usually facilitated by rigid constraints or by the presence of a body of unsympathetic observers. The importance of favorable ambience and mood for such efforts is intuitively and demonstrably clear, and little creative achievement is likely to occur in overly sterile or hostile environments, a truth Richard Wagner vividly conveyed to his own critics by his portrayal of the fate of young Walther attempting his avant-garde "Trial Song" before the assembled Meistersingers. Virtually every creative artist preserves some form of retreat or sanctuary, and even the most rigorous of scientists will concede the role of unstructured mental imagery in enhancing their technical insights.

The analogy of the quantum mechanical measurement process is somewhat more strained, in that it requires generalization of the concept to the macroscopic level of information or energy exchange between two persons or between a person and a physical system. The point will not be developed here, other than to note that if there is any validity to the application of quantum mechanical logic to this class and scale of intellectual/intuitive process, as discussed earlier and in the references, some form of "uncertainty principle" could predicate a limit to the precision with which psychic effects could be observed. More specifically, if the "hard" and "soft" coordinates of representation are canonically conjugate, some form of $\Delta_q \Delta_p \sim h$ rule may apply, so that attempts at excessive precision in specification of a psychic effect could dissipate its cause, and vice-versa [210].

The final two reservations regarding inconsistency of the phenomena with established scientific and personal views, while constituting powerful professional and personal discriminators and properly predicating great caution and discipline in venturing into any anomalous field, also cannot be allowed total veto authority if new domains of conceptual experience are ever to be challenged. In responding to a critic of an earlier paper who stood on these points I wrote, perhaps too floridly,

Authoritarianism such as this encourages established knowledge to sit smugly on its duff and categorically reject all new evidence that does not support or fill in its contemporary "world-view compatability criterion"—whatever that is. Worst of all, it stifles the most precious attribute of human consciousness, the yearning for ever new, ever higher wisdom that has driven the mind and spirit of man to evolve upward, rather than merely to replicate [232].

More persuasive to this issue, however, would be a simple historical count of the number of leaps of scientific insight, from Aristotle to this day, which would have been, and in most cases were, for a time, rejected on the basis of these criteria. Curiously, it has often been those giants of science who with soaring insight and courage of conviction violated such tenets to lead their fields to new plateaus of understanding, who also, in a later day, led the recalcitrance of the establishment against comparably sacrilegious visions of their successors, while still endorsing in general terms the importance of visionary thought. Galileo, early champion of scientific methodology and revolutionary concepts in terrestrial and celestial mechanics against vicious dogmatic opposition, rejected Kepler's elliptical orbits as "occult fantasy"; Thomas Young, whose brilliant interference experiments finally established the wave character of light, contended with Fresnel's theoretical formulations of the same processes; Ernst Mach disputed relativity and atomic theory; Rutherford, who showed the world the nuclear atom, dismissed any practical significance for nuclear energy; Lavoisier and Ostwald disputed atomic theories of chemistry; D'Alembert opposed probability theory; Edison discounted alternating current; Lindberg despaired of Goddard's rocketry; and Albert Einstein retained an enduring uneasiness about quantum theory despite his many contributions to its evolution [233]–[235]. Incidentally, the same Albert Einstein who would invoke the establishment criteria against Upton Sinclair's clairvoyance data:

> . . . the results of the telepathic experiments carefully and plainly set forth in this book stand surely far beyond those which a nature investigator holds to be thinkable [152].

could in quite another tone testify eloquently to the importance of the aesthetic dimension in creative science:

> The most beautiful and most profound emotion we can experience is the sensation of the mystical. It is the sower of all true science. He to whom this emotion is a stranger, who can no longer wonder and stand rapt in awe, is as good as dead. To know that what is impenetrable to us really exists, manifesting itself as the highest wisdom and the most radiant beauty which our dull faculties can comprehend only

in their most primitive forms—this knowledge, this feeling is at the center of true religiousness.

The cosmic religious experience is the strongest and noblest mainspring of scientific research [236].

Individually and collectively, these critical challenges to psychic research raise valid concerns which merit deliberate attention and predicate great caution, and can also help to illuminate some of the subtle phenomenological features. However, they can perform these functions well only if they themselves are informed, reasoned, and fair. Regrettably, from my reading of the critical literature, this has not invariably been the case, and instances of naiveté, selective representation of data and protocol, and excessive generalization also appear therein.

The role of the critic in psychic research is a most essential one, perhaps more so than in any field of scholarship yet broached. When the criticism is based in fact and experience and is objective and fair, it can instill healthy discipline in the study of this or any other difficult field and ensure that the fundamental requisites of scientific methodology, e.g., dispassionate rigor, humility in the face of observations, limitation on extrapolation of results, and openness of mind will prevail in the search. But it is equally essential that the process of criticism play by these same rules. If it violates any of them, if it lapses into categorical rejection, guilt by association, or sloppy logic, it can become as suspect as the object of its complaint, and thus fail in its proper role [237].

## Implications

Despite their compounded length, the foregoing historical outline, survey of contemporary activity, and selected examples of ongoing research and theoretical efforts are still far from adequate to convey the full essence of this complex and contradictory field. Fortunately an extensive body of reference literature exists, including a number of comprehensive general volumes, whereby an interested reader may flesh out this sketch and extend it to many aspects not broached here [6], [44], [45], [56], [57], [92], [130], [238]–[242]. Hopefully, such more thorough study would tend to confirm the general impressions of the status and prospects of the field conveyed above. To restate these in summary, it appears that once the illegitimate research and invalid criticism have been set aside, the remaining accumulated evidence of psychic phenomena comprises an array of experimental observations, obtained under reasonable protocols in a variety of scholarly disciplines, which compound to a philosophical dilemma. On the one hand, effects inexplicable in terms of established scientific theory, yet having numerous common characteristics, are frequently and widely observed; on the other hand, these effects have so far proven qualitatively and quantitatively irreplicable, in the strict scientific sense, and appear to be sensitive to a variety of psychological and environmental factors that are difficult to specify, let alone control. Under these circumstances, critical experimentation has been tedious and frustrating at best, and theoretical modeling still searches for vocabulary and concepts, well short of any useful formalisms.

Given these difficulties, what then are the motivations, if any, to proceed? As for most speculative topics, three potential generic benefits could be considered:

a) acquisition of fundamental knowledge,

b) practical applications,

c) humanistic benefits.

In this particular field, basic knowledge might accrue in two ways—the attainment of new scientific information in the usual sense, and the broadening of scientific methodology to deal more effectively with irregular phenomena of this type. In other words, study of this topic not only might provide certain phenomenological answers, but also might serve to broaden the context in which science can formulate its questions. New mechanisms for transfer of information or energy might be identified, or broader understanding of those properties, and how they are perceived and measured might emerge. The latter half of the opportunity clearly is a major challenge to science, but hardly a new one. William James posed it rather bluntly some eighty-five years ago:

> The spirit and principles of science are mere affairs of method; there is nothing in them that need hinder science from dealing successfully with a world in which personal forces are the starting point of new effects. The only form of thing that we concretely have is our own personal life. The only completed category of our thinking, our professors of philosophy tell us, is the category of personality, every other category being one of the abstract elements of that. And this systematic denial on science's part of personality as a condition of events, this rigorous belief that in its own essential and innermost nature our world is a strictly impersonal world, may, conceivably, as the whirligig of time goes round, prove to be the very defect that our descendants will be most surprised at in our boasted science, the omission that to their eyes will most tend to make it look perspectiveless and short [24].

The potential applications of psychic process are best considered with conservatism and restraint, especially given the tendency of certain elements of the public media and private exploiters to extrapolate the possibilities far beyond any demonstrated accomplishments. Clearly, the process of remote perception described earlier, along with other forms of clairvoyance, could hold some potential interest for intelligence agencies, law enforcement units, and any other activity relying on surveillance, as well as for archaeological searches, natural resource prospecting, and the like, and such operations have indeed engaged in empirical efforts to evaluate the efficacy of such strategies in their particular domains. From a strictly engineering standpoint, however, the potential efficiency and precision of such tactics are unclear, given their apparent tendency to trade more effectively in impressionistic generalities than in analytical detail.

Low-level PK effects, such as the REG distortions indicated above, could have more pervasive implications for high technology. If, for example, the basic functions of microelectronic elements could be even slightly disturbed by intentional or inadvertent intervention of human consciousness, it would seem important to obtain some assessment of the potential magnitude of such effects, and of the factors favoring or inhibiting such interference, before much more elaborate integrated circuit arrays, graphic display systems, and other sensitive man/machine interfaces are committed to delicate or critical operations. To focus our assessment of such possibilities, we are now examining PK disturbance of the memory function of a single microelectronic chip [243]. If the indications that psychological and environmental factors bear on the precipitation of such effects are sustained, it may be necessary to expand consideration of such parameters beyond the usual scope of human factors engineering, especially in situations involving high psychological stress.

The potential humanistic benefits of better comprehension of psychic phenomena could be addressed on either a personal or social level, but to do so in any detail would far exceed the purview of this article. Again, extensive references on various facets of the issue abound [244]–[252]. Ultimately, most of these philosophical excursions arrive at the same monumental question, namely whether convincing demonstration of the capability of human consciouness to influence its reality to a significant degree would substantially alter individual and collective perception of the human state, its value system, and its behavior pattern, and thereby facilitate its evolution to a higher life form. Such projections have been offered from a variety of perspectives. Engineer/futurist Willis Harman forecasts an "inner experience" paradigm:

> Just as conventional science depends upon a prior consensus on how knowledge of the sense-perceived world shall be publicly tested and validated, so the complementary paradigm will have to include consensus on how knowledge relating to the world of inner experience shall be publicly tested and validated.

Its essential characteristic would be that consciousness and its contents are primary data, rather than being secondary and derivative as in the conventional paradigm. Where the conventional paradigm involves reductionistic models the complementary paradigm would add holistic models; where the first employs deterministic (or stochastic) explanations of events the second would add teleological, purpose-recognizing explanations; where the first is little involved with matters of values and meaning, the second finds these of central concern; where the first is dominated by technology-focused values of prediction and control, the second would tend to value understanding relating to human well-being, development and evolution [221].

Biologist/immunologist Jonas Salk phrases it more in terms of a resonance of human volition with natural processes:

Man has come to the threshold of a state of consciousness, regarding his nature and his relationship to the Cosmos, in terms that reflect 'reality.' By using the processes of Nature as metaphor, to describe the forces by which it operates upon and within Man, we come as close to describing 'reality' as we can within the limits of our comprehension. Men will be very uneven in their capacity for such understanding, which, naturally, differs for different ages and cultures, and develops and changes in the course of time. For these reasons it will always be necessary to use metaphor and myth to provide 'comprehensible' guides to living. In this way, Man's imagination and intellect play vital roles in his survival and evolution [249].

And philosopher/paleontologist Teilhard de Chardin states his hope in terms of a collective consciousness of the human race:

Thus we find ourselves in the presence, in actual possession, of the super-organism we have been seeking, of whose existence we were intuitively aware. The collective mankind which the sociologists needed for the furtherance of their speculations and formulations now appears scientifically defined, manifesting itself in its proper time and place, like an object entirely new and yet awaited in the sky of life. It remains for us to observe the world by the light it sheds, which throws into astonishing relief the great ensemble of everyday phenomena with which we have always lived, without perceiving their reality, their immediacy or their vastness [253].

On a somewhat less lofty, but possibly more functional level, a recent lengthy study prepared for the House of Representatives Science and

Technology Committee, in a section encouraging serious assessment of further research on "the physics of consciousness," stated that recent experiments:

> suggest that there exists an 'interconnectiveness' of the human mind with other minds and with matter; . . . that the human mind may be able to obtain the information independent of geography and time

and later concluded that:

> . . . a general recognition of the degree of interconnectiveness of minds could have far-reaching social and political implications for this nation and the world [254].

The details and tones of these visions clearly are matters of individual heritage, experience, and intuition, but the messages share a common theme: the next stage in human evolution may involve expansion and interconnection of human consciousness, features clearly central to the psychic concept.

Beyond the difficulty of the phenomena and potential benefits of the knowledge, a more prosaic factor to be considered in contemplating further psychic research is the requisite cost of the effort. To date, such experimentation has been extraordinarily inexpensive by usual scientific standards. The primitive level of comprehension, the lack of organized interest within the established scientific communities, and the Bohemian status of many of the investigators have predicated projects of very low budgets compounding to a total annual national investment of the order of one million dollars or less [255]. Clearly, if more incisive progress is to be attempted, some increase in the sophistication and interaction of the principal programs must be funded, but it is most unlikely, and for the time probably undesirable, that this will consume any magnitude of resources comparable with, or distractive from, the better established research domains. A comparable statement could be made with respect to commitments of the requisite scholarly personnel.

If on the basis of such cost/risk/benefit considerations a modest ongoing program of research seems justified, it remains to consider the selection of topics, experimental styles, and evaluation criteria which would optimize the effort at this stage. In addition to the obvious desiderata that the specific experiments be clearly posed, conceptually simple, lend themselves logistically to rigorous, tightly controlled protocols, and focus on the more tractable and potentially applicable effects, three more specific recommendations could be offered.

First, given the irregularity of the phenomena, their possible dependence upon a broad range of physical, psychological, physiological, and environmental parameters, and their tendency to display effects as marginal deviations from some "normal" distributions, some premium should probably be placed on the capacity of the experiments for large data base accumulation and processing. While less prolific studies may continue to provide interesting anecdotal effects and suggest procedures for more detailed programs, it is unlikely that much correlation of those effects with pertinent prevailing parameters can be achieved without large quantities of data. More specifically, the favored experiments should 1) deal with processes found to have relatively high intrinsic yields; 2) employ equipment and protocols which permit data acquisition at rapid rates; and 3) have access to computational equipment and software which allow storage of large data arrays and processing of that data in many selective cross-concatenations. As an example, the latest refinement of the REG experiment described earlier allows acquisition, storage, and primary processing of several hundred experimental trials ($\sim 10^5$–$10^6$ bits) per hour, and subsequent concatenation of all previously stored data by any permutation of ten parametric indices, e.g., sampling rate, manual/automatic, volitional/instructed, operator characteristics, etc. For any such parametric explorations to be indicative, the pertinent data subset must be adequately large to display any systematic deviation from the baseline distribution beyond the statistical noise background. This we have found to require at least several thousand trials; the implication for the total data base is clear.

This very large data capability inevitably predicates a sophistication in equipment and software which, beyond the initial and operating expenses, may introduce some undesirable effects of complicating the phenomenological processes and clouding the experimental ambiences. Specifically, one needs to consider whether any observed effects, in either the PK or ESP categories, still trace unequivocally to the primary physical processes, or whether there now might arise confounding interactions with elements of the data collection and processing equipment or techniques. Related to this concern are possible uncertainties of the participants in defining and focusing on the primary tasks.

Reservations of this sort lead directly to a second general recommendation for effective psychic experimentation. Namely, if the phenomena derive to any significant degree from conscious or subconscious processes of the human mind, it is important that such not be inhibited or excessively complicated by the design and operation of the experiments. For this and numerous other reasons, it is probably essential in planning and implementing the experimental programs to include the insights, interpretations, and intuitions of the human operators, especially those who have demonstrated some success in the generation of the phenomena. It is quite possible that the difference between a sterile experiment and an effective one of equal rigor lies as much in the impressionistic aspects of its ambience and feedback as in the elegance of its instrumentation, and the former need to be well-tuned to the participants who are asked to function as components of the experimental system. On occasion, there seems to have been some tendency in this field to treat the experimental participants in rather perfunctory fashion, discounting any insights they might offer on the tasks at hand. If one subscribes at all to the concept of the phenomena emerging from some interpenetration of analytic and intuitive processes as suggested by the holistic models, there would seem no better place to combine perceptions and insights from these two domains than in the design, operation, and interpretation of the experiments addressed to illumination of the interface.

Finally, it seems most evident that given the intrinsic transdisciplinary nature of the business, research on this topic in any established sector should become much more communicative and interactive across traditional scholarly boundaries if it is to have any hope of rendering the phenomena into comprehensible and serviceable terms. This cross-talk cannot be limited to naturally contiguous fields, à la the usual exchange between physicist and engineer, or between psychologist and sociologist. As its lengthy heritage illustrates, in this domain the interests and insights of the theologian, philosopher, statistician, technologist, hard scientist, and creative holistic thinker are all potentially valid, and need to be melded in scholarly symbiosis and common respect. No insular approach is likely to prevail.

This requisite has implications for the staffing of particular projects, for the institutional environment in which they operate, and for the professional societies and publications which choose to attend to this topic. Individual laboratory personnel groups should comprise a broader range of experience and insight than the conventional hierarchy of technical specialists, and their cognizance of other contemporary work should be broader. The institution housing that laboratory needs to display considerable tolerance and support for the unusual tone and special requirements of the research and not force its conformity to established scientific subdivisions and research styles. Likewise, the professional community at large cannot at this time profitably ask for total adherence to its own reductionistic superstructure, but can only inquire dispassionately regarding the respective implications of this conglomerate field for the traditional areas of endeavor.

In this last regard, I should like to express my personal respect for this particular Society, and for this particular Journal, for the openness and generosity of spirit with which they have solicited and presented the results of legitimate scholarly effort in this difficult field. Their attitude could well stand as a model for other institutions and organs in dealing with this topic or with any other present or future projective area of human inquiry.

## Acknowledgment

The author would like to express his indebtedness to his research colleague, Ms. B. J. Dunne, who has provided immense logistical help in the preparation of this manuscript and who, as laboratory manager of the Princeton Engineering Anomalies Research program, has played a primary role in the generation and interpretation of much of the data reported herein. Dr. R. D.

Nelson also contributed heavily to the experimental program and to the refinement of the manuscript. Prof. W. H. Surber designed much of the REG circuitry and software, and wrote the original programs for the remote perception analytical judging procedure.

The program has also benefitted immensely from the interests and efforts of several present and past students and staff, most notably C. K. Curry (Dunham), E. G. Jahn, T. A. Curtis, and I. A. Cook.

# References

[1] M. Ebon, "A history of parapsychology," in *Psychic Exploration*, E. D. Mitchell et al., J. White, Ed. New York: Putnam, 1974.

[2] A. Gould, *The Founders of Psychical Research*. New York: Schocken, 1968.

[3] J. B. Rhine and associates, *Parapsychology from Duke to FRNM*. Durham, NC: Parapsychology Press, 1965.

[4] H. Carrington, *The Story of Psychic Science (Psychical Research)*. New York: Ives Washburn, 1931.

[5] R. C. LeClair, Ed., *The Letters of William James and Théodore Flournoy*. (Foreword by Gardner Murphy.) Madison, WI: University of Wisconsin Press, 1966.

[6] B. B. Wolman, Ed., *Handbook of Parapsychology*. New York: Van Nostrand Reinhold, 1977.

[7] D. S. Rogo, *Parapsychology: A Century of Inquiry*. New York: Taplinger, 1975.

[8] F. Hartmann, *Paracelsus: Life and Prophecies*. Blauvelt, NY: Rudolf Steiner Publications, 1973, pp. 103–131.

[9] M. Bell, "Francis Bacon: Pioneer in parapsychology," *Int J. Parapsychol.*, VI, no. 2, pp. 199–208, Spring, 1964.

[10] J. Glanvill, *Saducismus Triumphatus*, Introduction by C. O. Parsons, Facsimiles edit. Gainesville, FL: Scholars' Facsimiles and Reprints, 1966. (Originally published in 1689.)

[11] R. Haynes, *Philosopher King—The Humanist Pope Benedict XIV*. London, England. Weidenfeld & Nicholson, 1970.

[12] C. Richet, "La suggestion mentale et le calcul des probabilités," *Rev. Philosoph.*, 18, pp. 608–674, 1884.

[13] C. Richet, "Further experiments in hypnotic lucidity or clairvoyance," in *Proc. Soc. for Psychical Research*, 6, pp. 66–83, 1889.

[14] E. Swedenborg, *Divine Love and Wisdom*. New York: Swedenborg Foundation, Inc., 1979.

[15] G. Trobridge, *Swedenborg, Life and Teaching*. New York: Swedenborg Foundation, Inc., 1976.

[16] I. Ross, *The President's Wife, Mary Todd Lincoln*. New York: Putnam, 1973.

[17] F. W. H. Myers, *Human Personality and Its Survival of Bodily Death*. (Abridged and edited by S. Smith.) Secaucus, NJ: University Books, 1961. (Originally published in 1903, 2 vols.)

[18] W. F. Barrett, "Appendix to the report on thought–reading," in *Proc. Soc. for Psychical Research,* 1, pp. 47–64, 1882.

[19] O. J. Lodge, "An account of some experiments in thought-transference," in *Proc. Soc. for Psychical Research,* 2, pp. 189–200, 1884.

[20] The American Society for Psychical Research, Inc., 5 W. 73 St., New York, NY 10023.

[21] W. James, *Human Immortality: Two Supposed Objections to the Doctrine.* Boston, MA: Houghton Mifflin, 1898.

[22] ———, "Report of the Committee on Mediumistic Phenomena," in *Proc. American Soc. for Psychical Research,* 1, pp. 102–106, 1896.

[23] G. Murphy and R. O. Ballou, *William James on Psychical Research.* New York: Viking Press, 1969.

[24] W. James, "Psychical research," in *The Will to Believe and Other Essays in Popular Philosophy.* New York: Longmans, Green, and Co., 1897.

[25] ———, "Review of human personality and its survival of bodily death by F. W. H. Myers," in *Proc. Soc. for Psychical Research,* 18, p. 23, 1903.

[26] S. Freud, "A note on the unconscious in psycho-analysis," in *Proc. Soc. for Psychical Research,* 26, pp. 312–318, 1912.

[27] ———, *Studies in Parapsychology.* New York: Collier Books, 1963.

[28] C. G. Jung, *Synchronicity.* Princeton, NJ: Princeton University Press (Bollingen Series #20), 1973.

[29] ———, *On the Psychology and Pathology of So-Called Occult Phenomena.* Princeton, NJ: Princeton University Press (Bollingen Series # 20), 1957. (Originally published in 1902, doctoral dissertation, University of Basel.)

[30] ———, *Memories, Dreams, Reflections.* (Recorded and edited by A. Jaffe, translated by Richard and Clara Winston.) New York: Vintage Books, 1965, p. 137.

[31] W. Pauli and C. G. Jung, Eds., *The Interpretation of Nature and the Psyche.* Princeton, NJ: Princeton University Press (Bollingen Series #51), 1955.

[32] J. Ehrenwald, "Psi, psychotherapy, and psychoanalysis," in *Handbook of Parapsychology,* B. B. Wolman, Ed. New York: Van Nostrand Reinhold, 1977, pp. 529–540.

[33] M. Ullman, "Psychopathology and psi phenomena," in *Handbook of Parapsychology,* B. B. Wolman, Ed. New York: Van Nostrand Reinhold, 1977, pp. 557–574.

[34] J. G. Pratt, J. B. Rhine, C. E. Stuart, and B. M. Smith, *Extra-Sensory Perception After Sixty Years.* New York: Holt, 1940.

[35] J. B. Rhine, *New World of the Mind.* New York: William Morrow and Co., 1953.

[36] J. B. Rhine, Ed., *Progress in Parapsychology.* Durham, NC: Parapsychology Press, 1971.

[37] L. E. Rhine, *Mind Over Matter: Psychokinesis.* New York: Macmillan, 1970.

[38] J. B. Rhine, "Psi and psychology: Conflict and solution," *J. Parapsychol.,* 32, pp. 101–128, 1968.

[39] *Eur. J. Parapsychol., Int. J. Parapsychol.* (defunct), *J. Parapsychol., J. Amer. Soc. Psychical Research, J. Soc. for Psychical Research, Parapsychol. Rev., Proc. Soc. for Psychical Research.*

[40] US Universities/Colleges: Chicago; Colorado; Columbia; CUNY; Delaware; Denver; Drexel; Duke; Finch; Harvard; Illinois; John F. Kennedy; Kent State; Michigan; Missouri; Mundelein; Newark College of Engineering; New School for Social Research; NYU; North Carolina; Oakland; Pittsburgh; Princeton; St. John's; St. Joseph's; South West Minnesota; Syracuse; UC/Berkeley; UC/Davis; UC/Irvine; UC/LA; UC/Santa Barbara; Virginia; Wesleyan; West Florida; West Georgia; Wisconsin; Yale. Foreign: Amsterdam; Andhra; Argentina; Benares; Bonn; Cambridge; Chile; Copenhagen; Edinburgh; Freiburg; Ghana; Halifax; Iceland; Jung Inst.; Leningrad; Leyden; London; Loyola; Lund; McGill; Munich; Mysore; New South Wales; Oxford; Paris; Peking; Rhodes; South Africa; Tasmania; Tel Aviv; Utkal; Utrecht; Warsaw; Waterloo; Zurich.

[41] List available upon request.

[42] Research Institutions: Amer. Soc. for Psychical Research, New York; Ballistic Research Labs., Aberdeen, MD; Foundation for Research on the Nature of Man, Durham, NC; Inst. for Noetic Sciences, San Francisco, CA; Menninger Foundation, Topeka, KS; Midwest Psi Research Inst., Chicago, IL; Mind Science Foundation, San Antonio, TX; Parapsychology Foundation, NY; Psychical Research Foundation, Durham, NC; Psychophysical Research Labs, Princeton, NJ; Science Unlimited Research Foundation, San Antonio, TX; SRI International, Menlo Park, CA; Society for Psychical Research, London; Forschungsinstit für Psychotronik, West Berlin; Matsui Hospital, Kasahara, Japan; Inst. of Pharmacology, Polish Academy of Sciences, Krakow; Shanghai Municipal Human Exception Functions Research Society. Corporations: Airesearch Company of California; Boeing Scientific Research Laboratories.

[43] J. G. Pratt, "Soviet research in parapsychology," in *Handbook of Parapsychology,* B. B. Wolman, Ed. New York: Van Nostrand Reinhold, 1977, pp. 883–903.

[44] E. K. Naumov and L. V. Vilenskaya, *Bibliographies on Parapsychology (Psychoenergetics) and Related Subjects.* Arlington, VA: Joint Publications Research Service, 1972. (Originally published in Moscow, 1971.)

[45] E. K. Naumov and L. V. Vilenskaya, *Bibliography of Parapsychology (Psychotronics, Psychoenergetics, Psychoblophysics) and Related Problems.* (Literature published in the USSR), 1979 (in manuscript).

[46] E. C. Wortz, A. J. Bauer, R. F. Blackwelder, J. W. Eerkins, and A. J. Sour, "An investigation of Soviet psychical research," in *Proc. Special Session: The State of the Art in Psychic Research; Electro 77 Professional Program.* New York: Apr. 19–21, 1977.

[47] A. J. Lewis, *A Report.* Document EW-76-011, Airesearch Manufacturing Co. of California, January 1976. (A supplement to Wortz *et al.,* #46 above.)

[48] M. Johnson (Chairman) *et al.,* "Symposium: Current directions in European parapsychology," in *Research in Parapsychology 1978.* Metuchen, NJ: Scarecrow Press, 1979, pp. 1–10.

[49] S. Ostrander and L. Schroeder, *Psychic Discoveries Behind the Iron Curtain.* Englewood Cliffs, NJ: Prentice-Hall, 1970.

[50] L. L. Vasiliev, *Experiments in Distant Influence* (Edited with Introduction by A. Gregory). New York: Dutton, 1976.

[51] T. Moss, "Psychic research in the Soviet Union," in *Psychic Exploration*, E. D. Mitchell et al., J. White, Ed. New York: Putnam, 1974, pp. 469–486.

[52] R. A. McConnell, "Parapsychology in the USSR," *J. Parapsychol.*, 39 pp. 129–134, 1975.

[53] V. P. Zinchenko, A. N. Leont'yev, B. F. Lomov, and A. R. Luria, "Parapsychology: Fiction or reality?" *Voprosy Filosofii* (Questions of Philosophy), 9, pp. 128–136, 1973.

[54] Zhang Feng, "New advances made in study of exceptional human functions," Shanghai *Ziran Zazki* (Nature Journal) in Chinese, no. 8, p. 606, Aug. 1980.

[55] J. Palmer, "Attitudes and personality traits in experimental ESP research," in *Handbook of Parapsychology*, B. B. Wolman, Ed. New York: Van Nostrand Reinhold, 1977, pp. 175–201.

[56] S. Krippner, Ed., *Advances in Parapsychological Research: II, Extrasensory Perception*. New York: Plenum Press, 1978.

[57] K. R. Rao, *Experimental Parapsychology: A Review and Interpretation*. Springfield, IL: Charles C. Thomas, 1966.

[58] G. Schmeidler, "The psychic personality," in *Psychic Exploration*, C. Mitchell et al., J. White, Ed. New York: Putnam, 1974.

[59] H. J. Eysenck, "Personality and extrasensory perception," *J. Soc. Psychical Research*, 44, pp. 55–71, 1967.

[60] G. R. Schmeidler and R. A. McConnell, *ESP and Personality Patterns*. Westport, CT: Greenwood Press, 1973 (originally published 1958).

[61] J. Palmer, "Scoring in ESP tests as a function of belief in ESP. Part I. The sheep-goat effect," *J. Amer. Soc. Psychical Research*, 65, pp. 373–408, 1971.

[62] A. Parker, *States of Mind: ESP and Altered States of Consciousness*. New York: Taplinger, 1975.

[63] R. L. Van de Castle, "Sleep and dreams," in *Handbook of Parapsychology*, B. B. Wolman, Ed. New York: Van Nostrand Reinhold, 1977, pp. 473–499.

[64] M. Ullman, S. Krippner, and A. Vaughan, *Dream Telepathy*. New York: Macmillan, 1973.

[65] I. Strauch, "Dreams and psi in the laboratory," in *Psi Favorable States of Consciousness*, R. Cavanna, Ed. New York: Parapsychology Foundation, 1970, pp, 46–54.

[66] C. Honorton, "Psi and internal attention states," in *Handbook of Parapsychology*, B. B. Wolman, Ed. New York: Van Nostrand Reinhold, 1977, pp. 435–472.

[67] W. Braud, "Psi conducive conditions: Explorations and interpretations," in *Psi and States of Awareness: Proc. Int. Conf. held in Paris, France, Aug. 24–26, 1977*, B. Shapin and L. Coly, Eds. New York: Parapsychology Foundation, 1978.

[68] E. Dingwall, Ed., *Abnormal Hypnotic Phenomena* (4 Vols.). New York: Barnes and Noble, 1968.

[69] C. Honorton and S. Krippner, "Hypnosis and ESP performance: A review of the experimental literature," in *Surveys in Parapsychology*, R. White, Ed. Metuchen, NJ: Scarecrow Press, 1976, pp. 227–270.

[70] C. Sargent, "Hypnosis as a psi conducive state: A controlled replication study," *J. Parapsychol.*, 4, pp. 257–275, 1978.

[71] C. Tart, "Drug induced states of consciousness," in *Handbook of Parapsychology*, B. B. Wolman, Ed. New York: Van Nostrand Reinhold, 1977, pp. 500–525.

[72] J. Eccles, "The human person in its two-way relationship to the brain," Invited address to the Parapsychological Association Convention, State University of Utrecht, The Netherlands, Aug. 20, 1976. *Research in Parapsychology 1976*. Metuchen, NJ: Scarecrow Press, 1977, pp. 251–262.

[73] J. Beloff, "ESP: The search for a physiological index," *J. Amer. Soc. Psychical Research*, 47, Sept. 1974.

[74] J. Ehrenwald, "Psi phenomena and brain research," in *Handbook of Parapsychology*, B. B. Wolman, Ed. New York: Van Nostrand Reinhold, 1977, pp. 716–729.

[75] D. Dean, "The plethysmograph as an indicator of ESP," *J. Soc.Psychical Research*, 41, pp. 351–353, 1962.

[76] J. C. Carpenter, "Intrasubject and subject-agent effects in ESP experiments," in *Handbook of Parapsychology*, B. B. Wolman, Ed. New York: Van Nostrand Reinhold, 1977, pp. 202–272.

[77] R. A. White, "The influence of experimenter motivation, attitudes, and methods of handling subjects on psi test results," in *Handbook of Parapsychology*, B. B. Wolman, Ed. New York: Van Nostrand Reinhold, 1977, pp. 273–301.

[78] C. Honorton, M. Ramsey, and C. Cabibbo, "Experimenter effects in extrasensory perception," *J. Amer. Soc. Psychical Research*, 69, pp. 135–149, 1975.

[79] G. Murphy, "Psychical research and human personality," *Proc. Soc. Psychical Research*, 48, pp. 1–15, 1949.

[80] J. B. Rhine, "Conditions favoring success in psi tests," *J. Parapsychol.*, 12, pp. 58–75, 1948.

[81] G. R. Schmeidler and M. Maher, "The non-verbal communications of psi-conducive and psi-inhibitory experimenters," *J. Amer. Soc. Psychical Research*, 75, pp. 241–257, 1981.

[82] W. Crookes, *Crookes and the Spirit World*, collected by R. G. Medhurst. New York: Taplinger, 1972.

[83] B. J. T. Dobbs, *The Foundations of Newton's Alchemy*. Cambridge, MA: Cambridge University Press, 1975, pp. 7–8.

[84] C. Honorton, "Has science developed the competence to confront claims of the paranormal?" in *Research in Parapsychology 1975*. Metuchen, NJ: Scarecrow Press, 1976, pp. 199–223.

[85] B. Musicante, *Experiments in Psychokinesis: Critique and Proposed Study*, Senior Thesis submitted to the Department of Psychology, Princeton University, May 1979.

[86] R. Jungerman and J. Jungerman, "Computer controlled random number generator PK tests," in *Research in Parapsychology 1977*. Metuchen NJ: Scarecrow Press, 1978, pp. 157–162.

[87] H. Schmidt, "A PK test with electronic equipment," *J. Parapsychol.*, 34, pp. 175–181, 1970.

[88] H. Schmidt and L. Pantas, "Psi tests with internally different machines," *J. Parapsychol.*, 36, pp. 222–232, 1972.

[89] H. Schmidt, "PK effect on pre-recorded targets," *J. Amer. Soc. Psychical Research*, 70, pp. 267–291, 1976.

[90] ———, "PK tests with pre-recorded and pre-inspected seed numbers," in *Research in Parapsychology 1980.* Metuchen, NJ: Scarecrow Press, 1981, pp. 47–50.

[91] E. C. May, B. S. Humphrey, and G. S. Hubbard, "Electronic system perturbation techniques," SRI Int., Final Rep., Sept. 30, 1980.

[92] S. Krippner, Ed. *Advances in Parapsychological Research,* Vol. 1, Psychokinesis. New York: Plenum Press, 1977.

[93] B. Dunne, R. G. Jahn, and R. Nelson, "An REG experiment with large data-base capability," in *Research in Parapsychology 1981.* Metuchen, NJ: Scarecrow Press (in press).

[94] H. Puthoff and R. Targ, *Mind-Reach.* New York: Delacorte, 1977.

[95] ———, "Physics, entropy, and psychokinesis," in *Quantum Physics and Parapsychology,* L. Oteri, Ed. New York: Parapsychological Foundation, 1975.

[96] W. W. Eidson, D. L. Faust, K. Getsla, J. McClay, and B. Conoway, "An investigation of possible anomalous interaction between a human being and a polarized laser beam," preliminary rep. on investigations June–Sept. 1977, Drexel University, Physics Dep. (unpublished.)

[97] R. D. Nelson, B. J. Dunne, and R. G. Jahn, "Psychokinesis studies with a Fabry-Perot interferometer," in *Research in Parapsychology 1981.* Metuchen, NJ: Scarecrow Press (in press).

[98] J. B. Hasted, "Physical aspects of paranormal metal bending," *J. Soc. Psychical Research,* 49, pp. 583–607, 1977.

[99] ———, *The Metal-Benders.* London, Boston and Henley: Routledge and Kegan Paul, 1981.

[100] M. Ryzl, "A model for parapsychological communication," *J. Parapsychol.,* 30, pp. 18–31, 1966.

[101] M. A. Persinger, "Geophysical models for parapsychological experiences," *Psychoenergetic Syst.,* 1, pp. 63–74, 1975.

[102] G. E. Wolstenholme and E. C. P. Millar, Eds., *Extrasensory Perception: A CIBA Foundation Symposium.* New York: Citadel, 1966.

[103] O. C. de Beauregard, "Time symmetry and interpretation of quantum mechanics," *Foundations Phys.,* 6, pp. 539–559, 1976.

[104] G. Feinberg, "Possibility of faster-than light particles," *Phys. Rev.,* 159, p. 1089, 1967.

[105] W. A. Tiller, "A lattice model of space and its relationship to multidimensional systems," in *Proc. A.R.E. Medical Symp.,* Phoenix, AZ, Jan. 1977.

[106] L. Oteri, Ed., *Quantum Physics and Parapsychology: Proceedings of an International Conference held in Geneva, Switzerland, August 26–27,1974.* New York: Parapsychological Foundation, 1975.

[107] J. H. M. Whiteman, "Quantum theory and parapsychology," *J. Amer. Soc. for Psychical Research,* 67, pp. 341–360, 1973.

[108] E. H. Walker, "Consciousness and quantum theory," in *Psychic Exploration,* E. D. Mitchell *et al.,* J. White, Ed. New York: Putnam, 1974, pp. 544–568.

[109] R. D. Mattuck, "A quantum mechanical theory of the interaction between consciousness and matter," *Colloque International "Science et Conscience,"* Cordoba, Spain, Oct. 1–5, 1979.

[110] D. Bohm, "The enfolding-unfolding universe and consciousness," *Colloque International "Science et Conscience,"* Cordoba, Spain, Oct. 1–5, 1979.

[111] H. Margenau, "ESP in the framework of modern science," *J. Amer. Soc. Psychical Research,* 60, pp. 214–228, 1966.

[112] J. H. M. Whiteman, "Parapsychology and physics," in *Handbook of Parapsychology,* B. B. Wolman, Ed. New York: Van Nostrand Reinhold, 1977, pp. 730–756.

[113] A. Puharich, Ed., *The Iceland Papers: Select Papers on Experimental and Theoretical Research on the Physics of Consciousness.* Foreword by B. D. Josephson. Amherst, WI: Essentia Research Associates, 1979.

[114] A. H. Klopf, *Mental and Physical Phenomena: Toward a Unified Theory.* July 1977. (Unpublished manuscript.)

[115] Duke University, Dep. of Electrical Engineering; Princeton University, School of Engineering/Applied Science; Syracuse University, School of Computer and Information Science.

[116] S. S. Wilks, "Statistical aspects of experiments in telepathy," H. C. L. R. Lieber, Ed. A lecture by Samuel S. Wilks given at the Galois Institute of Mathematics, Long Island University, Mimeographed, 1938, 18 pp.

[117] P. Diaconis, "Statistical problems in ESP research," *Science,* 201, pp. 131–136, July 14, 1978.

[118] C. E. M. Hansel, *ESP and Parapsychology: A Critical Reevaluation.* Buffalo, NY: Prometheus Books, 1980.

[119] D. S. Burdick and E. F. Kelly, "Statistical Methods in Parapsychological Research," in *Handbook of Parapsychology,* B. B. Wolman, Ed. New York: Van Nostrand Reinhold, pp. 81–130, 1977.

[120] J. A. Greenwood and C. E. Stuart, "Mathematical techniques used in ESP research," *J. Parapsychol.,* 1, pp. 206–225, 1937.

[121] W. W. Carington, "Experiments on the paranormal cognition of drawings," *J. Parapsychol.,* 4, pp. 1–134, 1940.

[122] L. L. Gatlin, "A new measure of bias in finite sequences with applications to ESP data," *J. Amer. Soc. Psychical Research,* 1, pp. 29–43, 1979.

[123] C. T. Tart, "Randomicity, predictability, and mathematical inference strategies in ESP feedback experiments" (Discussion of Dr. Gatlin's paper.) *J Amer. Soc. Psychical Research,* 1, pp. 44–60, 1979.

[124] J. G. Pratt, "Is ESP only a misnomer for response sequences chosen to match inferred target sequences?" (Discussion of Dr. Gatlin's paper.) *J. Amer. Soc. Psychical Research,* 1, pp. 60–66,1979.

[125] D. S. Rogo, *Parapsychology: A Century of Inquiry.* New York: Taplinger, 1975, pp. 29–30.

[126] H. Bergson, "Presidential address to the Society for Psychical Research (1913)," *Proc. Soc. Psychical Research,* 27, pp. 157–175, 1914.

[127] ———, *Mind Energy.* New York: Henry Holt, 1920.

[128] C. D. Broad, *Religion, Philosophy and Psychical Research.* New York: Humanities Press, 1969.

[129] J. Ludwig, Ed., *Philosophy and Parapsychology.* Buffalo, NY: Prometheus Books, 1978.

[130] G. R. Schmeidler, Ed., *Parapsychology: Its Relation to Physics, Biology, Psychology, and Psychiatry.* Metuchen, NJ: Scarecrow Press, 1976.

[131] R. L. Van de Castle, "Parapsychology and anthropology," in *Handbook of Parapsychology,* B. B. Wolman, Ed. New York: Van Nostrand Reinhold, 1977, pp. 667–686.

[132] R. L. Morris, "Parapsychology, biology, and anpsi," in *Handbook of Parapsychology,* B. B. Wolman, Ed. New York: Van Nostrand Reinhold, 1977, pp. 687–715.

[133] W. H. Clark, "Parapsychology and religion," in *Handbook of Parapsychology,* B. B. Wolman, Ed. New York: Van Nostrand Reinhold, 1977, pp. 769–780.

[134] J. M. Backus, "Parapsychology and Literature," in *Handbook of Parapsychology,* B. B. Wolman, Ed. New York: Van Nostrand Reinhold, 1977, pp. 781–802.

[135] C. Panati, Ed., *The Geller Papers: Scientific Observations on the Paranormal Powers of Uri Geller.* Boston, MA: Houghton Mifflin, 1976.

[136] C. Crussard and J. Bouvaist, "Study of certain seemingly abnormal deformations and transformations of metals," *Memoires Scientifiques Revue Metallurgie,* Feb. 1978. (English translation H & P de Maigret, Nov. 1978).

[137] J. G. Pratt, *ESP Research Today: A Study of Developments in Parapsychology since 1960.* Metuchen, NJ: Scarecrow Press, 1973.

[138] J. G. Pratt, "The Pearisburg poltergeist," in *Research in Parapsychology 1977.* Metuchen, NJ: Scarecrow Press, 1978, pp. 174–182.

[139] J. Krieger, D. DalCorso, and G. Solfvin "RSPK in Philadelphia," in *Research in Parapsychology 1978.* Metuchen, NJ: Scarecrow Press, 1979, pp. 59–60.

[140] A. R. G. Owen, *Can We Explain the Poltergeist?* New York: Garrett Helix, 1964.

[141] W. G. Roll, *The Poltergeist.* Metuchen, NJ: Scarecrow Press, 1976.

[142] W. G. Roll, "Poltergeists," in *Handbook of Parapsychology,* B. B. Wolman, Ed. New York: Van Nostrand Reinhold, 1977, pp. 382–413.

[143] W. Tiller, "A technical report on some psychoenergetic devices," *A.R.E. J.,* 7, p. 81, 1972.

[144] G. Schmeidler, "PK effects upon continuously recorded temperature," *J. Amer. Soc. Psychical Research,* 67, p. 325, 1973.

[145] R. G. Stanford, "Experimental psychokinesis: A review from diverse perspectives" in *Handbook of Parapsychology,* B. B. Wolman, Ed. New York: Van Nostrand Reinhold, 1977, pp. 324–381.

[146] H. Schmidt, "Psychokinesis," in *Psychic Exploration,* E. D. Mitchell *et al.,* J. White, Ed. New York: Putnam, 1974, pp. 179–193.

[147] W. Cox, "The effect of PK on the placement of falling objects," *J. Parapsychol.*, 15, pp. 40–48, 1951.

[148] ———, "The effect of PK on electromechanical systems," *J. Parapsychol.*, 29, pp. 165–175, 1965.

[149] J. Hasted, *The Metal Benders*. London, Boston and Henley: Routledge and Kegan Paul, 1981, p. 131.

[150] M. G. Shafer, "PK metal bending in a semi-formal small group," in *Research in Parapsychology 1980*. Metuchen, NJ: Scarecrow Press, 1981, pp. 32–35.

[151] C. Honorton and L. Tremmel, "Psitrek: A preliminary effort toward development of psi-conducive computer software," *Research in Parapsychology 1979*. Metuchen, NJ: Scarecrow Press, 1980, pp. 159–160.

[152] U. Sinclair, *Mental Radio* (Rev. 2nd printing, Introduction by W. McDougall, Preface by A. Einstein, with a report by W. F. Prince). Springfield, IL: Charles C. Thomas, 1962.

[153] H. E. Puthoff and R. Targ, "A perceptual channel for information transfer over kilometer distances: Historical perspective and recent research," in *Proc. IEEE*, vol. 64, pp. 329–354, 1976.

[154] R. Targ and H. E. Puthoff, "Information, transmission under conditions of sensory shielding," *Nature*, 252, pp. 602–607, 1974.

[155] C. T. Tart, H. E. Puthoff, and R. Targ, Eds., *Mind at Large: IEEE Symposia on the Nature of Extrasensory Perception*. New York: Praeger Special Studies, 1979.

[156] H. E. Puthoff, R. Targ, and E. C. May, "Experimental psi research: Implication for physics," in *The Role of Consciousness in the Physical World*, R. G. Jahn, Ed. Boulder, CO: Westview Press, 1981, pp. 37–86.

[157] B. J. Dunne and J. P. Bisaha, "Precognitive remote viewing in the Chicago area," *J. Parapsychol.*, 43, pp. 17–30, 1979.

[158] ———, "Multiple subject precognitive remote viewing," in *Research in Parapsychology 1977*. Metuchen, NJ: Scarecrow Press, 1978, pp.146–151.

[159] ———, "Long distance precognitive remote viewing," in *Research in Parapsychology 1978*. Metuchen, NJ: Scarecrow Press, 1979, pp. 68–70.

[160] J. P. Bisaha and B. J. Dunne, "Long distance and multiple subject precognitive remote viewing of geographical locations," in *Mind at Large: IEEE Symposia on the Nature of Extrasensory Perception*, C. T. Tart, H. E. Puthoff, and R. Targ, Eds. New York: Praeger Special Studies, 1979, pp. 107–124.

[161] B. J. Dunne, *Precognitive Remote Perception*. M.A. thesis, Committee on Human Development, University of Chicago, 1979.

[162] B. J. Dunne and J. P. Bisaha, "Precognitive remote perception: A critical overview of the experimental program," in *Research in Parapsychology 1979*. Metuchen, NJ: Scarecrow Press, 19 80, pp. 117–120.

[163] R. G. Jahn, "Psychic process, energy transfer, and things that go bump in the night," *Princeton Alumni Weekly*, Dec. 4, 1978, S–1–12.

[164] E. A. Rauscher, G. Weissmann, J. Sarfatti, and S.-P. Sirag, "Remote

perception of natural scenes, shielded against ordinary perception," in *Research in Parapsychology 1975*. Metuchen, NJ: Scarecrow Press, pp. 41–45, 1976.

[165] S. Allen, P. Green, K. Rucker, R. Cohen, C. Goolsby, and R. L. Morris, "A remote viewing study using a modified version of the SRI procedure," in *Research in Parapsychology 1975*. Metuchen, NJ: Scarecrow Press, 1976, pp. 46–48.

[166] A. C. Hastings and D. B. Hurt, "A confirmatory remote viewing experiment in a group setting," *Proc. IEEE*, vol. 64, pp. 1544–1545, 1976.

[167] J. Vallee, A. C. Hastings, and G. Askevold, "Remote viewing through computer conferencing," *Proc. IEEE*, vol. 64, p. 1551, 1976.

[168] T. W. Whitson, D. N. Bogart, J. Palmer, and C. T. Tart, "Preliminary experiments in group remote viewing," *Proc. IEEE*, vol. 64, p.1550, 1976.

[169] H. Chotas, "Remote viewing in the Durham area," *J. Parapsychol.*, 1, pp. 61–62, 1978.

[170] M. Schlitz and S. Deacon, "Remote viewing: A conceptual replication of Targ and Puthoff," in *Research in Parapsychology 1979*. Metuchen, NJ: Scarecrow Press, 1980, pp. 124–126.

[171] E. Karnes and E. Sussman, "Remote viewing: A response bias interpretation," *Psycholog. Rep.*, 44, pp. 471–479, 1979.

[172] E. Karnes, J. Ballou, E. Sussman, and F. Swaroff, "Remote viewing: Failures to replicate with control comparisons," *Psycholog. Rep.*, 45, pp. 963–973, 1979.

[173] E. W. Karnes, E. P. Sussman, P. Klusman, and L. Turcotte, "Failures to replicate remote viewing using psychic subjects," *Zetetic Scholar*, 6, pp. 66–76, 1980.

[174] M. Schlitz and E. Gruber, "Transcontinental remote viewing," *J. Parapsychol.*, 4, pp. 305–317, 1980.

[175] C. Scott, "On the evaluation of verbal material in parapsychology: A discussion of Dr. Pratt's monograph," *J. Soc. Psychical Research*, 46, pp. 79–90, 1972.

[176] R. L. Morris, "An exact method for evaluating preferentially matched free-response material," *J. Amer. Soc. Psychical Research*, 66, p. 401, 1972.

[177] G. Solfvin, E. Kelly, and D. Burdick, "Some new methods of analysis for preferential ranking data," *J. Amer. Soc. Psychical Research*, 72, p. 93, 1978.

[178] D. Marks and R. Kammann, *The Psychology of the Psychic*. Buffalo, NY: Prometheus Books, 1980.

[179] R. G. Jahn, B. J. Dunne, E. G. Jahn, "Analytical judging procedure for remote perception experiments," *J. Parapsychol.*, 3, pp. 207–231, 1980.

[180] B. J. Winer, *Statistical Principles in Experimental Design*. New York: McGraw-Hill, 1962, pp. 43–45.

[181] R. G. Jahn, Ed., *The Role of Consciousness in the Physical World*. Boulder, CO: Westview Press, 1981.

[182] R. G. Stanford, "An experimentally testable model for spontaneous psi events. I. Extrasensory events," *J. Amer. Soc. Psychical Research*, 68, pp. 34–57, 1974. "II. Psychokinetic events," *Ibid*, pp. 321–356.

[183] C. T. K. Chari, "Some generalized theories and models of psi: A critical evaluation," in *Handbook of Parapsychology*, B. B. Wolman, Ed. New York: Van Nostrand Reinhold, 1977, pp. 803–822.

[184] R. G. Stanford, "Conceptual frameworks of contemporary psi research," in *Handbook of Parapsychology,* B. B. Wolman, Ed. New York: Van Nostrand Reinhold, 1977, pp. 823–858.

[185] B. B. Wolman, "Mind and body: A contribution to a theory of parapsychological phenomena," in *Handbook of Parapsychology,* B. B. Wolman, Ed. New York: Van Nostrand Reinhold, 1977, pp. 861–879.

[186] A. M. Young, *The Geometry of Meaning.* New York: Delacorte Press/Seymour Lawrence, 1976.

[187] B. Shapin and L. Coly, Eds., *Concepts and Theories of Parapsychology: Proceedings of an International Conference held in New York, NY, Dec. 6, 1980.* New York: Parapsychology Foundation, Inc., 1981.

[188] F. Cazzamalli, "Phénomenes télépsychiques et radiations cerebrales," *Rev. Métapsych.,* 4, p. 3, 1925.

[189] I. M. Kogan, "Is telepathy possible?" *Radio Eng.,* 21, p. 75, 1966.

———, "Telepathy, hypotheses and observations," *Radio Eng.,* 22, p. 141, 1967.

———, "Information theory analysis of telepathic communication experiments," *Radio Eng.,* 23, p. 122, 1968.

[190] M. A. Persinger, "ELF field mediation in spontaneous psi events: Direct information transfer or conditional elicitation?" in *Mind at Large,* C. T. Tart, H. E. Puthoff, and R. Targ, Eds. NewYork: Praeger Special Studies, 1979, pp. 189–204.

[191] L. L. Gatlin, *Information Theory and the Living System.* New York: Columbia University Press, 1972.

[192] W. von Lucadou and K. Kornwachs, "Development of the system-theoretic approach to psychokinesis," paper presented at the Parascience Conf., London, 1979.

[193] K. Kornwachs and W. von Lucadou, "Psychokinesis and the concept of complexity," *Psychoenergetic Syst.,* 3, pp. 327–342, 1979.

[194] G. Feinberg, "Precognition—A memory of things future," in *Quantum Physics and Parapsychology,* L. Oteri, Ed. New York: Parapsychology Foundation, 1975, pp. 54–64.

[195] E. A. Rauscher, "Some physical models potentially applicable to remote perception," in *The Iceland Papers,* A. Puharich, Ed. Amherst, WI: Essentia Research Associates, 1979, pp. 49–83.

[196] A. S. Eddington, *Space, Time and Gravitation: An Outline of the General Theory of Relativity.* Cambridge, MA: Cambridge University Press, 1920, pp. 198–201.

[197] A. S. Eddington, *The Nature of the Physical World.* Cambridge, MA: Cambridge University Press, 1928, p. 276.

[198] K. Pribram, *Languages of the Brain.* Englewood Cliffs, NJ: Prentice-Hall, 1971.

[199] K. Pribram, "Toward a holonomic theory of perception," in *Gestalttheorie Modernen Psychologie,* S. Ertel, Ed. Darmstadt: Steinkopff, 1975.

[200] K. Pribram, "Problems concerning the structure of consciousness," in *Consciousness and the Brain,* G. Globus, Ed. New York: Plenum Press, 1976.

[201] D. Bohm, "Quantum theory as an indication of a new order in physics. Part A. The development of new orders as shown through the history of physics," Foundations Phys., 1, pp. 359–381, 1971.

[202] D. Bohm, "Quantum theory as an indication of a new order in physics. Part B. Implicate and explicate order in physical law," *Foundations Phys.*, 1, pp. 139–168, 1971.

[203] A. Eddington, *Relativity Theory of Protons and Electrons.* New York: Macmillan, 1936, p. 329.

[204] O. C. de Beauregard, "The expanding paradigm of the Einstein paradox," in *The Iceland Papers*, A. Puharich, Ed. Amherst, WI: Essentia Associates, 1979, pp. 162–191.

[205] E. P. Wigner, "On hidden variables and quantum mechanical probabilities," *Amer. J. Phys.*, 38, p. 1005, 1970.

[206] J. S. Bell, "On the problem of hidden variables in quantum mechanics," *Rev. Modern Phys.*, 38, p. 447, 1966.

[207] D. Bohm and J. Bub, "A proposed solution of the measurement problem in quantum mechanics by a hidden variable theory," *Rev. Modern Phys.*, 38, p. 453, 1966.

[208] J. Mehra, "Quantum mechanics and the explanation of life," *Amer. Scientist,* 61, pp. 722–728, 1973.

[209] E. H. Walker, "Foundations of paraphysical and parapsychological phenomena," in *Quantum Physics and Parapsychology*, L. Oteri, Ed. New York: Parapsychology Foundation, 1975, pp. 1–44.

[210] R. G. Jahn and B. J. Dunne, "A quantum mechanical approach to the representation of paranormal phenomena," 1982 (to be published).

[211] T. N. E. Greville, "Are psi events random?" *J. A mer. Soc. Psychical Research,* 74, pp. 223–226, 1980.

[212] J. A. Greenwood and T. N. E Greville, "On requirements for using statistical analysis in psi experiments," *J. Parapsychol.,* 43, pp. 315–321, 1979.

[213] R. Jahn and B. Dunne, "Physical models of psychic process," in *Concepts and Theories of Parapsychology*, B. Shapin and L. Coly; Eds. New York: Parapsychology Foundation, Inc., 1981, pp. 69–79.

[214] R. May, "Creativity and encounter," in *The Creative Imagination,* H. M. Ruitenbeek, Ed. Chicago, IL: Quadrangle Books, 1965, pp. 283–291.

[215] F. Barron, "The needs for order and disorder as motives in creative activity," in the second (1957) University of Utah research conference on the identification of creative scientific talent, C. W. Taylor, Ed. Salt Lake City: University of Utah Press, 1958, pp. 119–128.

[216] D. McClelland, "The calculated risk: An aspect of scientific performance," in *Scientific Creativity, its Recognition and Development,* C. W. Taylor and F. Barron, Eds. New York: Wiley, 1963, pp. 184–192.

[217] S. D. Drell, "When is a particle?" *Phys. Today,* 31, pp. 23–32, 1978.

[218] W. Heisenberg, "The nature of elementary particles," *Phys. Today,* 29, pp. 32–39, 1976.

[219] F. Capra, Paper LBL-796, Lawrence Berkeley Laboratories, University of California, Berkeley, CA, 1978.

[220] J. A. Wheeler, "The universe as home for man," *Amer. Scientist,* 62, pp. 683–691, 1974.

[221] W. W. Harman, "Broader implications of recent findings in psychological

and psychic research," in *The Role of Consciousness in the Physical World*, R. G. Jahn, Ed. Boulder, CO: Westview Press, 1981, pp. 113–131.

[222] A. Angoff and B. Shapin, Eds., *A Century of Psychical Research: The Continuing Doubts and Affirmations*. New York: Parapsychology Foundation, 1971.

[223] C. A. Murchison, Ed. *The Case For and Against Psychical Belief.* New York: Arno Press, 1975. (Originally published in 1927.)

[224] W. F. Prince, *The Enchanted Boundary.* New York: Arno Press, 1975. (Originally published in 1930.)

[225] K. M. Goldney and S. G. Soal, "Report on a series of experiments with Mrs. Eileen Garrett," *Proc. Soc. Psychical Research,* 45, pp. 43–97, 1938.

[226] J. Beloff, "The 'sweethearts' experiment," *J. Soc. Psychical Research,* 45, pp. 1–7, 1969.

[227] M. Maher, D. Peratsakis, and G. R. Schmeidler, "Cerebral localization effects in ESP processing: An attempted replication," *J. Amer. Soc. for Psychical Research,* 73, pp. 167–177, 1979.

[228] S. Blackmore, "Correlation between ESP and memory," *Eur. J. Parapsychol.,* 3, pp. 127–147, 1980.

[229] J. Eisenbud, L. Hassel, H. Keely, and W. Sawrey, "A further study of teacher-pupil attitudes and results on clairvoyance tests in the fifth and sixth grades," *J. Amer. Soc. Psychical Research,* 54, pp. 72– 80, 1960.

[230] E. Belvedere and D. Foulkes, "Telepathy and dreams: A failure to replicate," *Perceptual Motor Skills,* 33, pp. 783–789, 1971.

[231] J. Beloff and D. Bate, "An attempt to replicate the Schmidt findings," *J. Soc. Psychical Research,* 46, pp. 21–31, 1971.

[232] R. G. Jahn, reply to Bradley Dowden, *Zetetic Scholar,* 7, p. 127, 1980.

[233] C. C. Gillispie, Ed., *Dictionary of Scientific Biography.* New York: Scribner's, 1970–1980.

[234] R. L. Weber, *A Random Walk in Science,* E. Mendoza, Ed., Foreword by W. Cooper. New York: Crane, Russak, 1973, pp. 66–67.

[235] R. S. de Ropp, *The New Prometheans.* New York: Delacorte, 1972, p. 2–28.

[236] L. Barnett, *The Universe and Dr. Einstein* (Rev. edit.). New York: The New American Library, 1952, p. 117.

[237] R. G. Jahn, "Psychic research: New dimensions or old delusions?" *Zetetic Scholar,* 6, pp. 5–16, 1980.

[238] J. Beloff, Ed., *New Directions in Parapsychology.* Metuchen, NJ: Scarecrow Press, 1975.

[239] J. B. Rhine and J. G. Pratt, *Parapsychology: Frontier Science of the Mind* (Rev. edit.). Springfield, IL: Charles C. Thomas, 1962.

[240] R. A. White, Ed., *Surveys in Parapsychology.* Metuchen, NJ: Scarecrow Press, 1976.

[241] R. A. White and L. A. Dale, *Parapsychology: Sources of Information.* Metuchen, NJ: Scarecrow Press, 1973. (Rev. edit. by R. A. White in preparation.)

[242] N. Bowles and F. Hynds with J. Maxwell, *Psi Search.* San Francisco, CA: Harper and Row, 1978.

[243] R. G. Jahn, B. J. Dunne, R. Nelson, and H. Mertz, "Anomalous operator influence on elementary microelectronic devices," Tech. note, School of Engineering/Applied Science, Princeton University, 1981.

[244] J. Bronowski, *Science and Human Values*. New York: Harper and Brothers, 1956.

[245] M. Polanyi, *Personal Knowledge*. Chicago, IL: University of Chicago Press, 1962.

[246] A. Korzybski, *Science and Sanity: An Introduction to Non-Aristotelian Systems and General Semantics*. Clinton, MA: The Colonial Press, 1933.

[247] W. Penfield, *The Mystery of the Mind*. Princeton, NJ: Princeton University Press, 1975.

[248] M. Ferguson, *The Aquarian Conspiracy*. Los Angeles, CA: J. P. Tarcher, 1980.

[249] J. Salk, *Survival of the Wisest*. New York: Harper and Row, 1973.

[250] A. M. Young, *The Reflexive Universe*. New York: Delacorte Press, 1976.

[251] E. Jantsch, *The Self-Organizing Universe: Scientific and Human Implications of the Emerging Paradigms of Evolution*. Elmsford, NY: Pergamon Press, 1980.

[252] D. Dean *et al.*, *Executive ESP*. Englewood Cliffs, NJ: Prentice-Hall, 1974.

[253] P. T. de Chardin, *The Future of Man*. New York: Harper and Row, 1964 (pp. 166–167 in Harper Torchbooks edit.).

[254] Report to the House of Representatives, Committee on Science and Technology, June 1981.

[255] C. T. Tart, "A survey of expert opinion on potentially negative uses of psi, United States government interest in psi, and the level of research funding of the field," in *Research in Parapsychology 1978*. Metuchen, NJ: Scarecrow Press, 1979, pp. 54–55.

# Index

# Hampton Roads Publishing Company

*. . . for the evolving human spirit*

Hampton Roads Publishing Company
publishes books on a variety of subjects,
including metaphysics, health, integrative medicine,
visionary fiction, and other related topics.

For a copy of our latest catalog, call toll-free
800-766-8009, or send your name and address to:

Hampton Roads Publishing Company, Inc.
1125 Stoney Ridge Road
Charlottesville, VA 22902

e-mail: hrpc@hrpub.com
www.hrpub.com